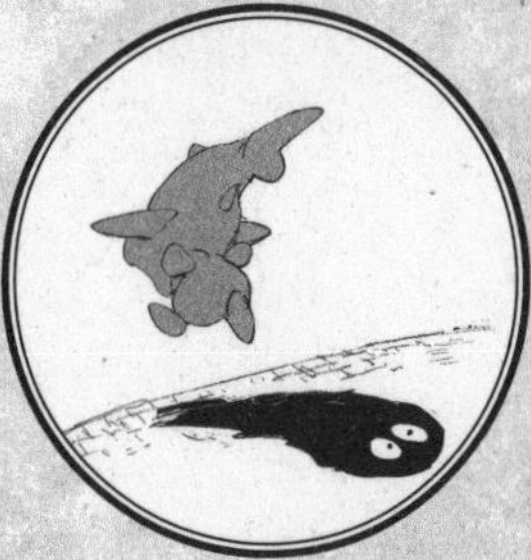

POSUKA DEMIZU

Shonen Jump graphic novels are usually 200 pages per volume, so if we're at volume 10, that would mean I've drawn about 2,000 pages. I'm going to catch up to the A.D. years! The lower half of my closet is a sea of manga paper.

By the way, I'm currently drawing the pages for volume 11, and Emma is...um, wow, what's going to happen to Emma?!

The outcome of the battle will be in the next volume!

From the seashore of manga paper, thank you for always supporting me!

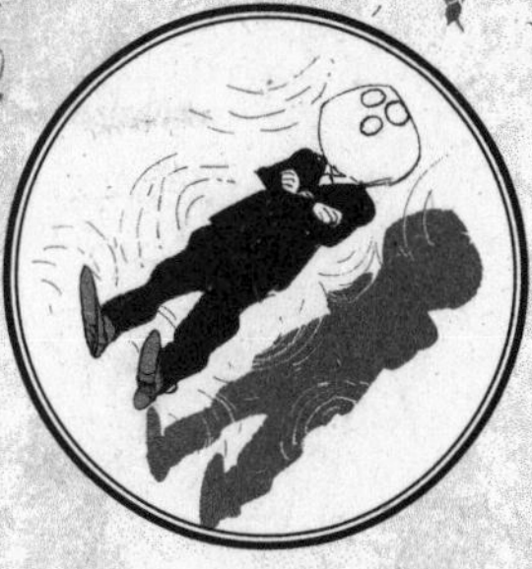

KAIU SHIRAI

Writer Shirai's personal highlights for *The Promised Neverland* fanatics, part 7!

1. I know it's sudden, but I'm revealing their blood types!
Ray: AB
Norman: B
Emma: O
Isabella: A

2. The design of Leuvis!
The motif for his mask was a crayfish. His overall motif was a fake Minerva. (When I heard that, I was like, Demizu Sensei, you're super amazing!!!!
It's like this every week.
Sheer happiness.)

Please enjoy this volume!

Posuka Demizu debuted as a manga artist with the 2013 *CoroCoro* series *Oreca Monster Bouken Retsuden*. A collection of illustrations, *The Art of Posuka Demizu*, was released in 2016 by PIE International.

Kaiu Shirai debuted in 2015 with *Ashley Gate no Yukue* on the *Shonen Jump+* website. Shirai first worked with Posuka Demizu on the two-shot *Poppy no Negai*, which was released in February 2016.

THE PROMISED NEVERLAND

VOLUME 10
SHONEN JUMP Manga Edition

STORY BY KAIU SHIRAI
ART BY POSUKA DEMIZU

Translation/Satsuki Yamashita
Touch-Up Art & Lettering/Mark McMurray
Design/Julian [JR] Robinson
Editor/Alexis Kirsch

YAKUSOKU NO NEVERLAND © 2016 by Kaiu Shirai, Posuka Demizu
All rights reserved.
First published in Japan in 2016 by SHUEISHA Inc., Tokyo.
English translation rights arranged by SHUEISHA Inc.

The stories, characters and incidents mentioned in this publication are entirely fictional.

Printed in the U.S.A.

Published by VIZ Media, LLC
P.O. Box 77010
San Francisco, CA 94107

10 9 8 7 6 5 4 3 2 1
First printing, June 2019

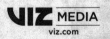
viz.com

PARENTAL ADVISORY
THE PROMISED NEVERLAND is rated T+ and is recommended for ages 16 and up. This volume contains fantasy violence and adult themes.

shonenjump.com

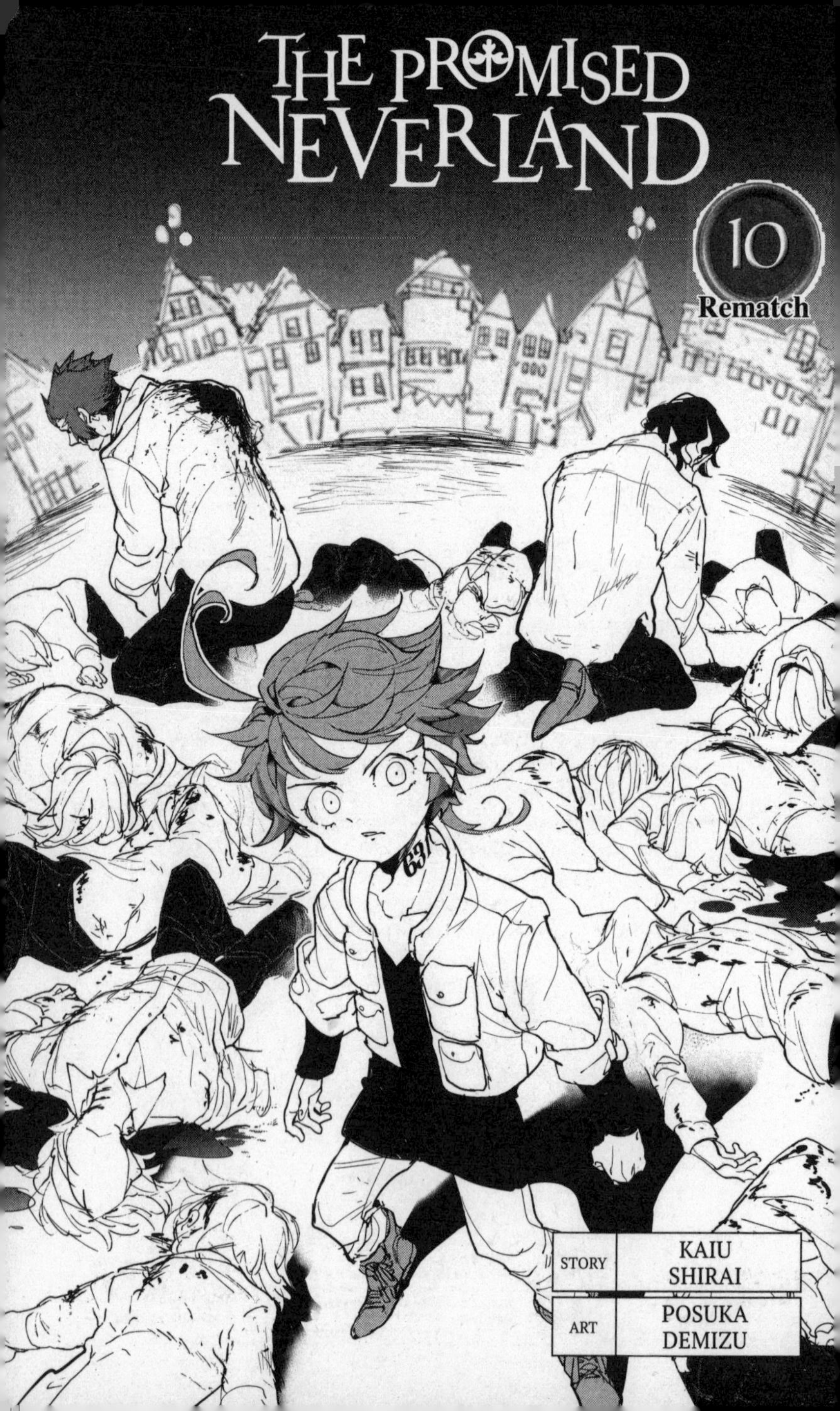
THE PROMISED NEVERLAND
10
Rematch
STORY
KAIU SHIRAI
ART
POSUKA DEMIZU

CHARACTERS

The Children of Grace Field House

They aim to free all of the children who are trapped in Grace Field House within two years.

RAY

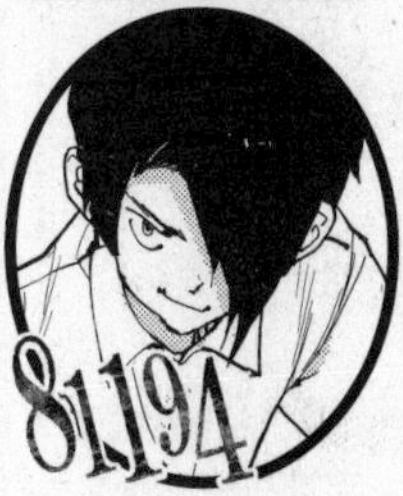
81194

The only one among the Grace Field House children who can match wits with Norman.

EMMA

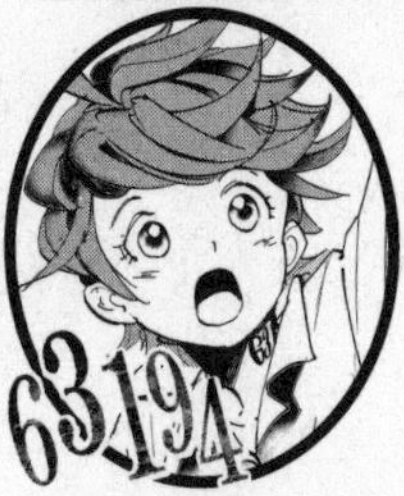
63194

An enthusiastic and optimistic girl with superb athletic and learning abilities.

NORMAN

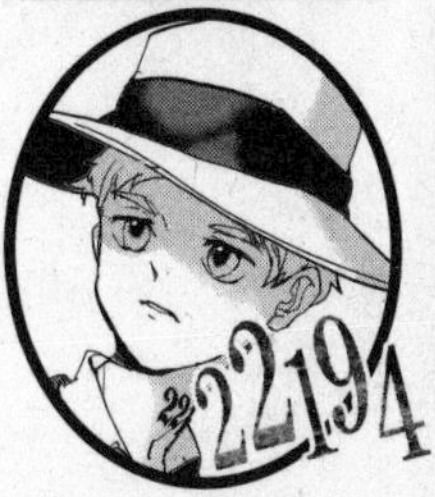
22194

A boy with excellent analytical and decision-making capabilities. He was the smartest child at Grace Field House.

The People of Goldy Pond

They plan to annihilate the demons of Goldy Pond, who hunt children for fun.

ZACK

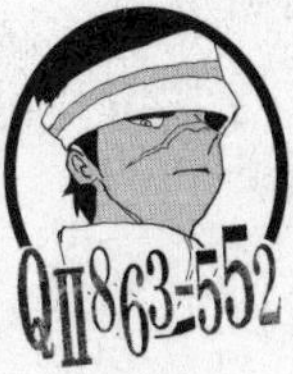
QII863=552

SONYA

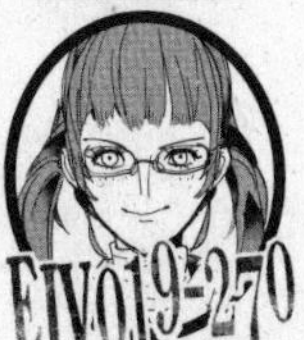
EIV019-270

OLIVER

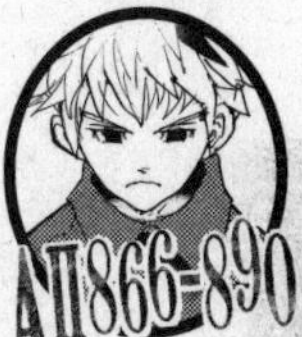
AII866=890

LUCAS

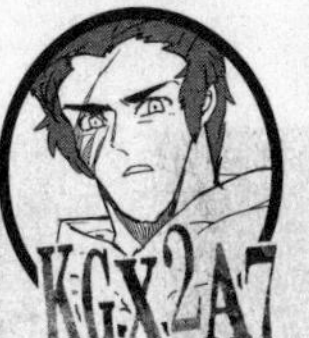
KGX2A7

VIOLET

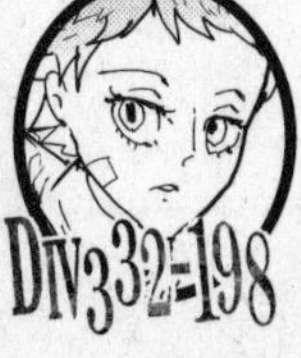
DIV332-198

NIGEL

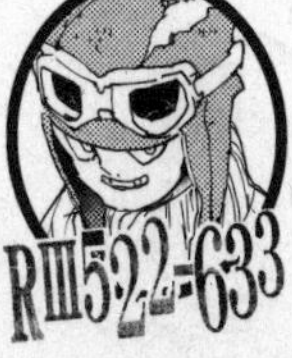
RIII522-633

PAULA

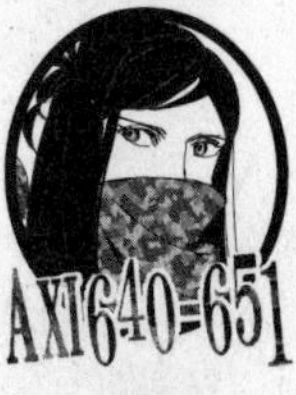
AXI640=651

SANDY

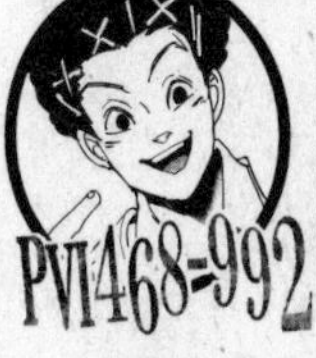
PVI468=992

ADAM

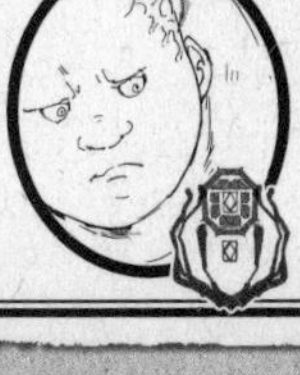

THEO

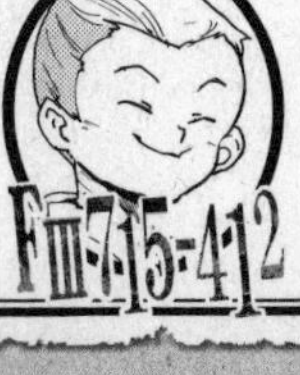
FIII715=412

PEPE

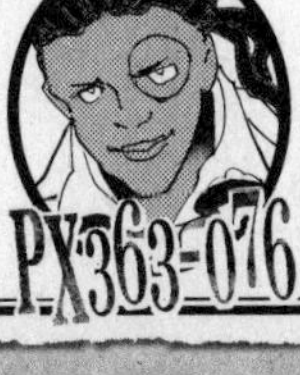
PX363=076

GILLIAN

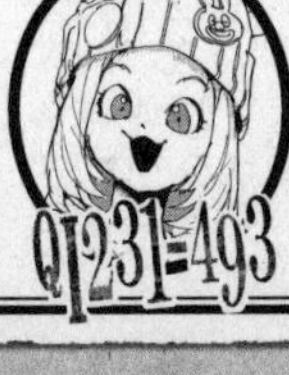
QI231=493

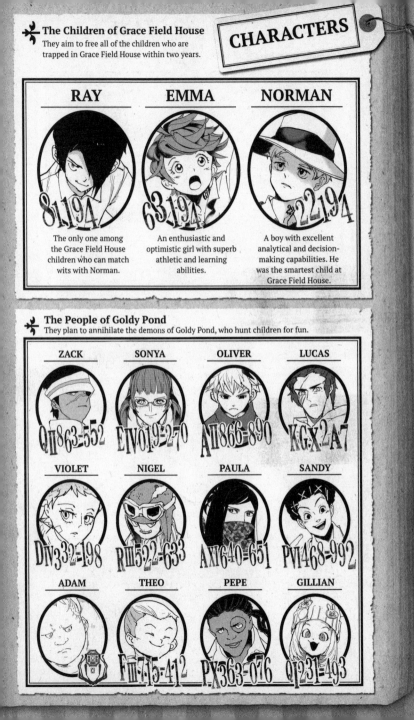

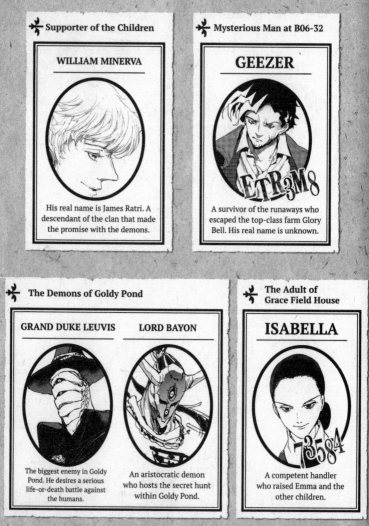

Supporter of the Children

WILLIAM MINERVA

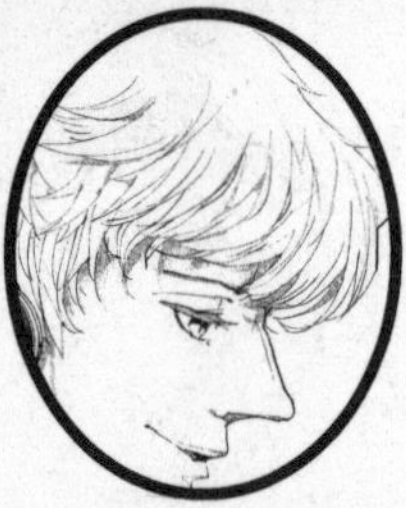

His real name is James Ratri. A descendant of the clan that made the promise with the demons.

Mysterious Man at B06-32

GEEZER

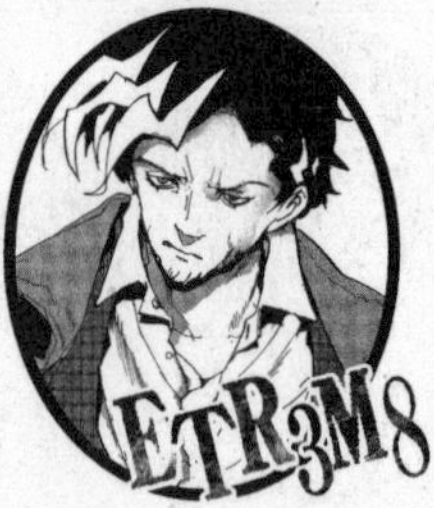

A survivor of the runaways who escaped the top-class farm Glory Bell. His real name is unknown.

The Demons of Goldy Pond

GRAND DUKE LEUVIS

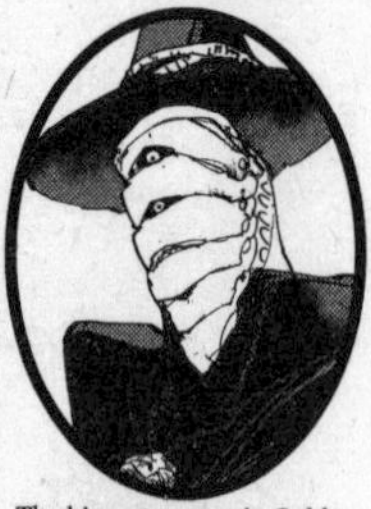

The biggest enemy in Goldy Pond. He desires a serious life-or-death battle against the humans.

LORD BAYON

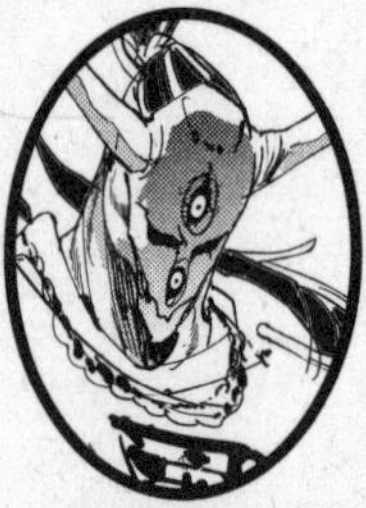

An aristocratic demon who hosts the secret hunt within Goldy Pond.

The Adult of Grace Field House

ISABELLA

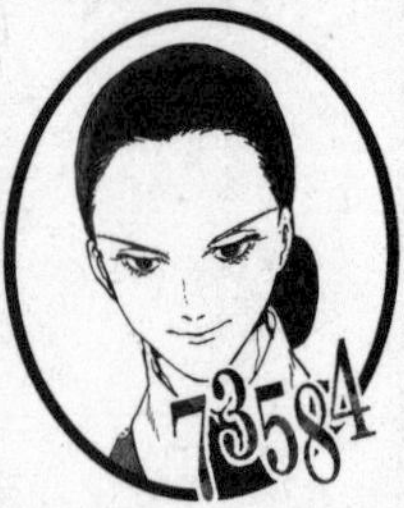
73584

A competent handler who raised Emma and the other children.

The Story So Far

Emma is living happily at Grace Field House with her foster siblings. One day, she realizes that they are being bred as food for demons and decides to escape with a group of other children. At a safe shelter, she meets a man who guides her and Ray to Goldy Pond, a location Minerva indicated in a letter. But Emma is kidnapped on the way and suddenly finds herself inside Goldy Pond. There, she meets other humans who are planning to destroy the demons that hunt them. In a secret room within Goldy Pond, she finds out more information about Minerva and what she must do. And then, the humans of Goldy Pond decide to begin their long-planned revolt against the demons.

THE PROMISED NEVERLAND 10

Rematch

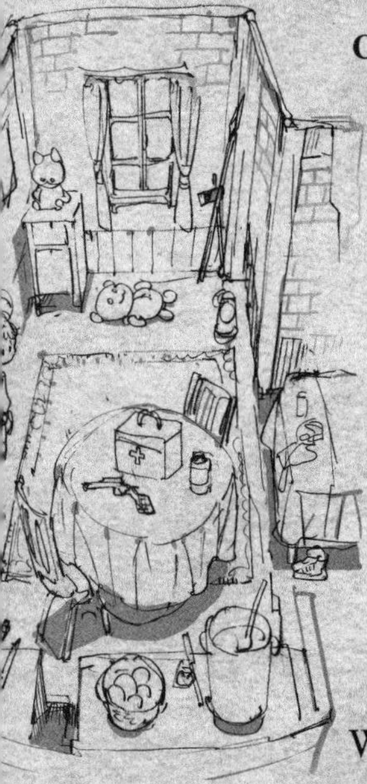

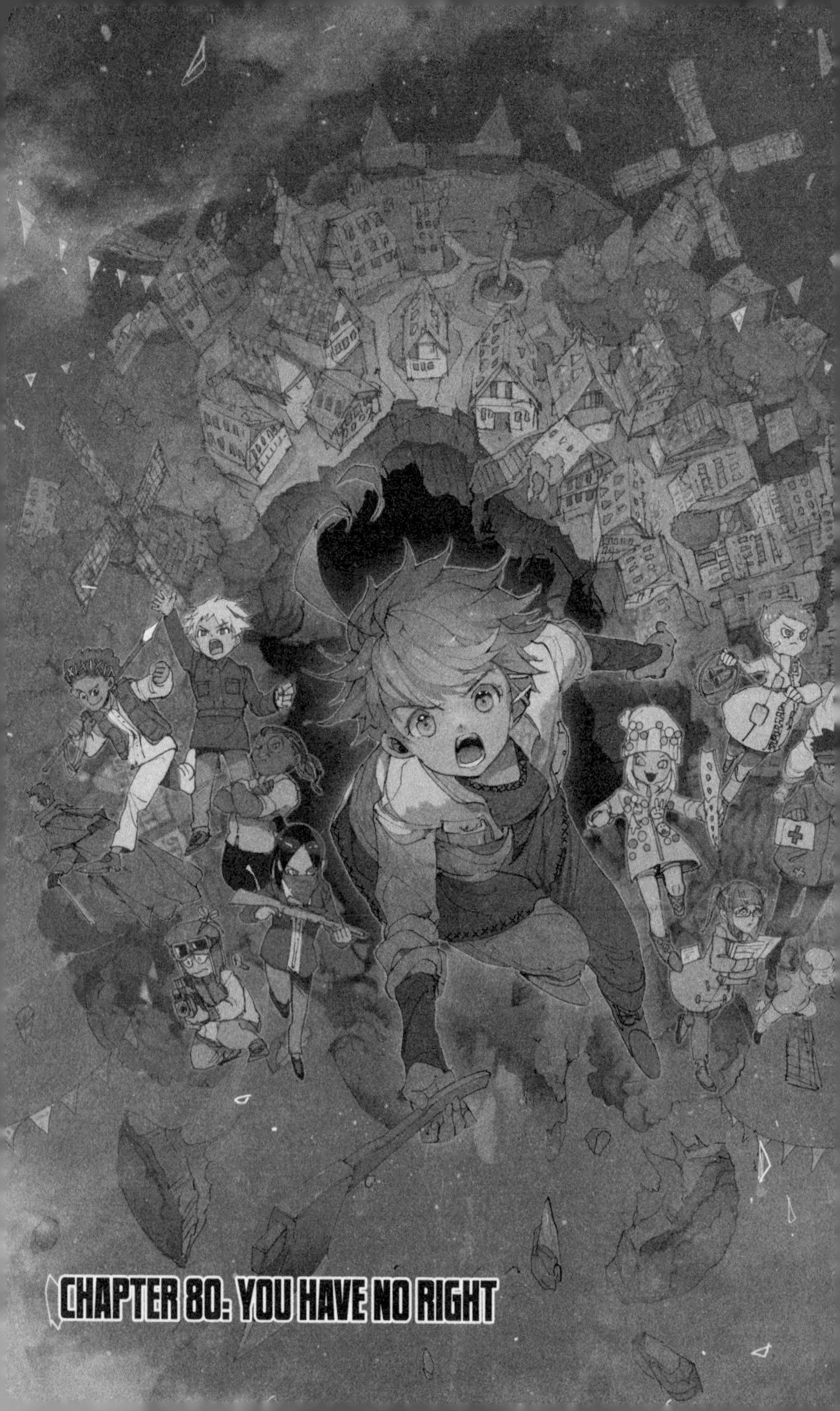
CHAPTER 80: YOU HAVE NO RIGHT

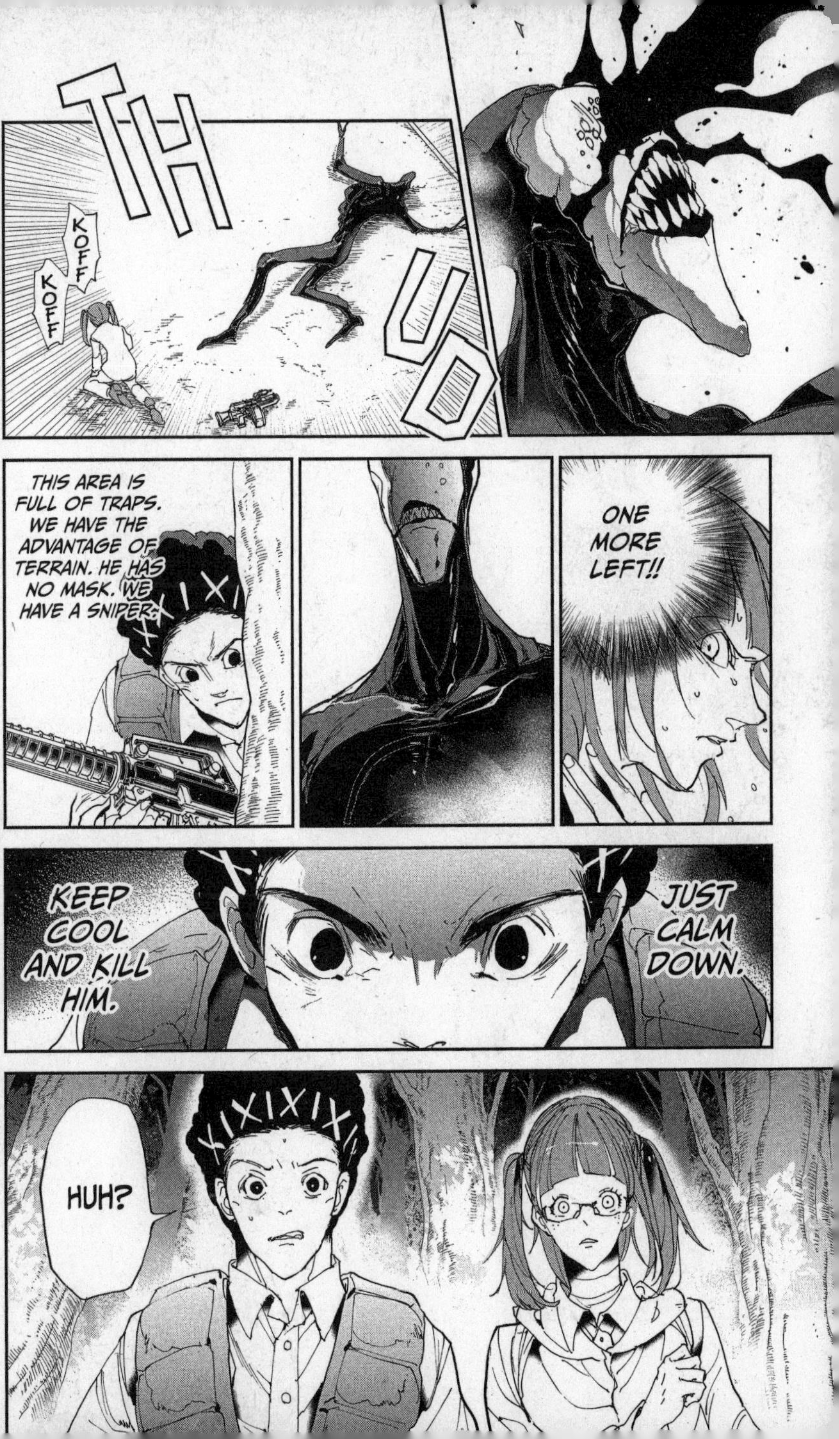
THUD
KOFF
KOFF
ONE MORE LEFT!!
THIS AREA IS FULL OF TRAPS. WE HAVE THE ADVANTAGE OF TERRAIN. HE HAS NO MASK. WE HAVE A SNIPER.
JUST CALM DOWN.
KEEP COOL AND KILL HIM.
HUH?

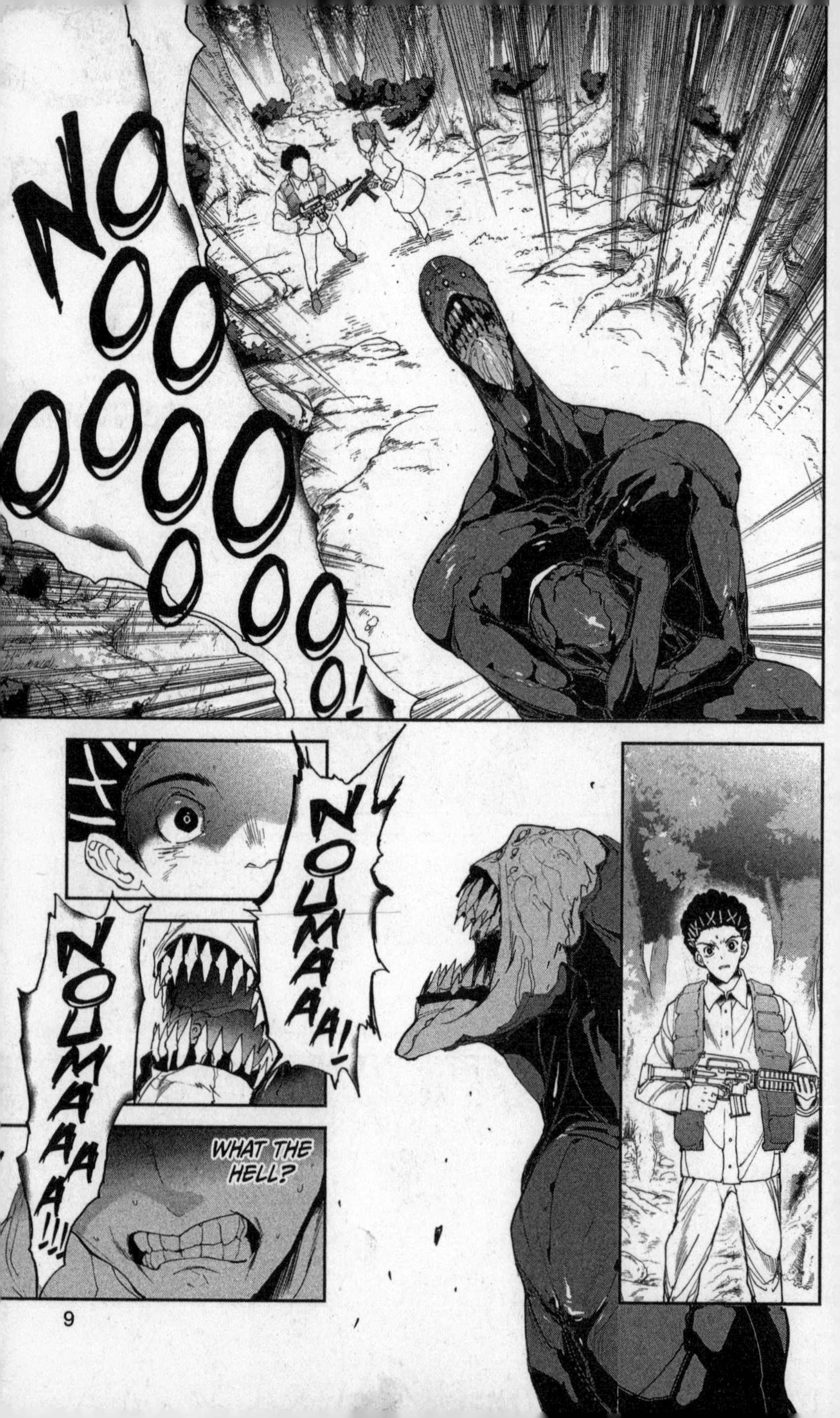
NOOOOOOOOOOOOOOOO!
NOUMAAAA!
NOUMAAAAAA!!!
WHAT THE HELL?

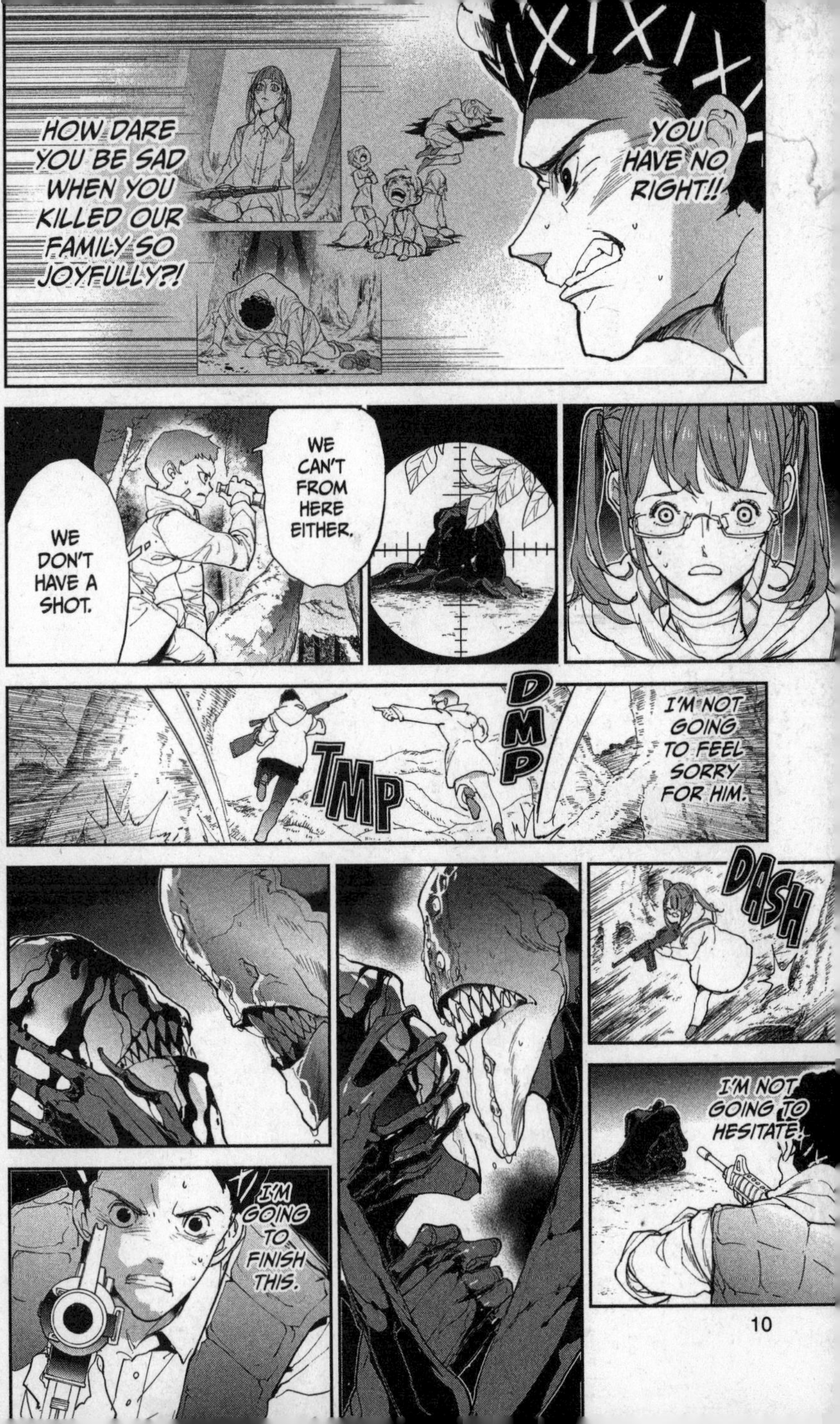
YOU HAVE NO RIGHT!!
HOW DARE YOU BE SAD WHEN YOU KILLED OUR FAMILY SO JOYFULLY?!
WE CAN'T FROM HERE EITHER.
WE DON'T HAVE A SHOT.
I'M NOT GOING TO FEEL SORRY FOR HIM.
DMP
TMP
DASH
I'M NOT GOING TO HESITATE.
I'M GOING TO FINISH THIS.

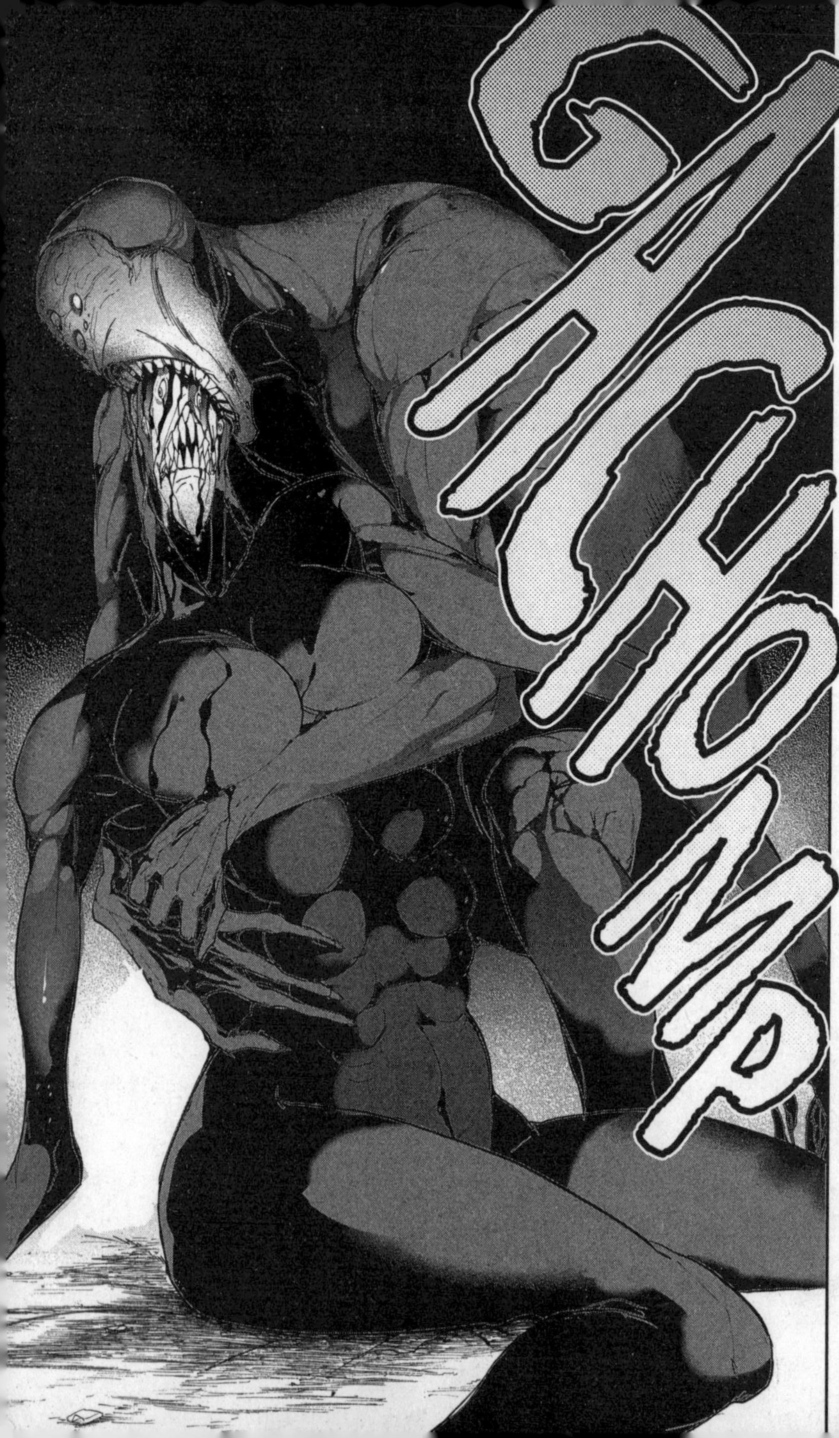
GACHOMP

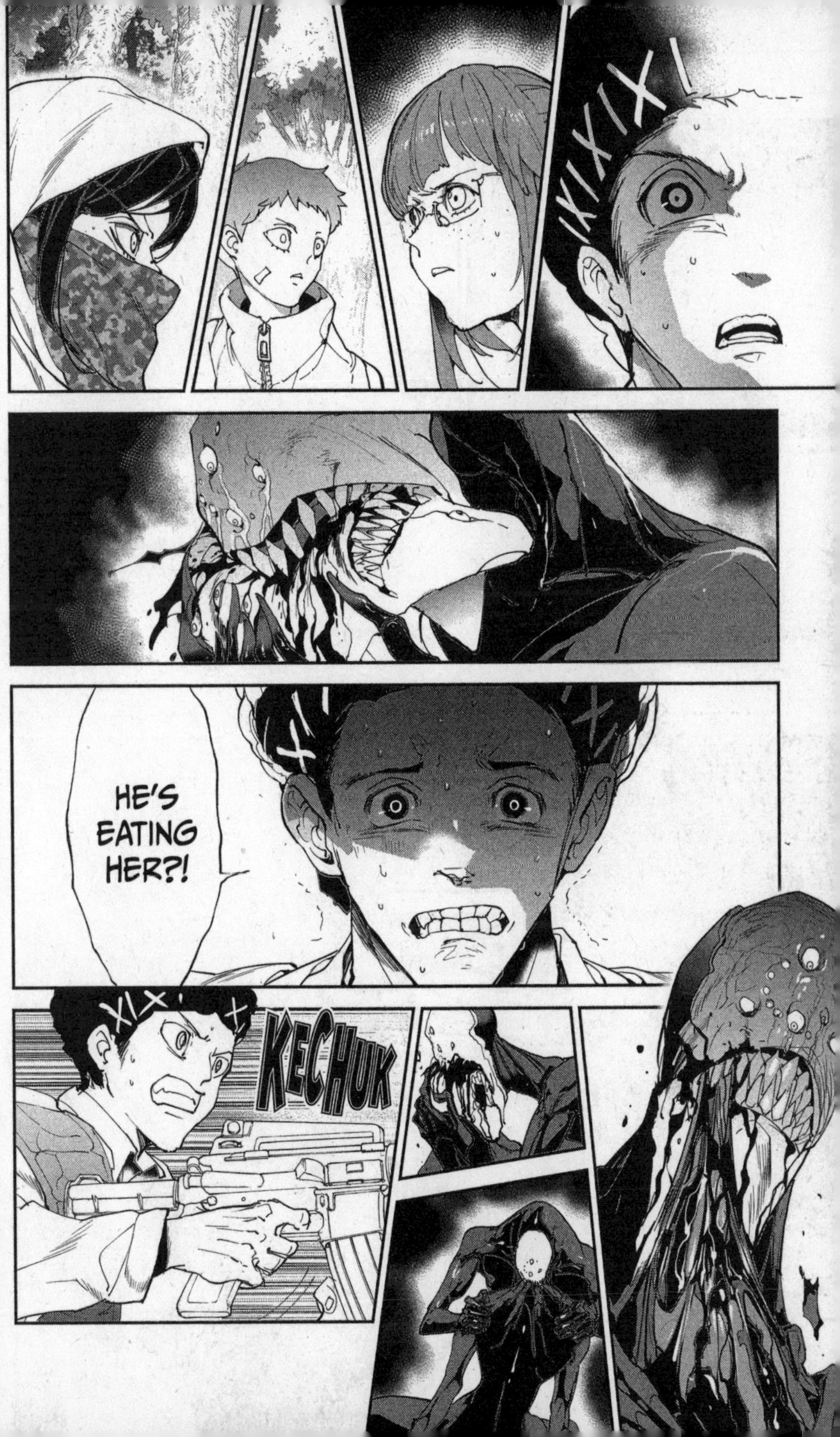
HE'S EATING HER?!
KECHUK

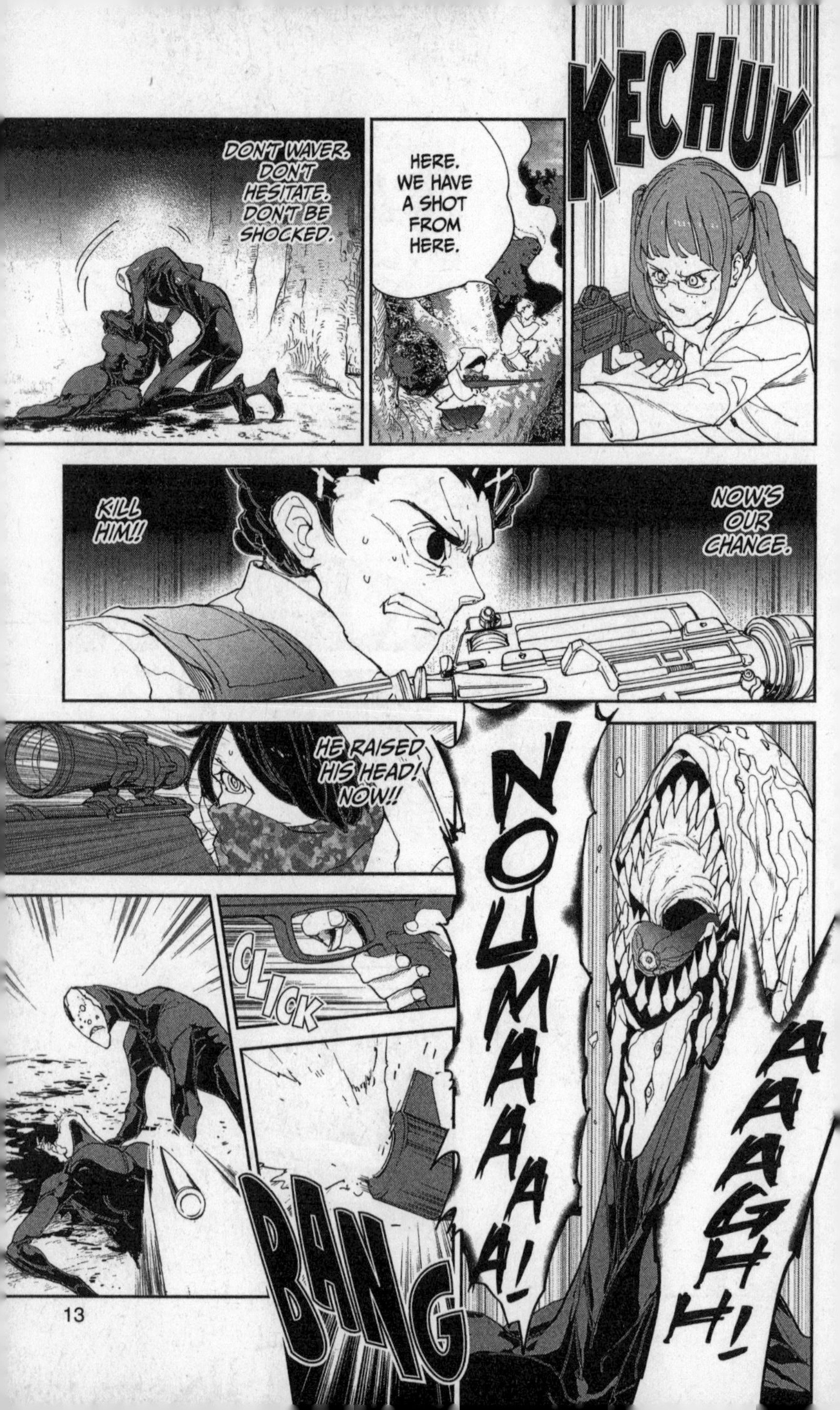
KECHUK
HERE. WE HAVE A SHOT FROM HERE.
DON'T WAVER. DON'T HESITATE. DON'T BE SHOCKED.
NOW'S OUR CHANCE.
KILL HIM!!
NOUMAAAAA!
AAAGHH!
HE RAISED HIS HEAD! NOW!!
CLICK
BANG

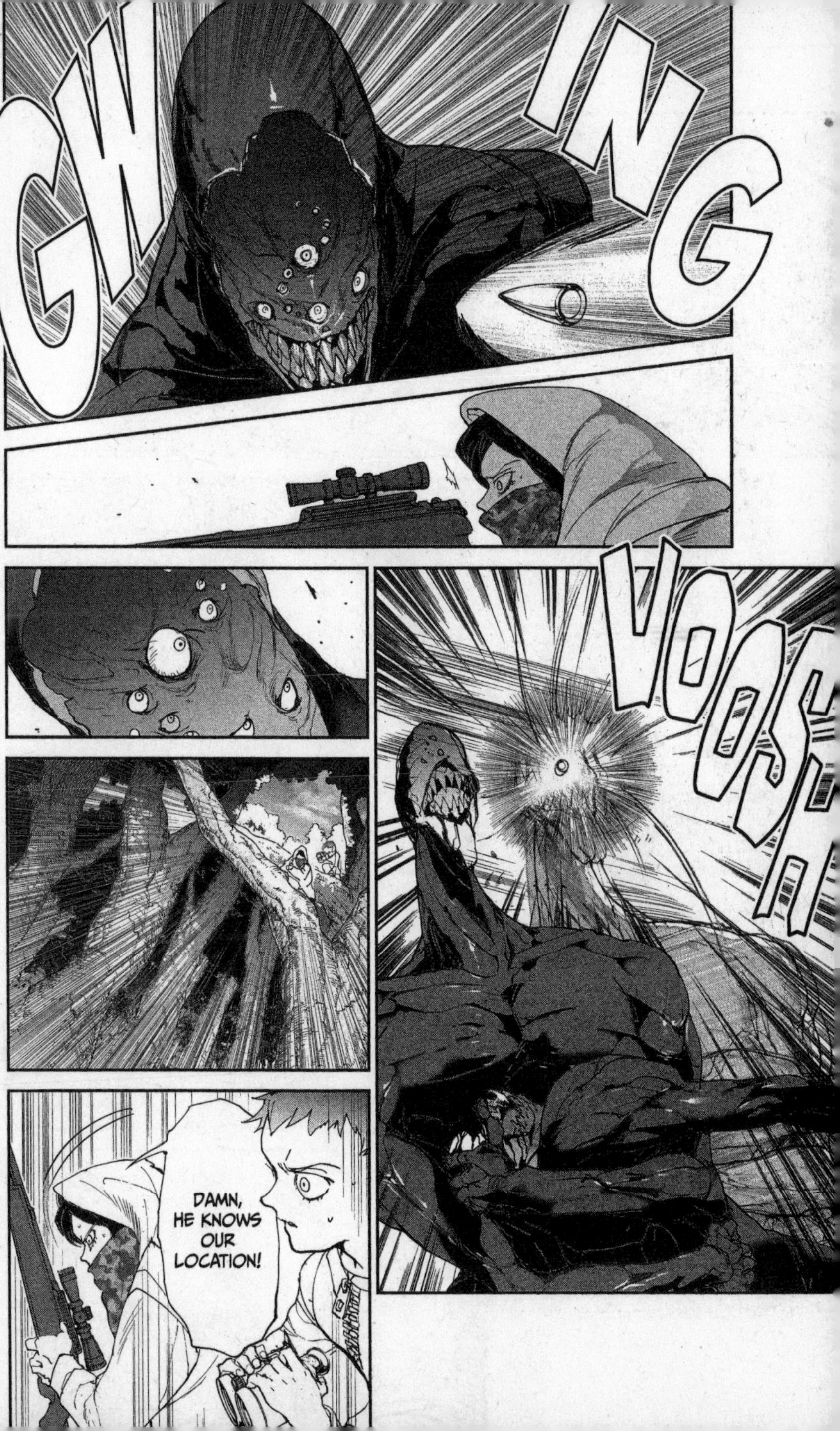
GWING
VOOSH
DAMN, HE KNOWS OUR LOCATION!

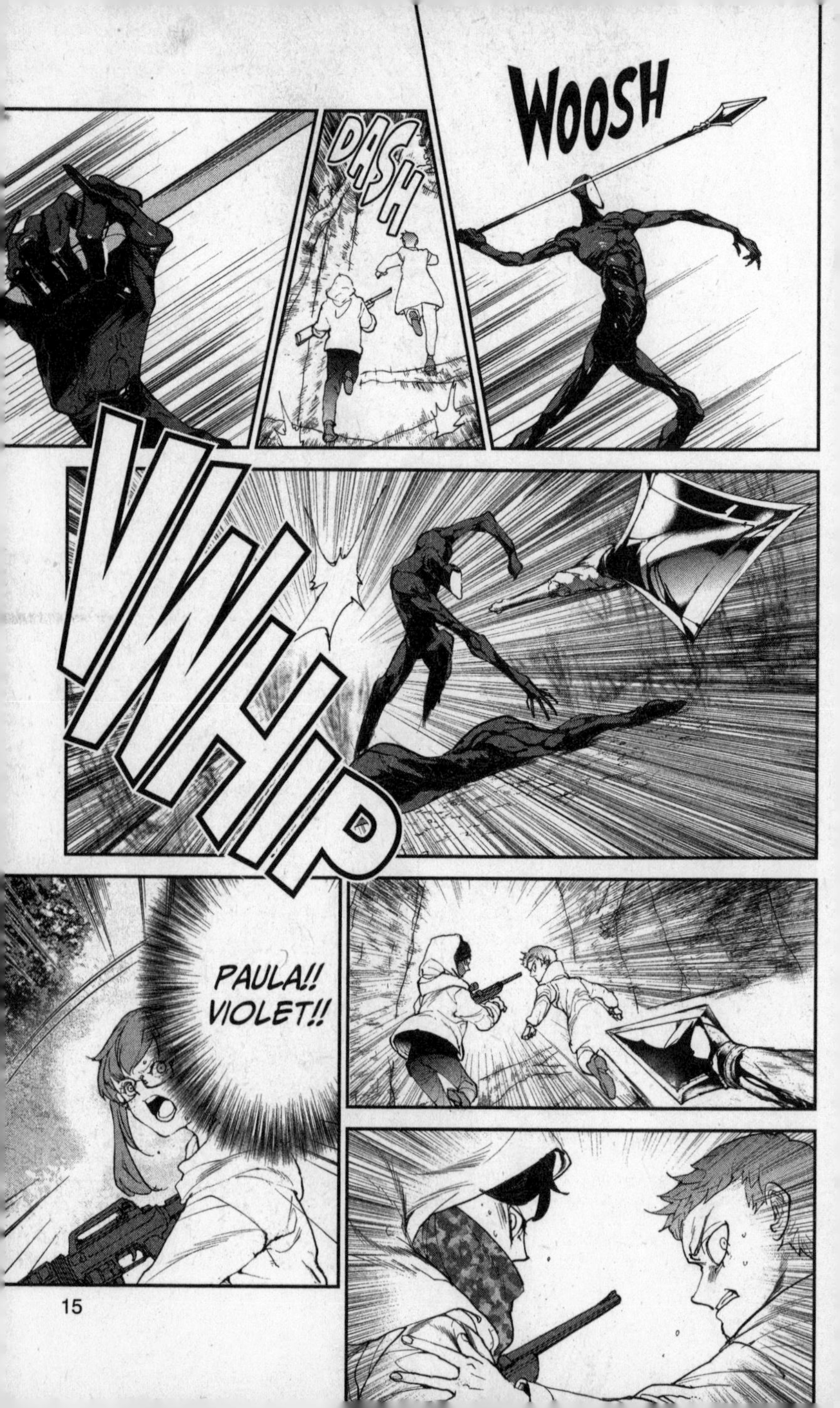
WOOSH
DASH
WHIP
PAULA!!
VIOLET!!

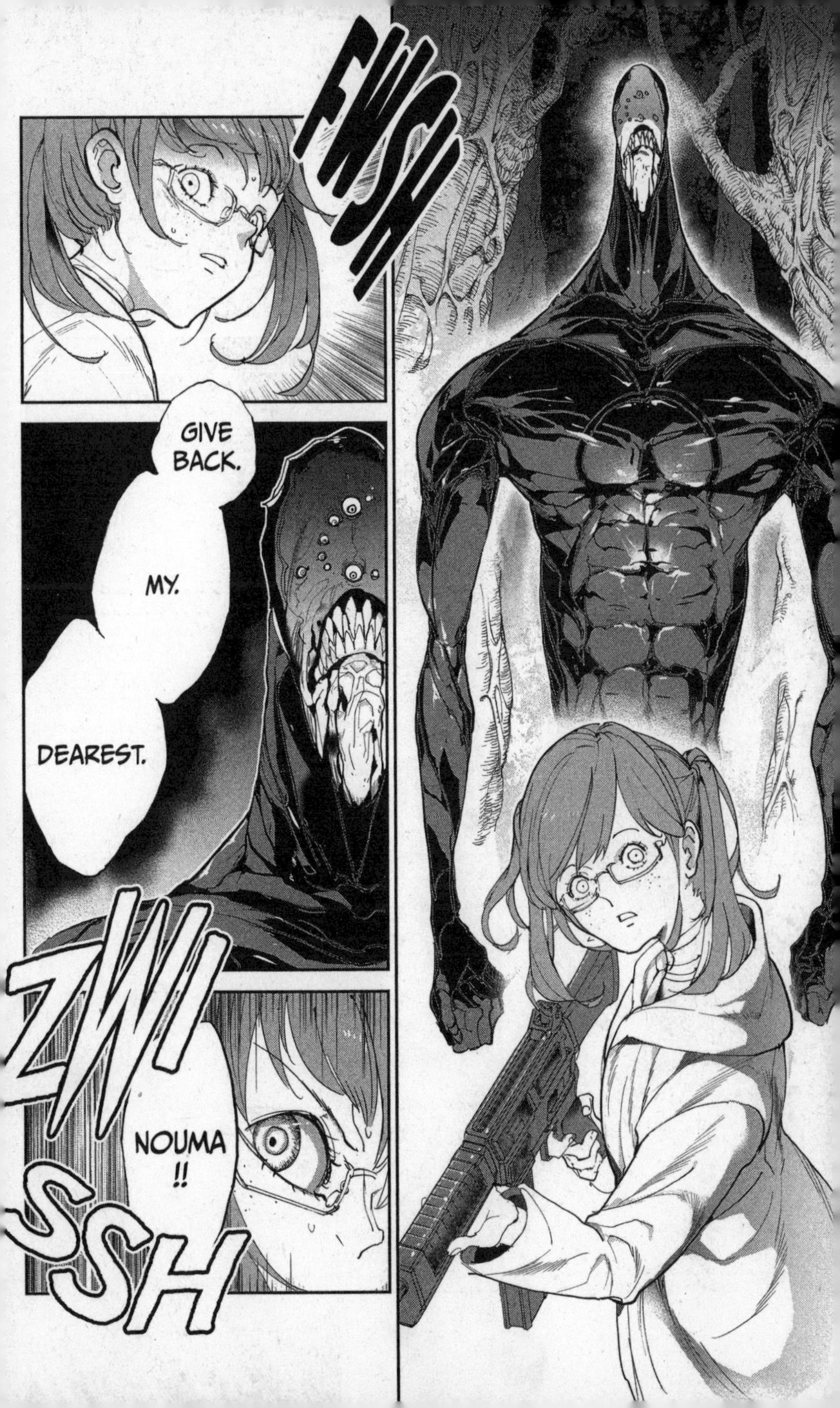
FWSH!!
GIVE BACK.
MY.
DEAREST.
ZWISSH
NOUMA!!

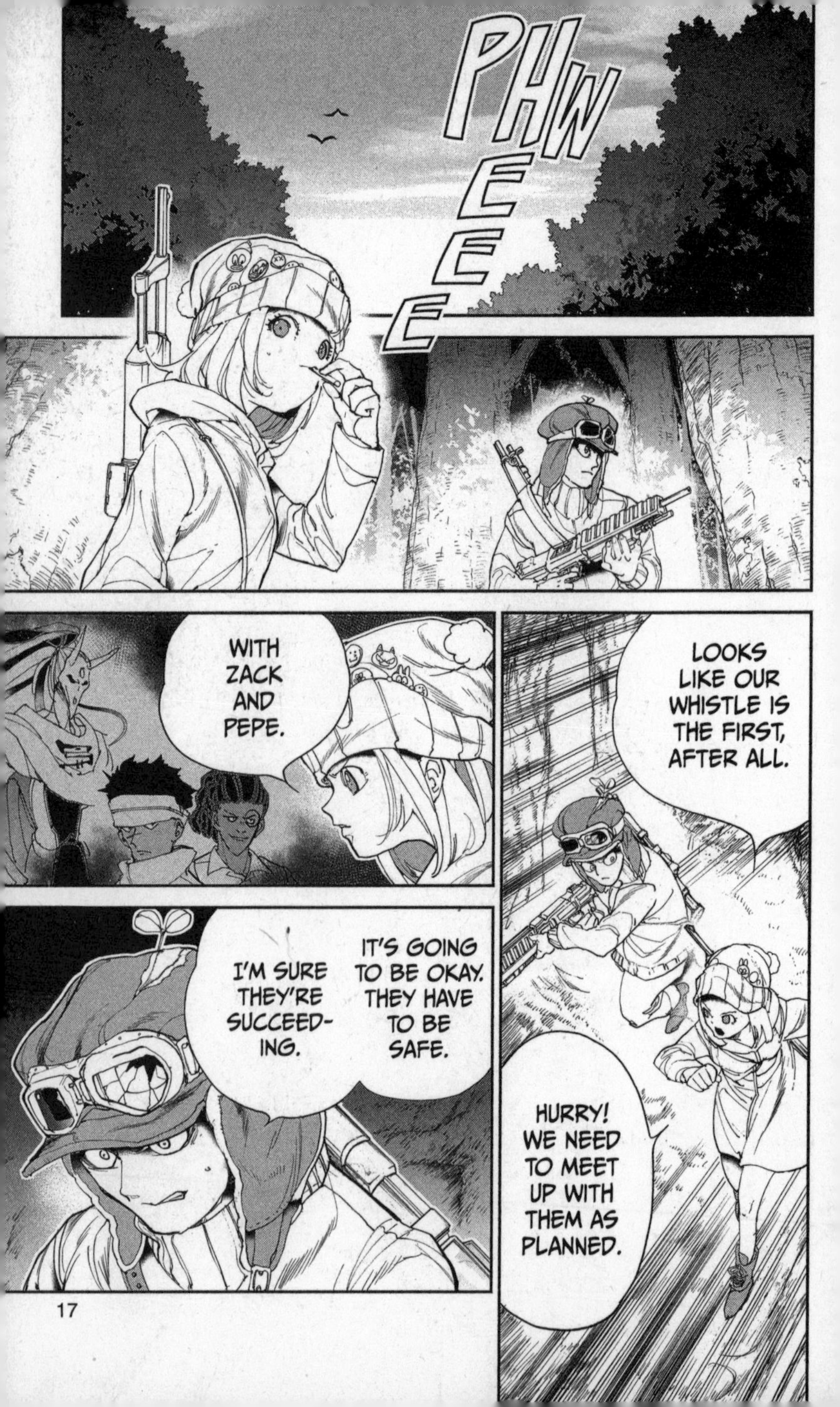
PHWEEEE
LOOKS LIKE OUR WHISTLE IS THE FIRST, AFTER ALL.
HURRY! WE NEED TO MEET UP WITH THEM AS PLANNED.
WITH ZACK AND PEPE.
IT'S GOING TO BE OKAY. THEY HAVE TO BE SAFE.
I'M SURE THEY'RE SUCCEED-ING.

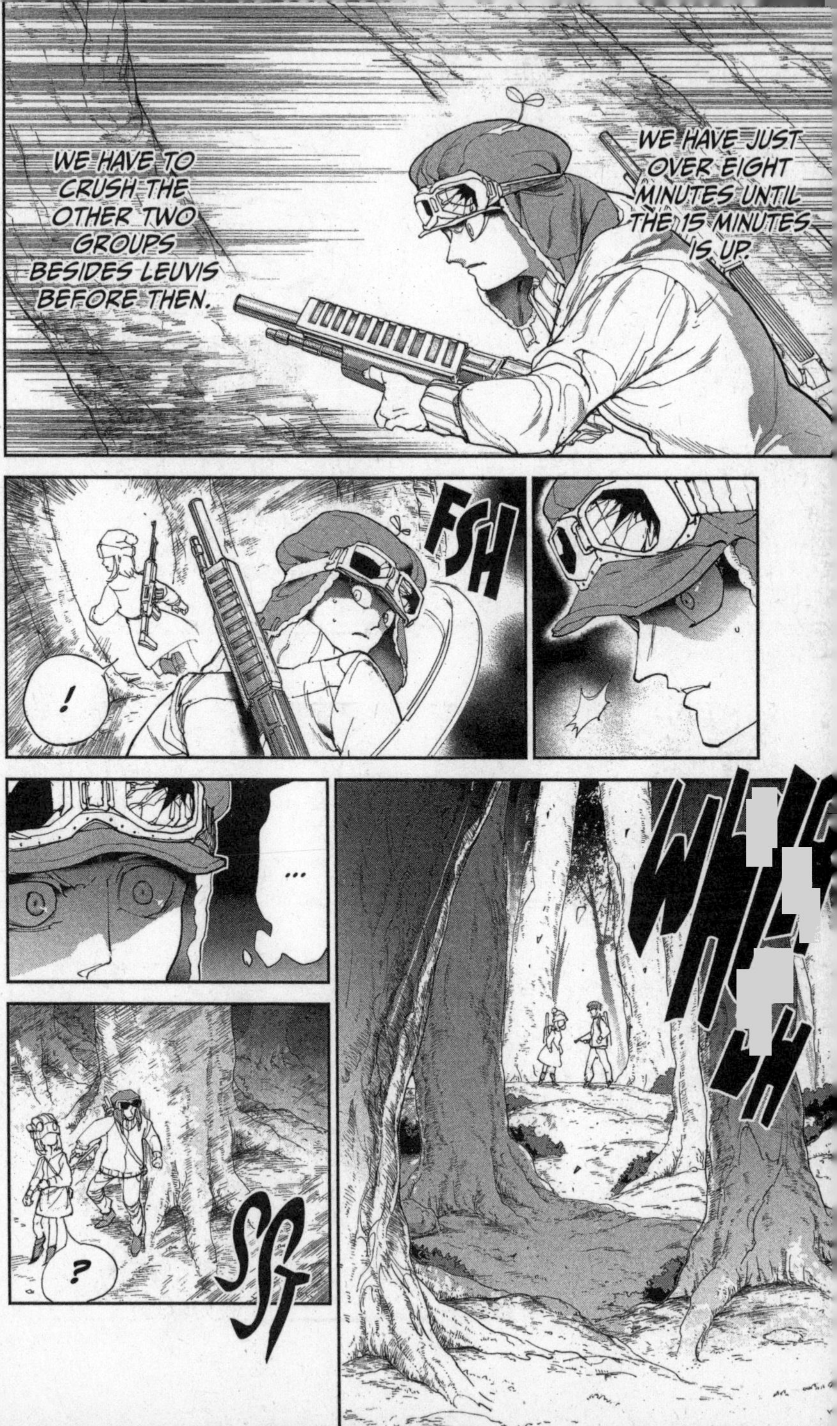

WE HAVE JUST OVER EIGHT MINUTES UNTIL THE 15 MINUTES IS UP.
WE HAVE TO CRUSH THE OTHER TWO GROUPS BESIDES LEUVIS BEFORE THEN.
FSH
!
...
?
SST

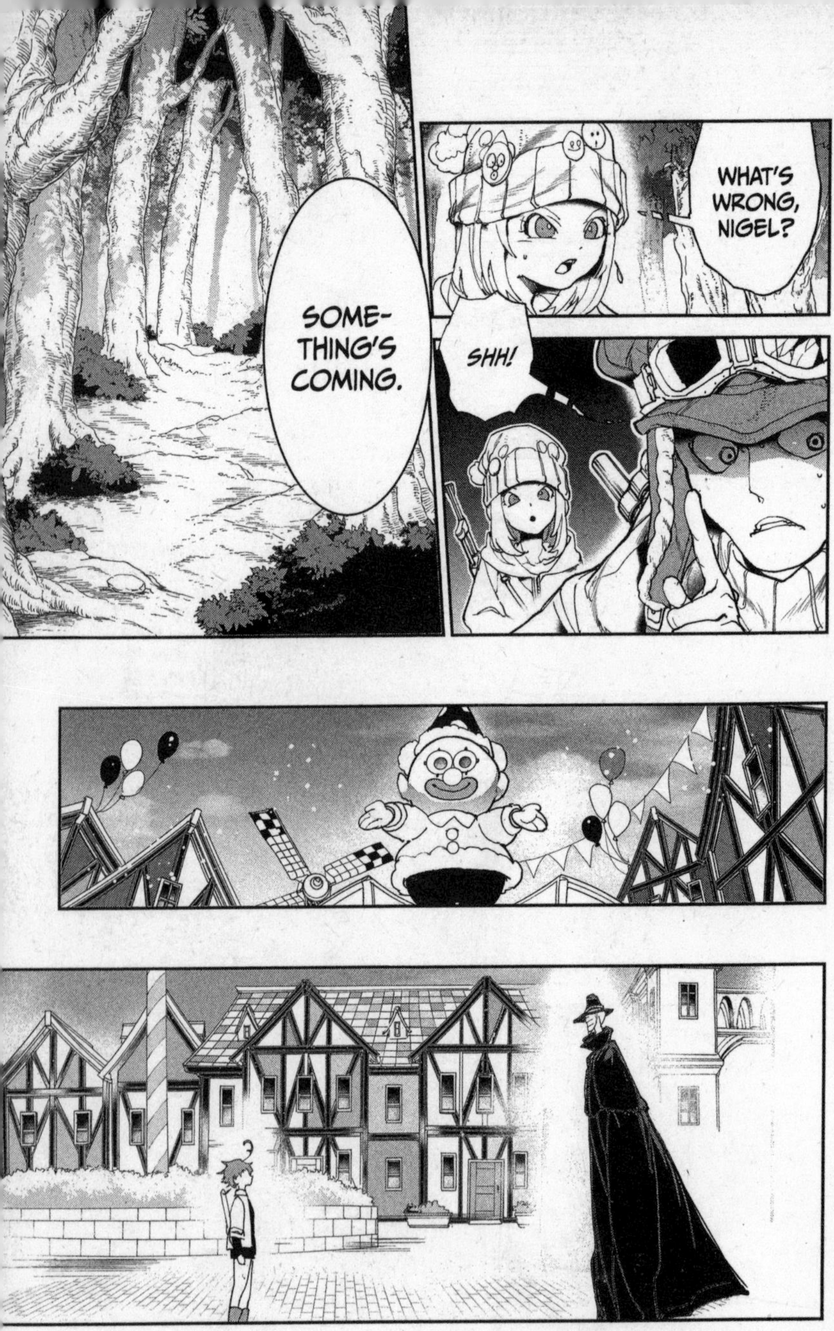
WHAT'S WRONG, NIGEL?
SHH!
SOME-THING'S COMING.

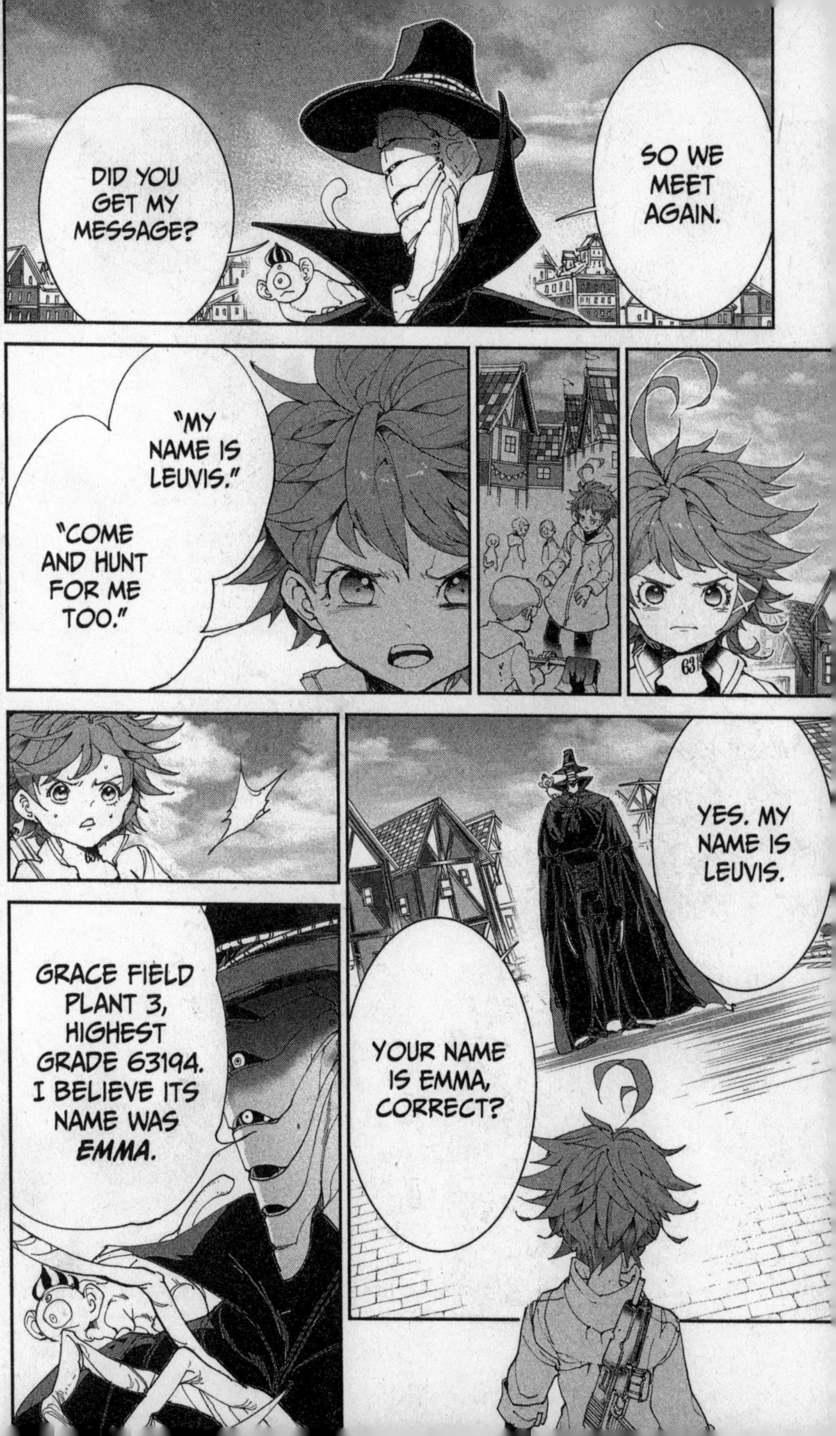
SO WE MEET AGAIN.
DID YOU GET MY MESSAGE?
"MY NAME IS LEUVIS."
"COME AND HUNT FOR ME TOO."
YES. MY NAME IS LEUVIS.
YOUR NAME IS EMMA, CORRECT?
GRACE FIELD PLANT 3, HIGHEST GRADE 63194. I BELIEVE ITS NAME WAS *EMMA*.

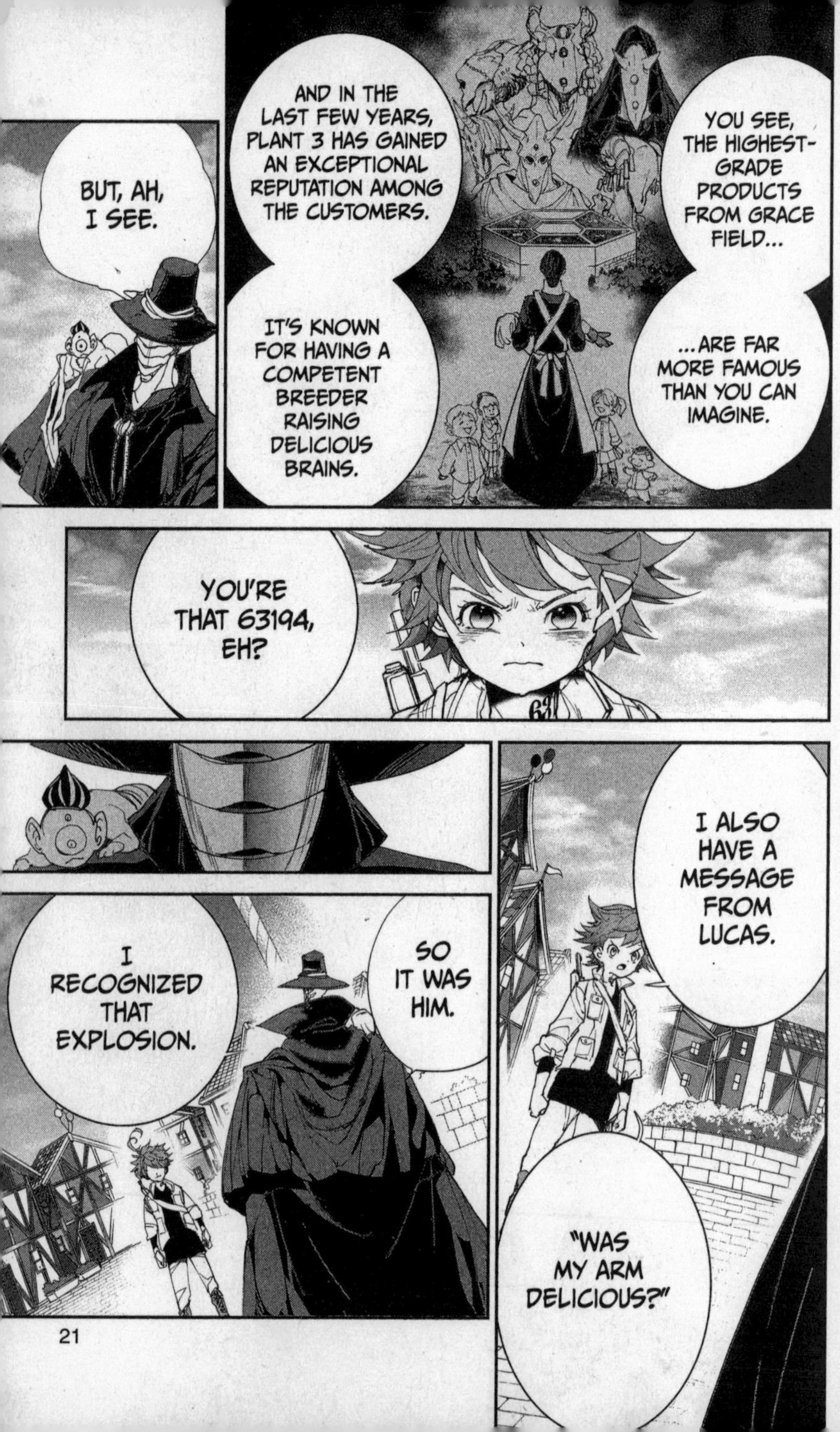
YOU SEE, THE HIGHEST-GRADE PRODUCTS FROM GRACE FIELD...
...ARE FAR MORE FAMOUS THAN YOU CAN IMAGINE.
AND IN THE LAST FEW YEARS, PLANT 3 HAS GAINED AN EXCEPTIONAL REPUTATION AMONG THE CUSTOMERS.
IT'S KNOWN FOR HAVING A COMPETENT BREEDER RAISING DELICIOUS BRAINS.
BUT, AH, I SEE.
YOU'RE THAT 63194, EH?
I ALSO HAVE A MESSAGE FROM LUCAS.
"WAS MY ARM DELICIOUS?"
SO IT WAS HIM.
I RECOGNIZED THAT EXPLOSION.

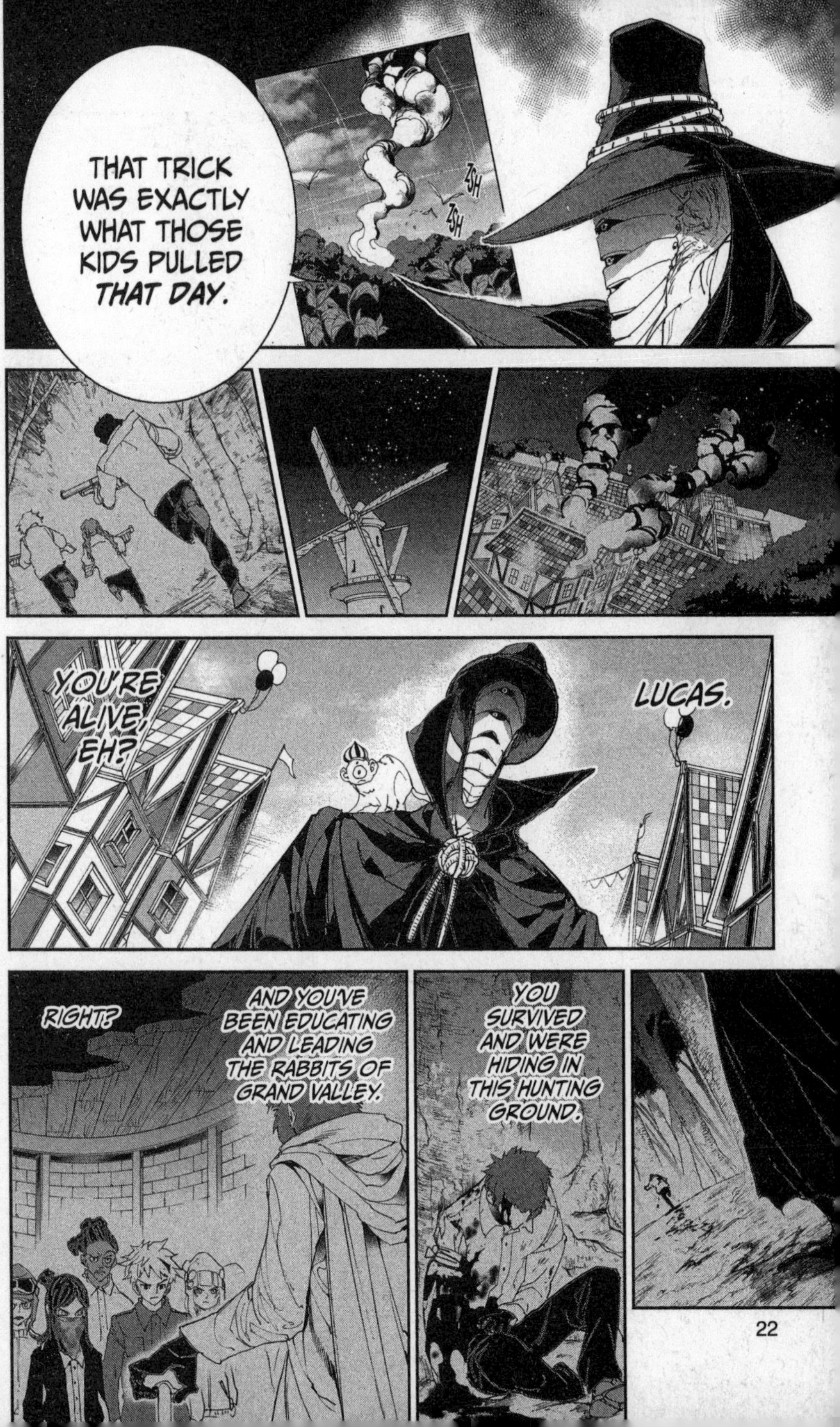
THAT TRICK WAS EXACTLY WHAT THOSE KIDS PULLED *THAT DAY.*
ZSH
ZSH
YOU'RE ALIVE, EH?
LUCAS.
YOU SURVIVED AND WERE HIDING IN THIS HUNTING GROUND.
AND YOU'VE BEEN EDUCATING AND LEADING THE RABBITS OF GRAND VALLEY.
RIGHT?

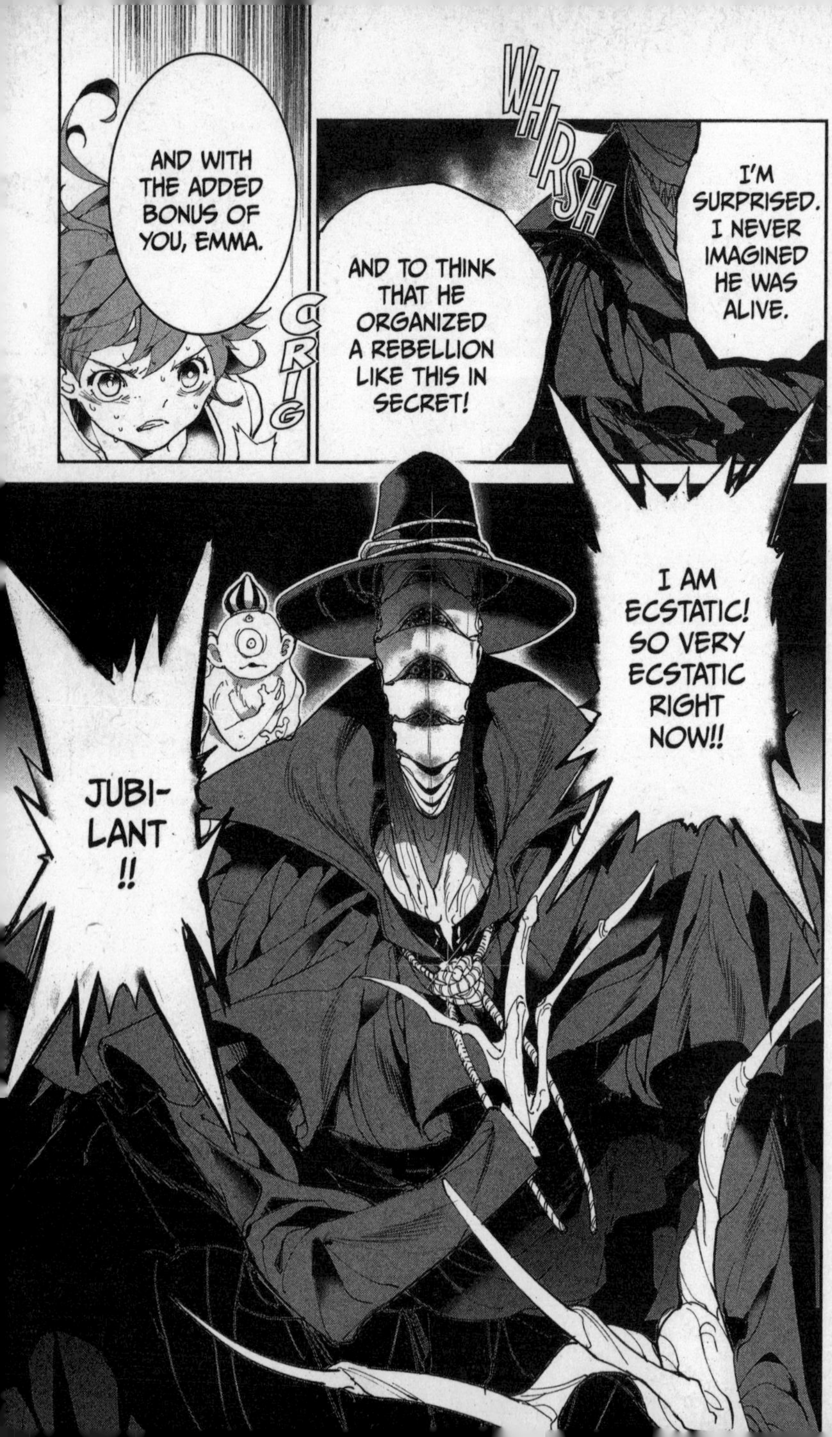

WHIRSH
I'M SURPRISED. I NEVER IMAGINED HE WAS ALIVE.
AND TO THINK THAT HE ORGANIZED A REBELLION LIKE THIS IN SECRET!
AND WITH THE ADDED BONUS OF YOU, EMMA.
CRIG
I AM ECSTATIC! SO VERY ECSTATIC RIGHT NOW!!
JUBI-LANT !!

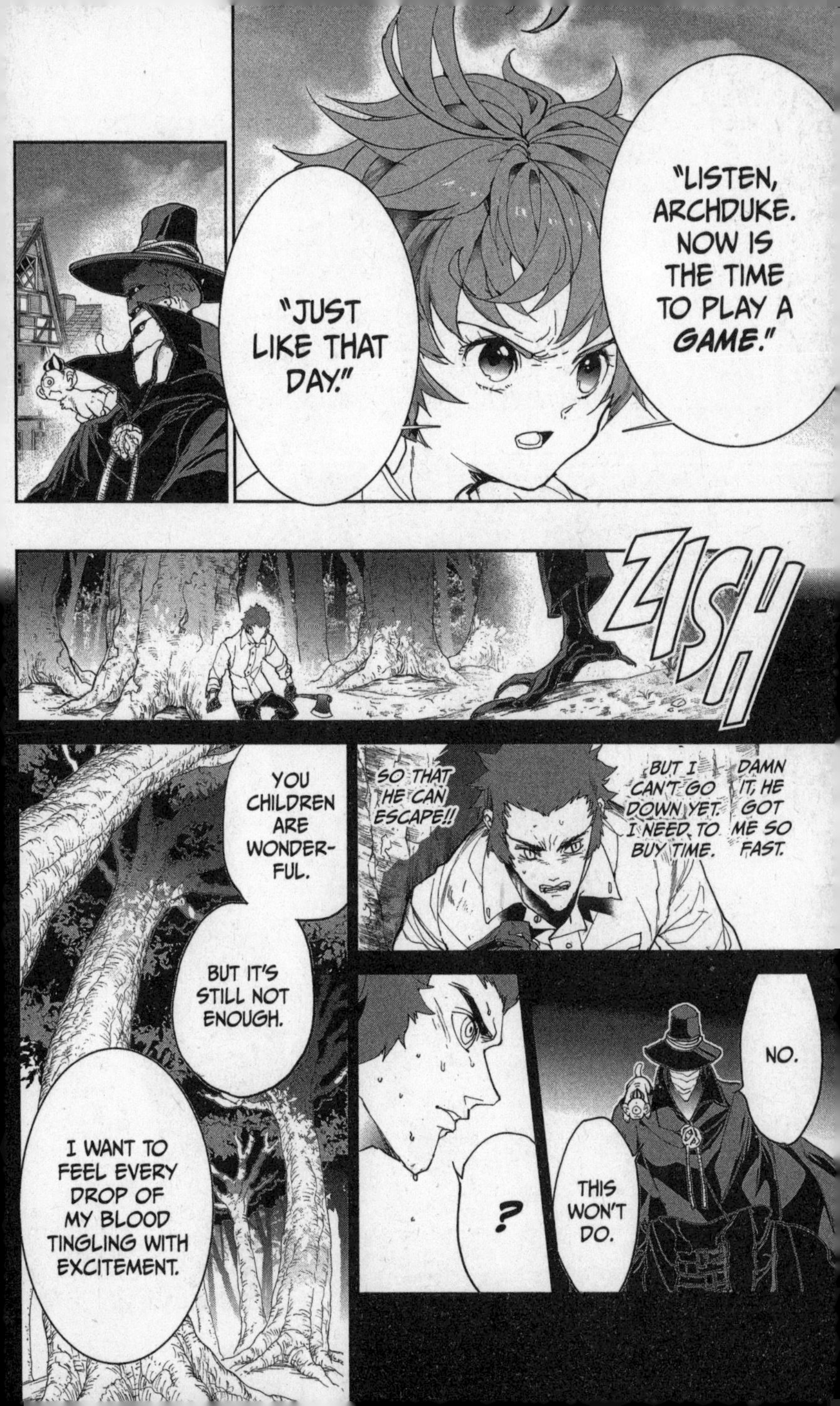
"LISTEN, ARCHDUKE. NOW IS THE TIME TO PLAY A GAME."
"JUST LIKE THAT DAY."
ZISH
DAMN IT, HE GOT ME SO FAST.
BUT I CAN'T GO DOWN YET. I NEED TO BUY TIME.
SO THAT HE CAN ESCAPE!!
NO.
THIS WON'T DO.
?
YOU CHILDREN ARE WONDER-FUL.
BUT IT'S STILL NOT ENOUGH.
I WANT TO FEEL EVERY DROP OF MY BLOOD TINGLING WITH EXCITEMENT.

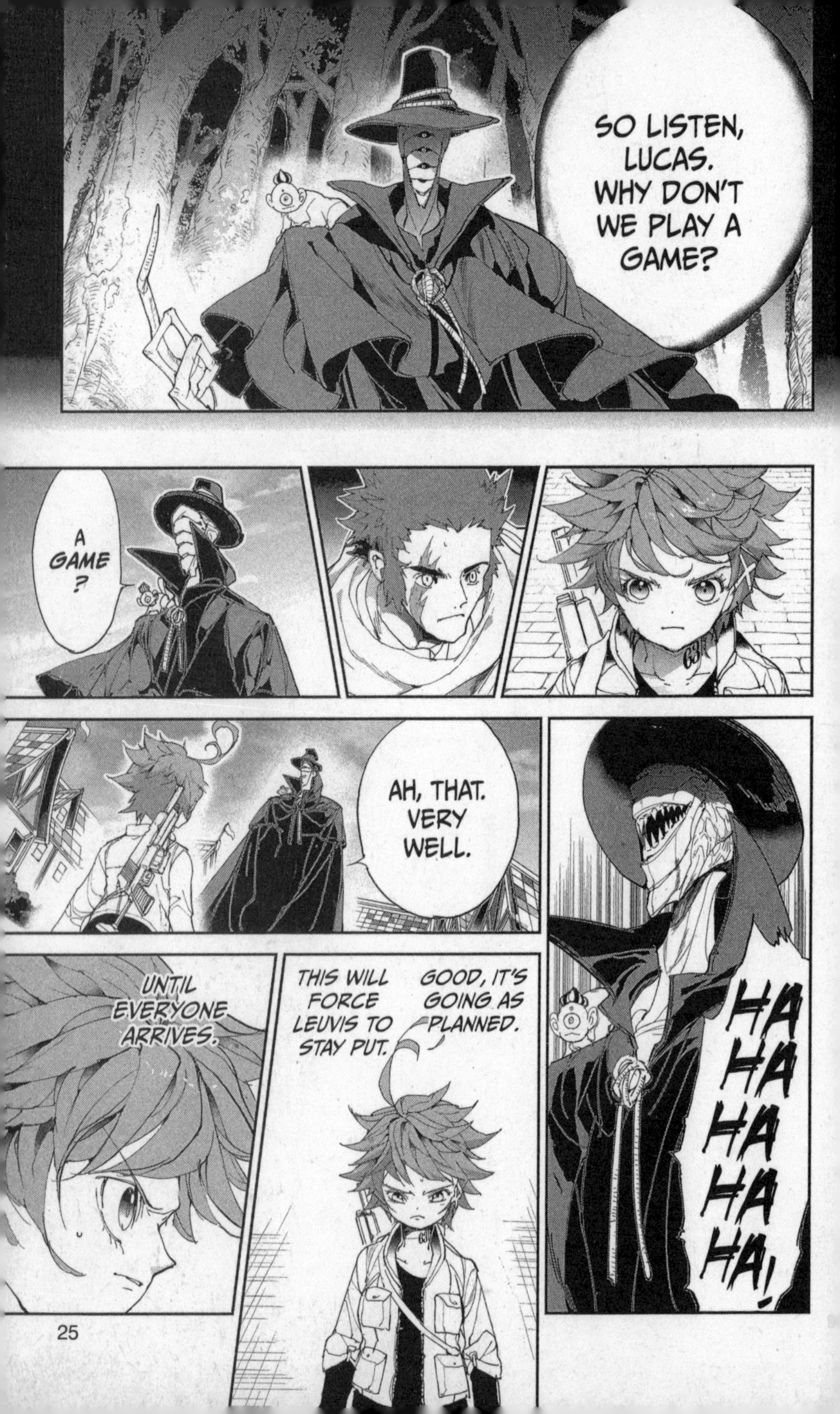
SO LISTEN, LUCAS. WHY DON'T WE PLAY A GAME?
A GAME?
HA HA HA HA HA HA HA HA HA HA!
AH, THAT. VERY WELL.
GOOD, IT'S GOING AS PLANNED.
THIS WILL FORCE LEUVIS TO STAY PUT.
UNTIL EVERYONE ARRIVES.

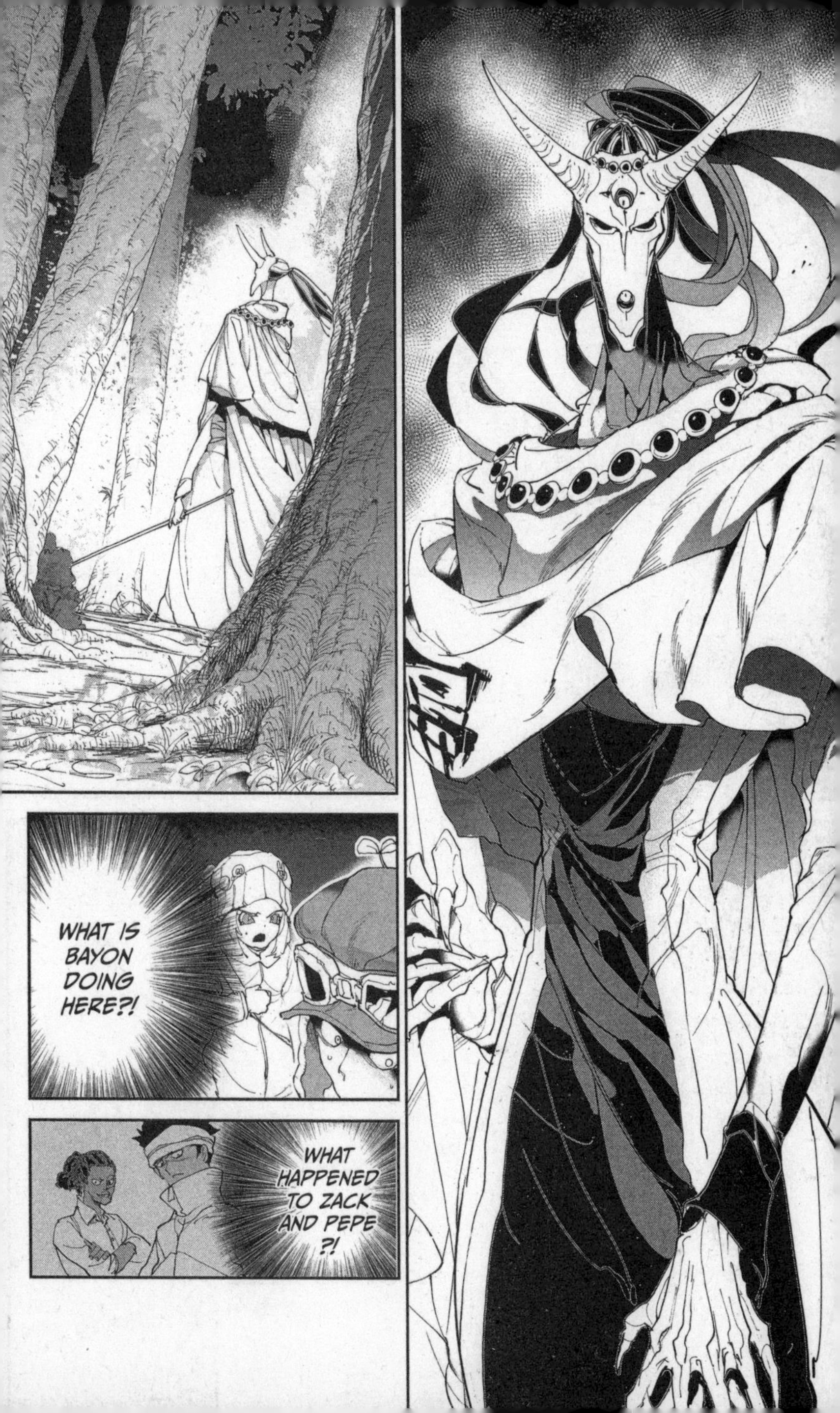
WHAT IS BAYON DOING HERE?!
WHAT HAPPENED TO ZACK AND PEPE ?!

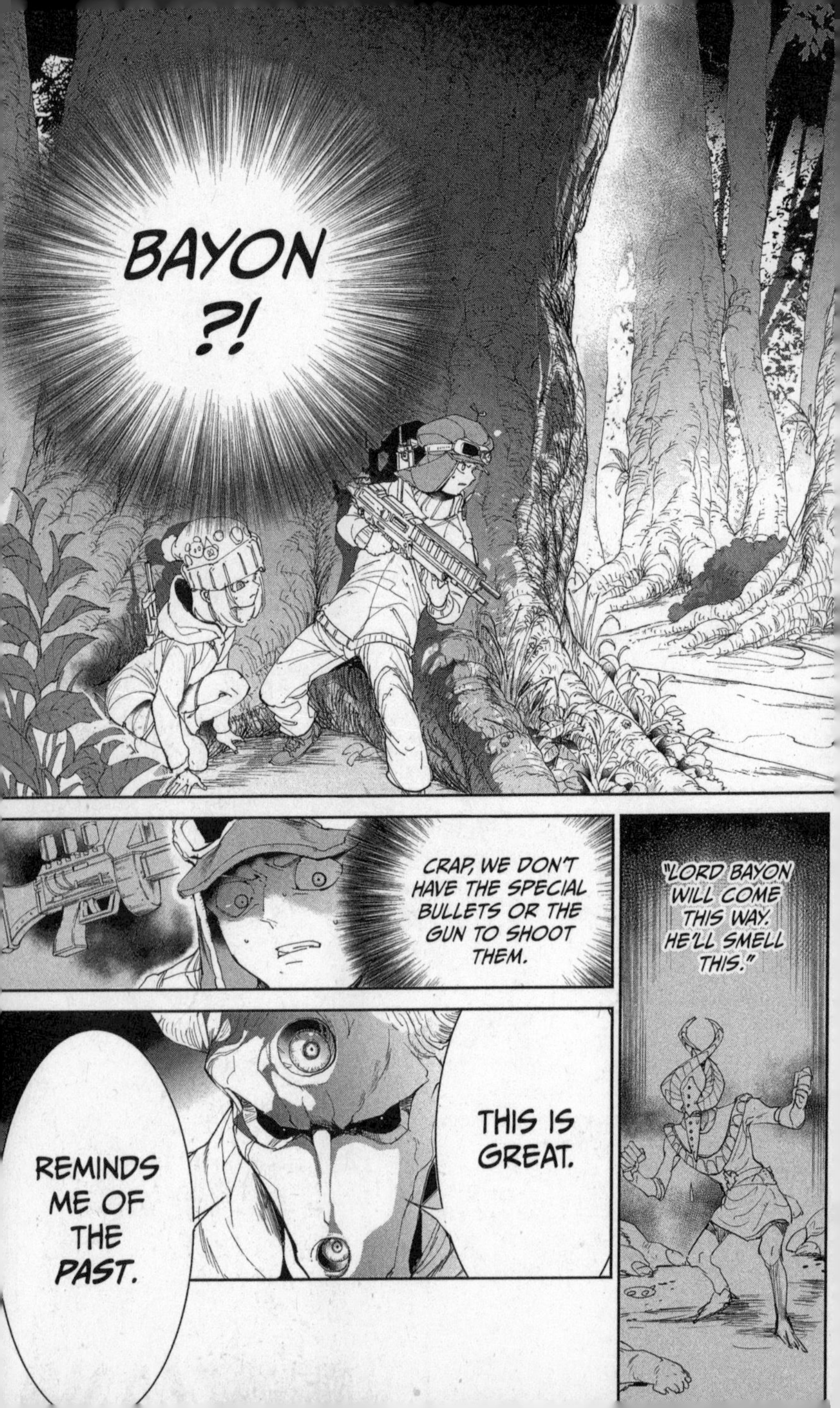
BAYON ?!
"LORD BAYON WILL COME THIS WAY. HE'LL SMELL THIS."
CRAP, WE DON'T HAVE THE SPECIAL BULLETS OR THE GUN TO SHOOT THEM.
THIS IS GREAT.
REMINDS ME OF THE PAST.

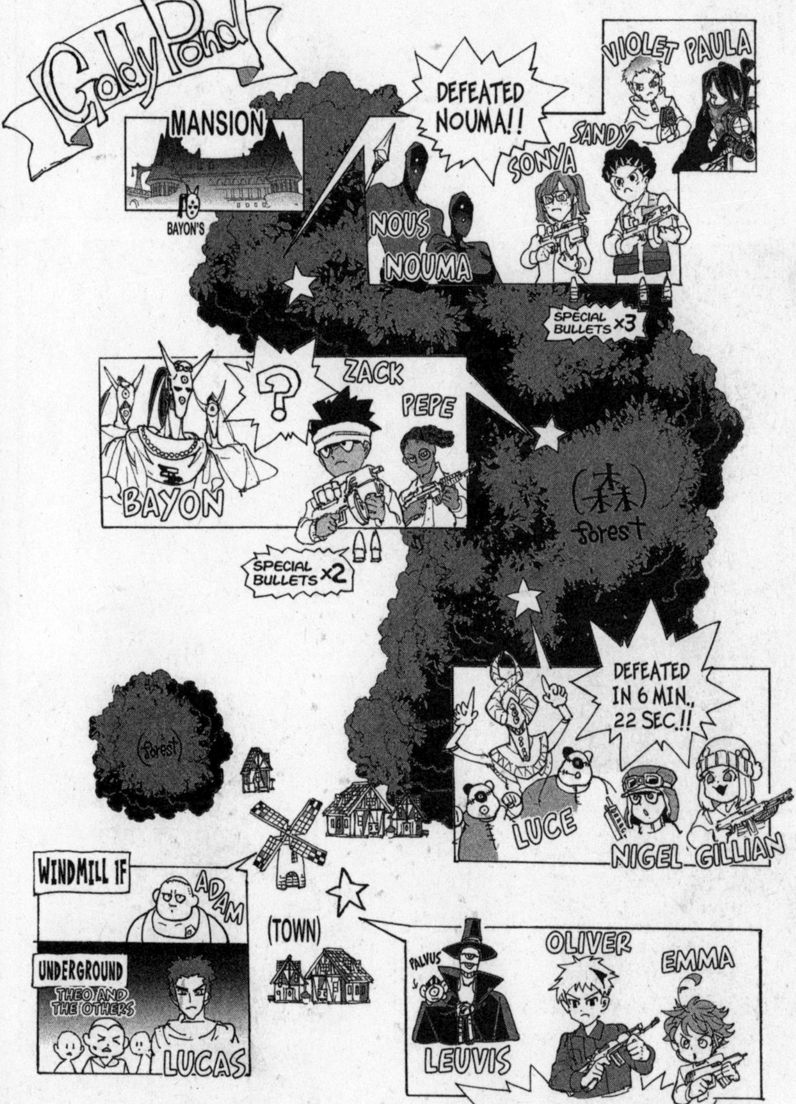

Goldy Pond
VIOLET
PAULA
DEFEATED NOUMA!!
MANSION
SANDY
SONYA
BAYON'S
NOUS
NOUMA
SPECIAL BULLETS ×3
ZACK
PEPE
?
BAYON
(森) forest
SPECIAL BULLETS ×2
DEFEATED IN 6 MIN., 22 SEC.!!
(forest)
LUCE
NIGEL
GILLIAN
WINDMILL 1F
ADAM
(TOWN)
OLIVER
EMMA
PALVUS
UNDERGROUND
THEO AND THE OTHERS
LUCAS
LEUVIS
BUY TIME FOR 15 MINUTES!

CHAPTER 81: DEFEND TO THE DEATH

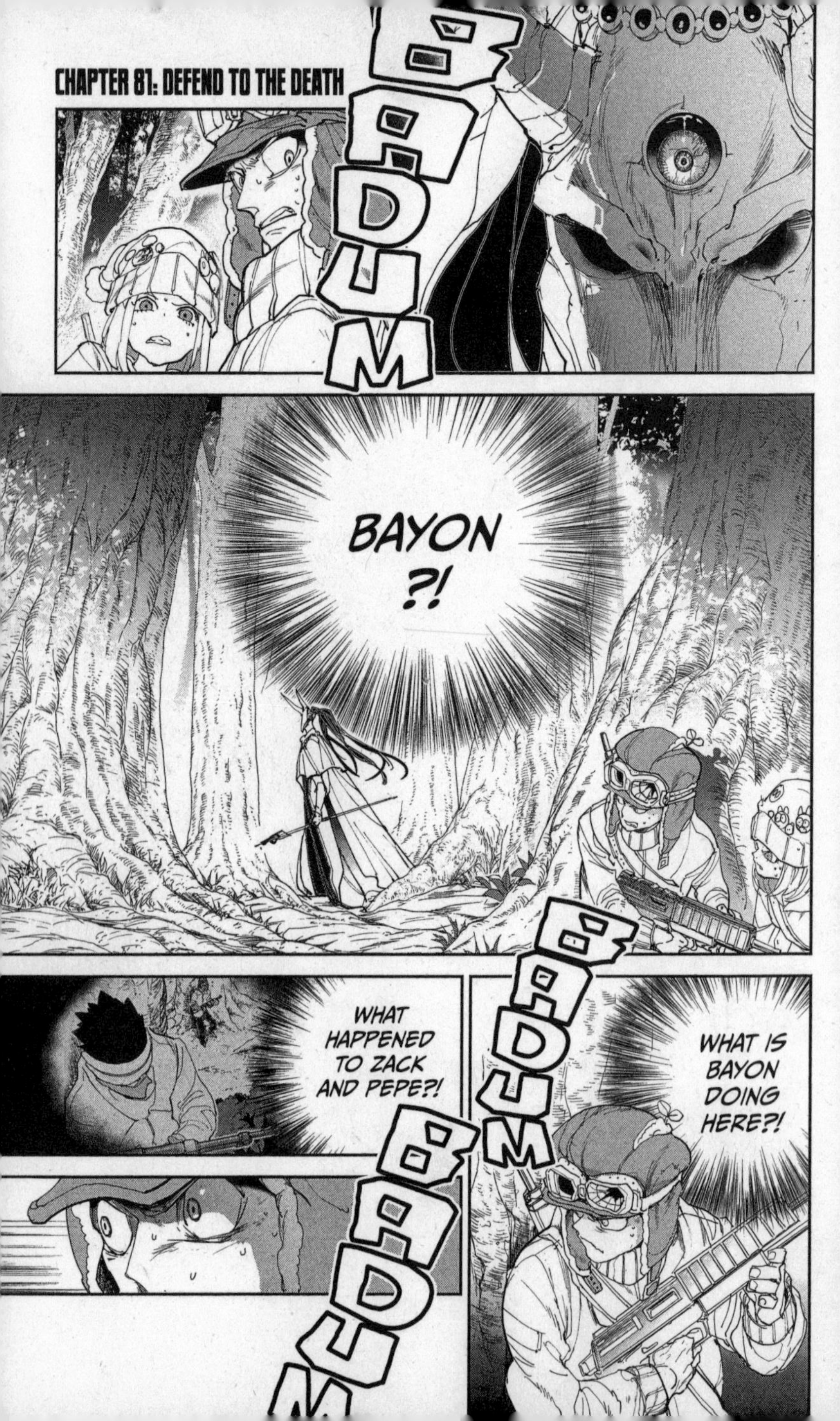
BADUM
BAYON ?!
BADUM
WHAT IS BAYON DOING HERE?!
WHAT HAPPENED TO ZACK AND PEPE?!
BADUM

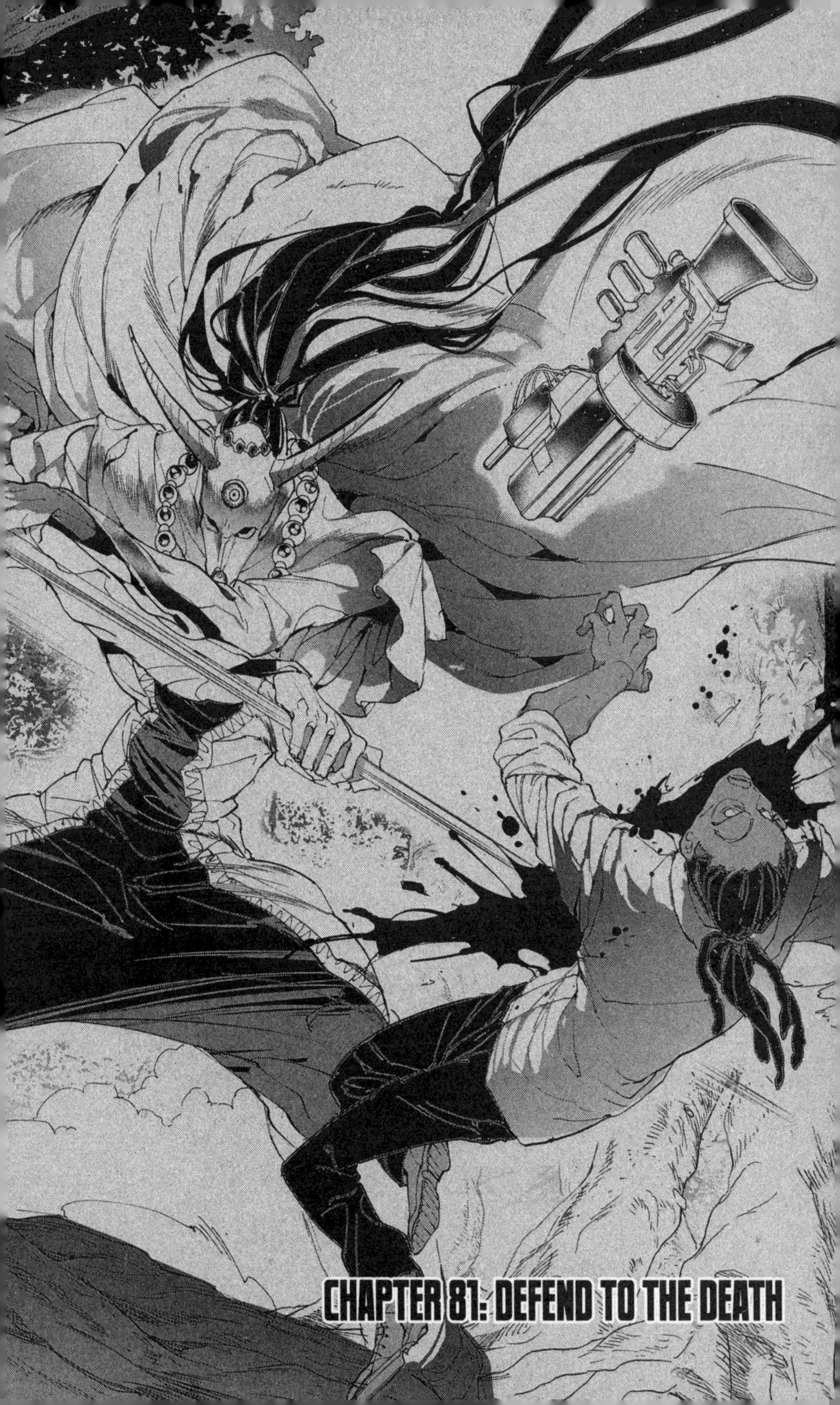
CHAPTER 81: DEFEND TO THE DEATH

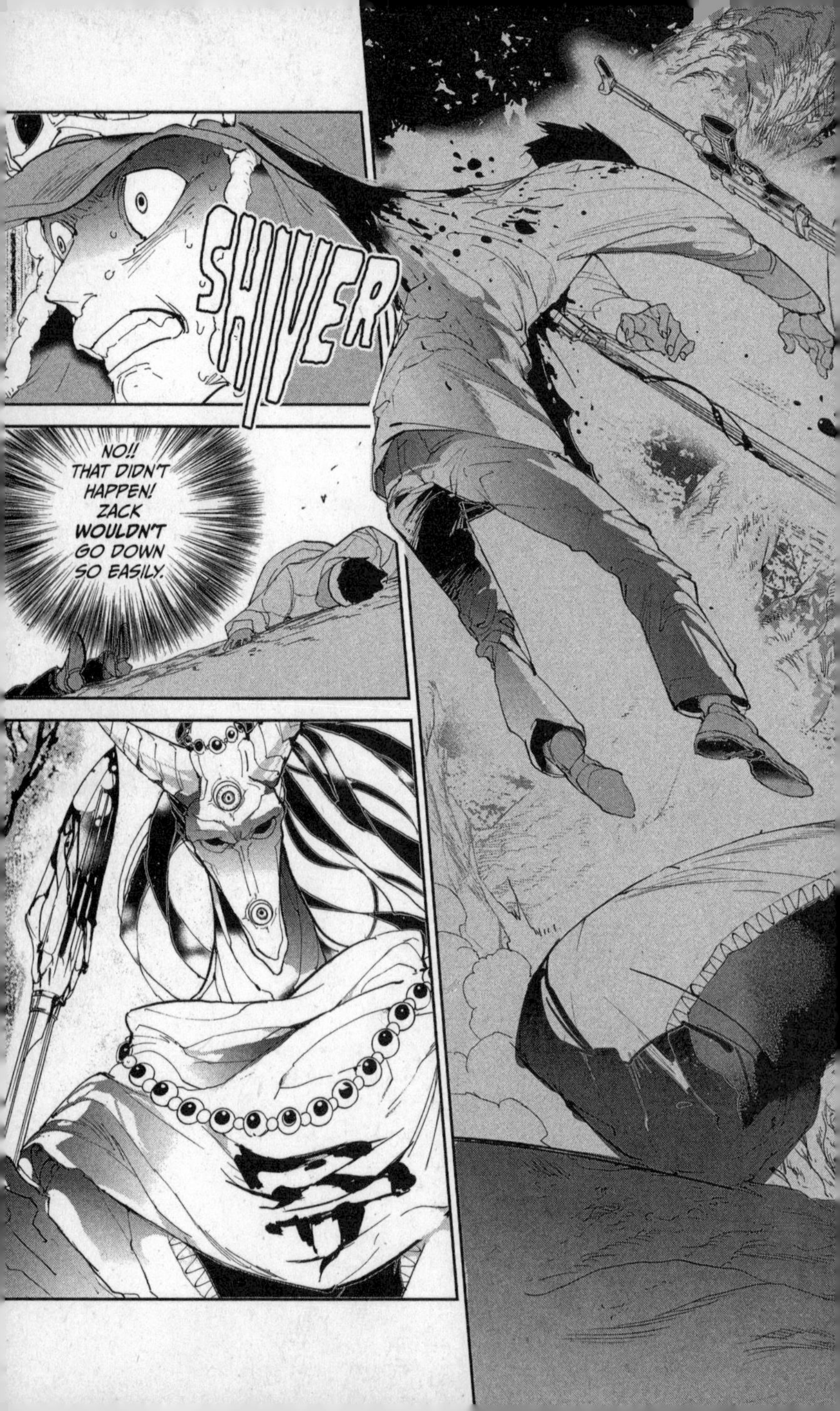
SHIVER
NO!! THAT DIDN'T HAPPEN! ZACK WOULDN'T GO DOWN SO EASILY.

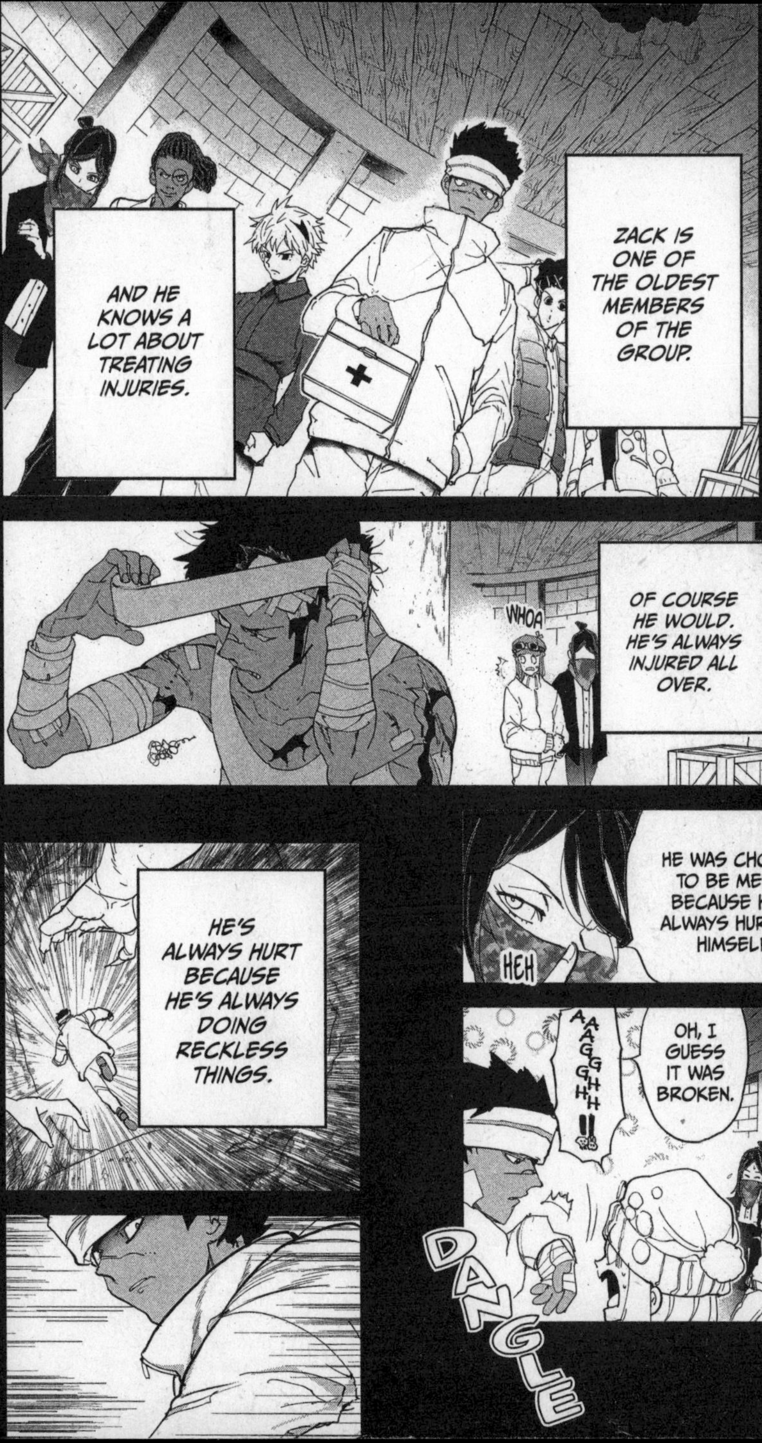
ZACK IS ONE OF THE OLDEST MEMBERS OF THE GROUP.
AND HE KNOWS A LOT ABOUT TREATING INJURIES.
OF COURSE HE WOULD. HE'S ALWAYS INJURED ALL OVER.
WHOA
HE WAS CHOSEN TO BE MEDIC BECAUSE HE'S ALWAYS HURTING HIMSELF.
HEH
HE'S ALWAYS HURT BECAUSE HE'S ALWAYS DOING RECKLESS THINGS.
OH, I GUESS IT WAS BROKEN.
AAAGGGHHH!!
DANGLE

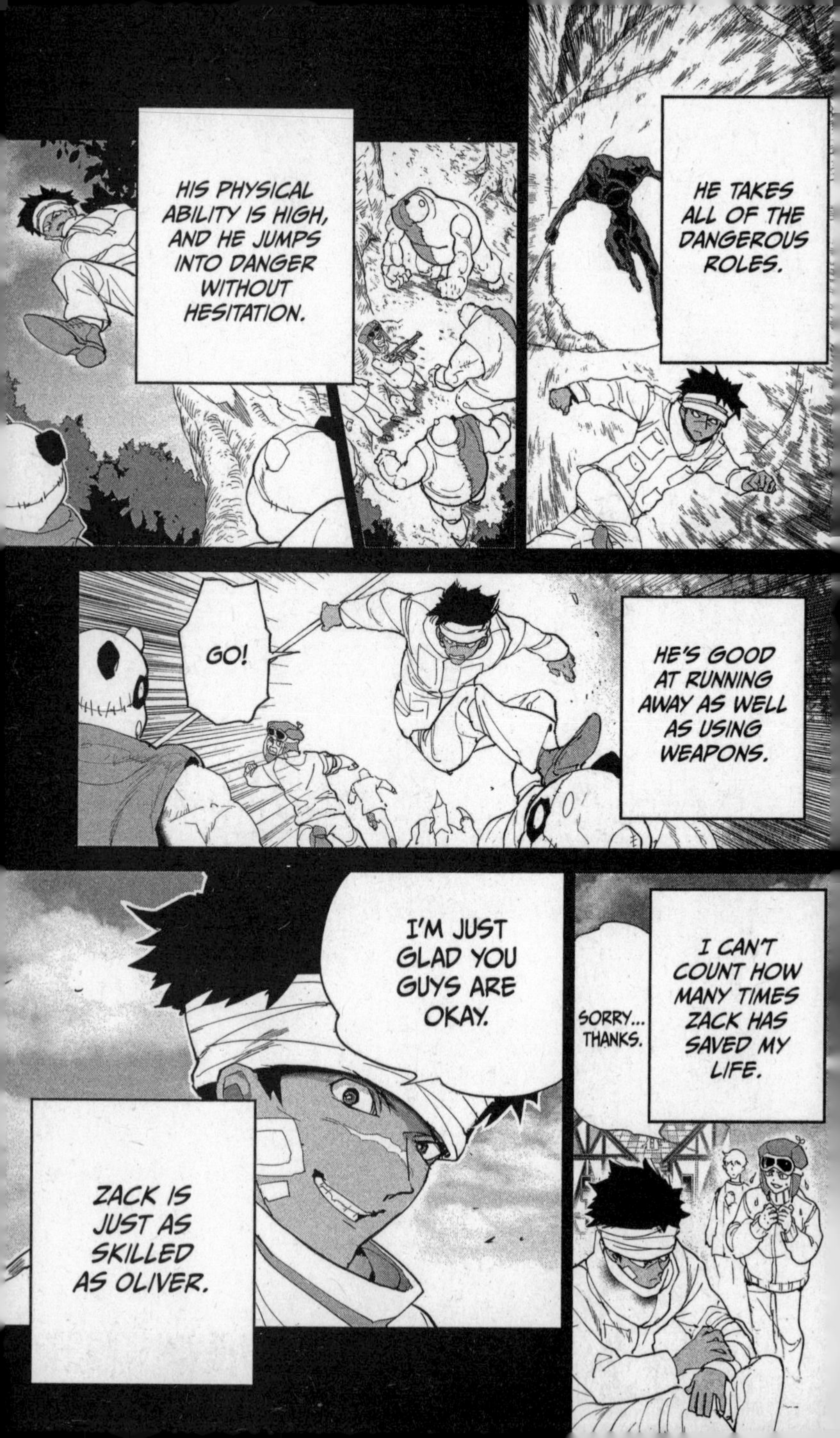
HE TAKES ALL OF THE DANGEROUS ROLES.
HIS PHYSICAL ABILITY IS HIGH, AND HE JUMPS INTO DANGER WITHOUT HESITATION.
HE'S GOOD AT RUNNING AWAY AS WELL AS USING WEAPONS.
GO!
I CAN'T COUNT HOW MANY TIMES ZACK HAS SAVED MY LIFE.
SORRY... THANKS.
I'M JUST GLAD YOU GUYS ARE OKAY.
ZACK IS JUST AS SKILLED AS OLIVER.

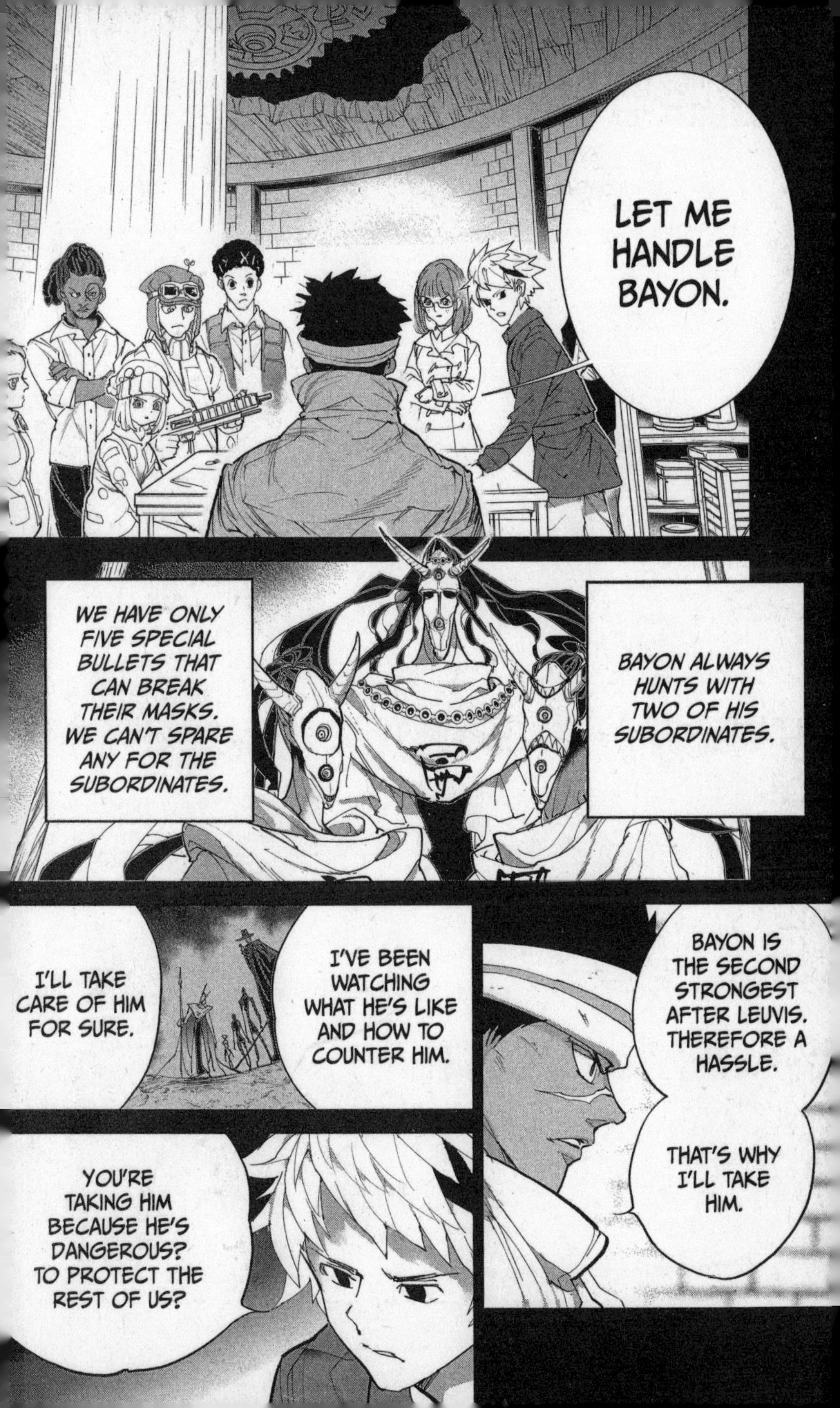
LET ME HANDLE BAYON.
BAYON ALWAYS HUNTS WITH TWO OF HIS SUBORDINATES.
WE HAVE ONLY FIVE SPECIAL BULLETS THAT CAN BREAK THEIR MASKS. WE CAN'T SPARE ANY FOR THE SUBORDINATES.
BAYON IS THE SECOND STRONGEST AFTER LEUVIS. THEREFORE A HASSLE.
THAT'S WHY I'LL TAKE HIM.
I'VE BEEN WATCHING WHAT HE'S LIKE AND HOW TO COUNTER HIM.
I'LL TAKE CARE OF HIM FOR SURE.
YOU'RE TAKING HIM BECAUSE HE'S DANGEROUS? TO PROTECT THE REST OF US?

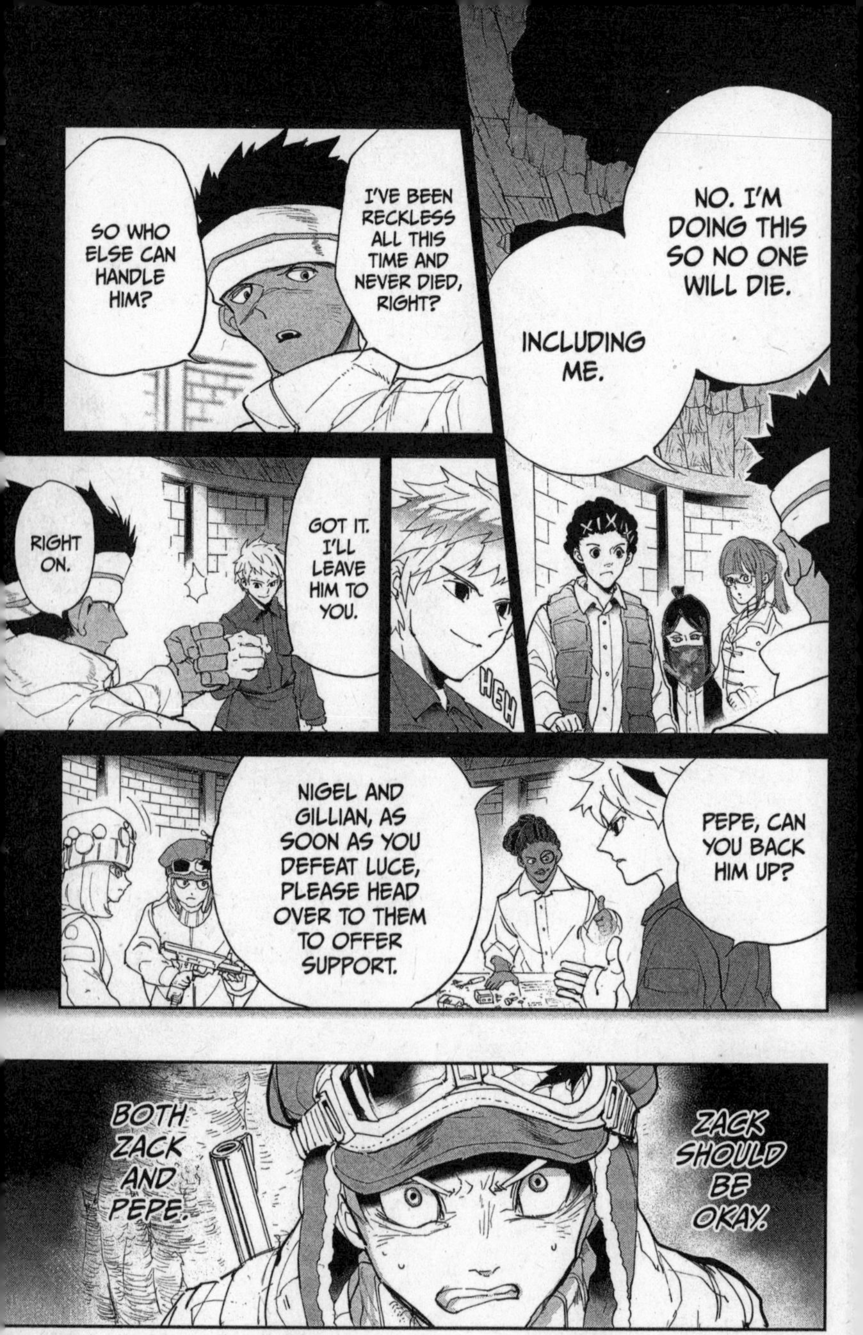
I'VE BEEN RECKLESS ALL THIS TIME AND NEVER DIED, RIGHT?
SO WHO ELSE CAN HANDLE HIM?
NO. I'M DOING THIS SO NO ONE WILL DIE.
INCLUDING ME.
GOT IT. I'LL LEAVE HIM TO YOU.
HEH
RIGHT ON.
PEPE, CAN YOU BACK HIM UP?
NIGEL AND GILLIAN, AS SOON AS YOU DEFEAT LUCE, PLEASE HEAD OVER TO THEM TO OFFER SUPPORT.
ZACK SHOULD BE OKAY.
BOTH ZACK AND PEPE.

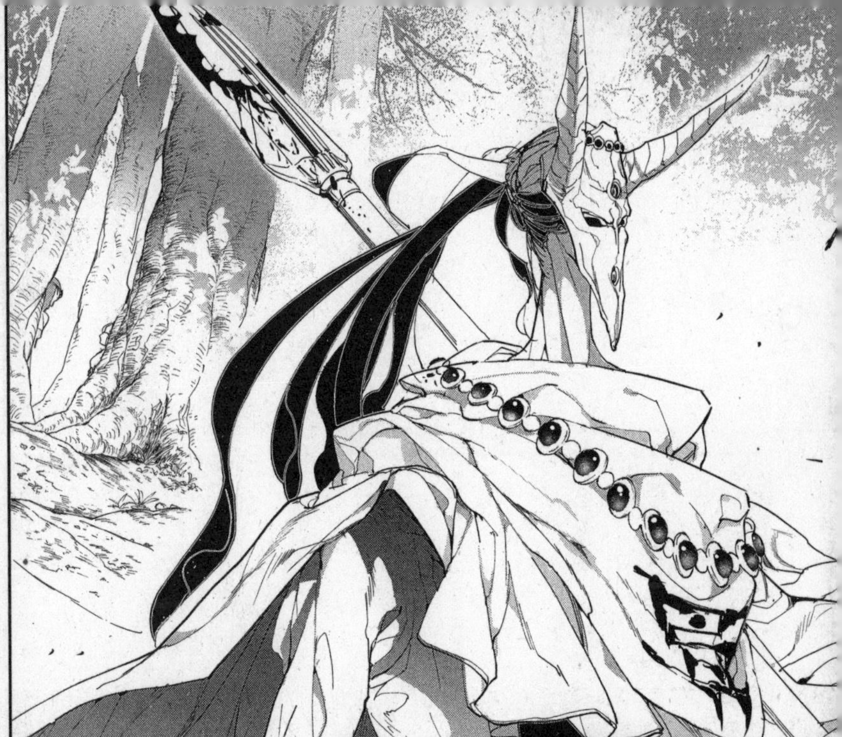

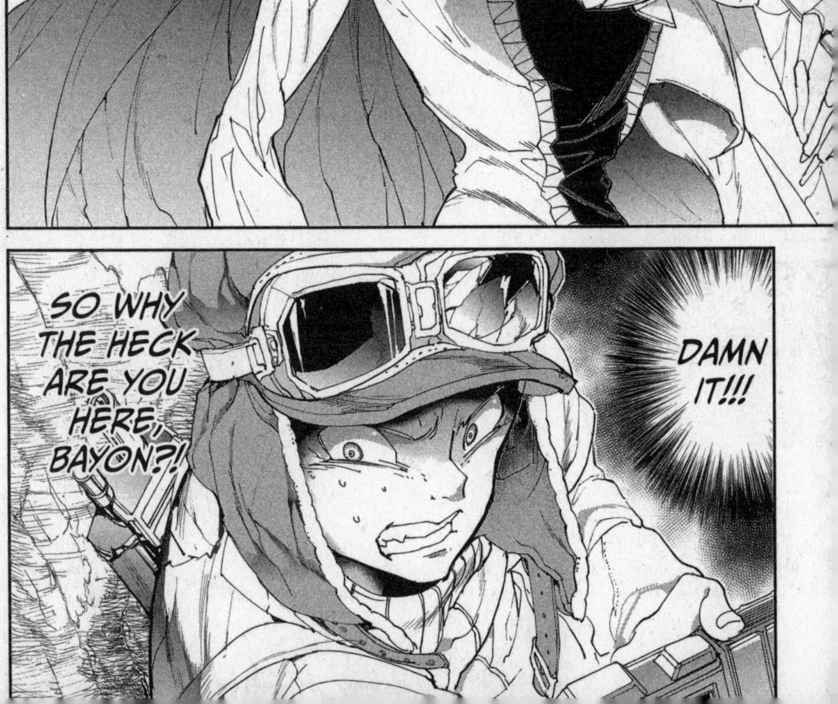
DAMN IT!!!
SO WHY THE HECK ARE YOU HERE, BAYON?!

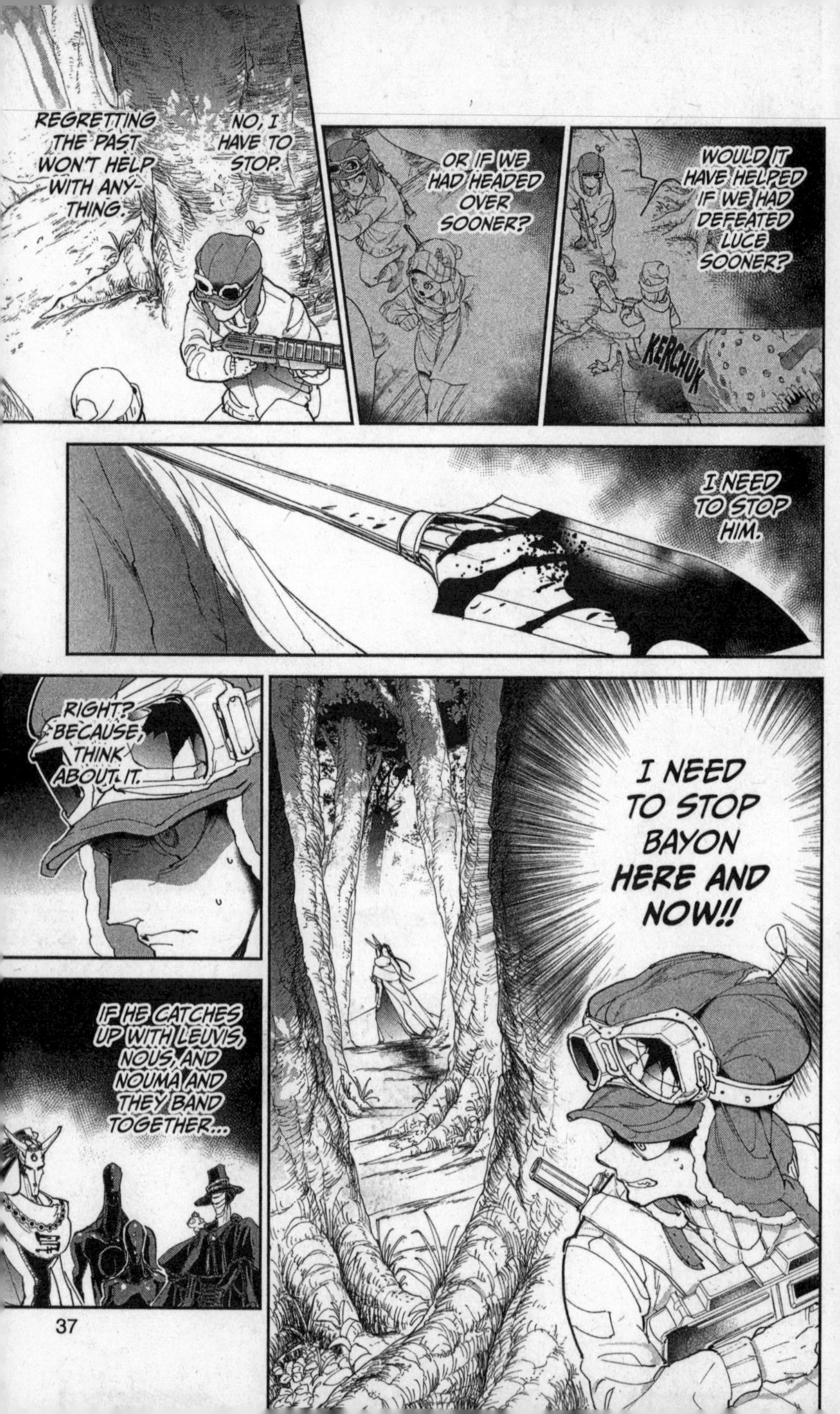
WOULD IT HAVE HELPED IF WE HAD DEFEATED LUCE SOONER?
KERCHUK
OR IF WE HAD HEADED OVER SOONER?
NO, I HAVE TO STOP.
REGRETTING THE PAST WON'T HELP WITH ANY-THING.
I NEED TO STOP HIM.
I NEED TO STOP BAYON HERE AND NOW!!
RIGHT? BECAUSE, THINK ABOUT IT.
IF HE CATCHES UP WITH LEUVIS, NOUS, AND NOUMA AND THEY BAND TOGETHER...

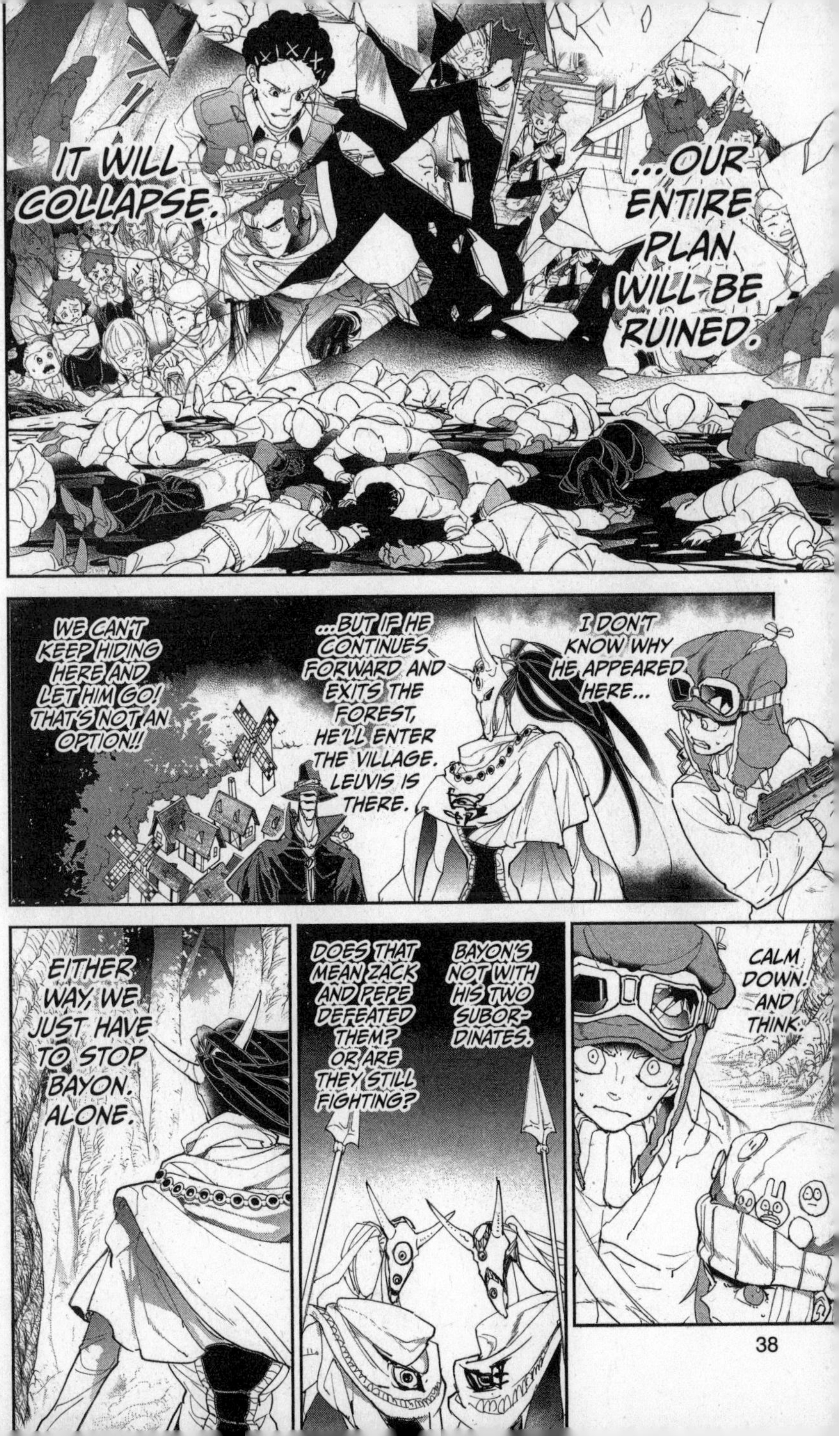

...OUR ENTIRE PLAN WILL BE RUINED.
IT WILL COLLAPSE.
I DON'T KNOW WHY HE APPEARED HERE...
...BUT IF HE CONTINUES FORWARD AND EXITS THE FOREST, HE'LL ENTER THE VILLAGE. LEUVIS IS THERE.
WE CAN'T KEEP HIDING HERE AND LET HIM GO! THAT'S NOT AN OPTION!!
CALM DOWN. AND THINK.
BAYON'S NOT WITH HIS TWO SUBOR-DINATES.
DOES THAT MEAN ZACK AND PEPE DEFEATED THEM? OR ARE THEY STILL FIGHTING?
EITHER WAY, WE JUST HAVE TO STOP BAYON. ALONE.

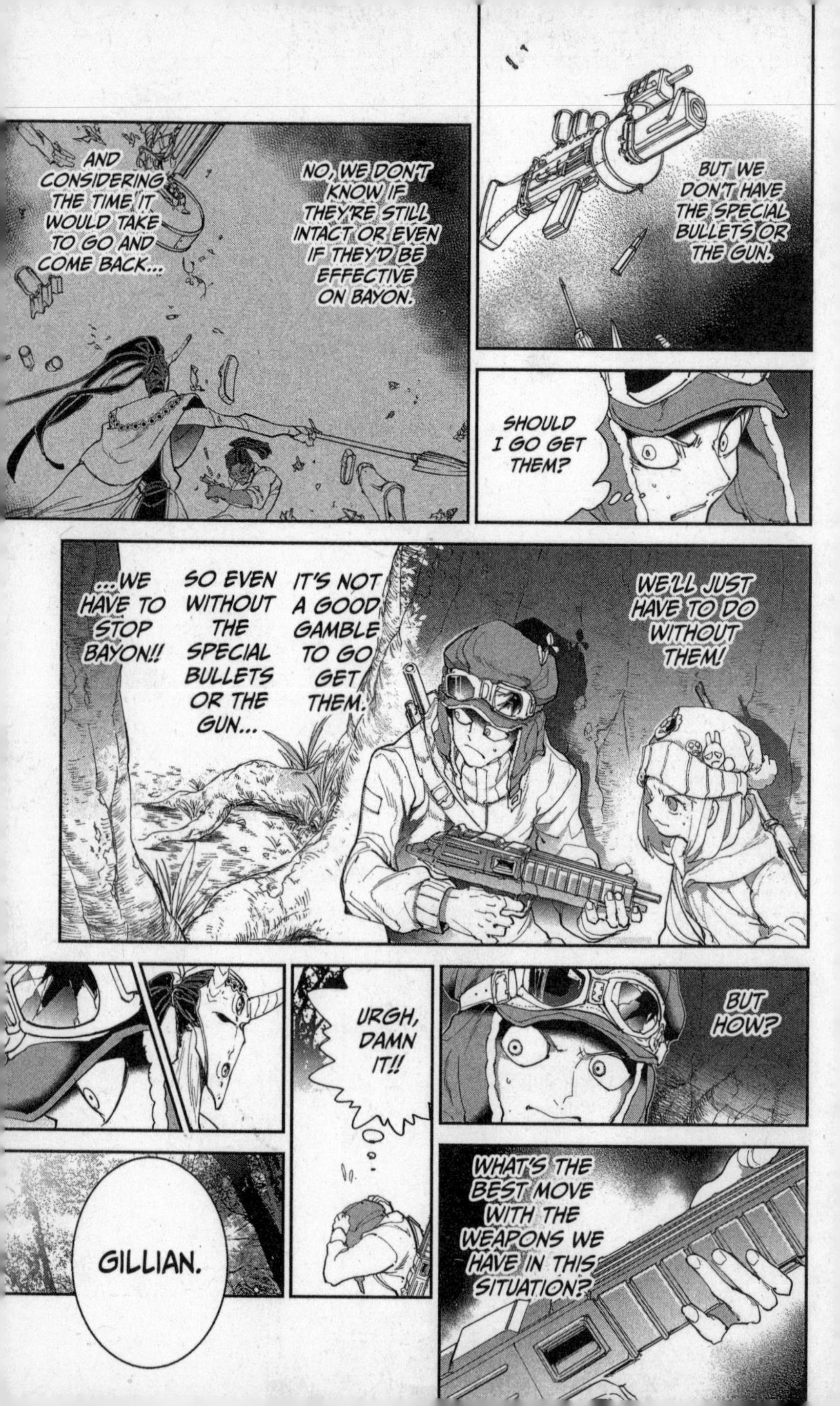
BUT WE DON'T HAVE THE SPECIAL BULLETS OR THE GUN.
SHOULD I GO GET THEM?
NO, WE DON'T KNOW IF THEY'RE STILL INTACT OR EVEN IF THEY'D BE EFFECTIVE ON BAYON.
AND CONSIDERING THE TIME IT WOULD TAKE TO GO AND COME BACK...
WE'LL JUST HAVE TO DO WITHOUT THEM!
IT'S NOT A GOOD GAMBLE TO GO GET THEM.
SO EVEN WITHOUT THE SPECIAL BULLETS OR THE GUN...
...WE HAVE TO STOP BAYON!!
BUT HOW?
WHAT'S THE BEST MOVE WITH THE WEAPONS WE HAVE IN THIS SITUATION?
URGH, DAMN IT!!
GILLIAN.

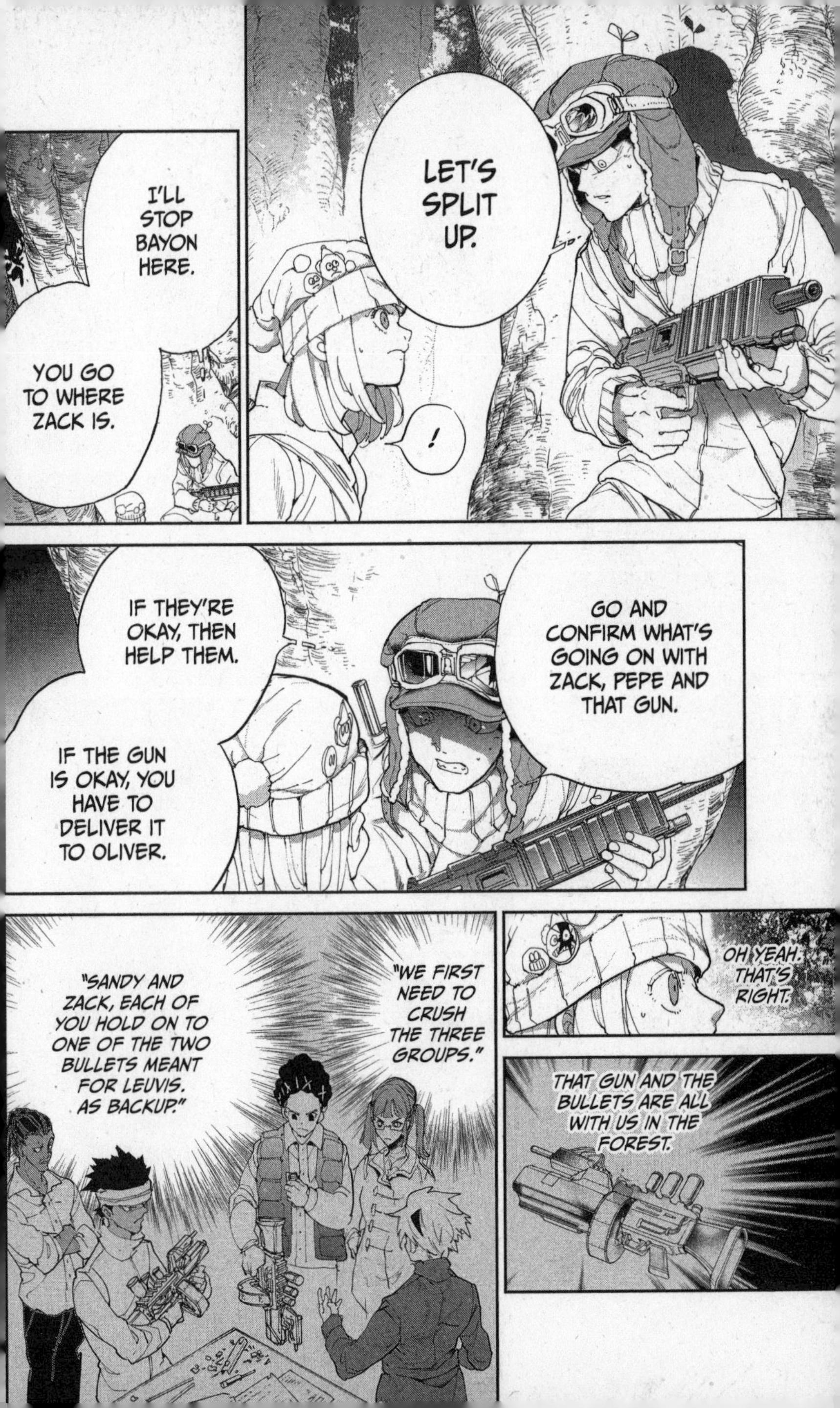
LET'S SPLIT UP.
!
I'LL STOP BAYON HERE.
YOU GO TO WHERE ZACK IS.
GO AND CONFIRM WHAT'S GOING ON WITH ZACK, PEPE AND THAT GUN.
IF THEY'RE OKAY, THEN HELP THEM.
IF THE GUN IS OKAY, YOU HAVE TO DELIVER IT TO OLIVER.
OH YEAH. THAT'S RIGHT.
THAT GUN AND THE BULLETS ARE ALL WITH US IN THE FOREST.
"WE FIRST NEED TO CRUSH THE THREE GROUPS."
"SANDY AND ZACK, EACH OF YOU HOLD ON TO ONE OF THE TWO BULLETS MEANT FOR LEUVIS. AS BACKUP."

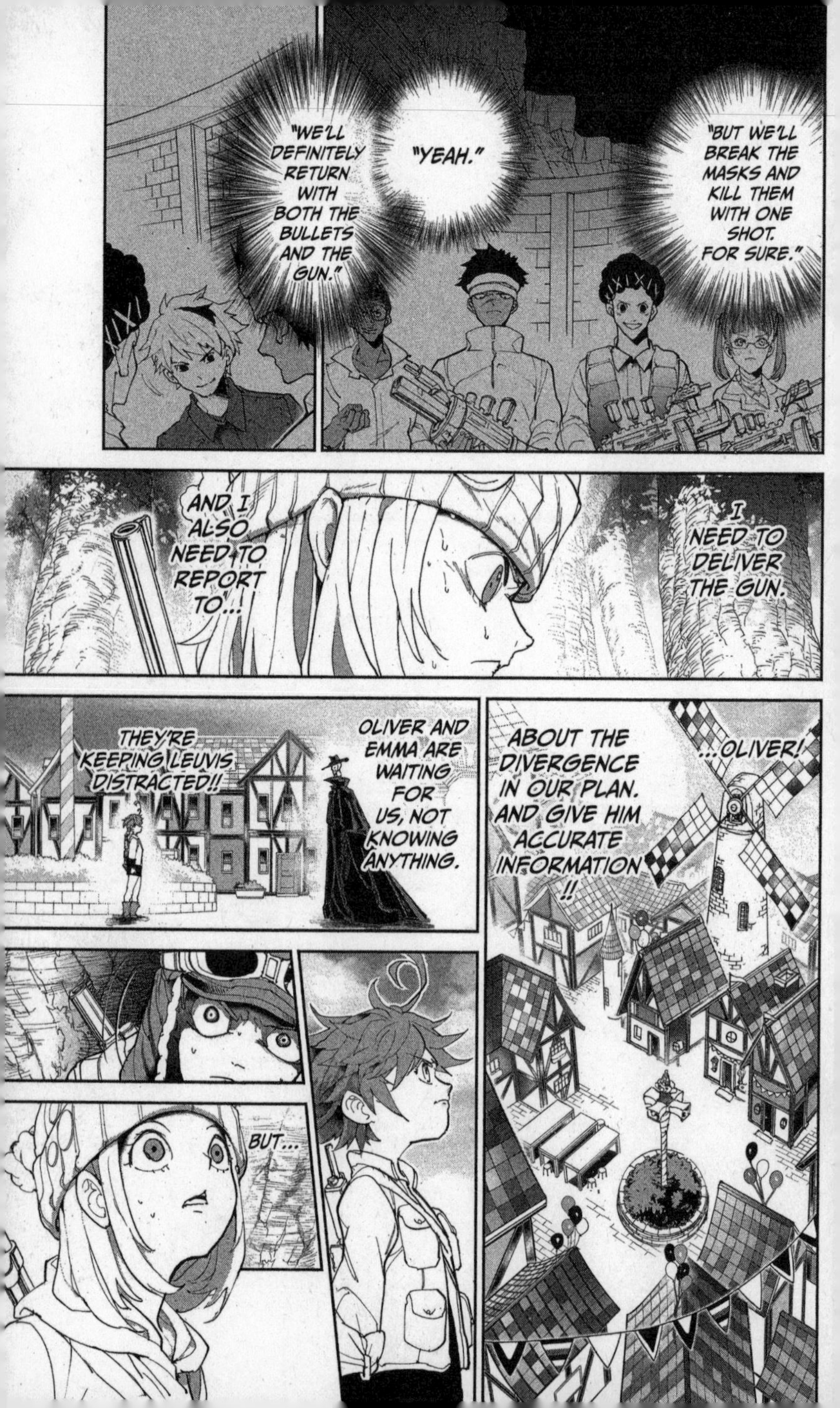
"BUT WE'LL BREAK THE MASKS AND KILL THEM WITH ONE SHOT. FOR SURE."
"YEAH."
"WE'LL DEFINITELY RETURN WITH BOTH THE BULLETS AND THE GUN."
I NEED TO DELIVER THE GUN.
AND I ALSO NEED TO REPORT TO...
...OLIVER!
ABOUT THE DIVERGENCE IN OUR PLAN. AND GIVE HIM ACCURATE INFORMATION!!
OLIVER AND EMMA ARE WAITING FOR US, NOT KNOWING ANYTHING.
THEY'RE KEEPING LEUVIS DISTRACTED!!
BUT...

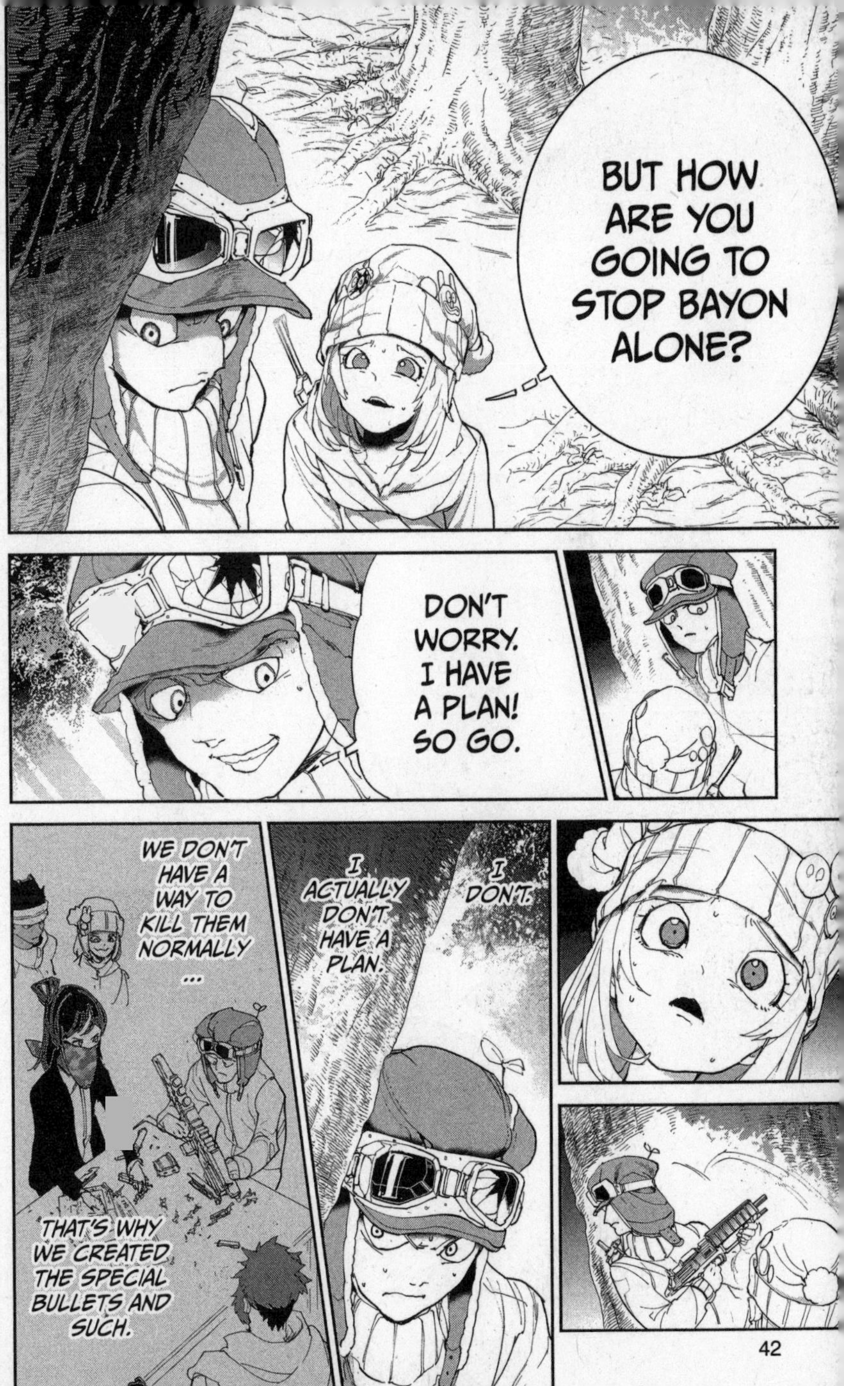
BUT HOW ARE YOU GOING TO STOP BAYON ALONE?
DON'T WORRY. I HAVE A PLAN! SO GO.
I DON'T.
I ACTUALLY DON'T HAVE A PLAN.
WE DON'T HAVE A WAY TO KILL THEM NORMALLY...
THAT'S WHY WE CREATED THE SPECIAL BULLETS AND SUCH.

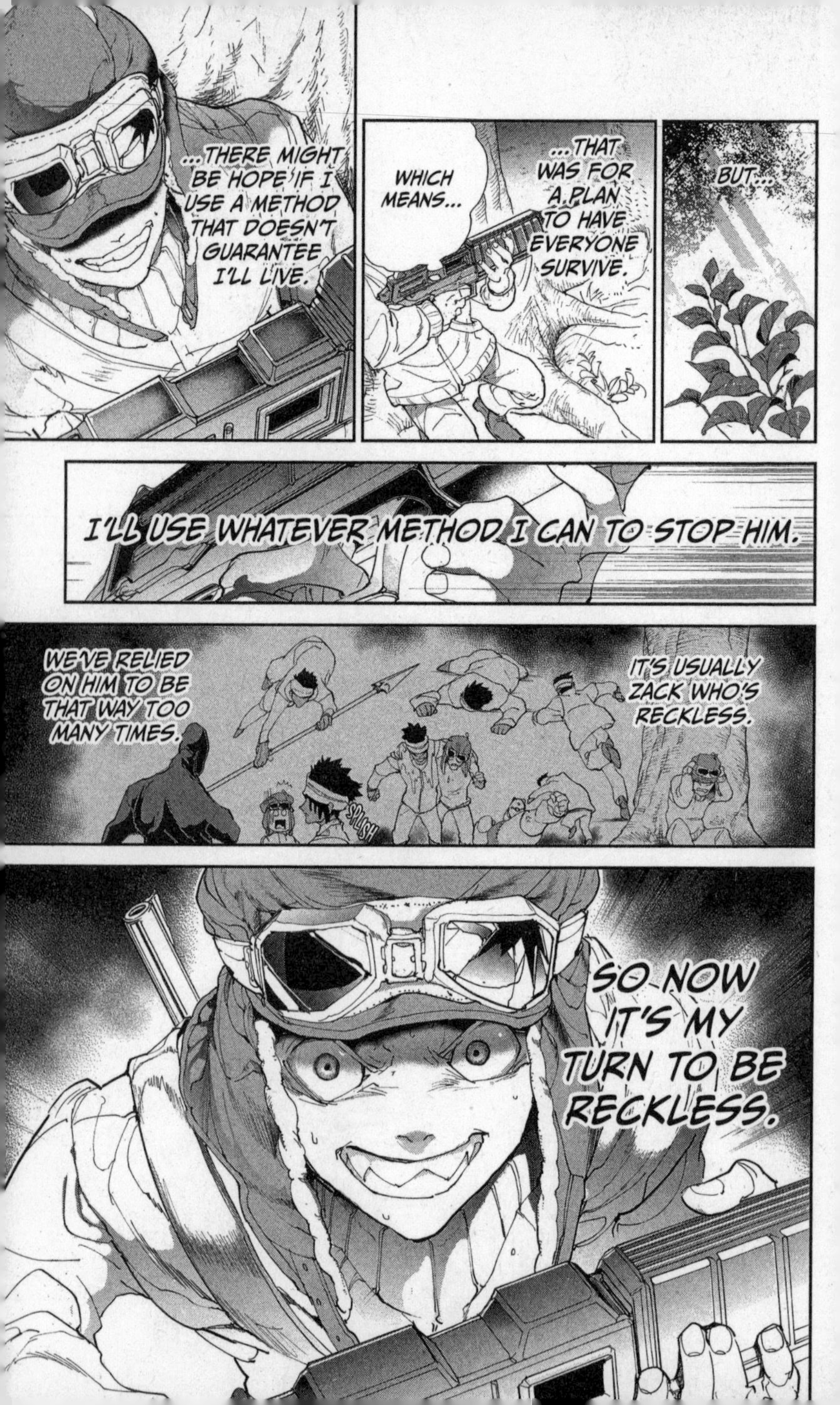
BUT...
...THAT WAS FOR A PLAN TO HAVE EVERYONE SURVIVE.
WHICH MEANS...
...THERE MIGHT BE HOPE IF I USE A METHOD THAT DOESN'T GUARANTEE I'LL LIVE.
I'LL USE WHATEVER METHOD I CAN TO STOP HIM.
IT'S USUALLY ZACK WHO'S RECKLESS.
WE'VE RELIED ON HIM TO BE THAT WAY TOO MANY TIMES.
SPLISH
SO NOW IT'S MY TURN TO BE RECKLESS.

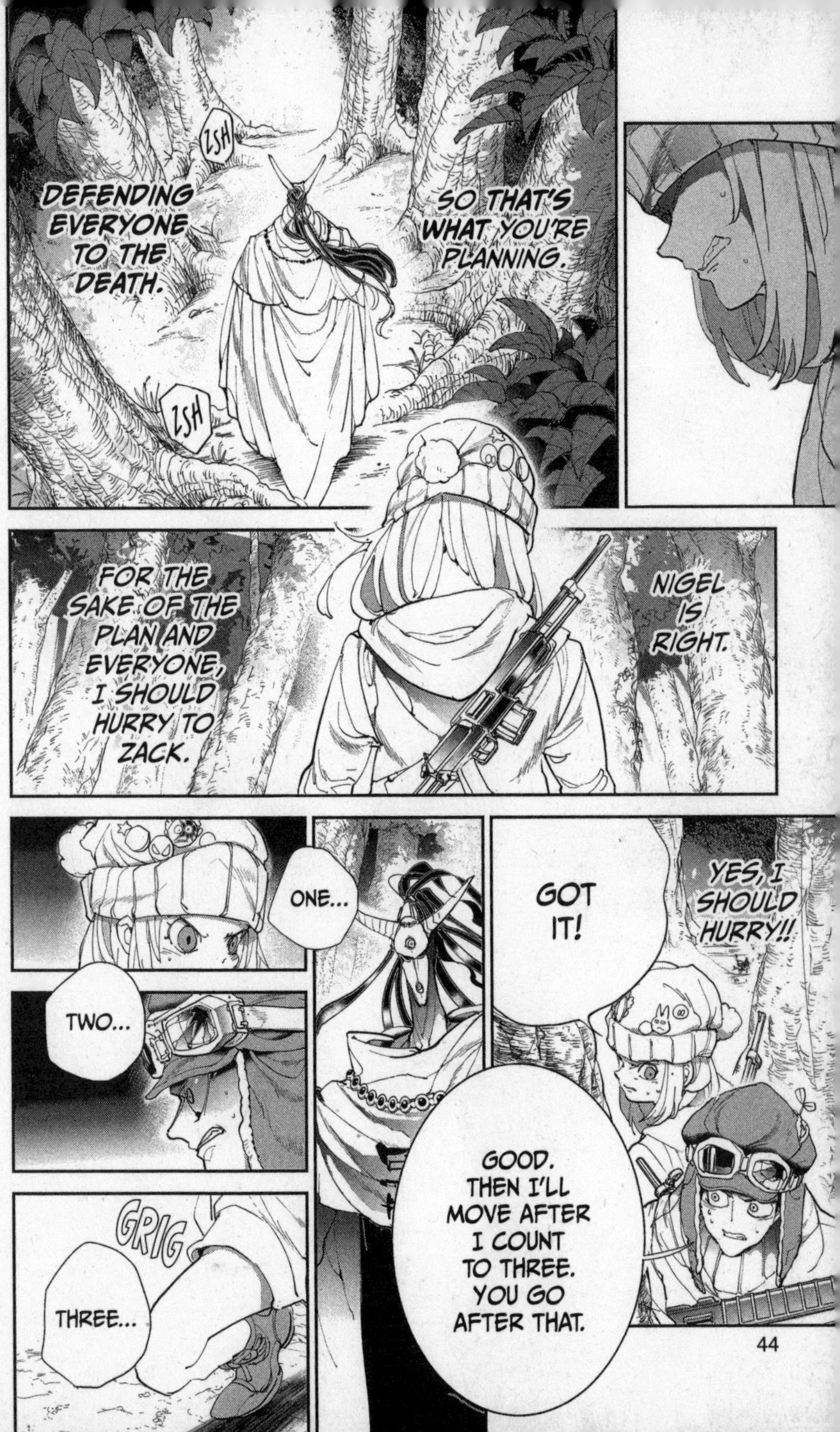
ZSH
SO THAT'S WHAT YOU'RE PLANNING.
DEFENDING EVERYONE TO THE DEATH.
ZSH
NIGEL IS RIGHT.
FOR THE SAKE OF THE PLAN AND EVERYONE, I SHOULD HURRY TO ZACK.
GOOD. THEN I'LL MOVE AFTER I COUNT TO THREE. YOU GO AFTER THAT.
GOT IT!
YES, I SHOULD HURRY!!
ONE...
TWO...
GRIG
THREE...

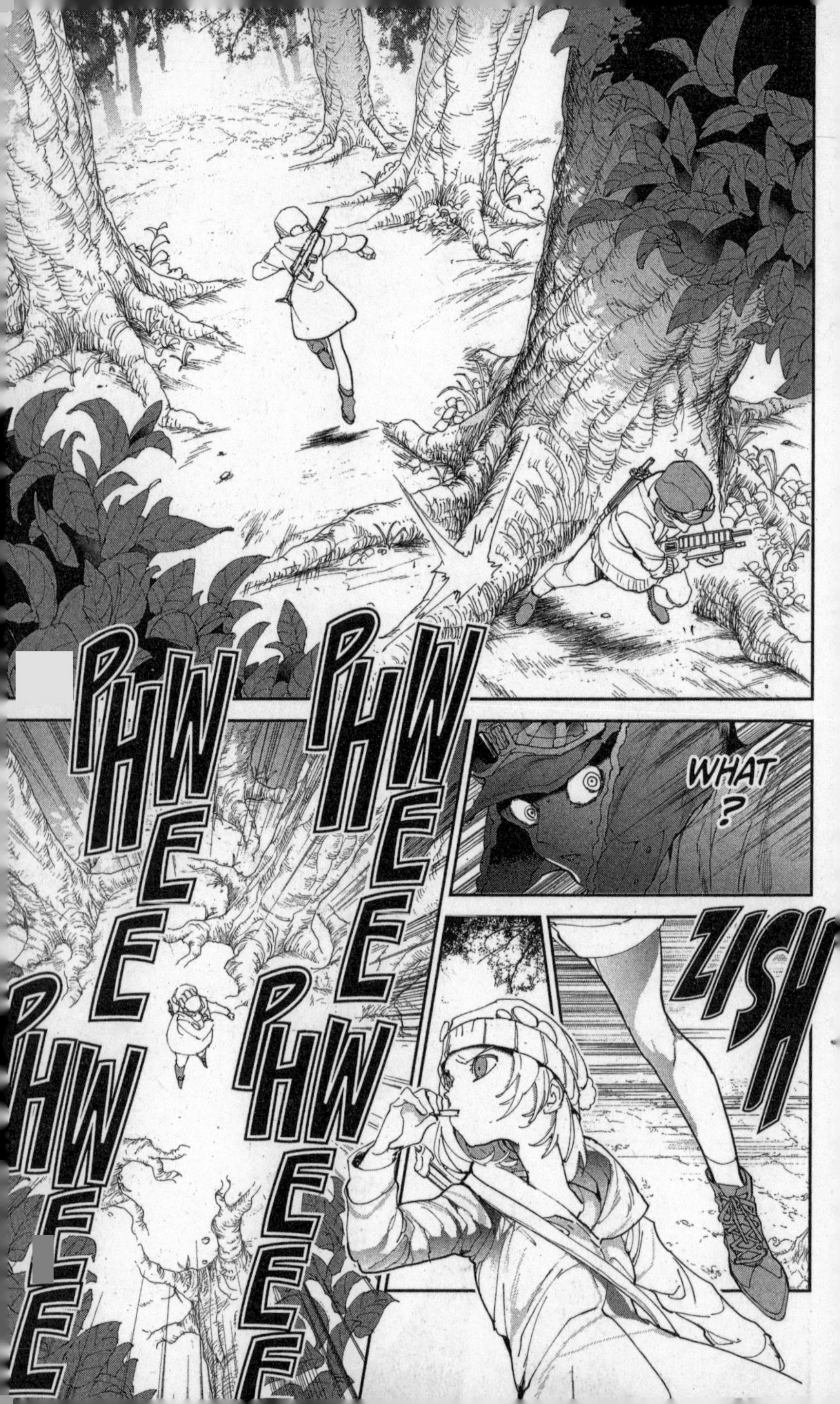

WHAT ?
ZISH
PHWEEE
PHWEEE
PHWEEE
PHWEEE

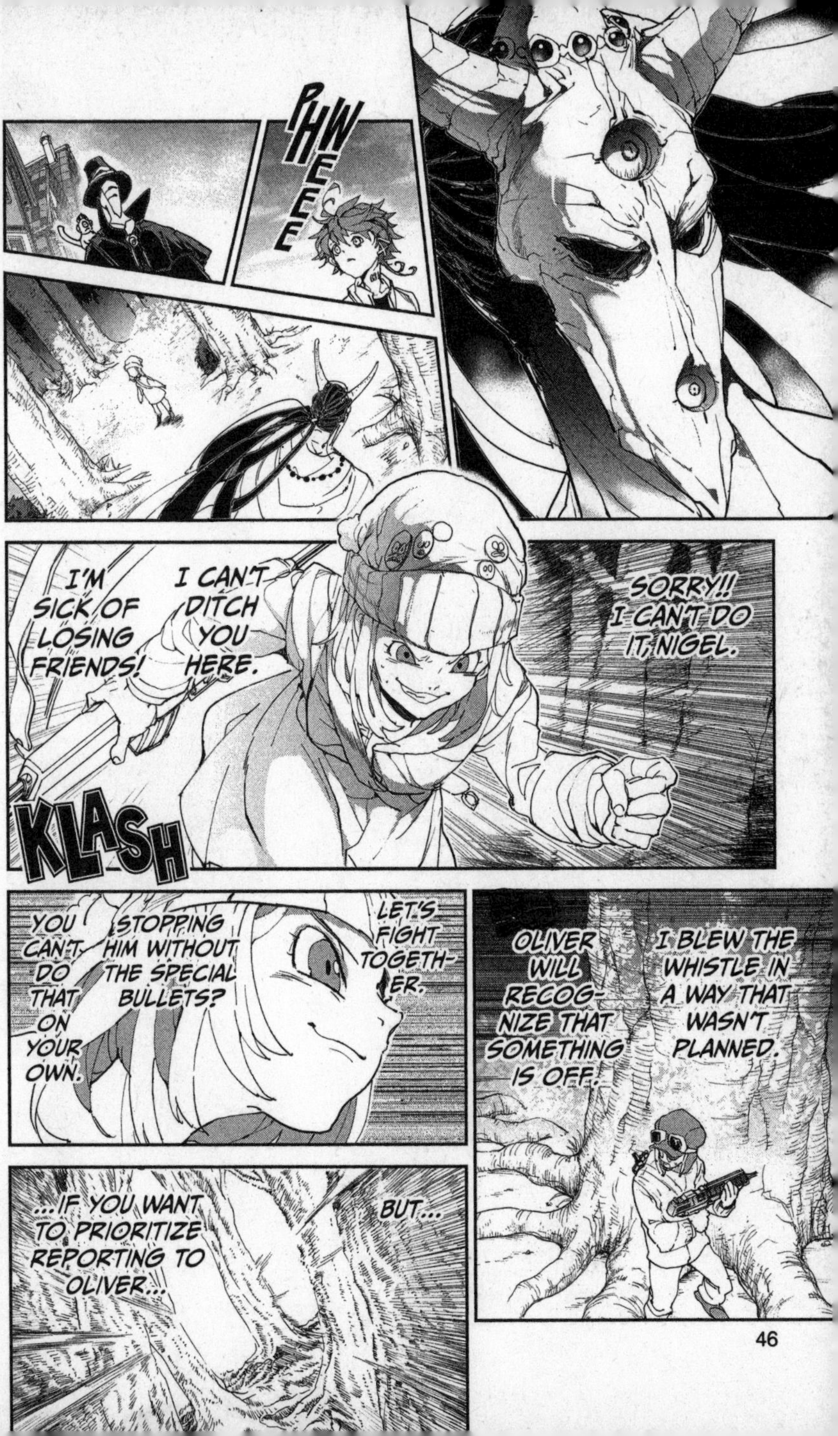
PHWEEEE
SORRY!! I CAN'T DO IT, NIGEL.
I CAN'T DITCH YOU HERE.
I'M SICK OF LOSING FRIENDS!
KLASH
I BLEW THE WHISTLE IN A WAY THAT WASN'T PLANNED.
OLIVER WILL RECOGNIZE THAT SOMETHING IS OFF.
LET'S FIGHT TOGETHER.
STOPPING HIM WITHOUT THE SPECIAL BULLETS?
YOU CAN'T DO THAT ON YOUR OWN.
BUT...
...IF YOU WANT TO PRIORITIZE REPORTING TO OLIVER...

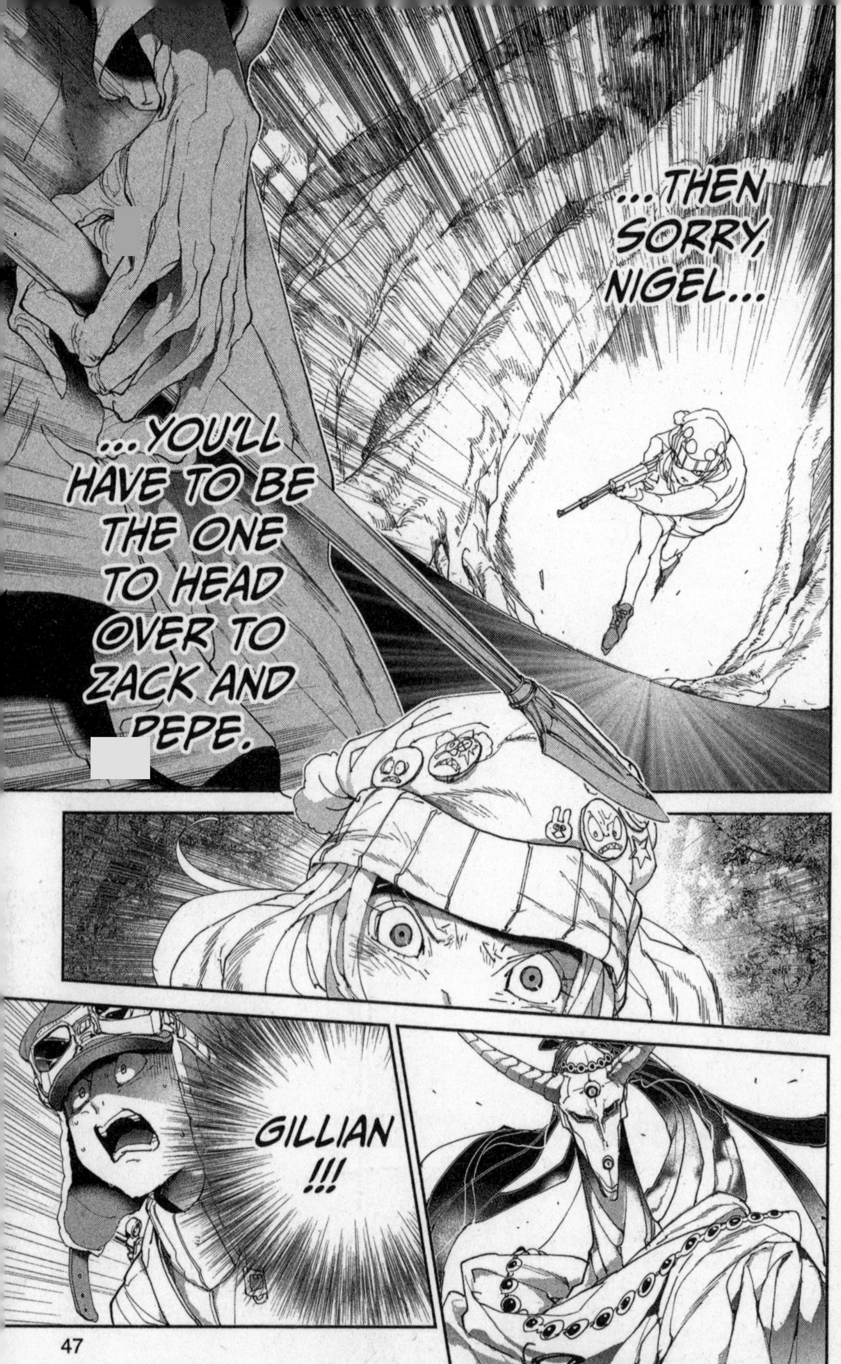
...THEN SORRY, NIGEL...
...YOU'LL HAVE TO BE THE ONE TO HEAD OVER TO ZACK AND PEPE.
GILLIAN !!!

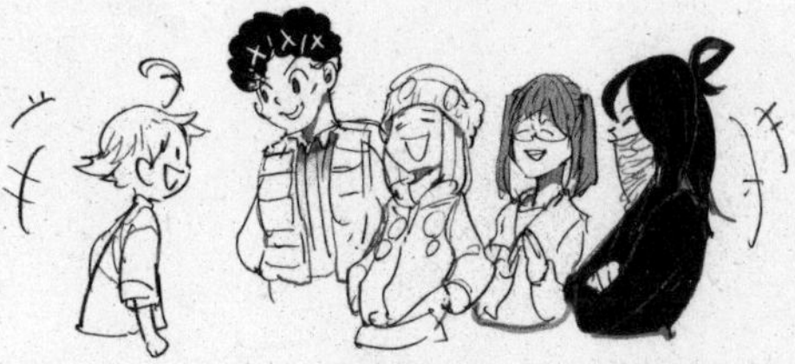

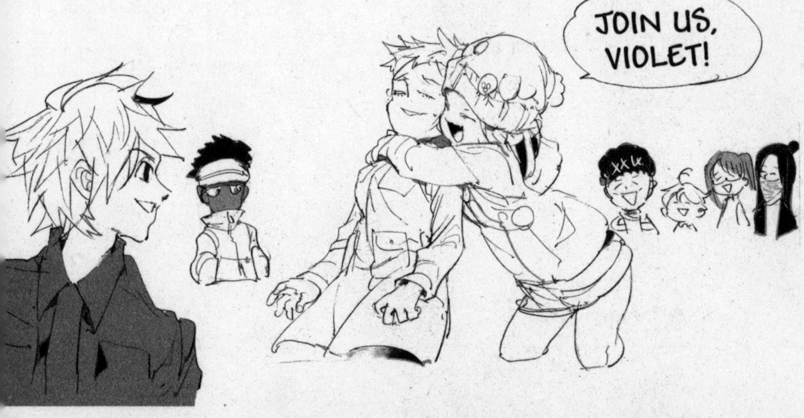
JOIN US, VIOLET!

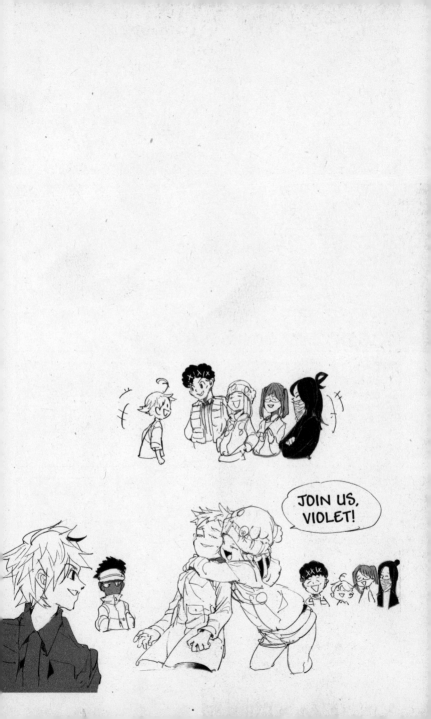

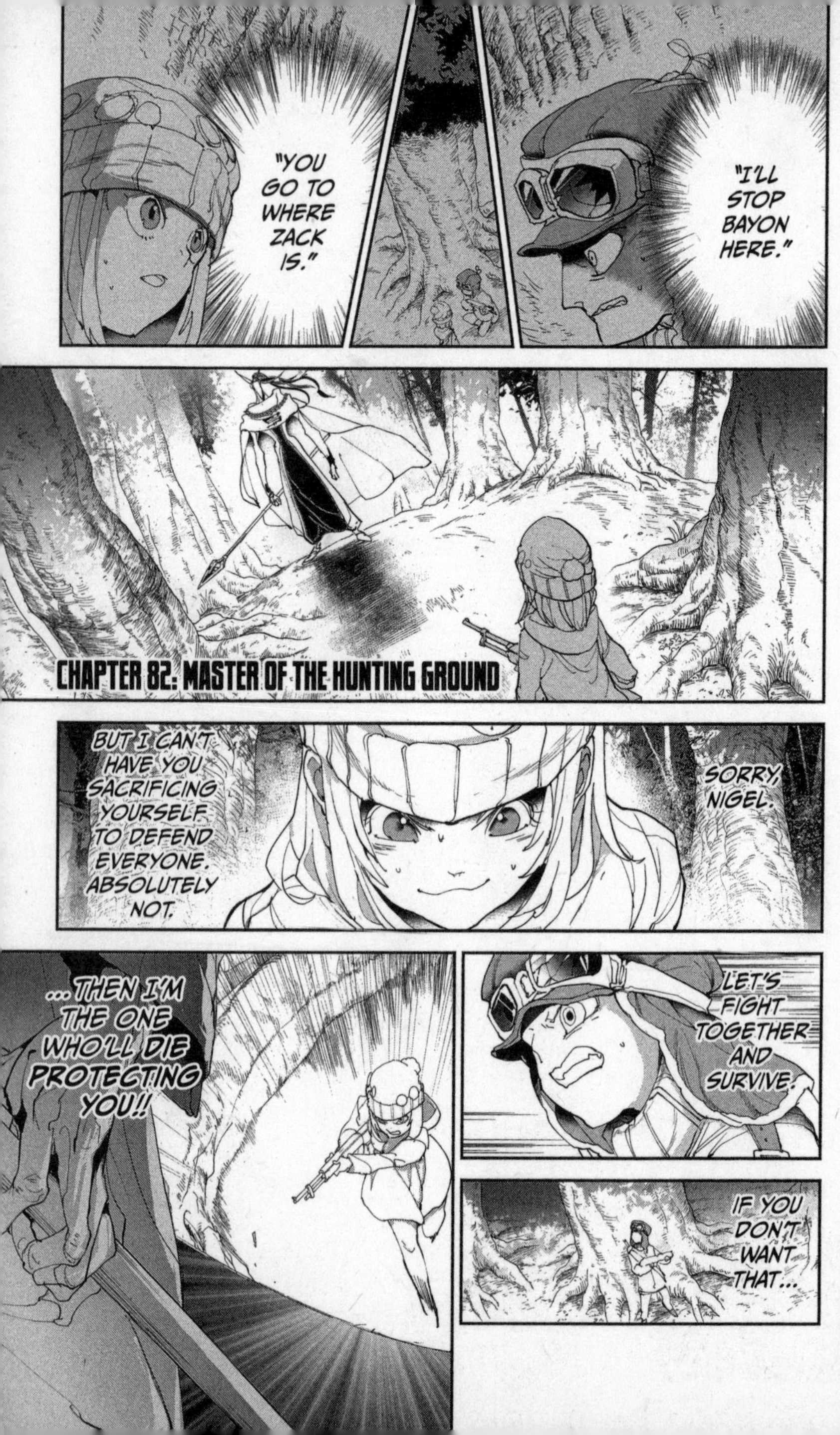
"I'LL STOP BAYON HERE."
"YOU GO TO WHERE ZACK IS."
CHAPTER 82: MASTER OF THE HUNTING GROUND
SORRY, NIGEL.
BUT I CAN'T HAVE YOU SACRIFICING YOURSELF TO DEFEND EVERYONE. ABSOLUTELY NOT.
LET'S FIGHT TOGETHER AND SURVIVE.
IF YOU DON'T WANT THAT...
...THEN I'M THE ONE WHO'LL DIE PROTECTING YOU!!

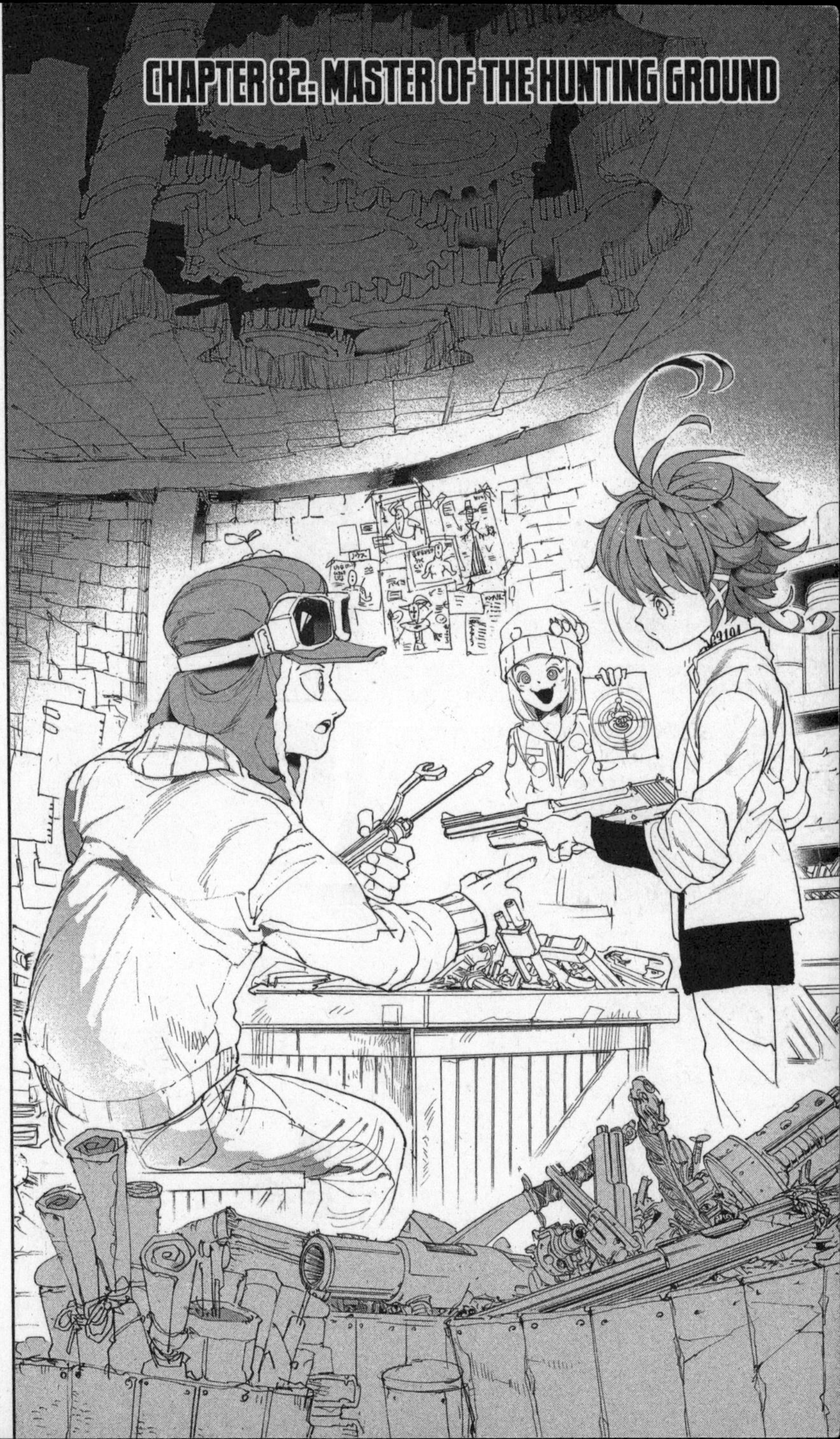
CHAPTER 82: MASTER OF THE HUNTING GROUND

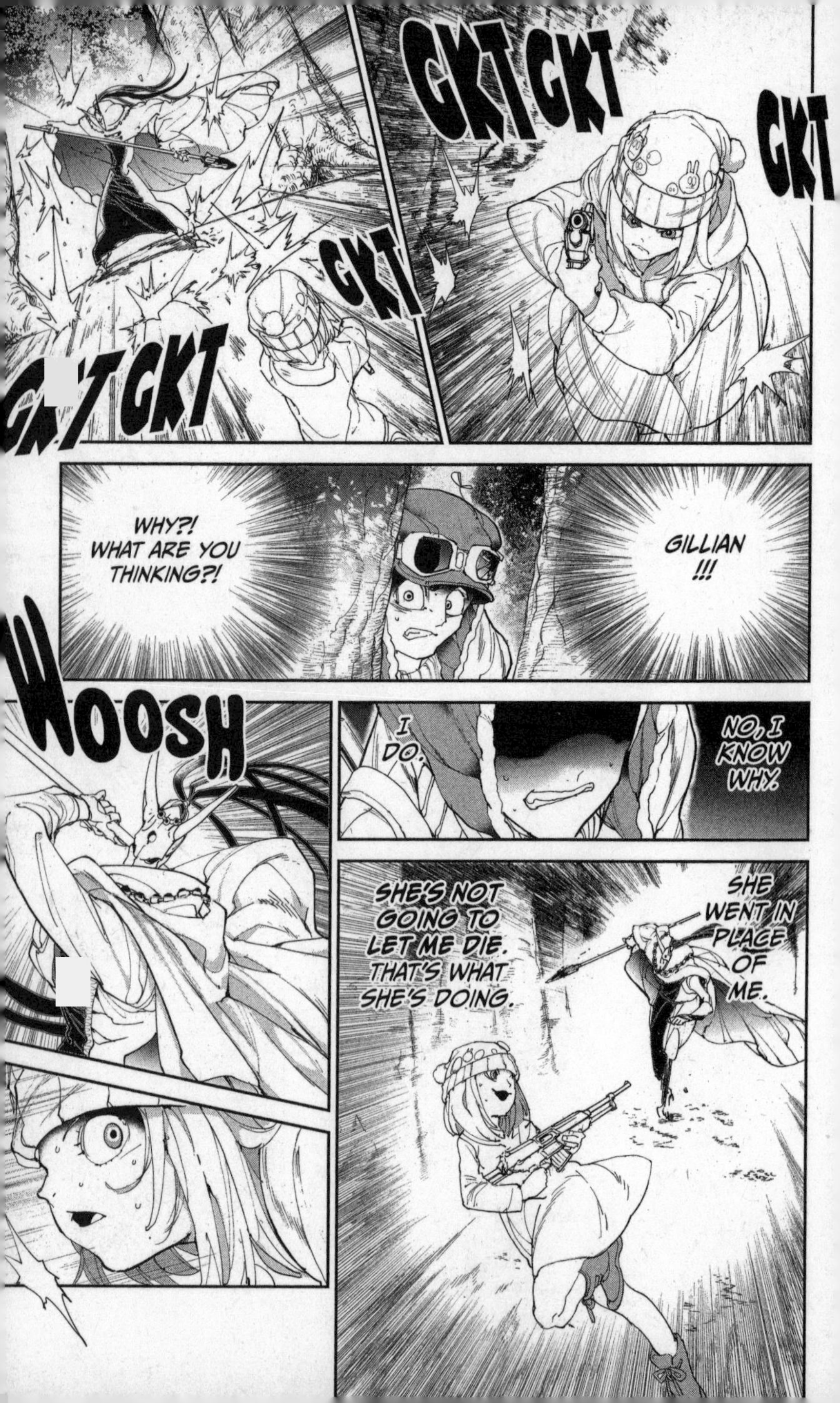

GCKT GCKT
GCKT
GCKT
GCKT
GILLIAN !!!
WHY?! WHAT ARE YOU THINKING?!
NO, I KNOW WHY.
I DO.
SHE WENT IN PLACE OF ME.
SHE'S NOT GOING TO LET ME DIE. THAT'S WHAT SHE'S DOING.
WOOSH

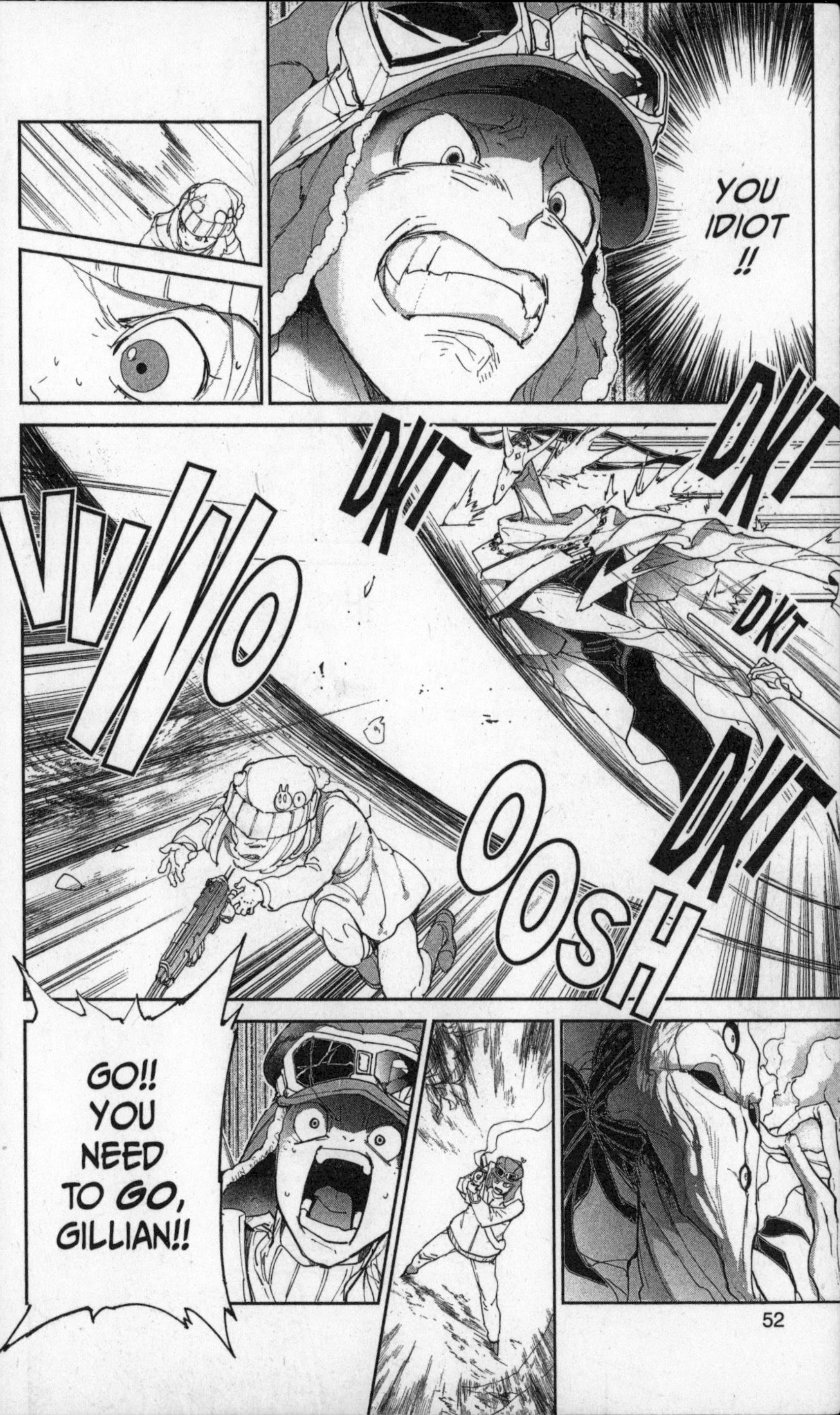
YOU IDIOT !!
DKT DKT
DKT DKT
DKT
DKT DKT
VVWOOOSH
GO!! YOU NEED TO GO, GILLIAN!!

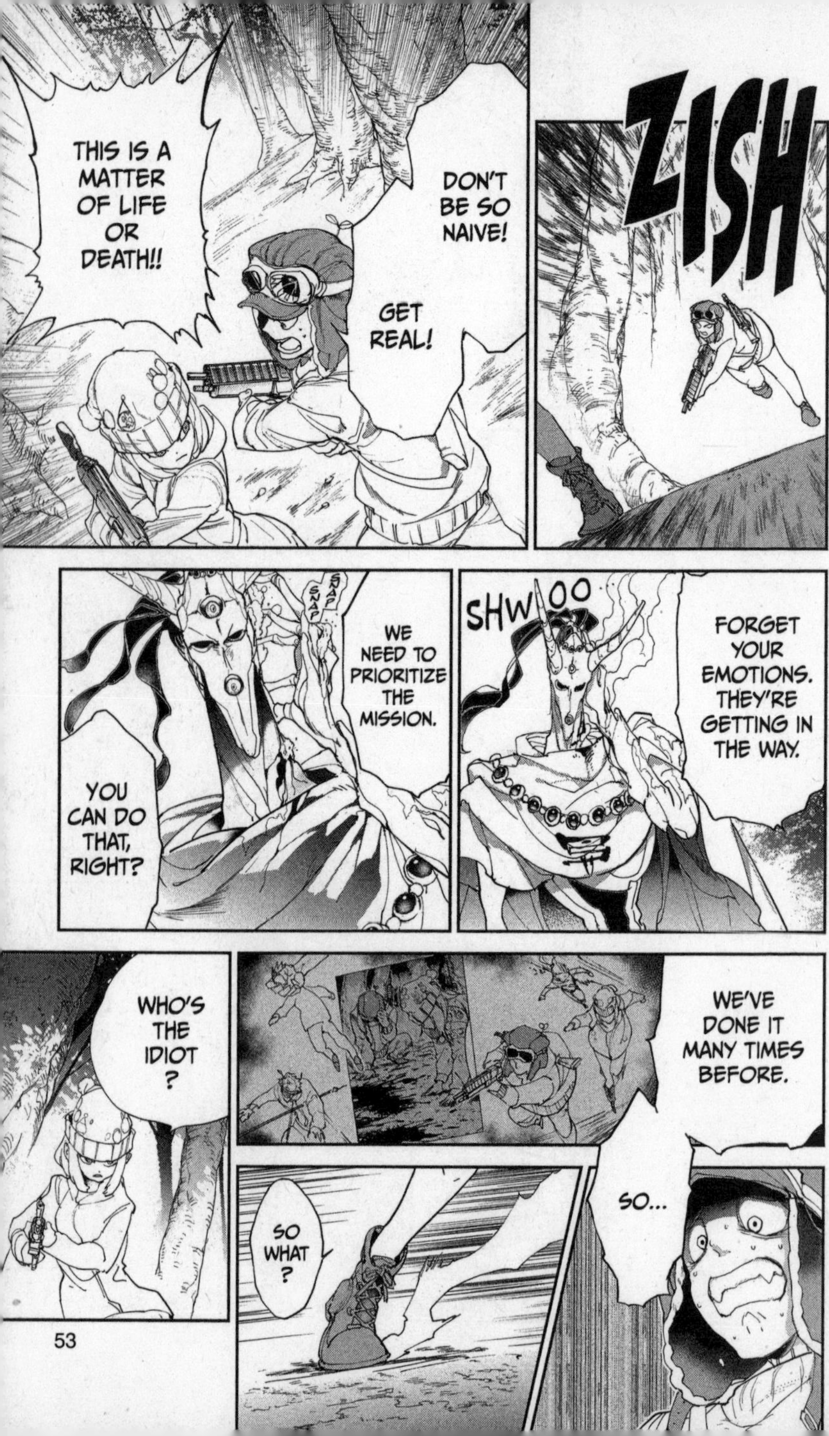
ZISH
DON'T BE SO NAIVE!
GET REAL!
THIS IS A MATTER OF LIFE OR DEATH!!
SHWOO
FORGET YOUR EMOTIONS. THEY'RE GETTING IN THE WAY.
SNAP SNAP
WE NEED TO PRIORITIZE THE MISSION.
YOU CAN DO THAT, RIGHT?
WE'VE DONE IT MANY TIMES BEFORE.
SO...
SO WHAT?
WHO'S THE IDIOT?

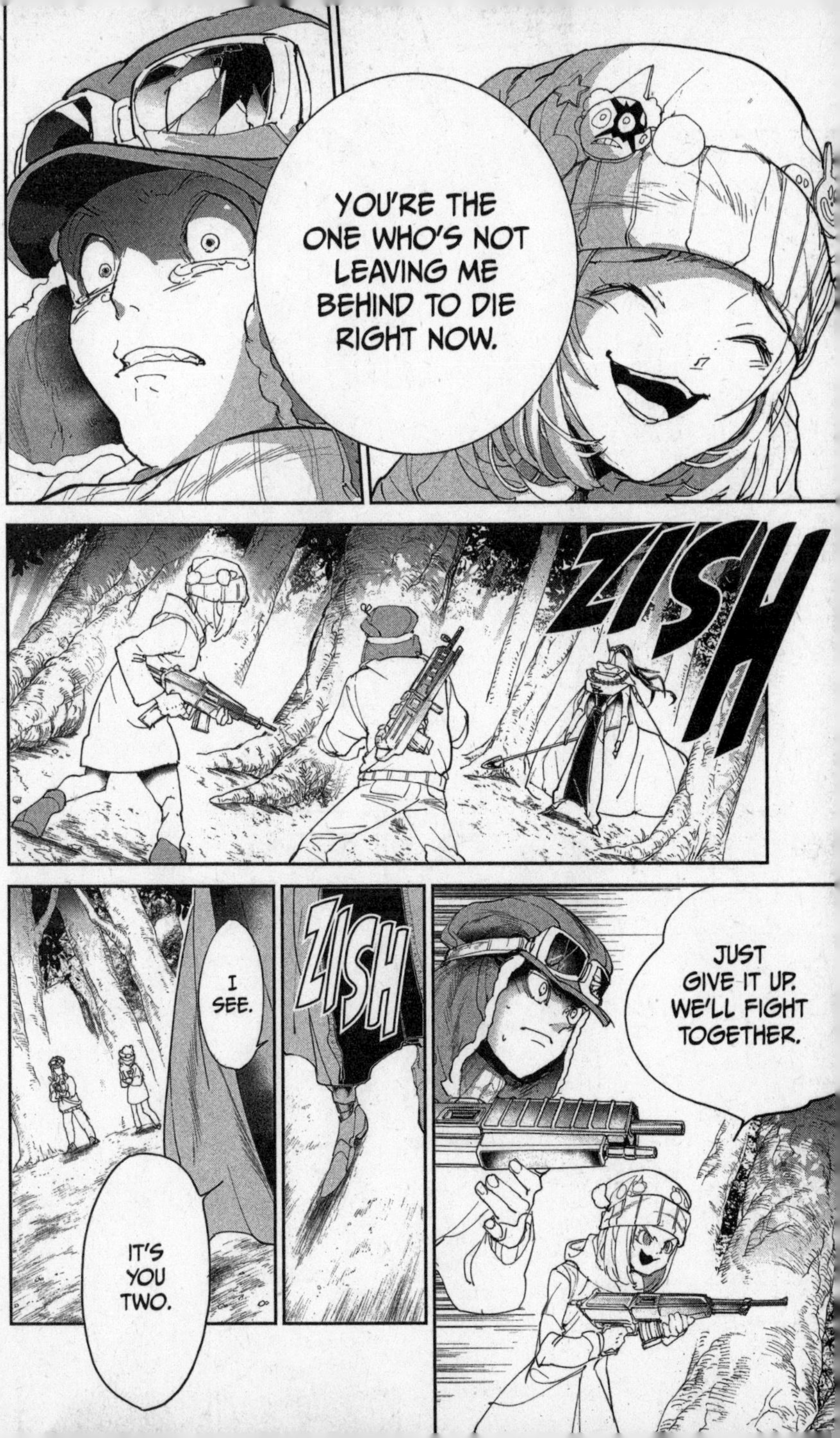
YOU'RE THE ONE WHO'S NOT LEAVING ME BEHIND TO DIE RIGHT NOW.
ZISH
JUST GIVE IT UP. WE'LL FIGHT TOGETHER.
ZISH
I SEE.
IT'S YOU TWO.

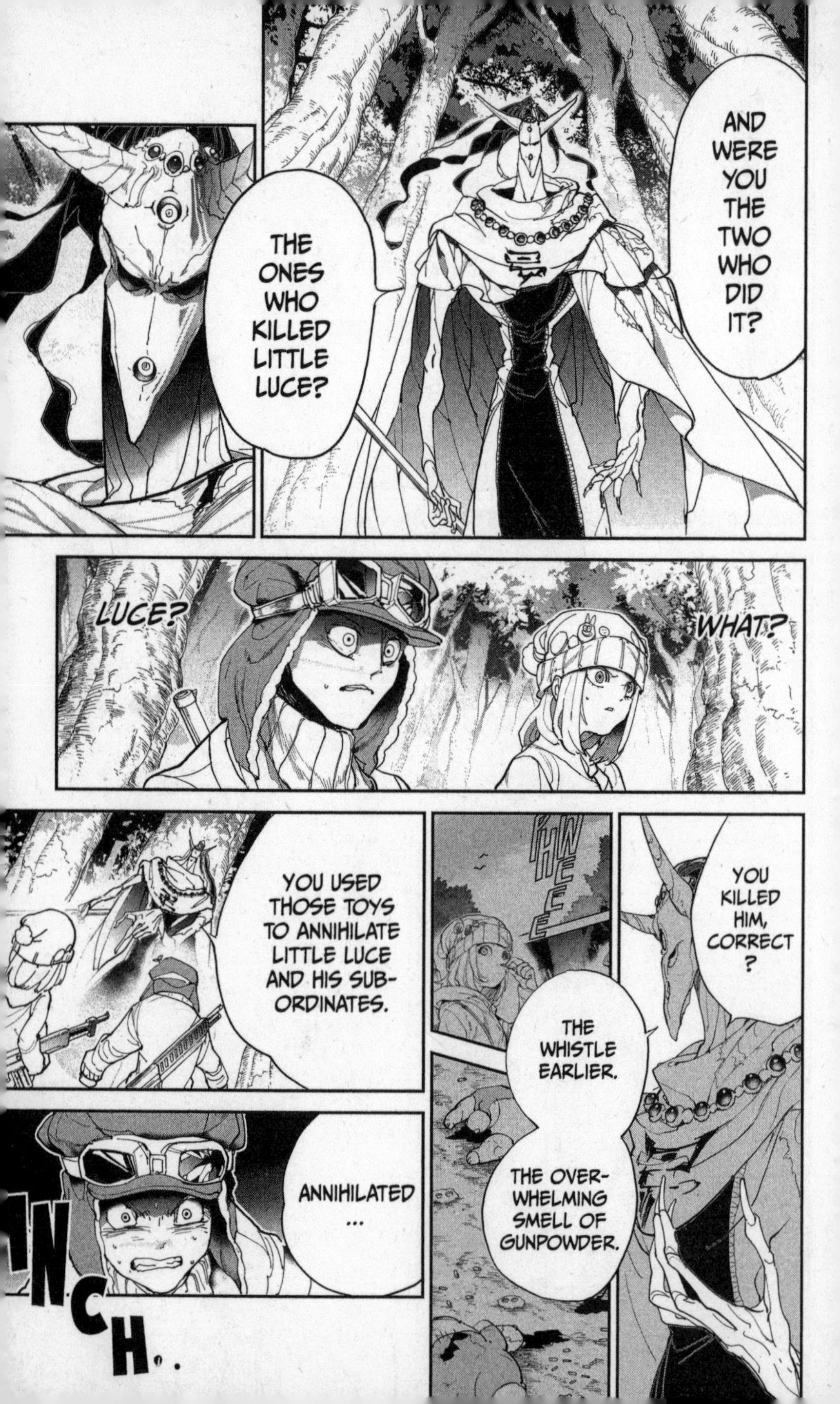
AND WERE YOU THE TWO WHO DID IT?
THE ONES WHO KILLED LITTLE LUCE?
WHAT?
LUCE?
YOU KILLED HIM, CORRECT?
PHWEEE
THE WHISTLE EARLIER.
THE OVER-WHELMING SMELL OF GUNPOWDER.
YOU USED THOSE TOYS TO ANNIHILATE LITTLE LUCE AND HIS SUB-ORDINATES.
ANNIHILATED ...
NCH..

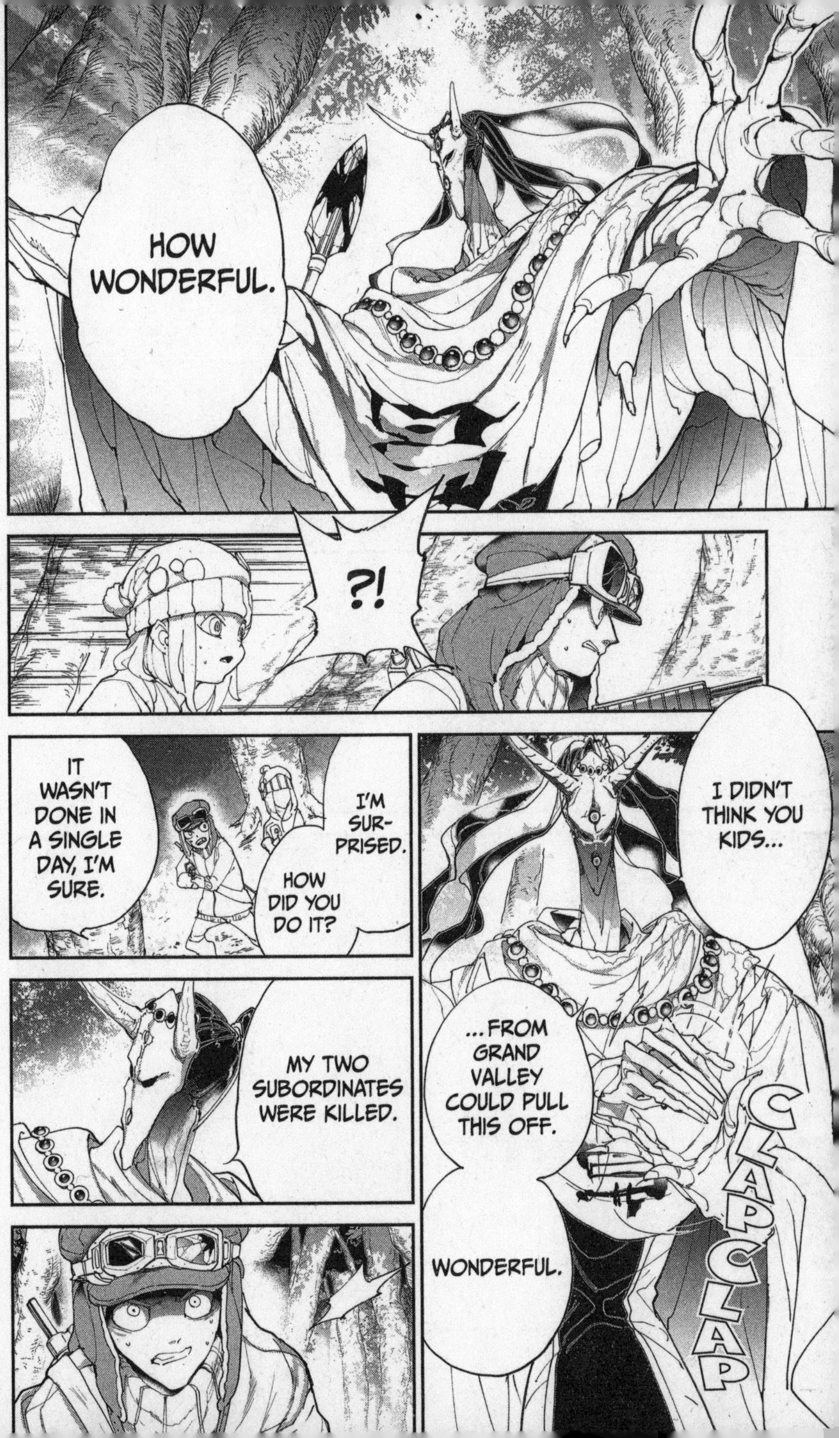
HOW WONDERFUL.
?!
I DIDN'T THINK YOU KIDS...
...FROM GRAND VALLEY COULD PULL THIS OFF.
WONDERFUL.
CLAP CLAP
I'M SURPRISED.
HOW DID YOU DO IT?
IT WASN'T DONE IN A SINGLE DAY, I'M SURE.
MY TWO SUBORDINATES WERE KILLED.

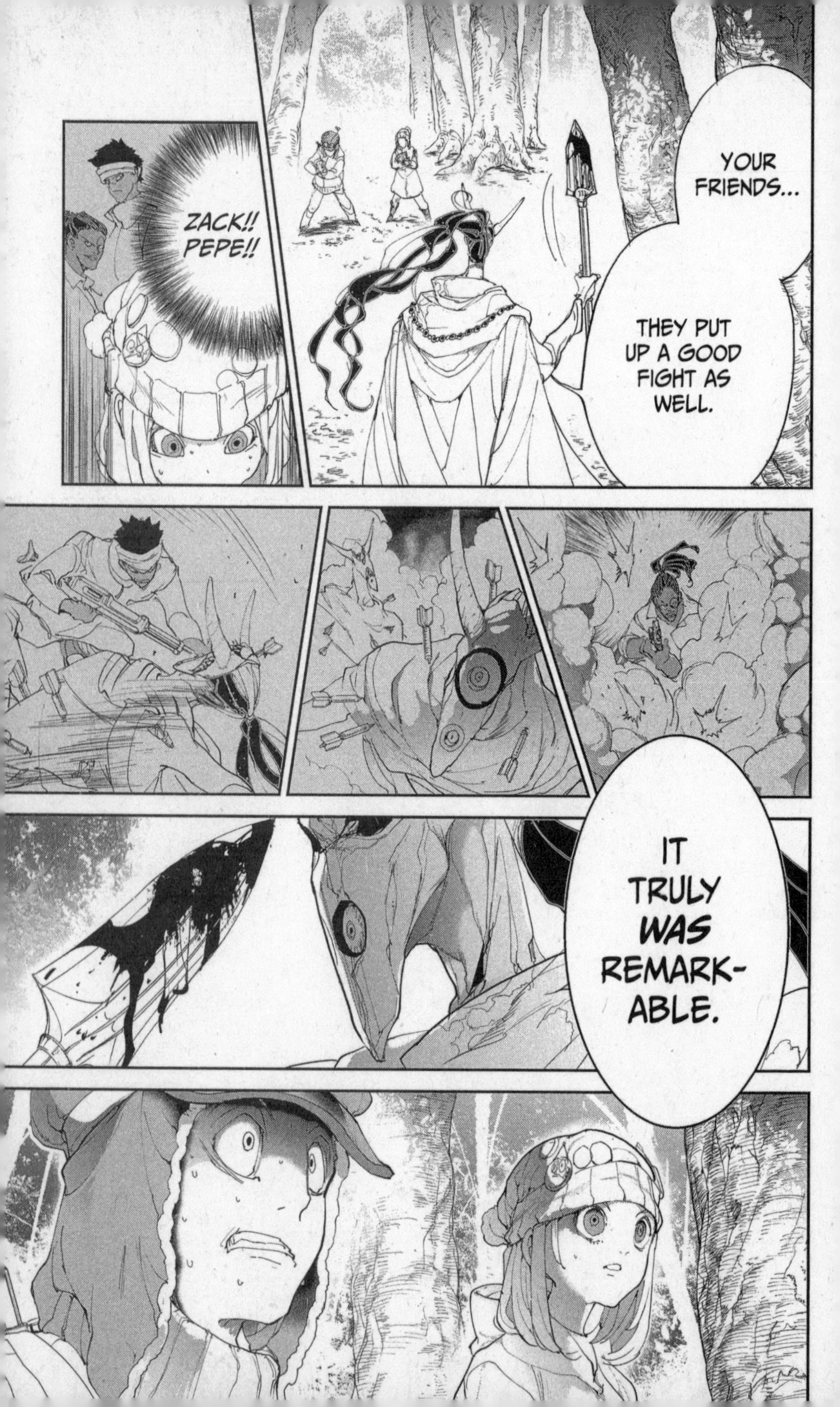
YOUR FRIENDS...
THEY PUT UP A GOOD FIGHT AS WELL.
ZACK!! PEPE!!
IT TRULY WAS REMARKABLE.

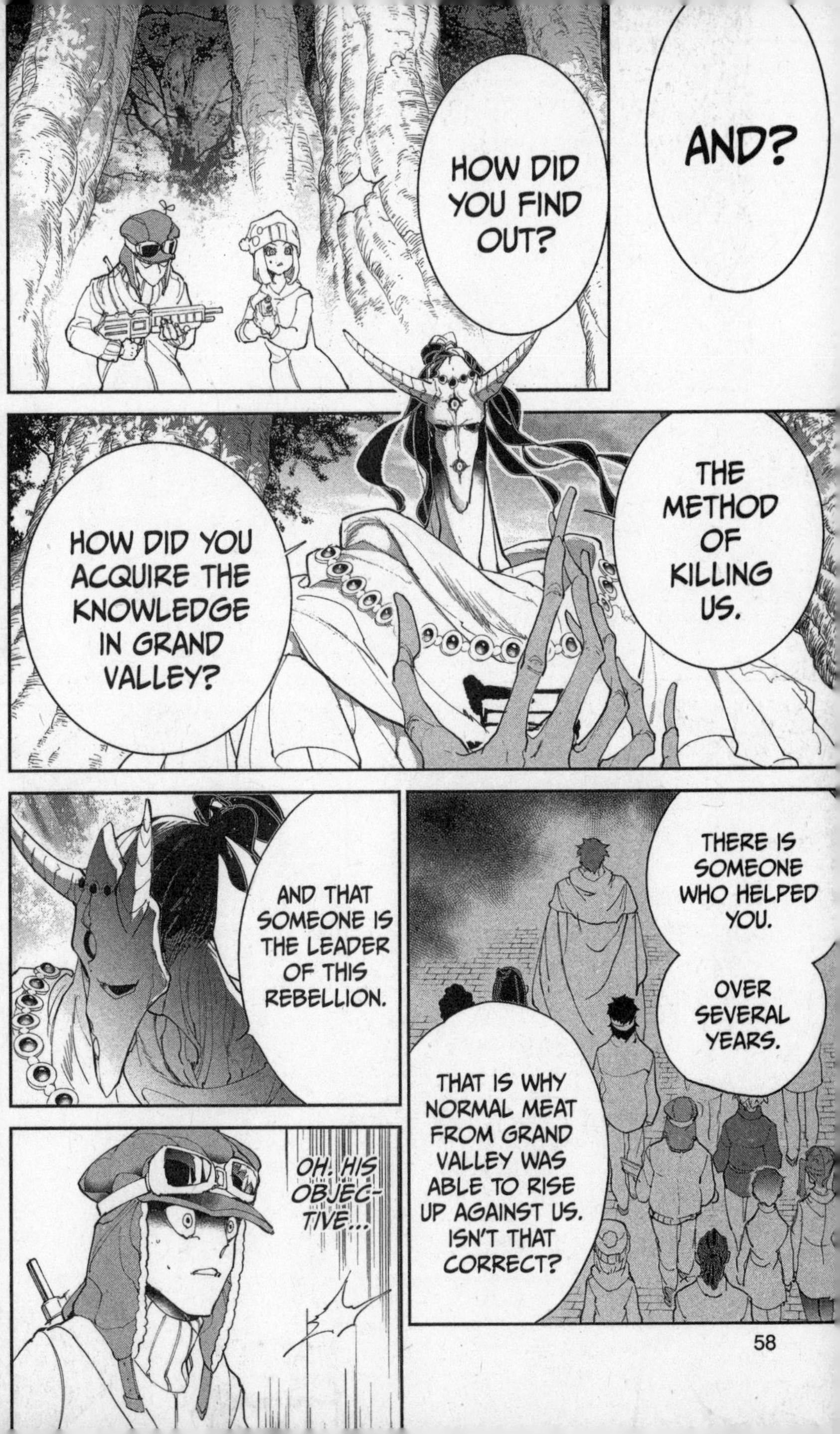
AND?
HOW DID YOU FIND OUT?
THE METHOD OF KILLING US.
HOW DID YOU ACQUIRE THE KNOWLEDGE IN GRAND VALLEY?
THERE IS SOMEONE WHO HELPED YOU.
OVER SEVERAL YEARS.
THAT IS WHY NORMAL MEAT FROM GRAND VALLEY WAS ABLE TO RISE UP AGAINST US. ISN'T THAT CORRECT?
AND THAT SOMEONE IS THE LEADER OF THIS REBELLION.
OH. HIS OBJEC-TIVE...

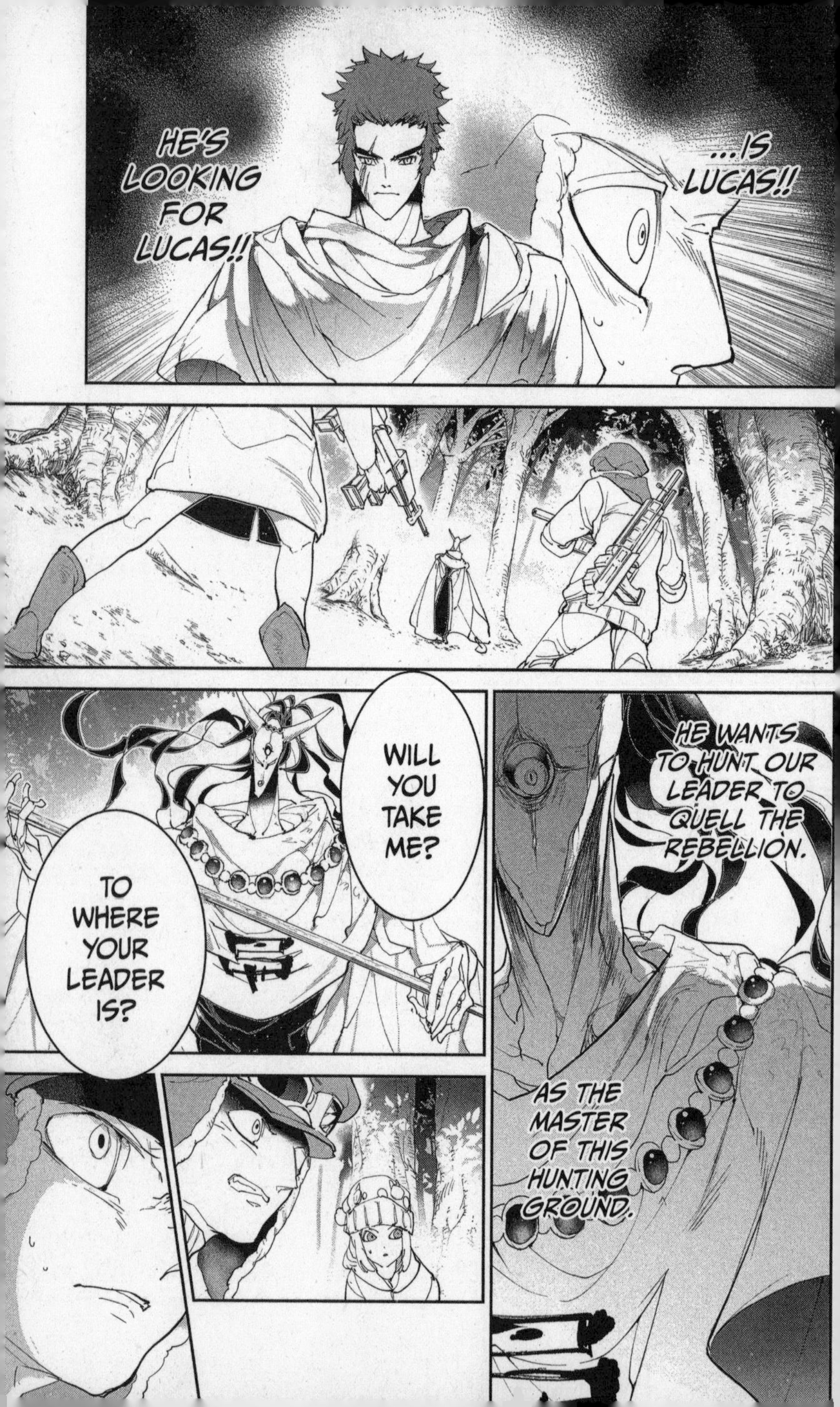
...IS LUCAS!!
HE'S LOOKING FOR LUCAS!!
HE WANTS TO HUNT OUR LEADER TO QUELL THE REBELLION.
AS THE MASTER OF THIS HUNTING GROUND.
WILL YOU TAKE ME?
TO WHERE YOUR LEADER IS?

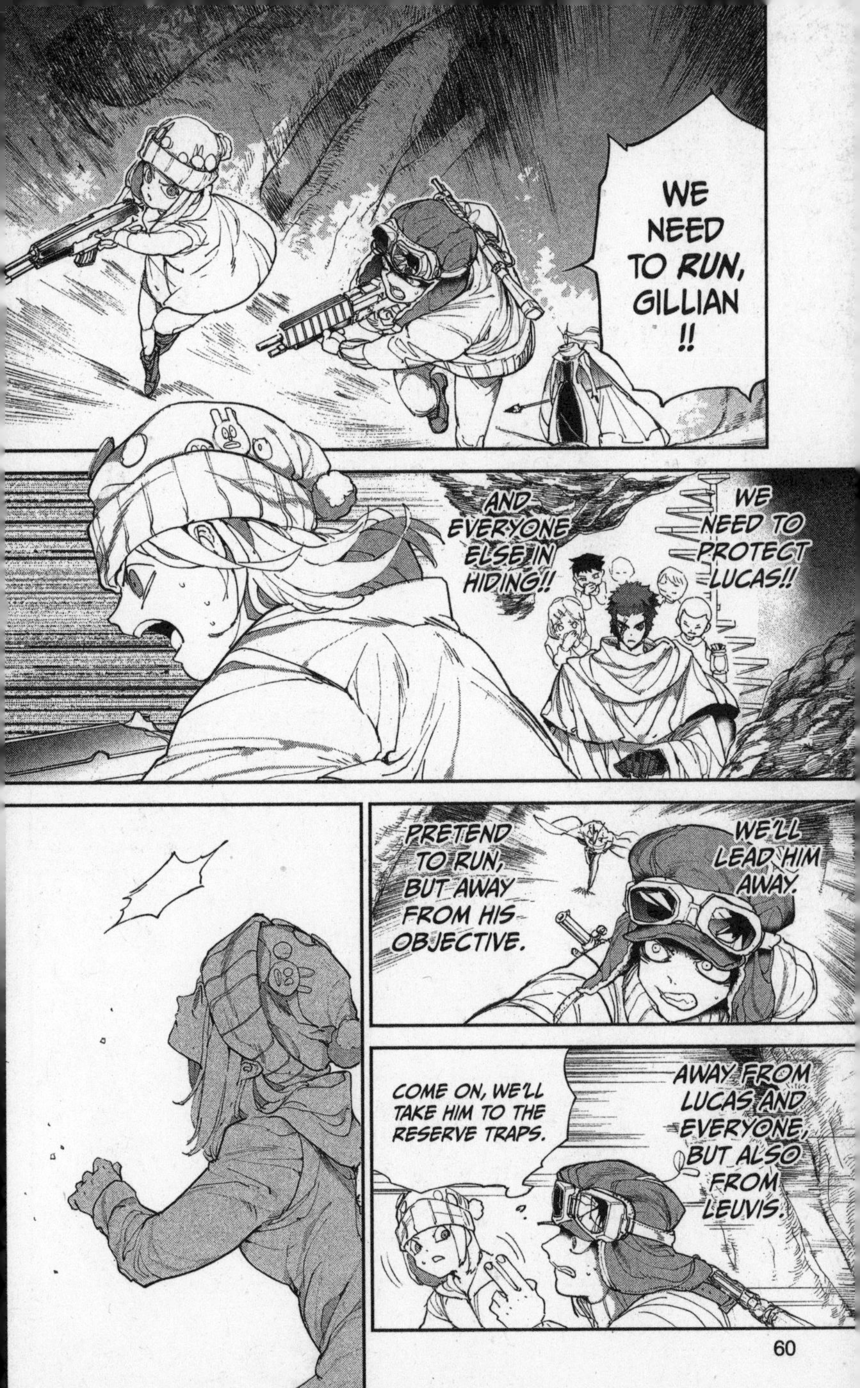

WE NEED TO RUN, GILLIAN !!
WE NEED TO PROTECT LUCAS!!
AND EVERYONE ELSE IN HIDING!!
WE'LL LEAD HIM AWAY.
PRETEND TO RUN, BUT AWAY FROM HIS OBJECTIVE.
AWAY FROM LUCAS AND EVERYONE, BUT ALSO FROM LEUVIS.
COME ON, WE'LL TAKE HIM TO THE RESERVE TRAPS.

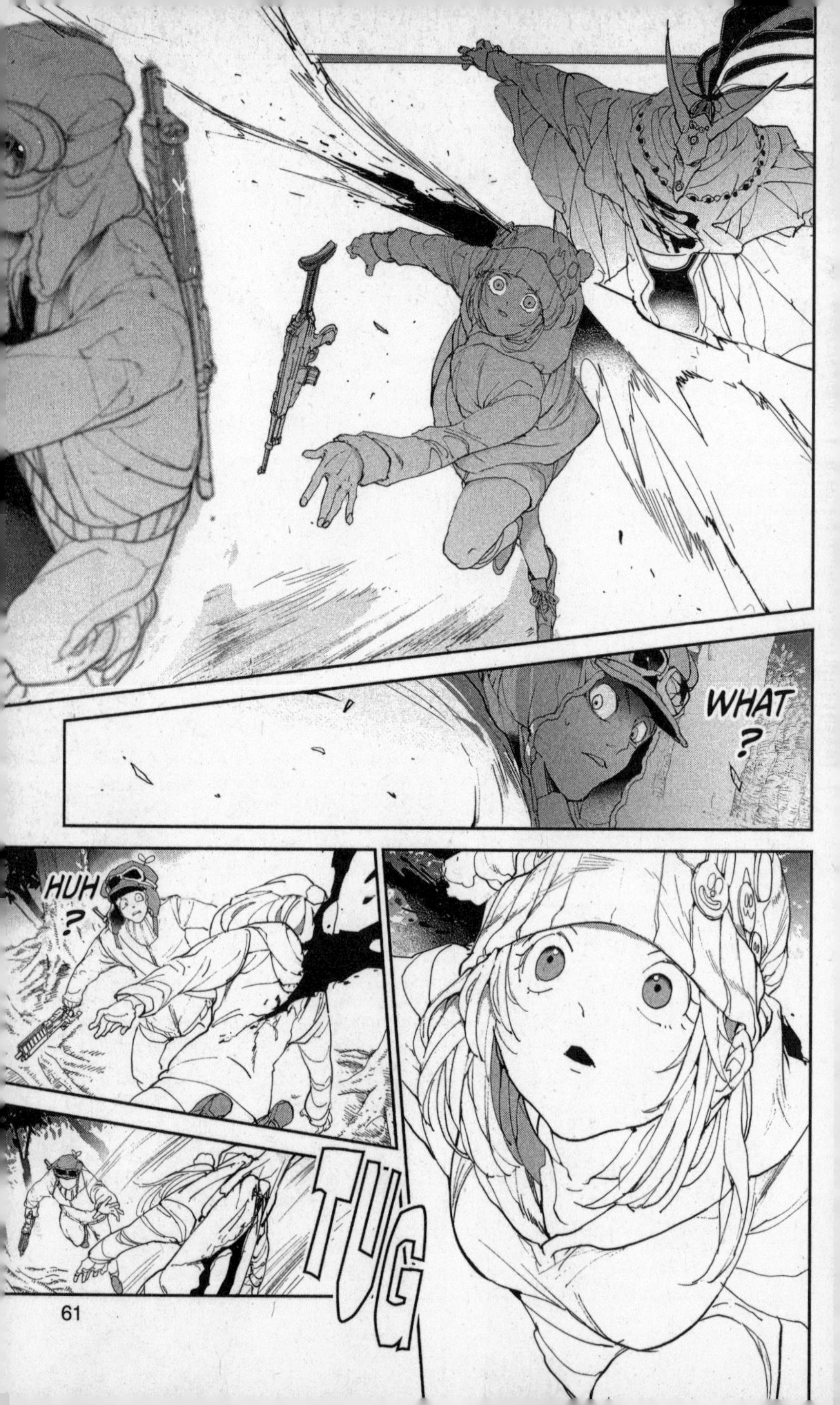
WHAT?
HUH?
TUG

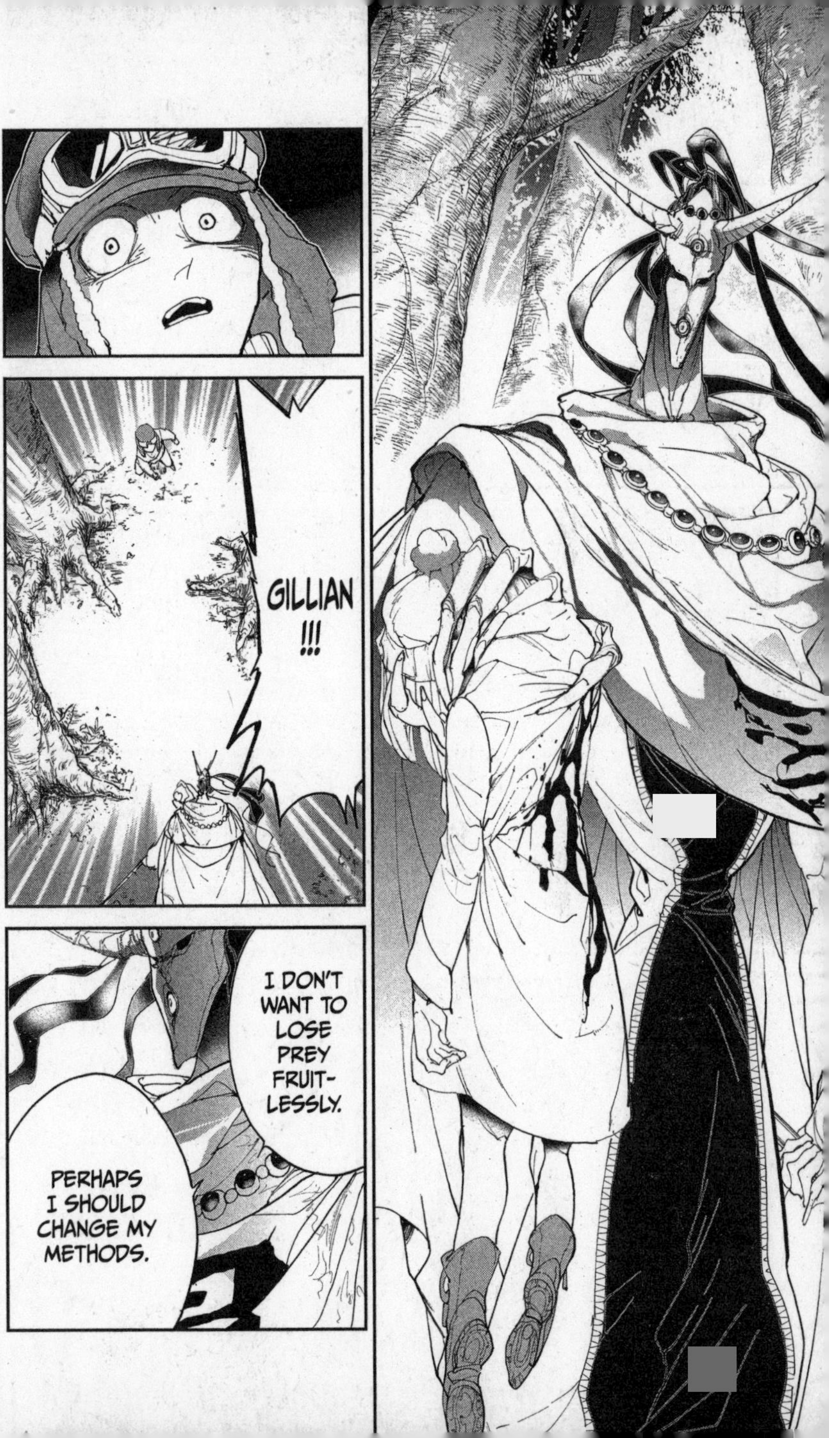
GILLIAN !!!
I DON'T WANT TO LOSE PREY FRUITLESSLY.
PERHAPS I SHOULD CHANGE MY METHODS.

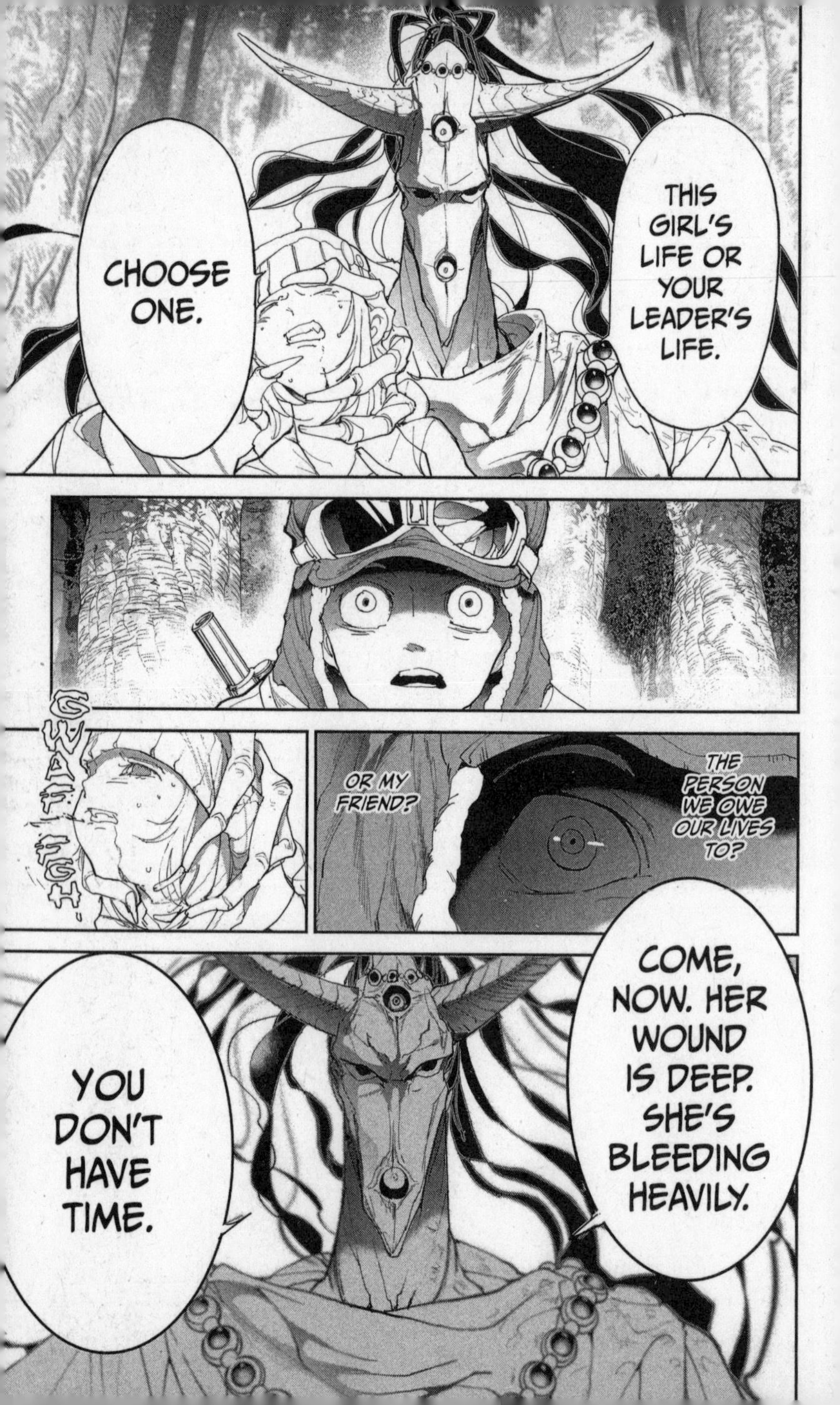
THIS GIRL'S LIFE OR YOUR LEADER'S LIFE.
CHOOSE ONE.
THE PERSON WE OWE OUR LIVES TO?
OR MY FRIEND?
GWAF FGH
COME, NOW. HER WOUND IS DEEP. SHE'S BLEEDING HEAVILY.
YOU DON'T HAVE TIME.

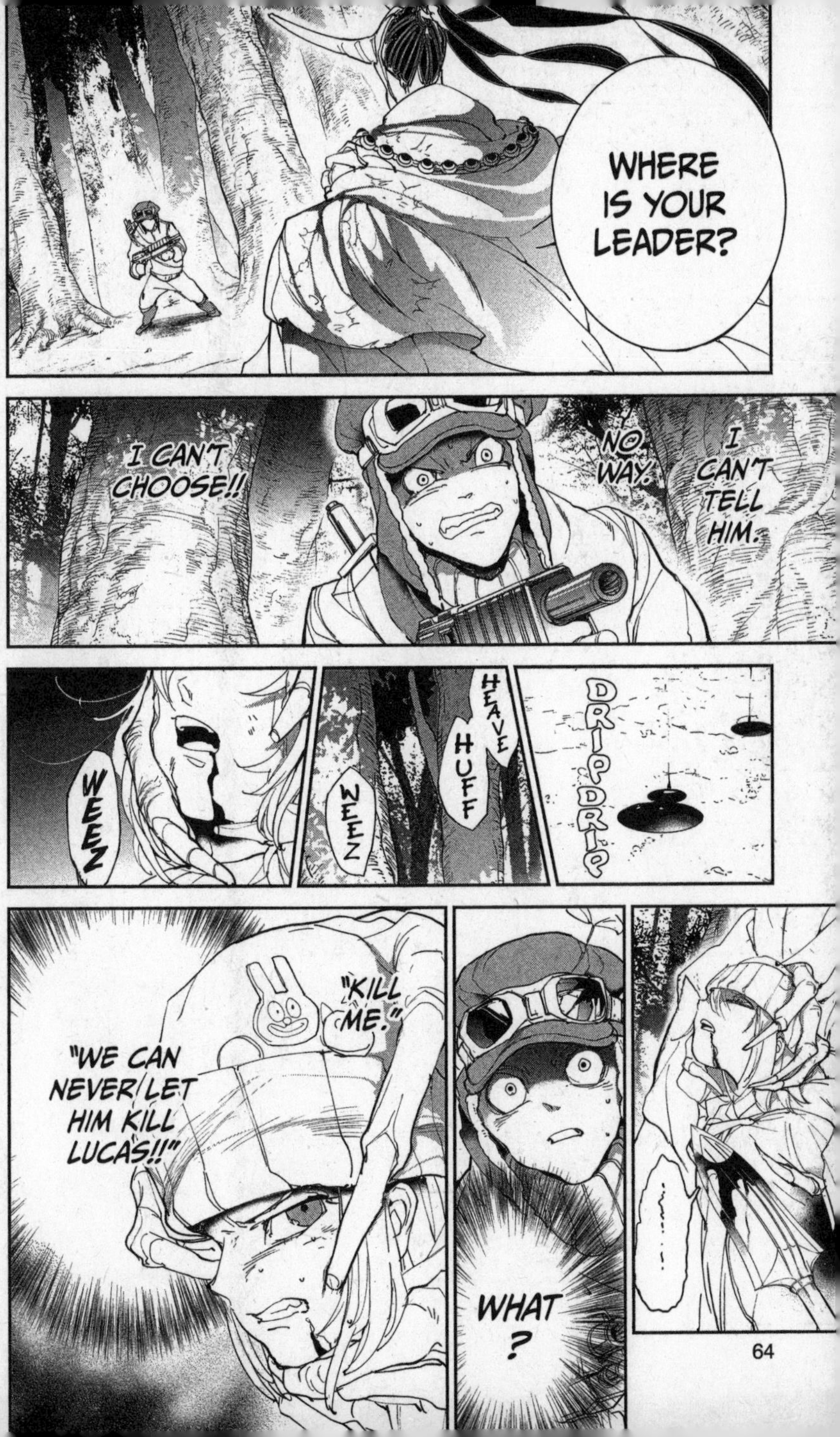
WHERE IS YOUR LEADER?
I CAN'T TELL HIM.
NO WAY.
I CAN'T CHOOSE!!
DRIP DRIP DRIP
HEAVE
HUFF
WEEZ
WEEZ
......
WHAT?
"KILL ME."
"WE CAN NEVER LET HIM KILL LUCAS!!"

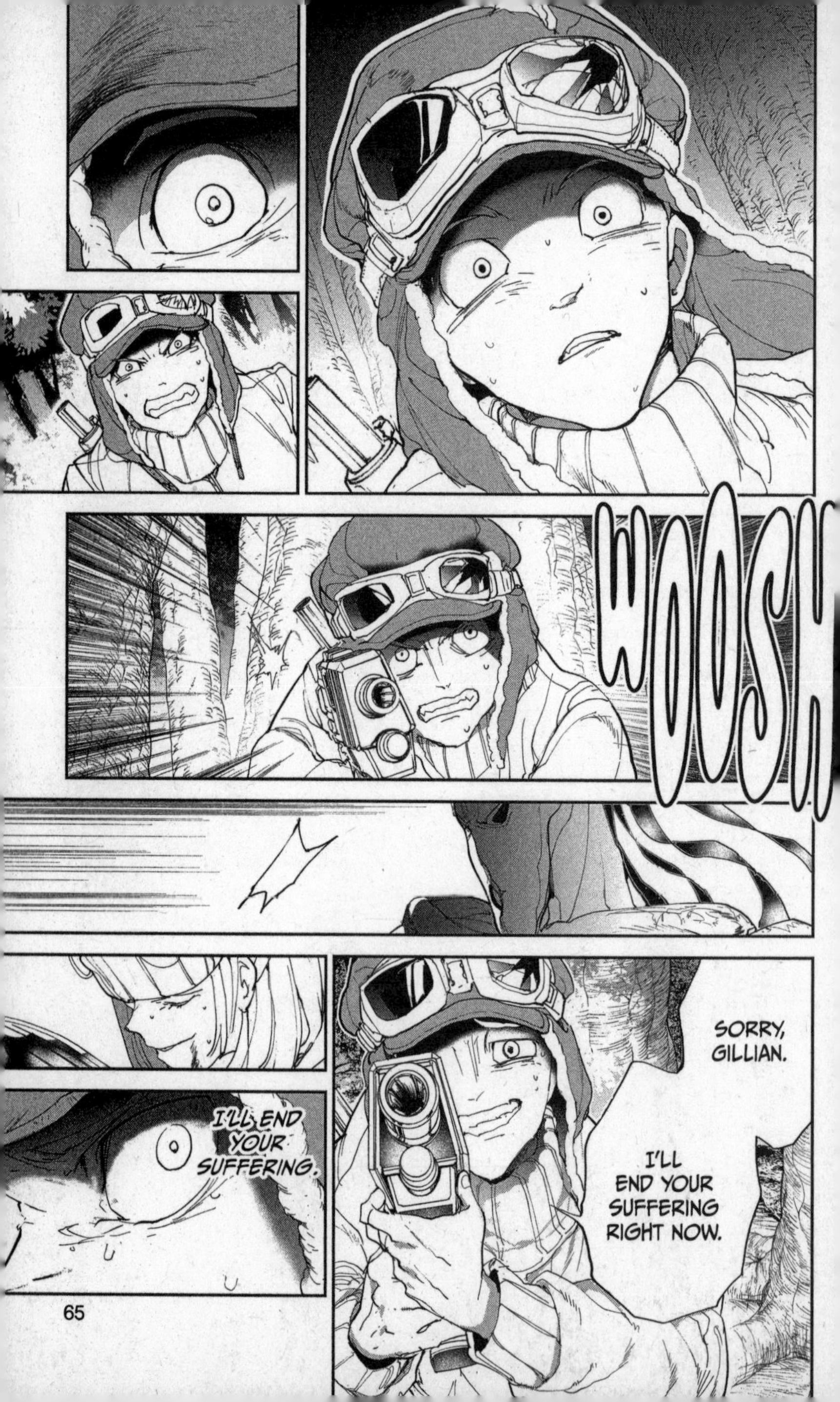
WOOSH
SORRY, GILLIAN.
I'LL END YOUR SUFFERING RIGHT NOW.
I'LL END YOUR SUFFERING.

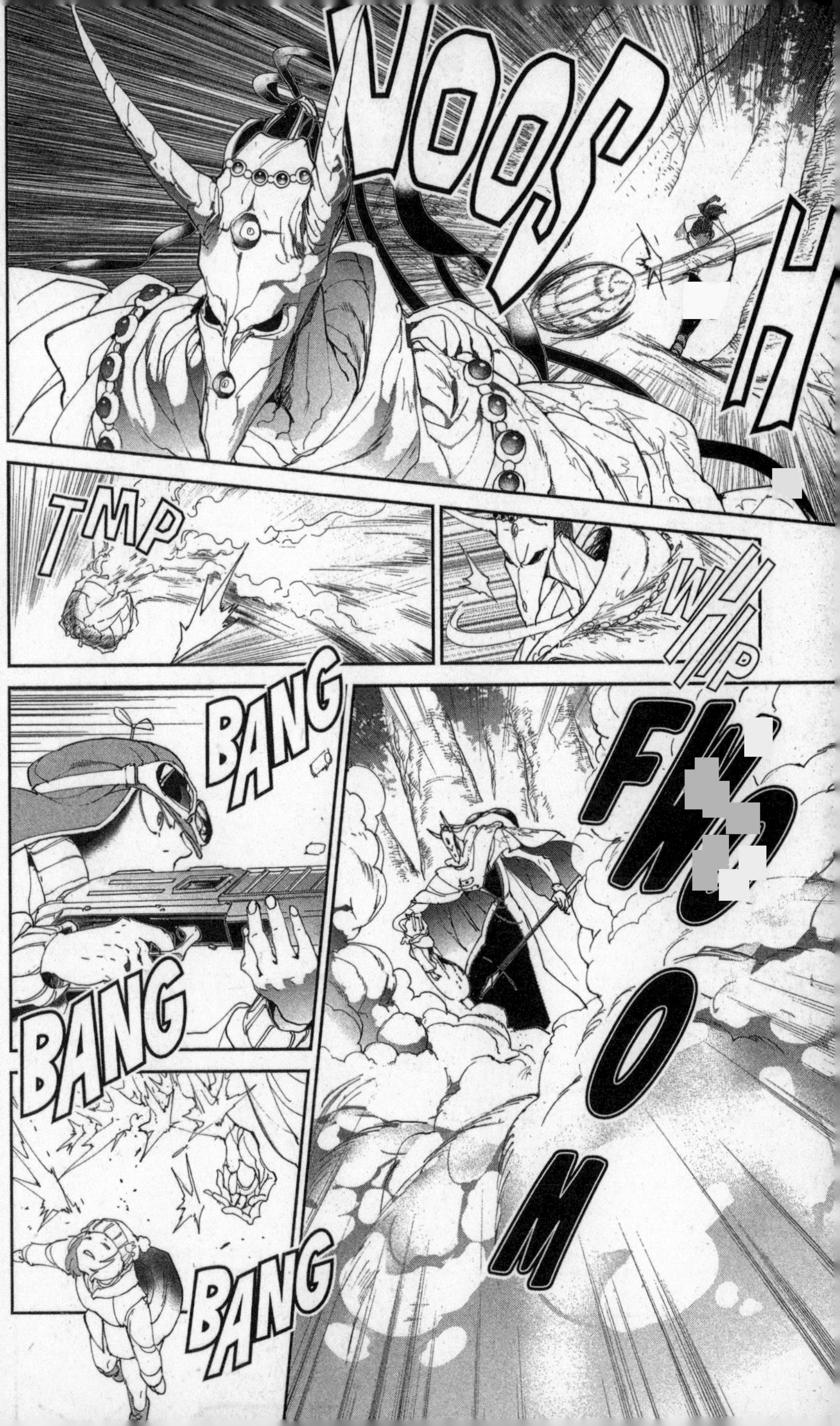
WOOSH
WHIP
TMP
FWOOM
BANG
BANG
BANG

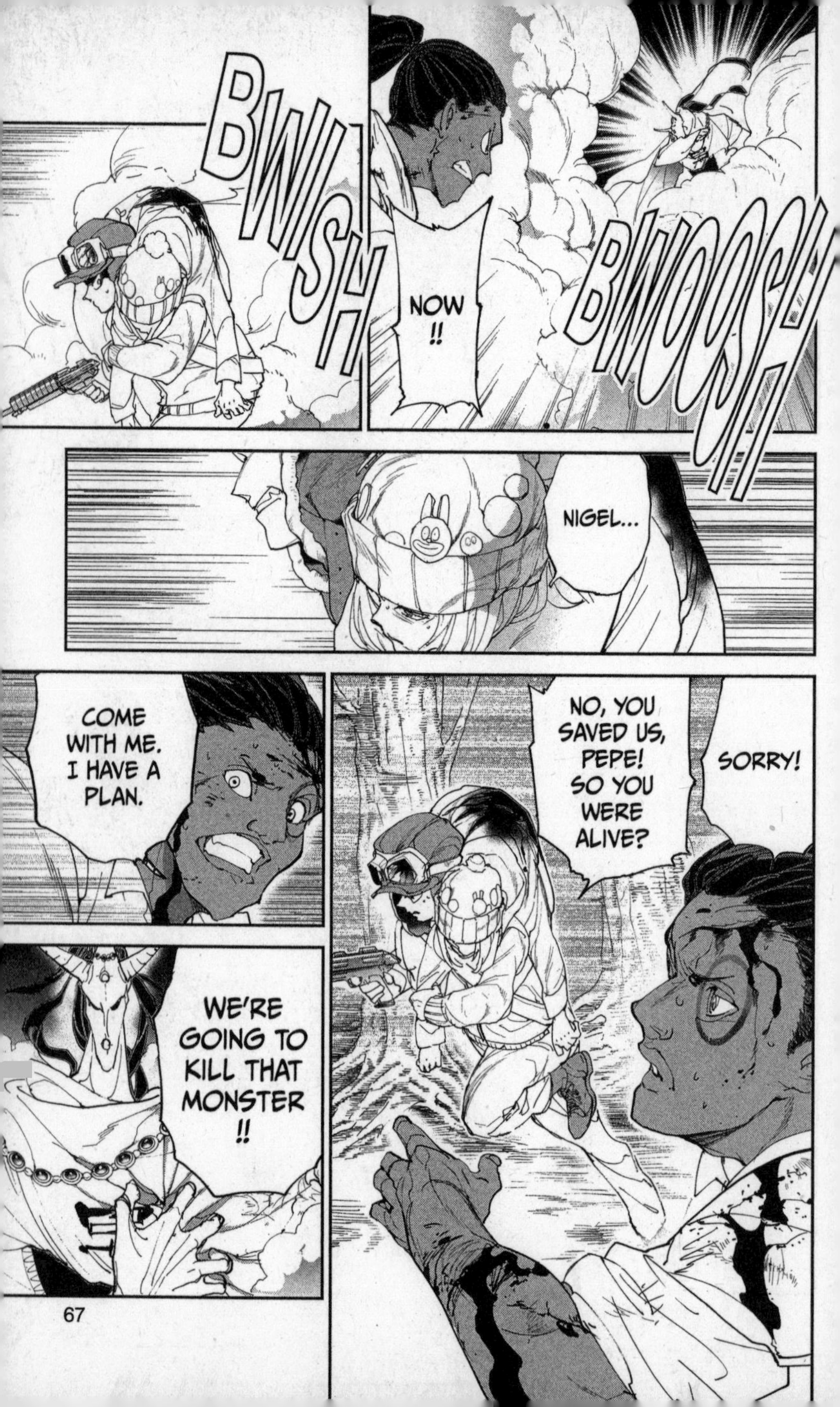

NOW !!
BWOOSH
BWISH
NIGEL...
SORRY!
NO, YOU SAVED US, PEPE! SO YOU WERE ALIVE?
COME WITH ME. I HAVE A PLAN.
WE'RE GOING TO KILL THAT MONSTER !!

SIDE STORY 7-1

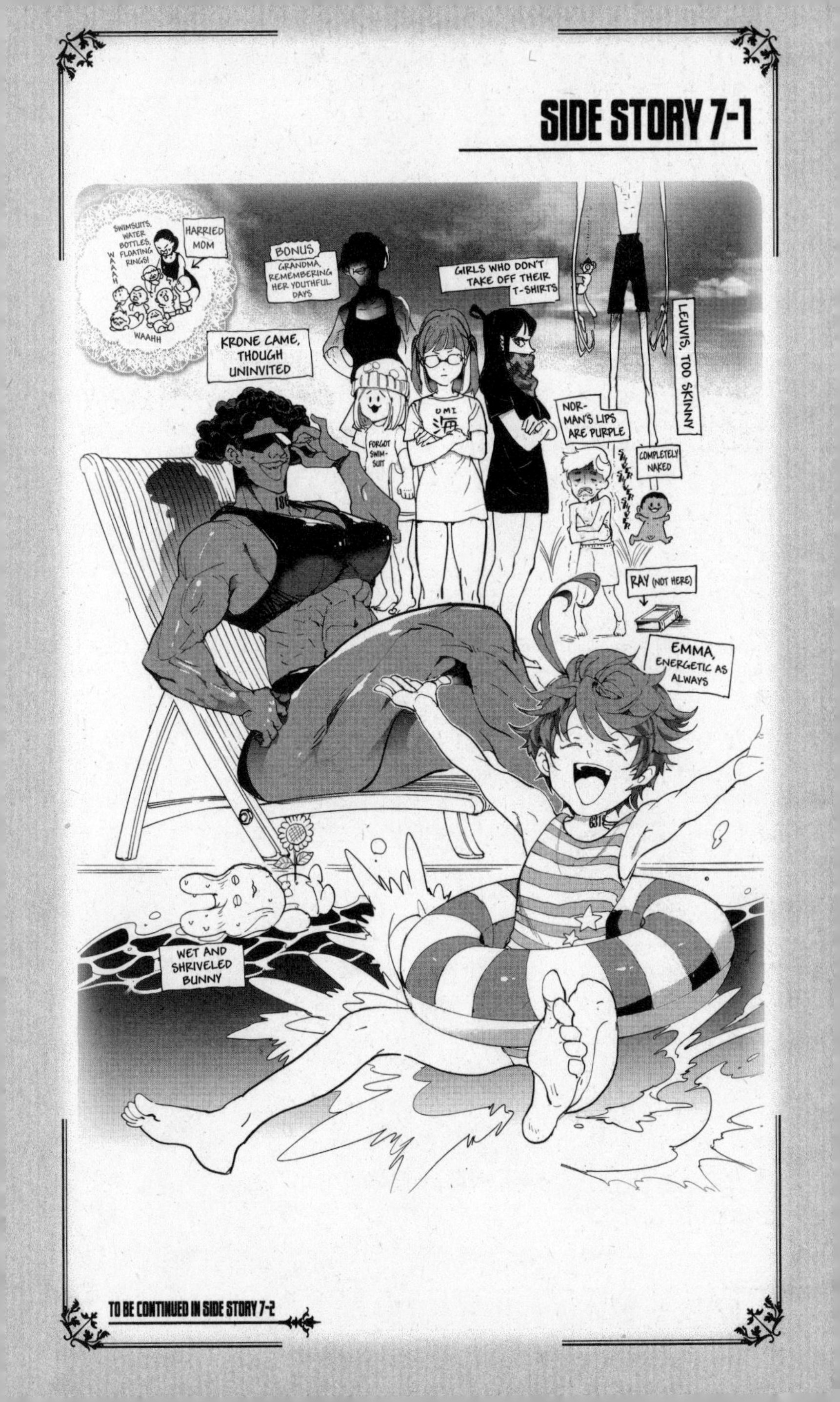
LEUVIS, TOO SKINNY
GIRLS WHO DON'T TAKE OFF THEIR T-SHIRTS
BONUS
GRANDMA, REMEMBERING HER YOUTHFUL DAYS
HARRIED MOM
SWIMSUITS, WATER BOTTLES, FLOATING RINGS!
WAAAH
WAAHH
KRONE CAME, THOUGH UNINVITED
NOR-MAN'S LIPS ARE PURPLE
COMPLETELY NAKED
UMI
海
FORGOT SWIM-SUIT
RAY (NOT HERE)
EMMA, ENERGETIC AS ALWAYS
WET AND SHRIVELED BUNNY

TO BE CONTINUED IN SIDE STORY 7-2

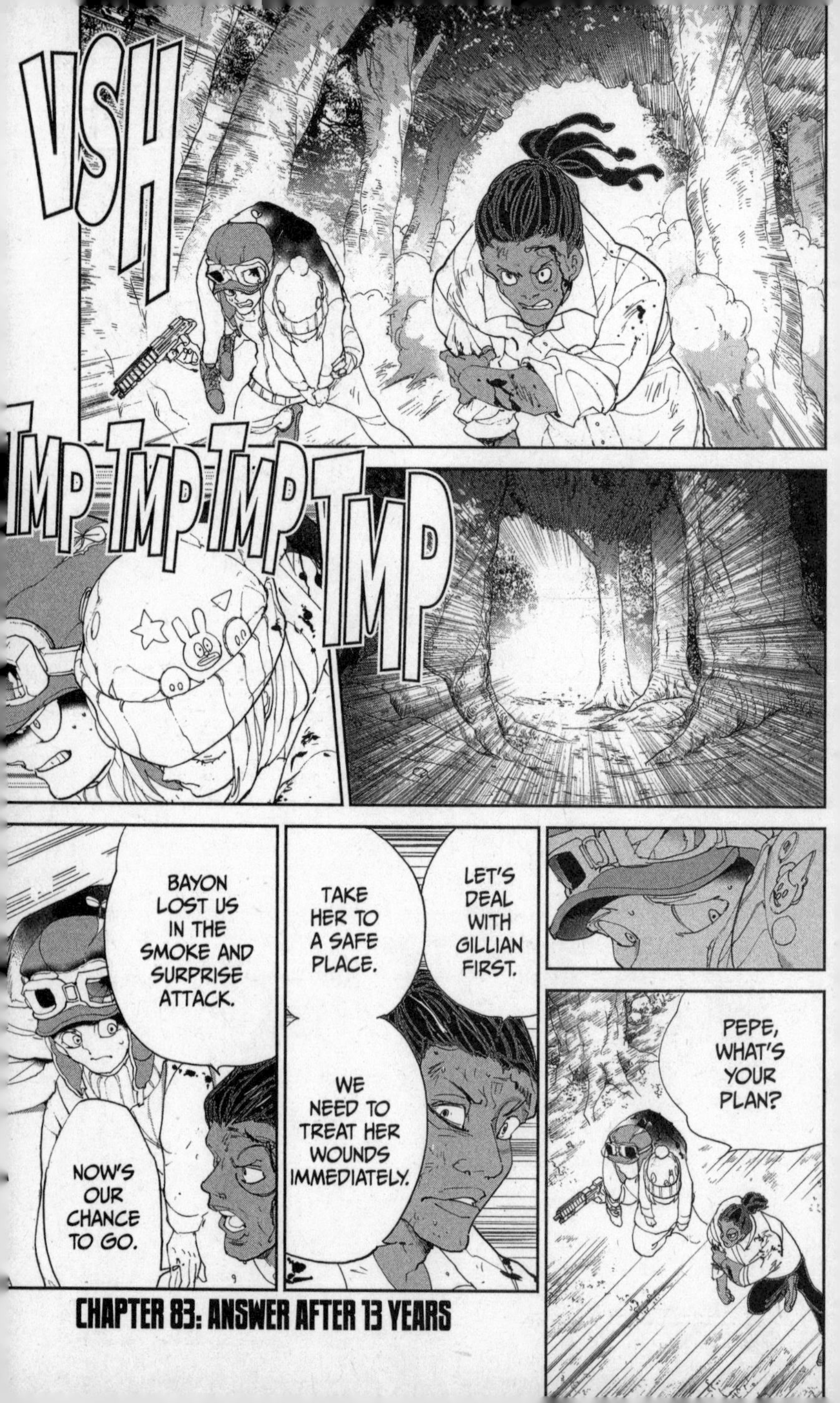
VSH
TMP TMP TMP TMP
PEPE, WHAT'S YOUR PLAN?
LET'S DEAL WITH GILLIAN FIRST.
TAKE HER TO A SAFE PLACE.
WE NEED TO TREAT HER WOUNDS IMMEDIATELY.
BAYON LOST US IN THE SMOKE AND SURPRISE ATTACK.
NOW'S OUR CHANCE TO GO.

CHAPTER 83: ANSWER AFTER 13 YEARS

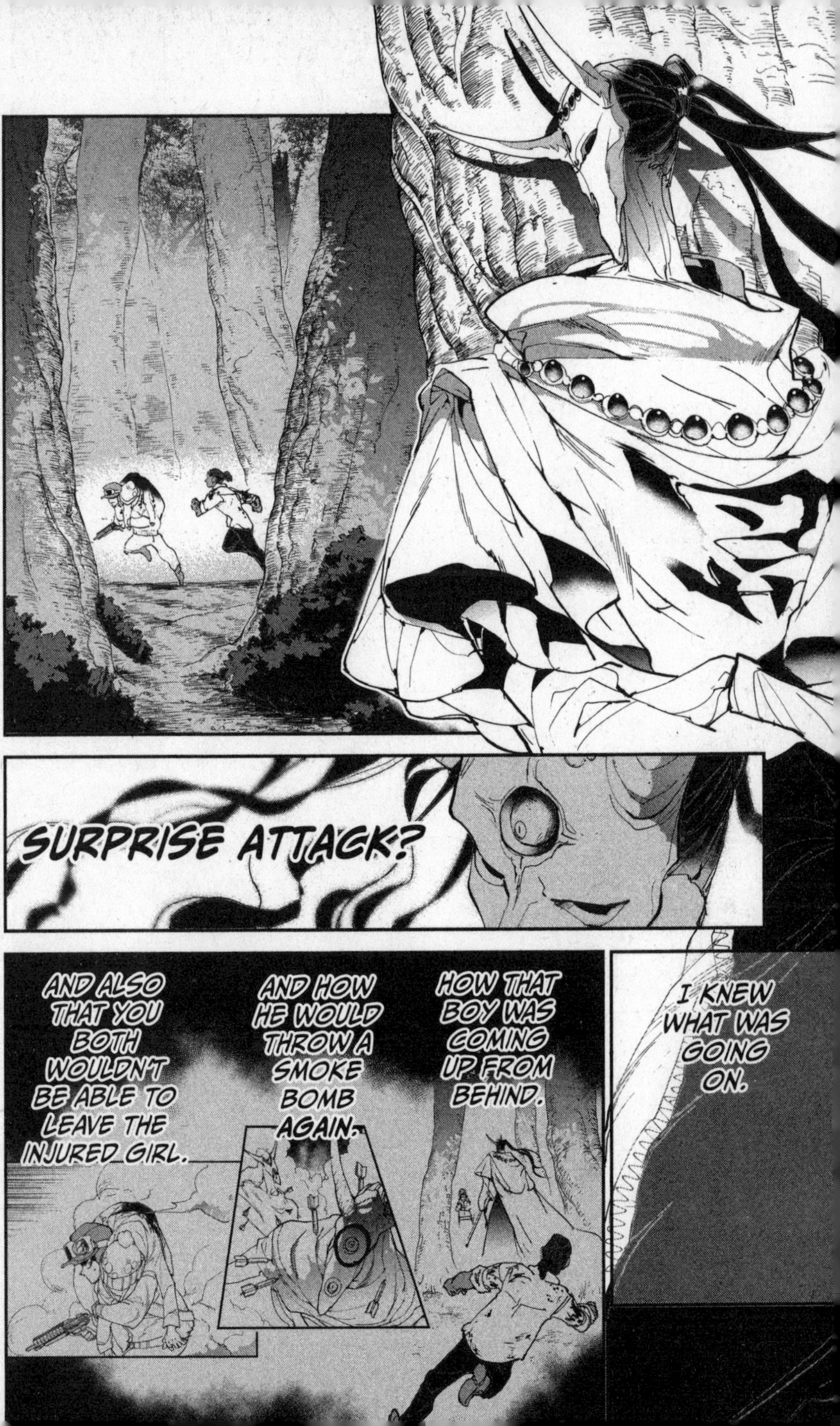
SURPRISE ATTACK?
I KNEW WHAT WAS GOING ON.
HOW THAT BOY WAS COMING UP FROM BEHIND.
AND HOW HE WOULD THROW A SMOKE BOMB AGAIN.
AND ALSO THAT YOU BOTH WOULDN'T BE ABLE TO LEAVE THE INJURED GIRL.

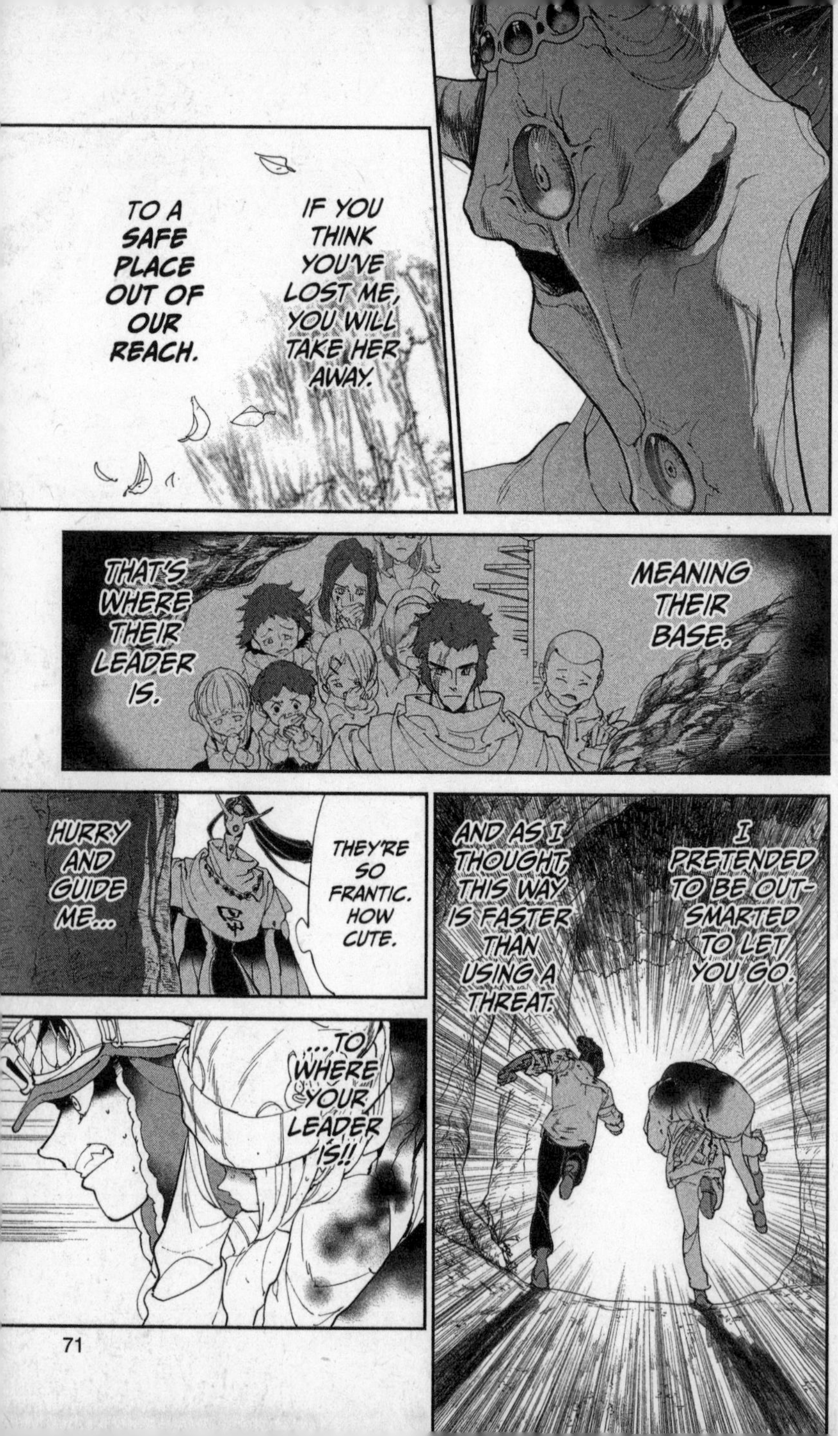
IF YOU THINK YOU'VE LOST ME, YOU WILL TAKE HER AWAY.
TO A SAFE PLACE OUT OF OUR REACH.
MEANING THEIR BASE.
THAT'S WHERE THEIR LEADER IS.
I PRETENDED TO BE OUT-SMARTED TO LET YOU GO.
AND AS I THOUGHT, THIS WAY IS FASTER THAN USING A THREAT.
THEY'RE SO FRANTIC. HOW CUTE.
HURRY AND GUIDE ME...
...TO WHERE YOUR LEADER IS!!

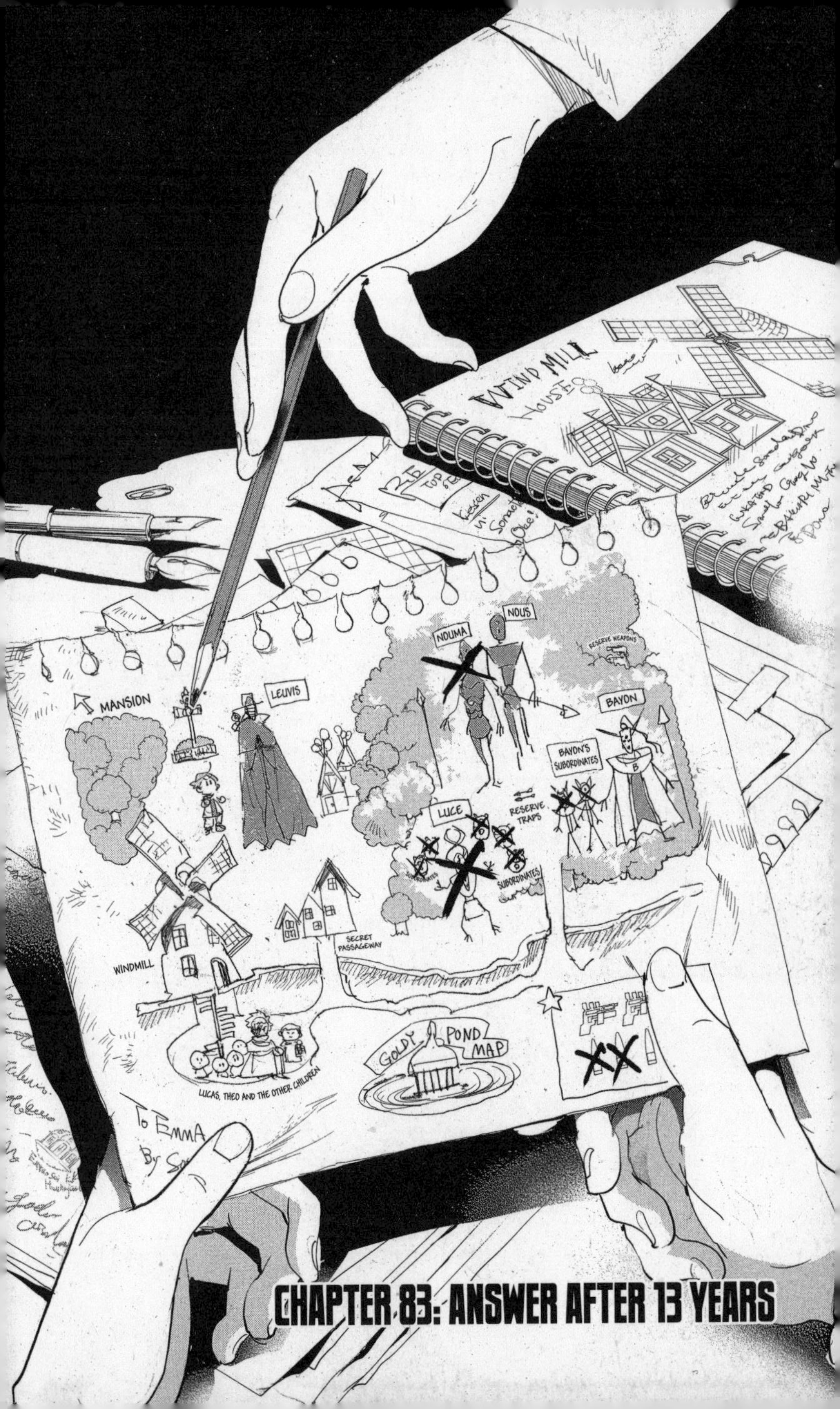
WIND MILL
HOUSE
NOUS
NOUMA
RESERVE WEAPONS
MANSION
LEUVIS
BAYON
BAYON'S SUBORDINATES
LUCE
RESERVE TRAPS
SUBORDINATES
SUBORDINATES
WINDMILL
SECRET PASSAGEWAY
GOLDY POND MAP
LUCAS, THEO AND THE OTHER CHILDREN
To EMMA

CHAPTER 83: ANSWER AFTER 13 YEARS

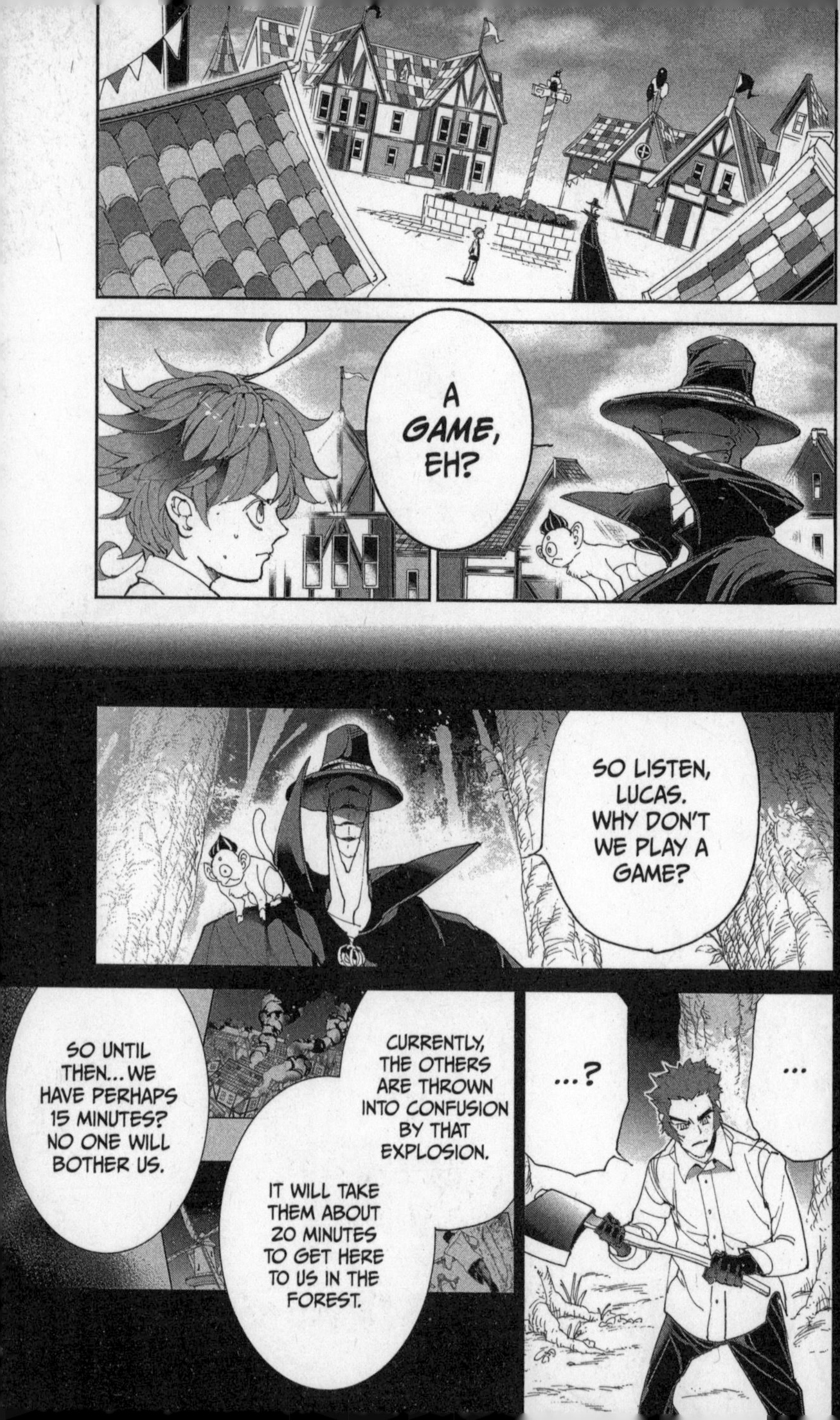
A GAME, EH?
SO LISTEN, LUCAS. WHY DON'T WE PLAY A GAME?
...
...?
CURRENTLY, THE OTHERS ARE THROWN INTO CONFUSION BY THAT EXPLOSION.
IT WILL TAKE THEM ABOUT 20 MINUTES TO GET HERE TO US IN THE FOREST.
SO UNTIL THEN... WE HAVE PERHAPS 15 MINUTES? NO ONE WILL BOTHER US.

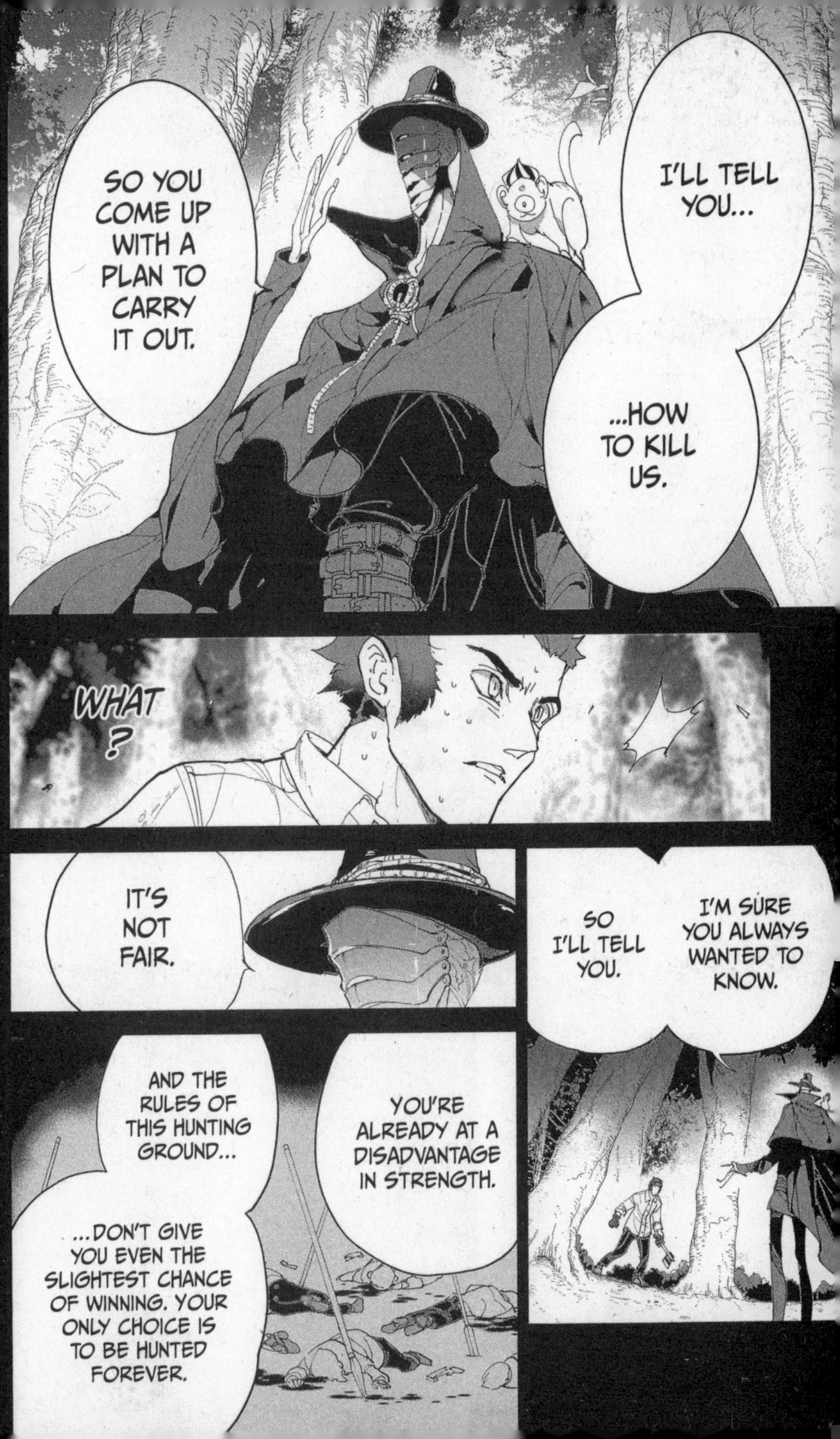
I'LL TELL YOU...
...HOW TO KILL US.
SO YOU COME UP WITH A PLAN TO CARRY IT OUT.
WHAT?
I'M SURE YOU ALWAYS WANTED TO KNOW.
SO I'LL TELL YOU.
IT'S NOT FAIR.
YOU'RE ALREADY AT A DISADVANTAGE IN STRENGTH.
AND THE RULES OF THIS HUNTING GROUND...
...DON'T GIVE YOU EVEN THE SLIGHTEST CHANCE OF WINNING. YOUR ONLY CHOICE IS TO BE HUNTED FOREVER.

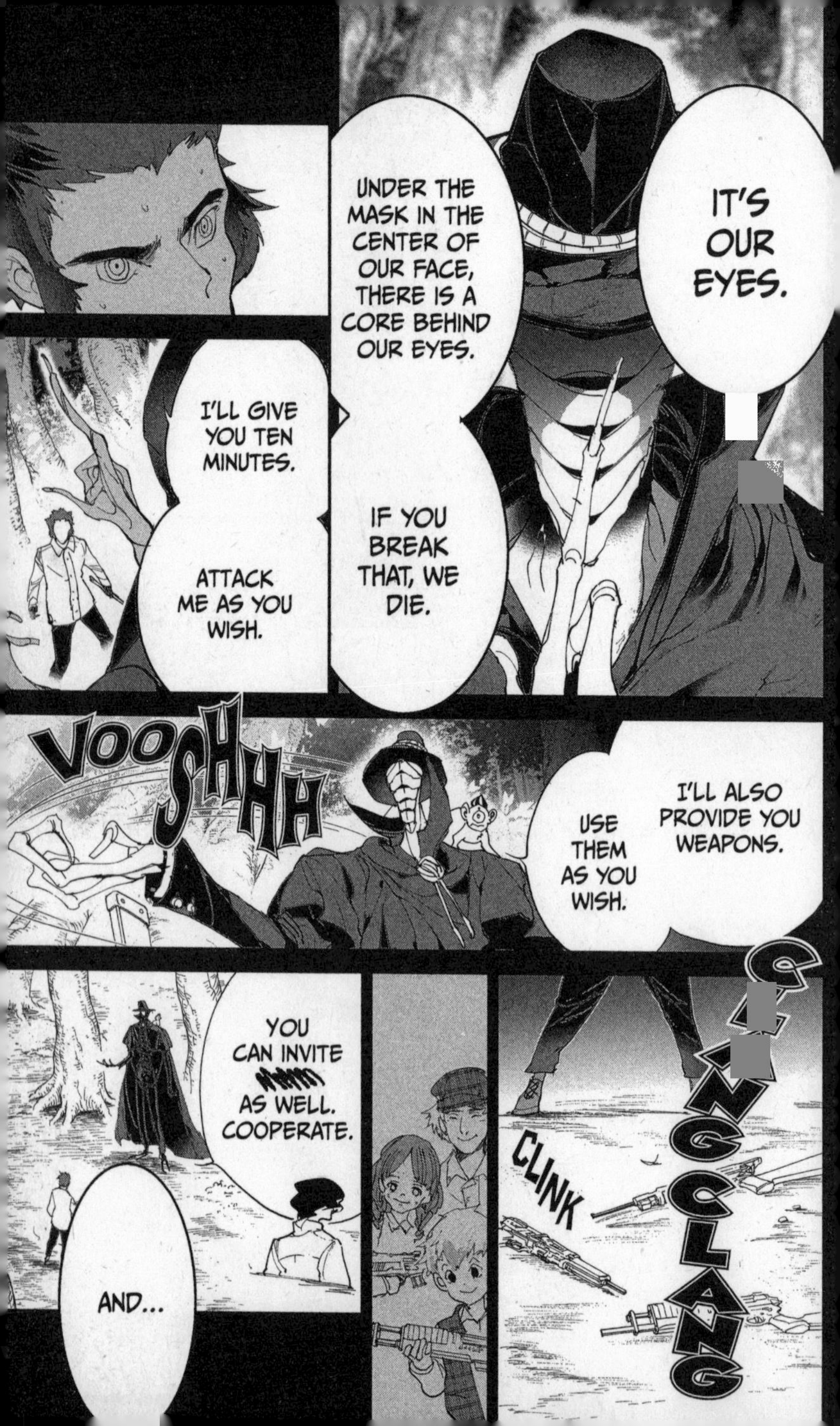
IT'S OUR EYES.
UNDER THE MASK IN THE CENTER OF OUR FACE, THERE IS A CORE BEHIND OUR EYES.
IF YOU BREAK THAT, WE DIE.
I'LL GIVE YOU TEN MINUTES.
ATTACK ME AS YOU WISH.
I'LL ALSO PROVIDE YOU WEAPONS.
USE THEM AS YOU WISH.
VOOSHHH
CLANG
CLINK
YOU CAN INVITE [redacted] AS WELL. COOPERATE.
AND...

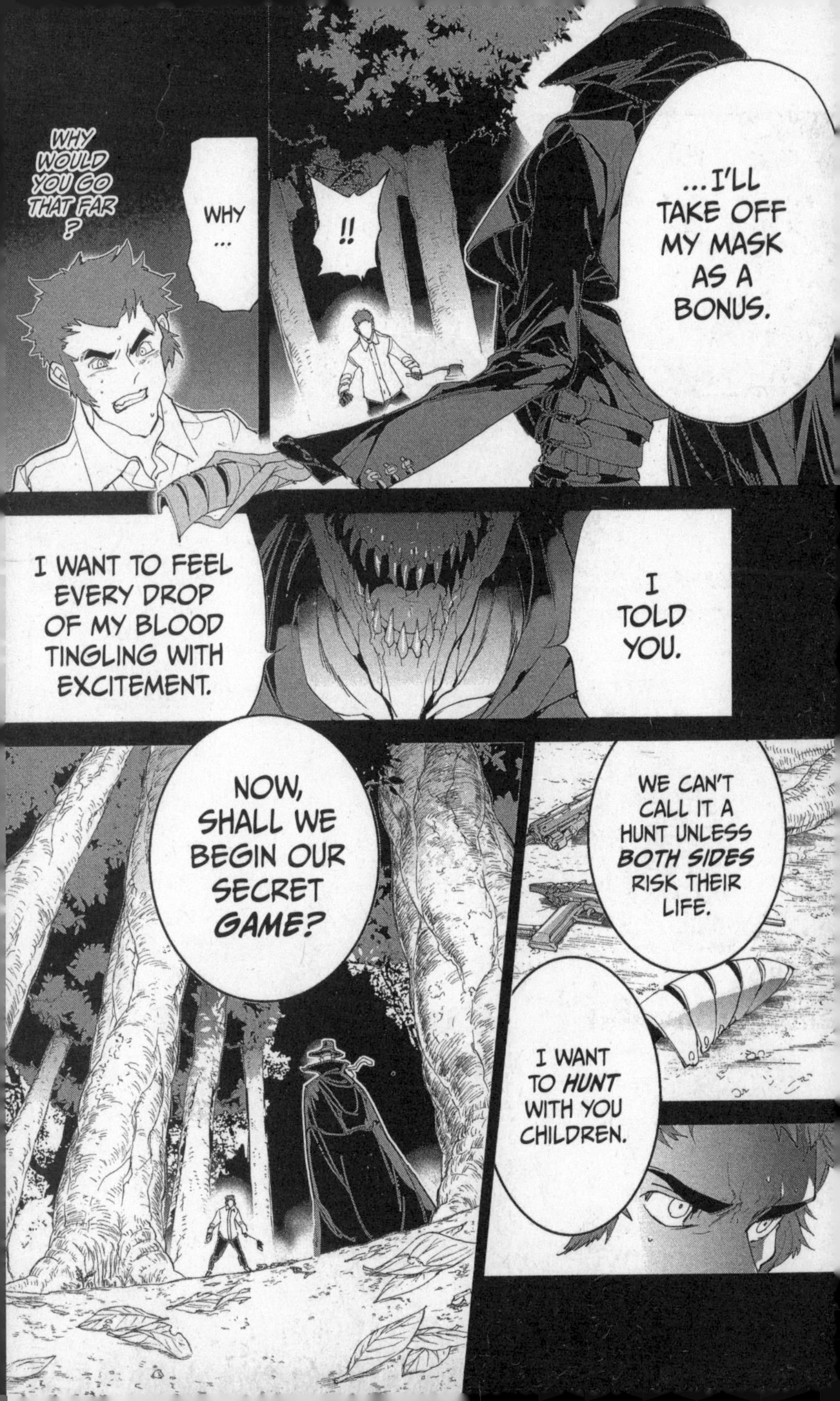
...I'LL TAKE OFF MY MASK AS A BONUS.
!!
WHY ...
WHY WOULD YOU GO THAT FAR?
I TOLD YOU.
I WANT TO FEEL EVERY DROP OF MY BLOOD TINGLING WITH EXCITEMENT.
WE CAN'T CALL IT A HUNT UNLESS *BOTH SIDES* RISK THEIR LIFE.
I WANT TO *HUNT* WITH YOU CHILDREN.
NOW, SHALL WE BEGIN OUR SECRET *GAME?*

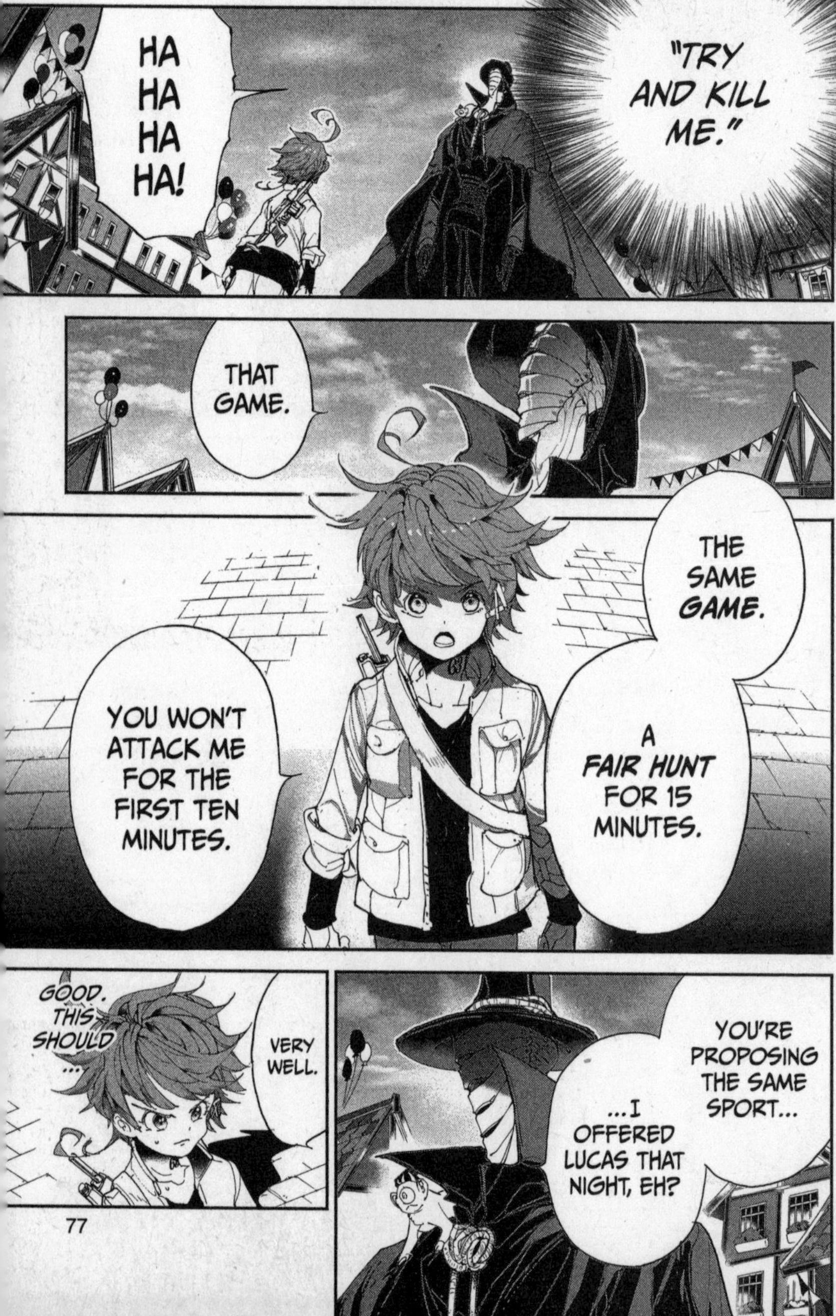
"TRY AND KILL ME."
HA HA HA HA!
THAT GAME.
THE SAME GAME.
A FAIR HUNT FOR 15 MINUTES.
YOU WON'T ATTACK ME FOR THE FIRST TEN MINUTES.
YOU'RE PROPOSING THE SAME SPORT...
...I OFFERED LUCAS THAT NIGHT, EH?
VERY WELL.
GOOD. THIS SHOULD ...

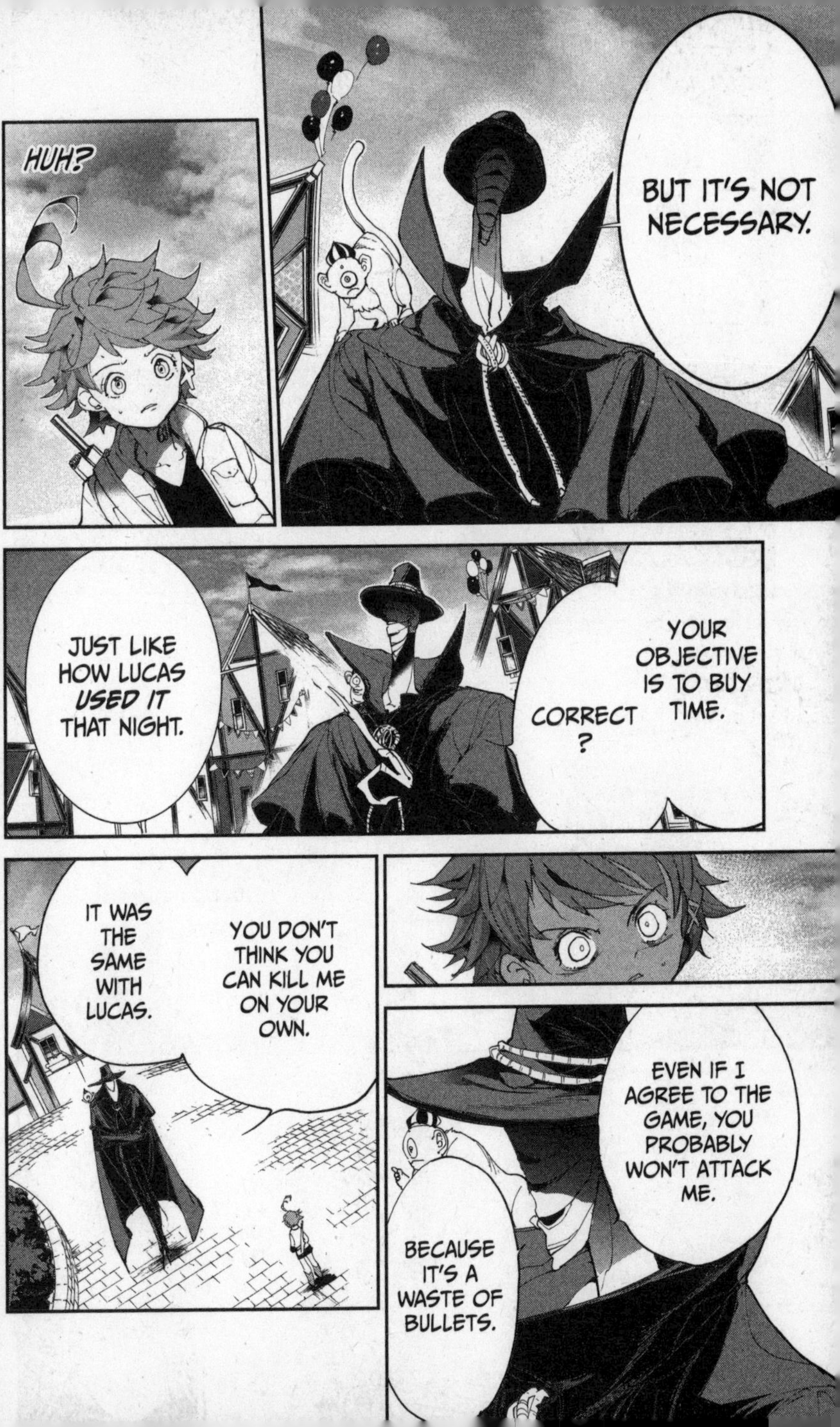
BUT IT'S NOT NECESSARY.
HUH?
YOUR OBJECTIVE IS TO BUY TIME.
CORRECT ?
JUST LIKE HOW LUCAS *USED IT* THAT NIGHT.
EVEN IF I AGREE TO THE GAME, YOU PROBABLY WON'T ATTACK ME.
BECAUSE IT'S A WASTE OF BULLETS.
YOU DON'T THINK YOU CAN KILL ME ON YOUR OWN.
IT WAS THE SAME WITH LUCAS.

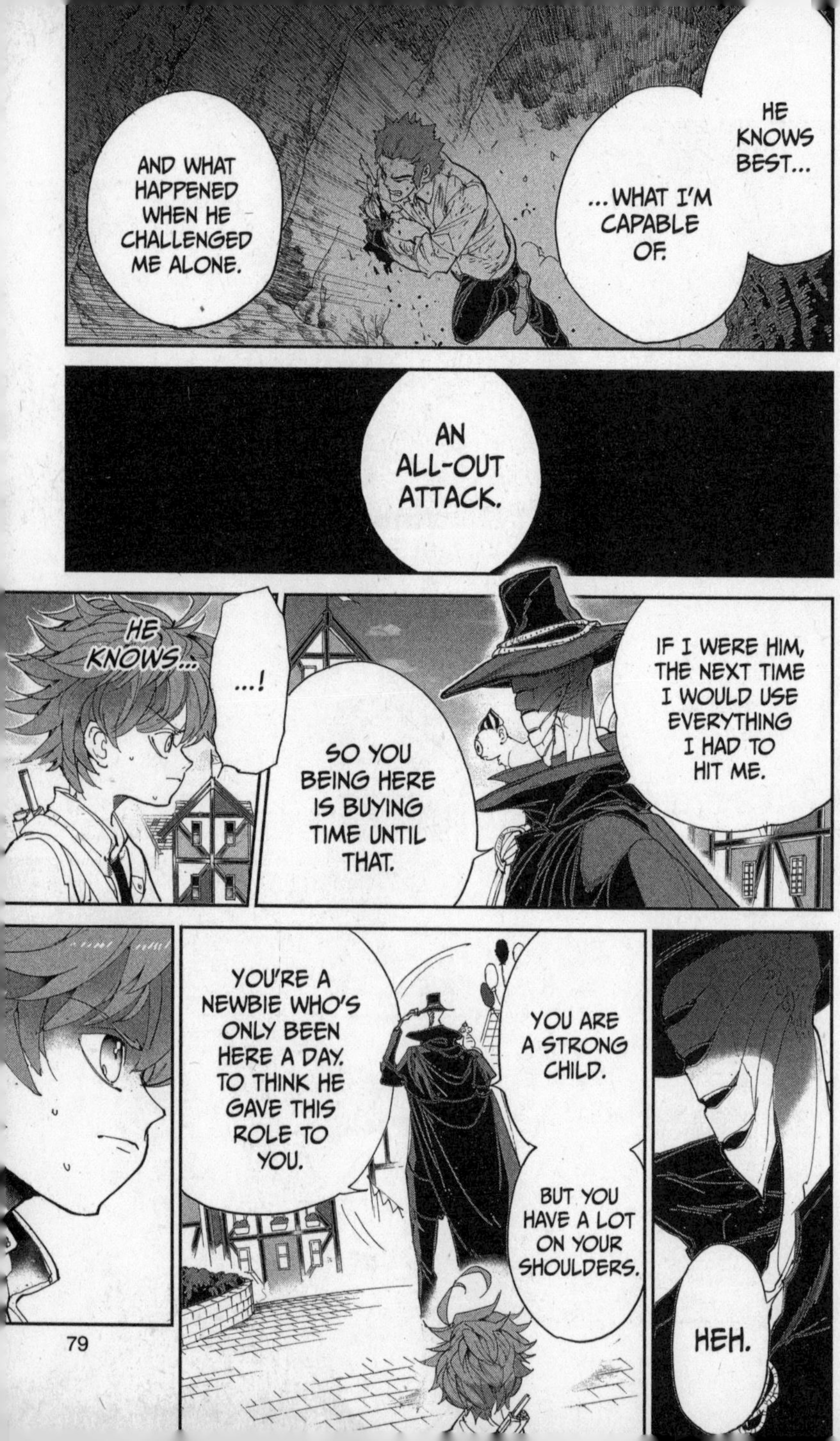
HE KNOWS BEST...
...WHAT I'M CAPABLE OF.
AND WHAT HAPPENED WHEN HE CHALLENGED ME ALONE.
AN ALL-OUT ATTACK.
IF I WERE HIM, THE NEXT TIME I WOULD USE EVERYTHING I HAD TO HIT ME.
SO YOU BEING HERE IS BUYING TIME UNTIL THAT.
...!
HE KNOWS...
HEH.
YOU'RE A NEWBIE WHO'S ONLY BEEN HERE A DAY. TO THINK HE GAVE THIS ROLE TO YOU.
YOU ARE A STRONG CHILD.
BUT YOU HAVE A LOT ON YOUR SHOULDERS.

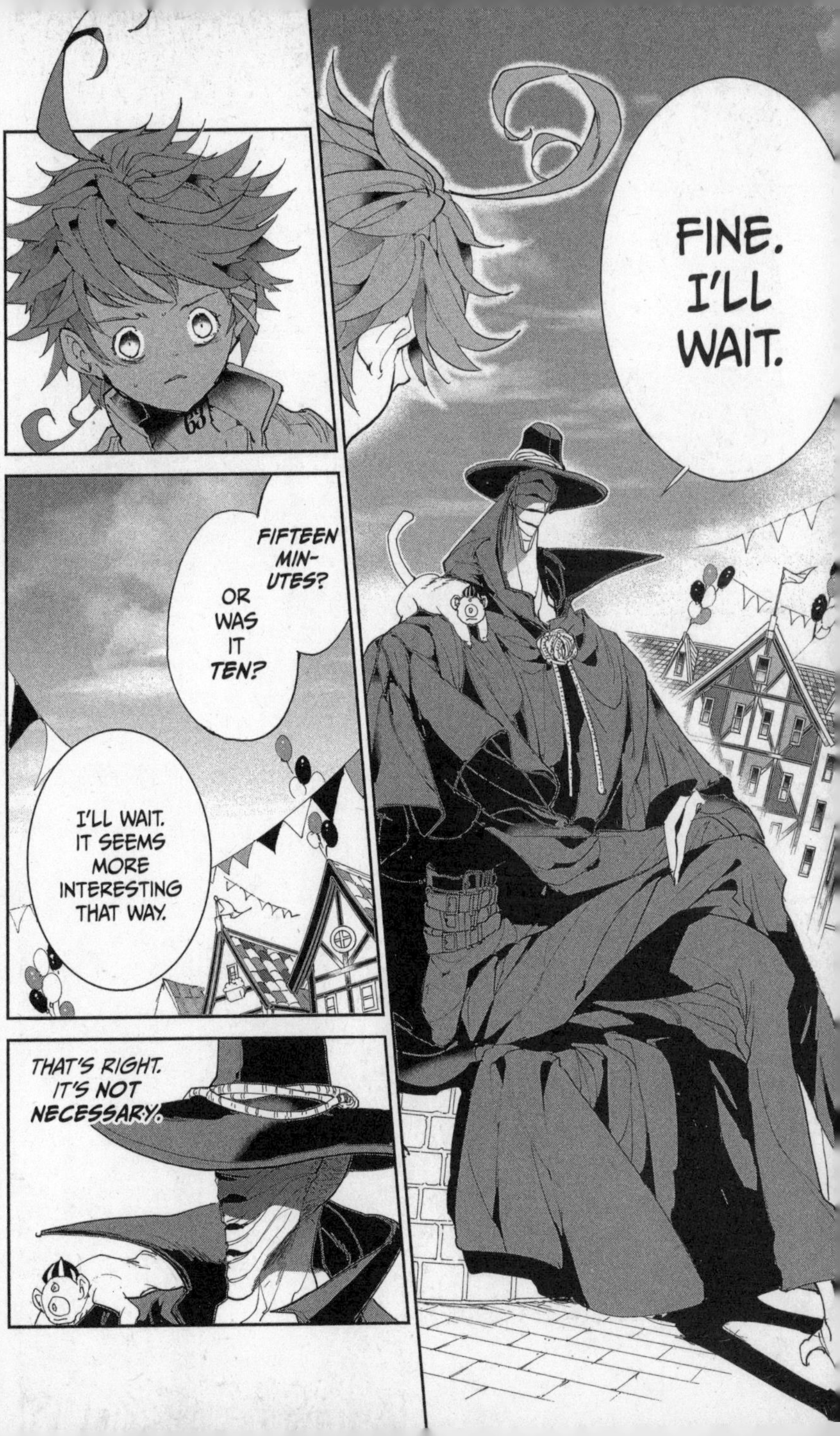
FINE. I'LL WAIT.
FIFTEEN MIN-UTES?
OR WAS IT TEN?
I'LL WAIT. IT SEEMS MORE INTERESTING THAT WAY.
THAT'S RIGHT. IT'S NOT NECESSARY.

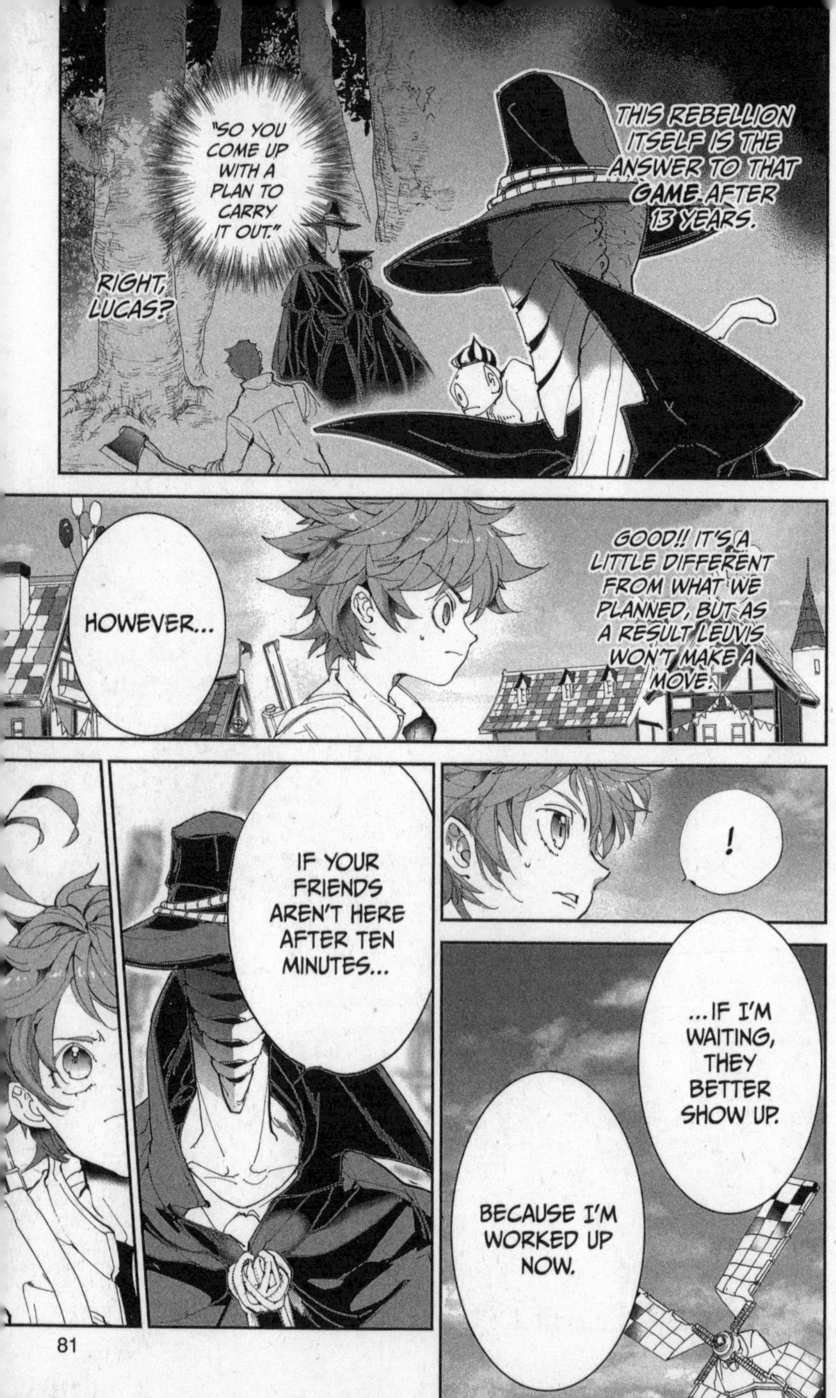
THIS REBELLION ITSELF IS THE ANSWER TO THAT GAME AFTER 13 YEARS.
"SO YOU COME UP WITH A PLAN TO CARRY IT OUT."
RIGHT, LUCAS?
GOOD!! IT'S A LITTLE DIFFERENT FROM WHAT WE PLANNED, BUT AS A RESULT LEUVIS WON'T MAKE A MOVE.
HOWEVER...
!
...IF I'M WAITING, THEY BETTER SHOW UP.
BECAUSE I'M WORKED UP NOW.
IF YOUR FRIENDS AREN'T HERE AFTER TEN MINUTES...

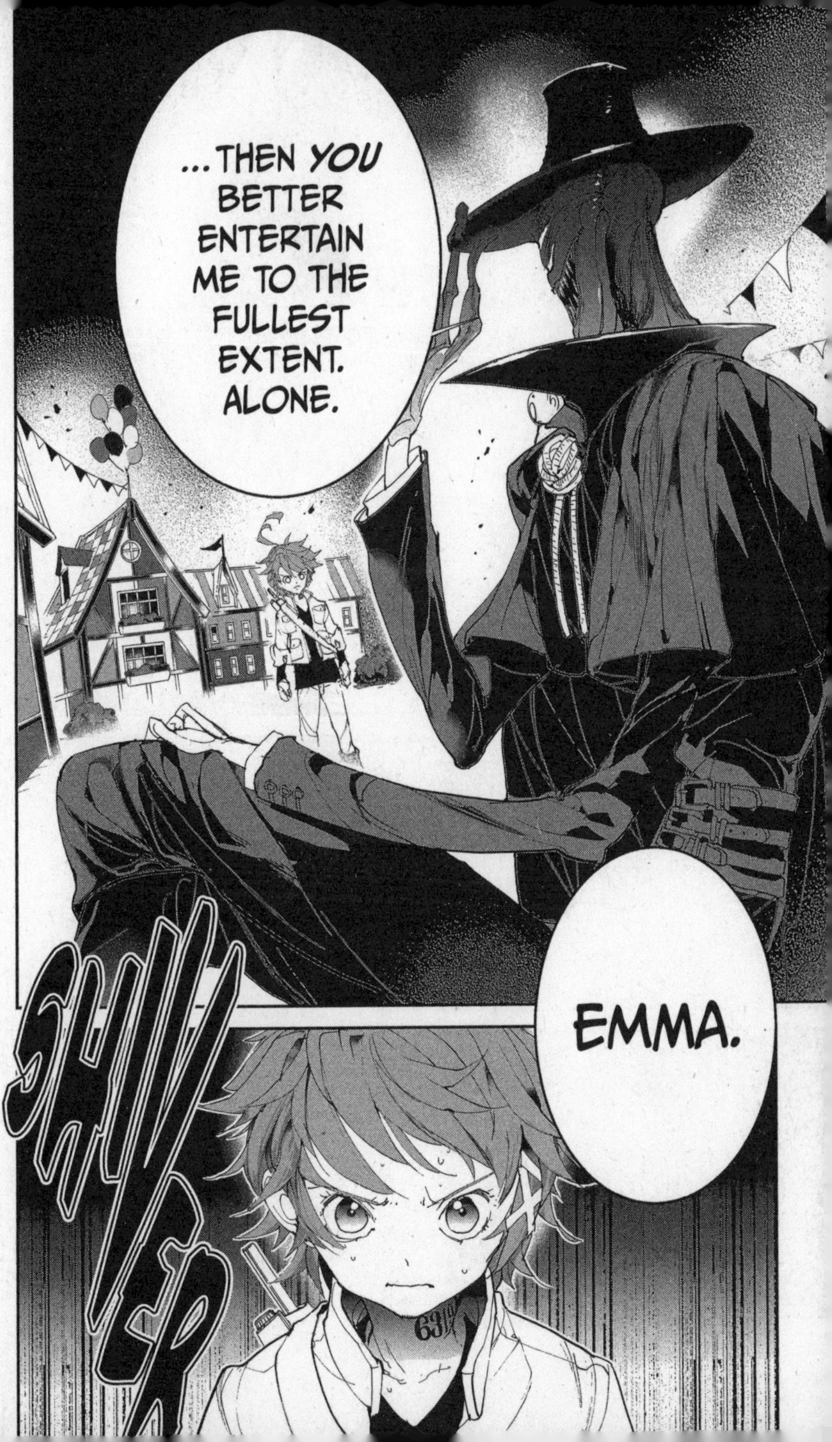
...THEN *YOU* BETTER ENTERTAIN ME TO THE FULLEST EXTENT. ALONE.
EMMA.
SHIVER

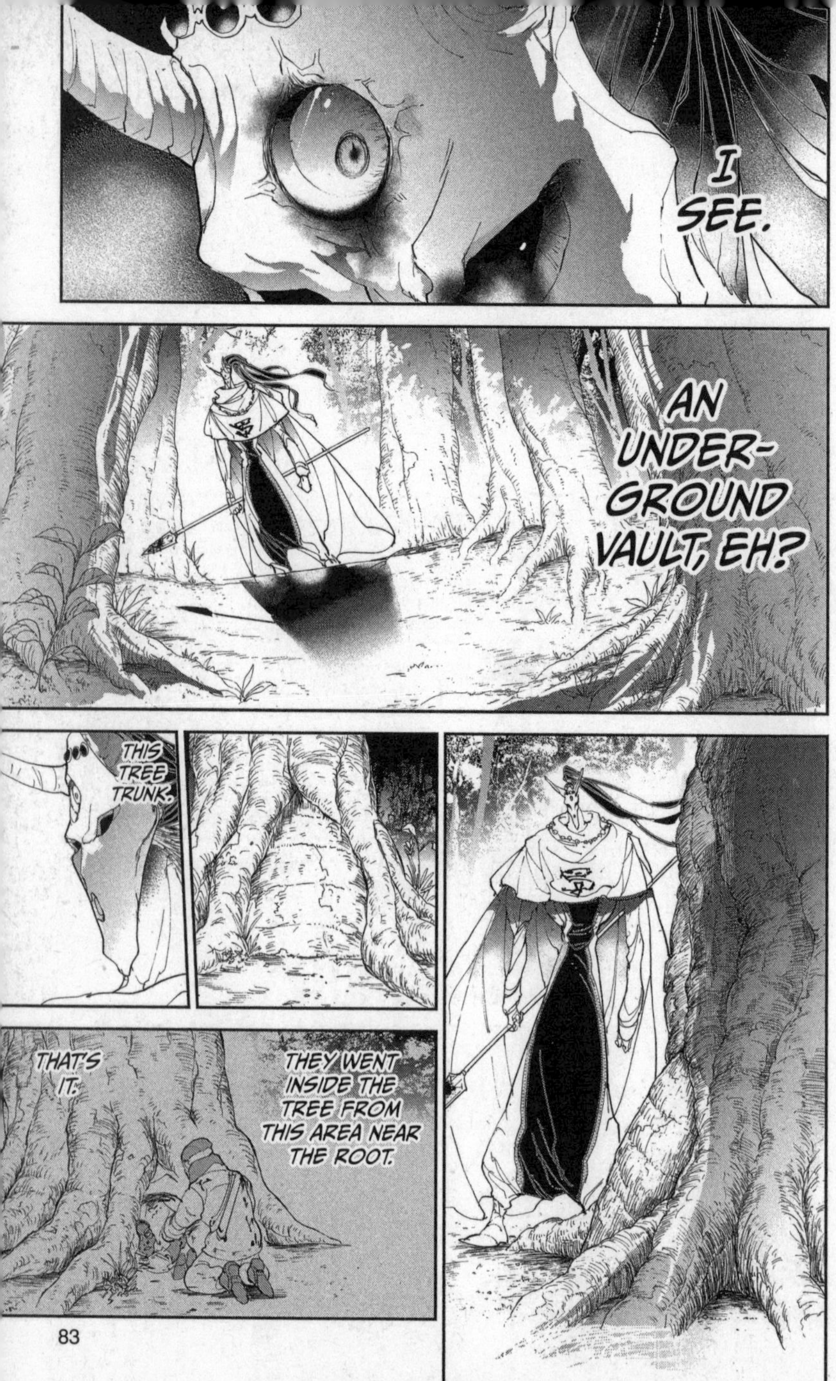
I SEE.
AN UNDER-GROUND VAULT, EH?
THIS TREE TRUNK.
THEY WENT INSIDE THE TREE FROM THIS AREA NEAR THE ROOT.
THAT'S IT.

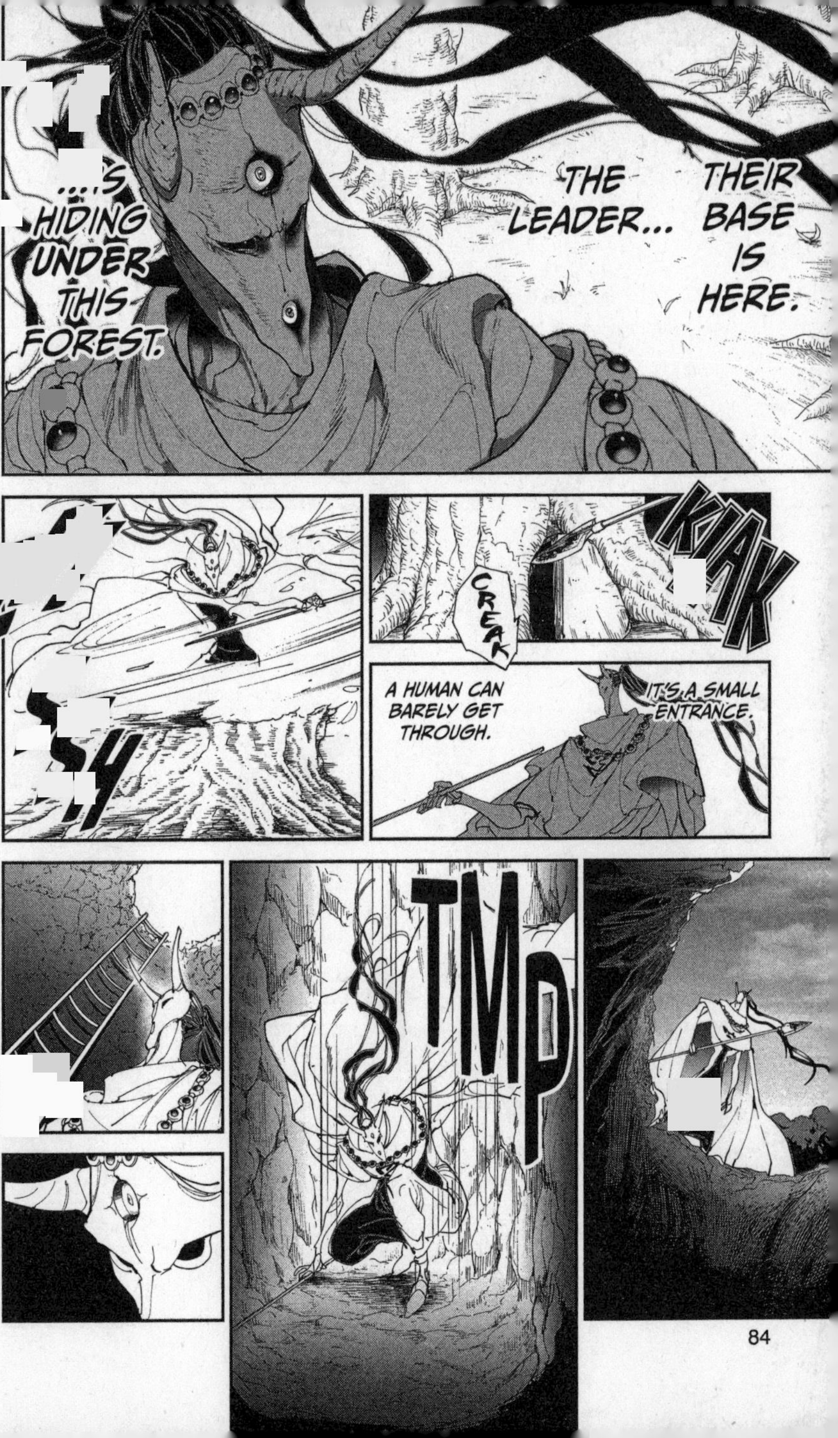
THEIR BASE IS HERE.
THE LEADER...
...'S HIDING UNDER THIS FOREST.
KIAK
CREAK
IT'S A SMALL ENTRANCE.
A HUMAN CAN BARELY GET THROUGH.
TMP

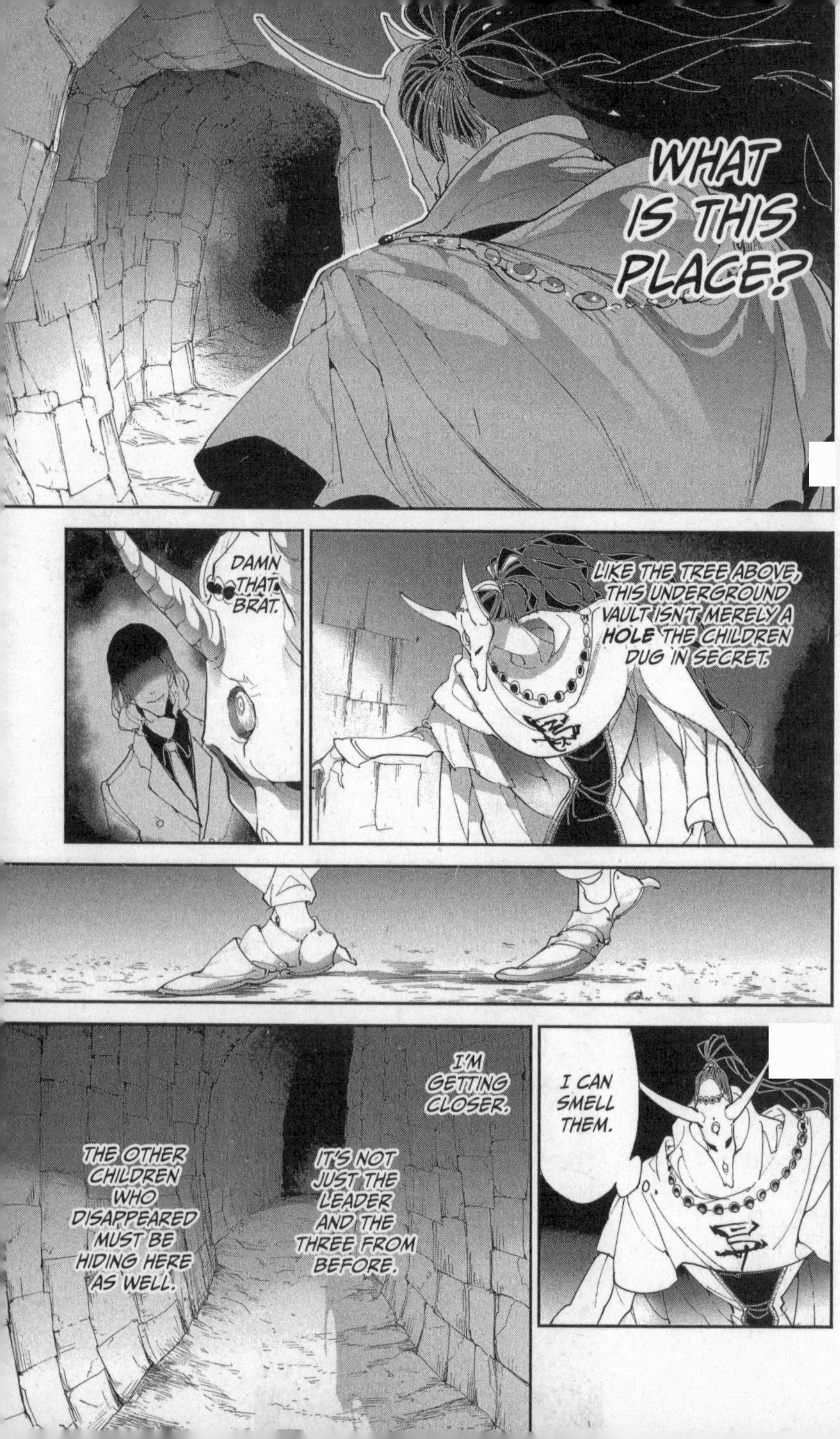
WHAT IS THIS PLACE?
LIKE THE TREE ABOVE, THIS UNDERGROUND VAULT ISN'T MERELY A **HOLE** THE CHILDREN DUG IN SECRET.
DAMN THAT BRAT.
I CAN SMELL THEM.
I'M GETTING CLOSER.
IT'S NOT JUST THE LEADER AND THE THREE FROM BEFORE.
THE OTHER CHILDREN WHO DISAPPEARED MUST BE HIDING HERE AS WELL.

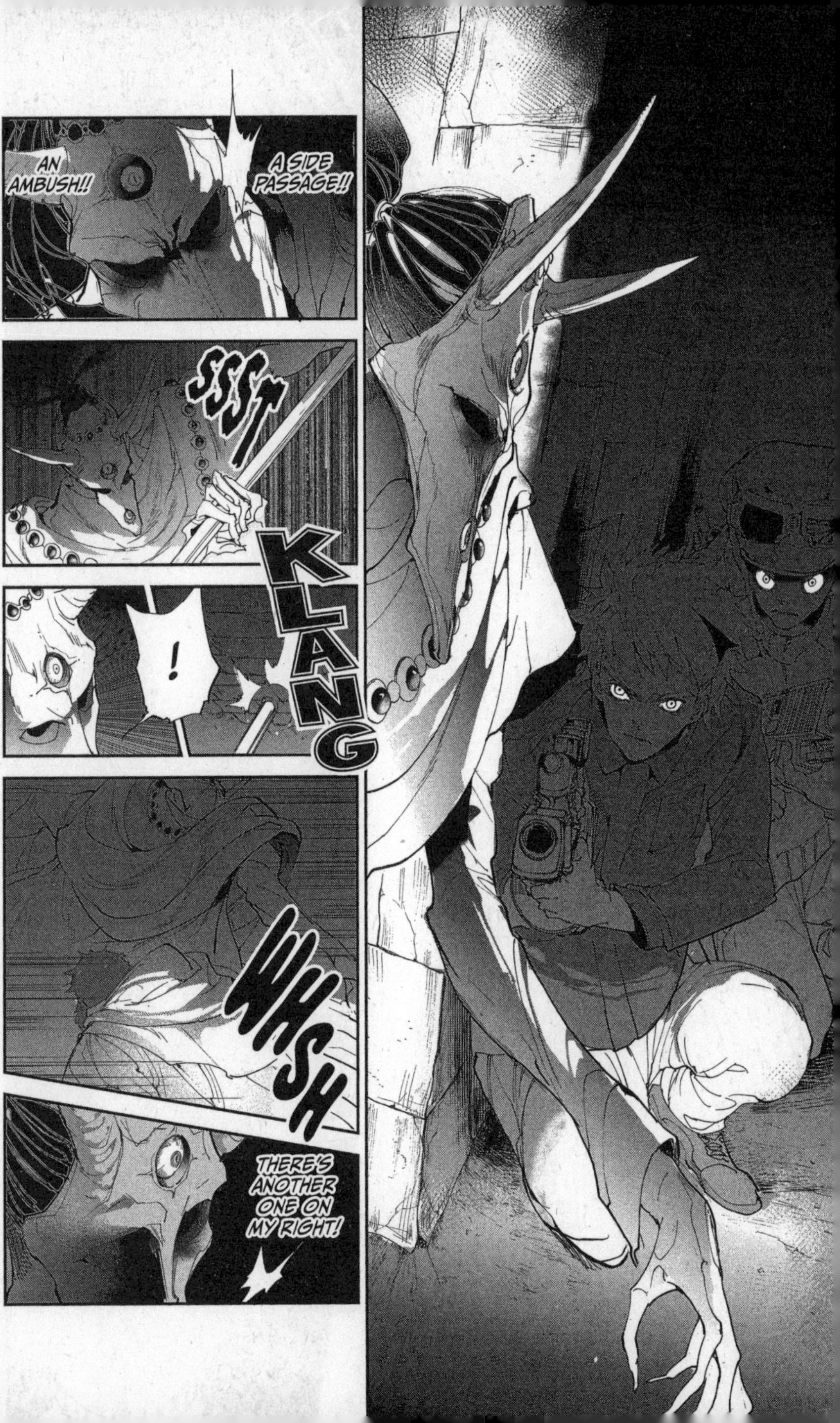
A SIDE PASSAGE!!
AN AMBUSH!!
SSST
KLANG
!
WHSH
THERE'S ANOTHER ONE ON MY RIGHT!

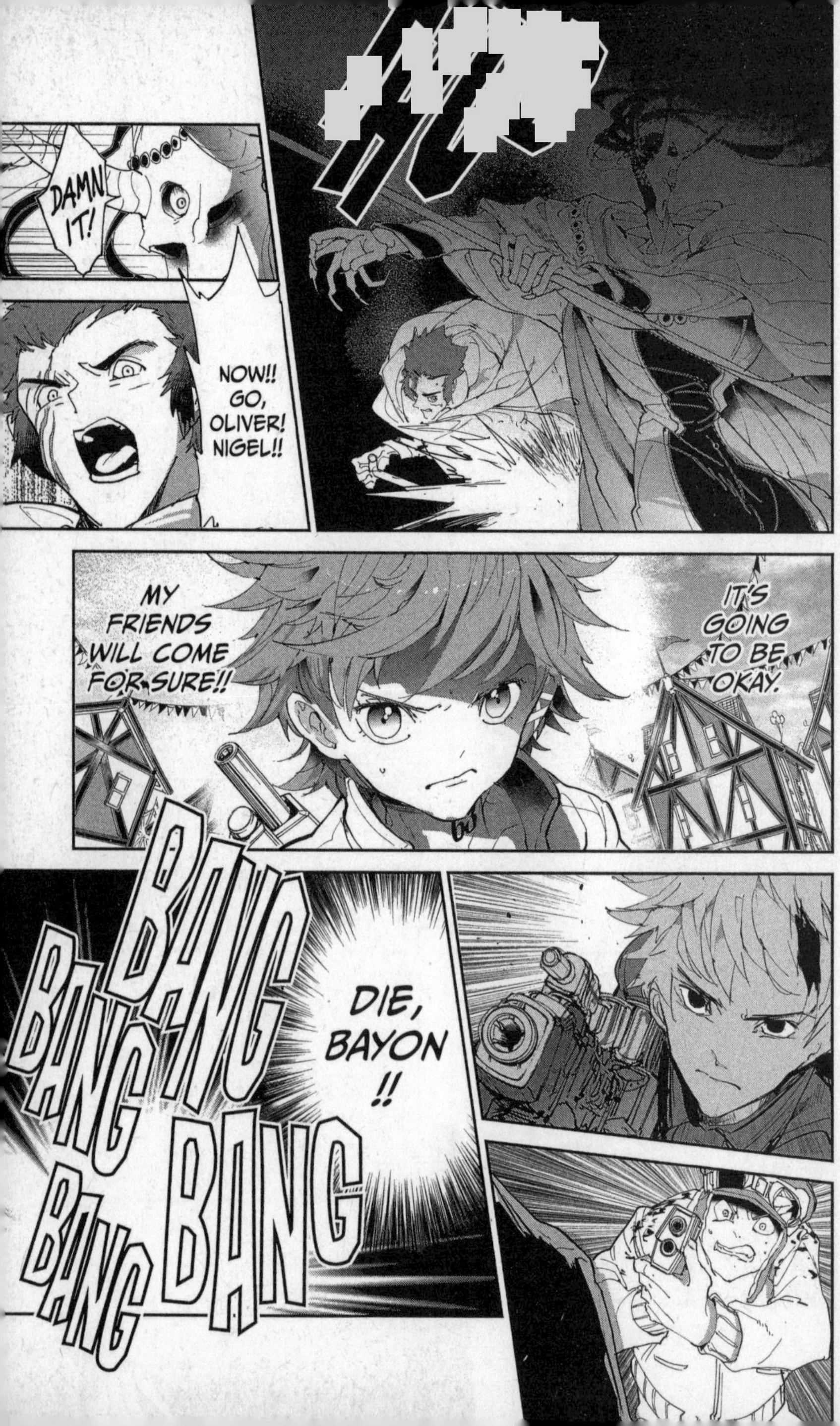
DAMN IT!
NOW!! GO, OLIVER! NIGEL!!
IT'S GOING TO BE OKAY.
MY FRIENDS WILL COME FOR SURE!!
DIE, BAYON!!
BANG
BANG
BANG
BANG

IT'S SUMMER!!!

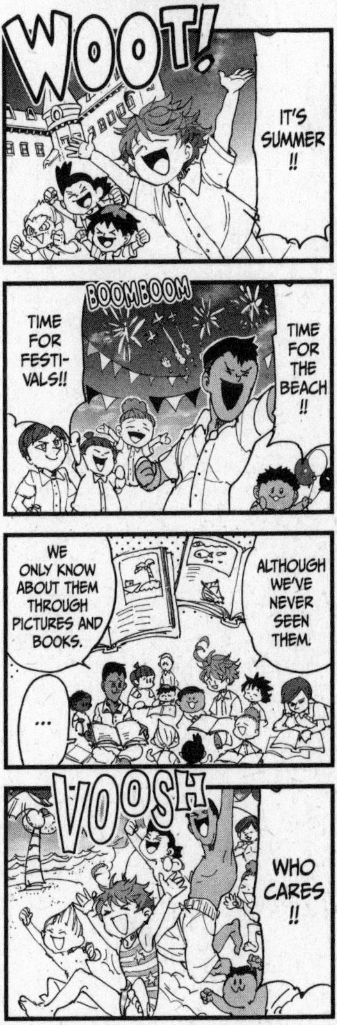
WOOT!
IT'S SUMMER !!
BOOMBOOM
TIME FOR THE BEACH !!
TIME FOR FESTI-VALS!!
ALTHOUGH WE'VE NEVER SEEN THEM.
WE ONLY KNOW ABOUT THEM THROUGH PICTURES AND BOOKS.
...
VOOSH
WHO CARES !!

RIDICULOUSLY FAST LEARNERS

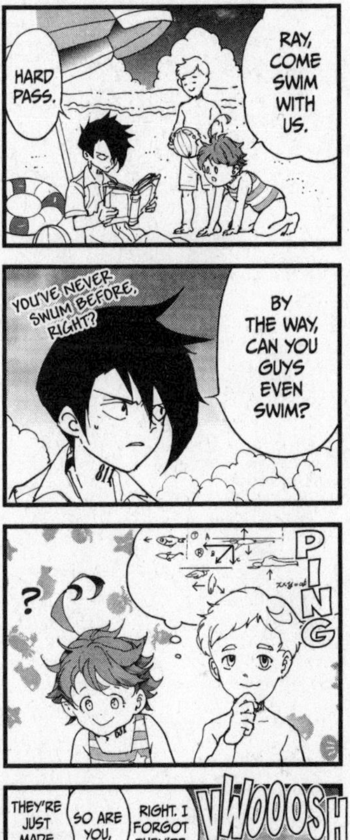
RAY, COME SWIM WITH US.
HARD PASS.
BY THE WAY, CAN YOU GUYS EVEN SWIM?
YOU'VE NEVER SWUM BEFORE, RIGHT?
PING
?
VWOOOSH
RIGHT. I FORGOT THEY'RE LIKE THAT.
SO ARE YOU, RAY!
THEY'RE JUST MADE DIFFER-ENTLY.

TO BE CONTINUED IN SIDE STORY 7-3

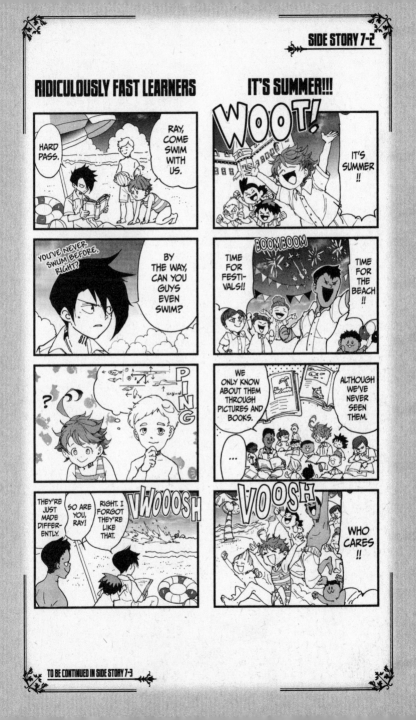

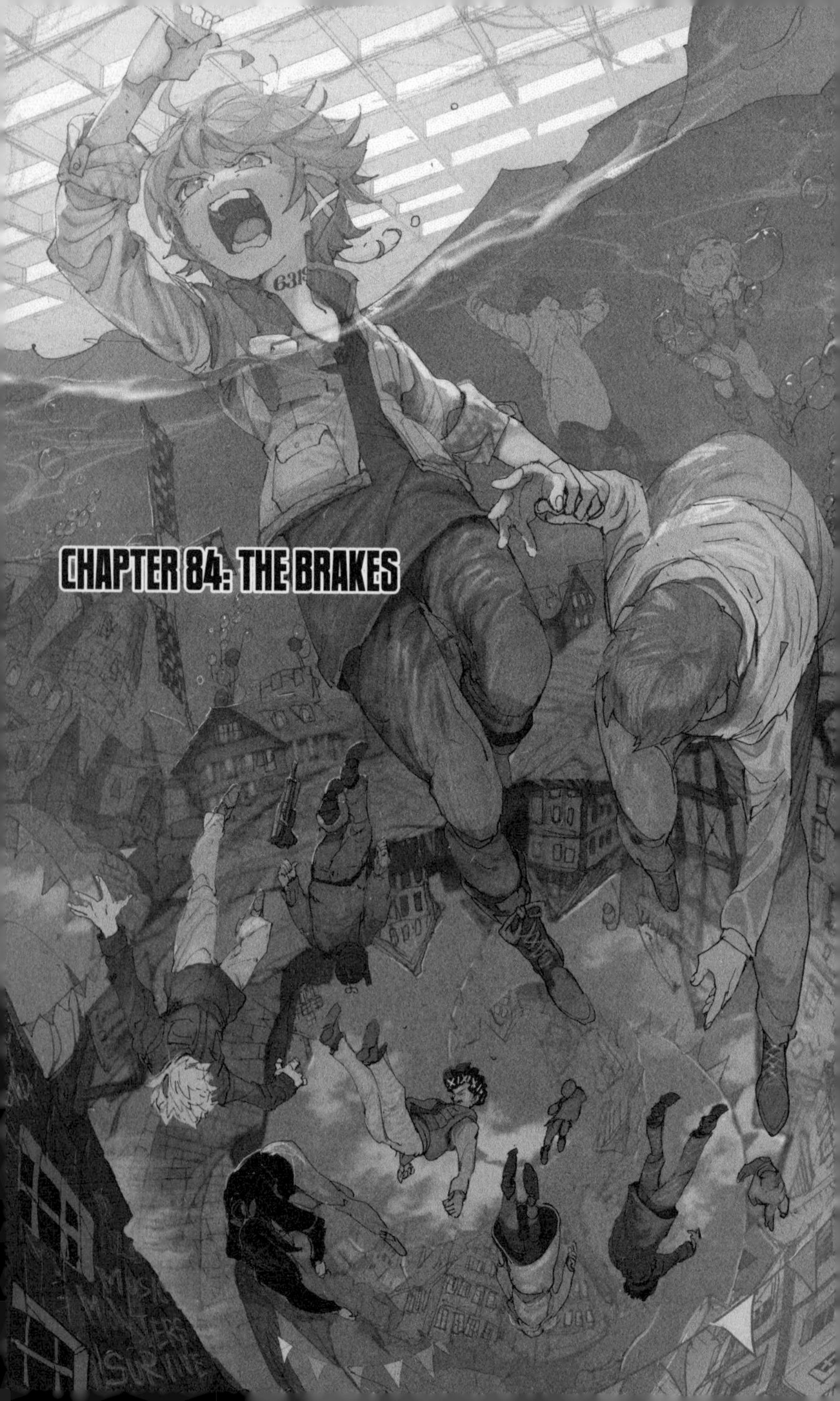
CHAPTER 84: THE BRAKES

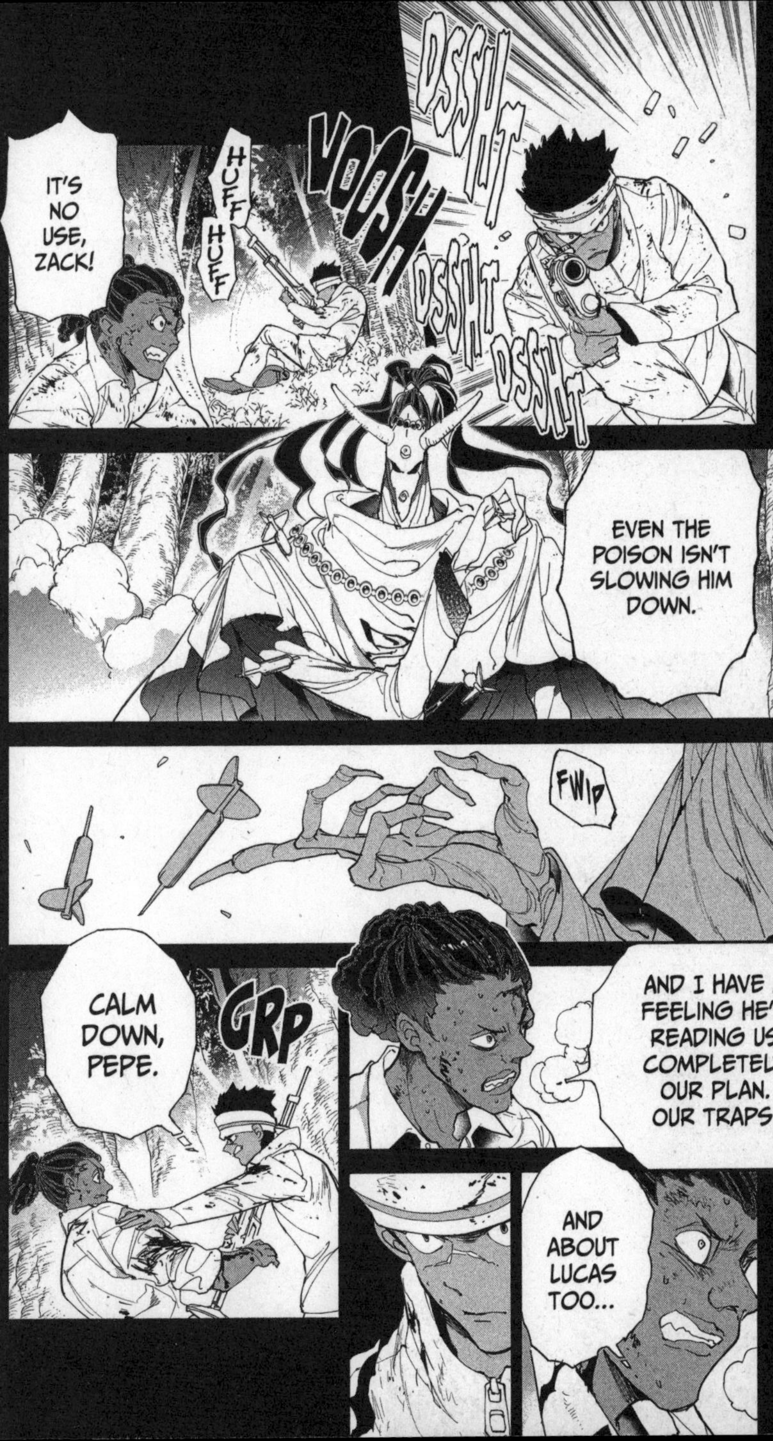
DSSHT
VOOSH
DSSHT
DSSHT
HUFF HUFF
IT'S NO USE, ZACK!
EVEN THE POISON ISN'T SLOWING HIM DOWN.
FWIP
AND I HAVE A FEELING HE'S READING US COMPLETELY. OUR PLAN. OUR TRAPS.
AND ABOUT LUCAS TOO...
GRP
CALM DOWN, PEPE.

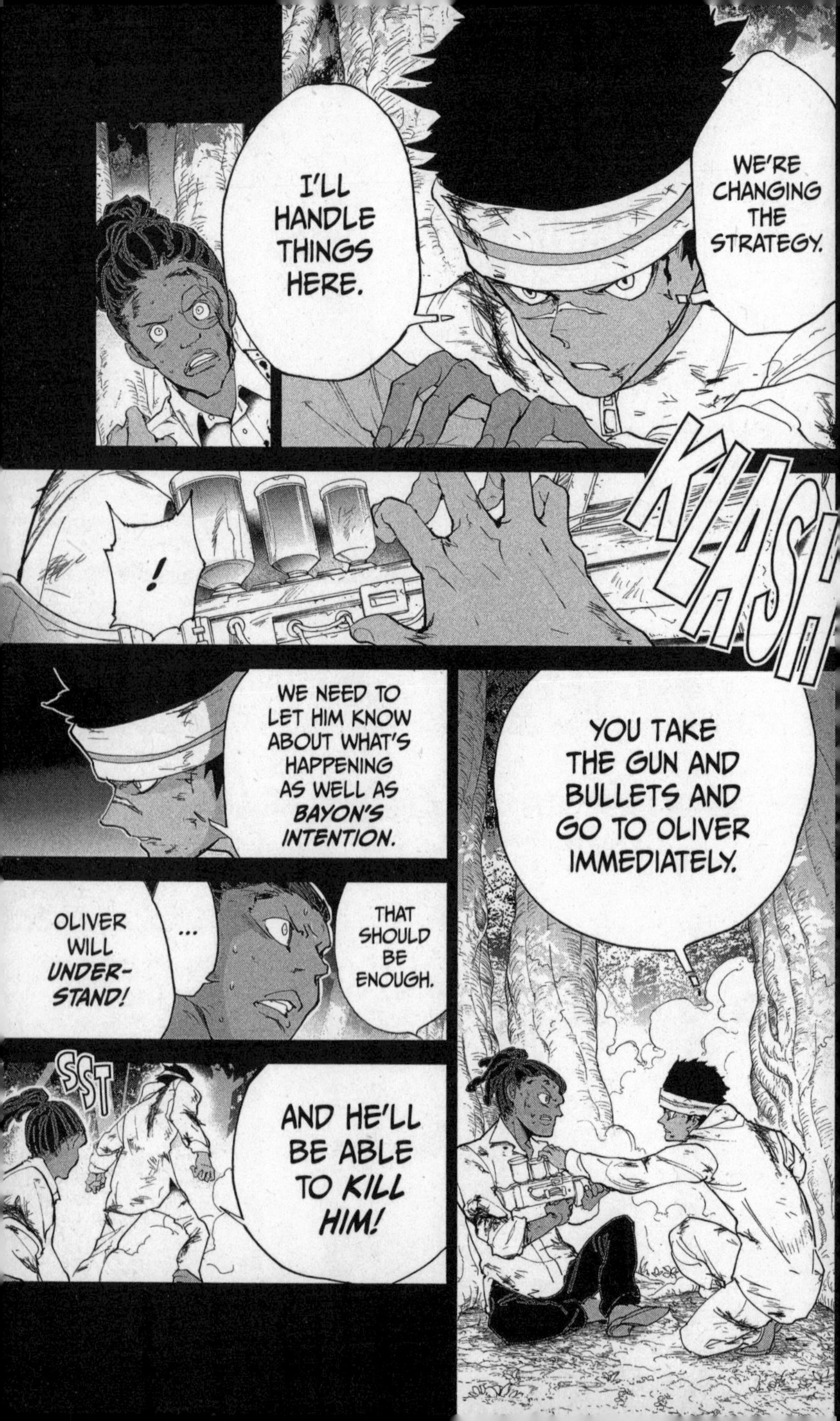
WE'RE CHANGING THE STRATEGY.
I'LL HANDLE THINGS HERE.
KLASH
!
YOU TAKE THE GUN AND BULLETS AND GO TO OLIVER IMMEDIATELY.
WE NEED TO LET HIM KNOW ABOUT WHAT'S HAPPENING AS WELL AS *BAYON'S INTENTION*.
THAT SHOULD BE ENOUGH.
...
OLIVER WILL *UNDER-STAND!*
SST
AND HE'LL BE ABLE TO *KILL HIM!*

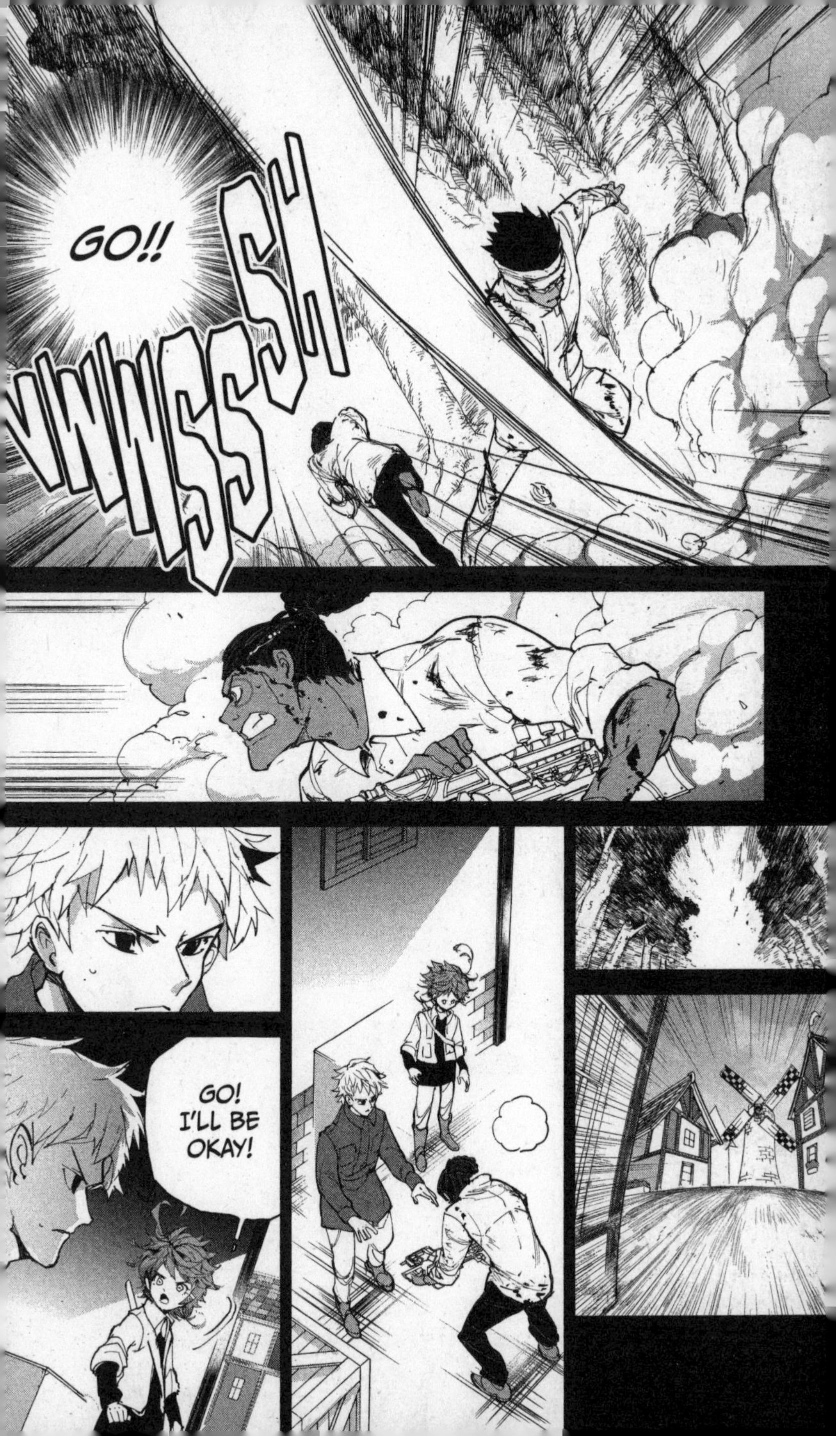
GO!!
VWWHSSSH
GO! I'LL BE OKAY!

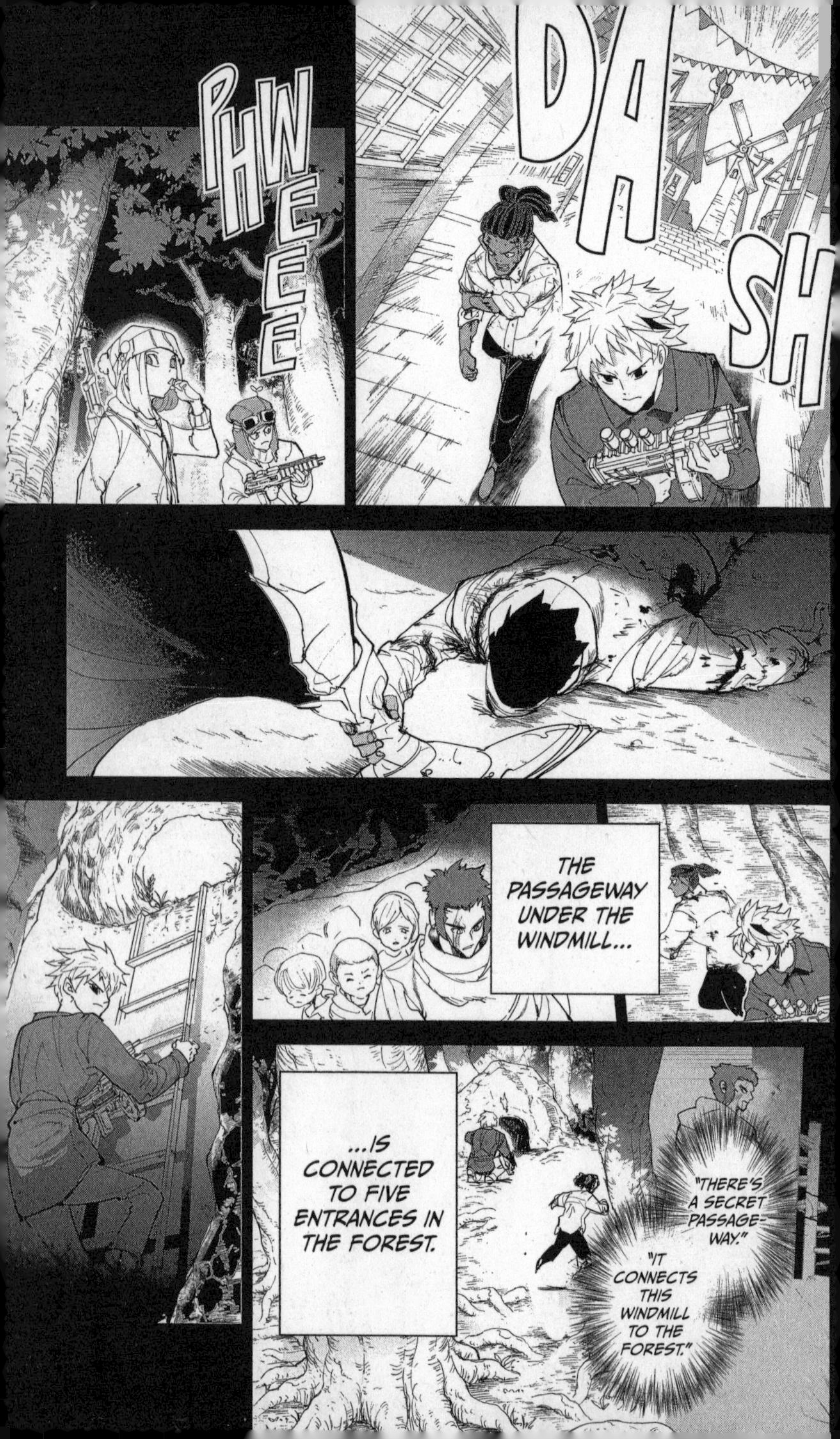
DASH
PHWEEE
THE PASSAGEWAY UNDER THE WINDMILL...
...IS CONNECTED TO FIVE ENTRANCES IN THE FOREST.
"THERE'S A SECRET PASSAGE-WAY."
"IT CONNECTS THIS WINDMILL TO THE FOREST."

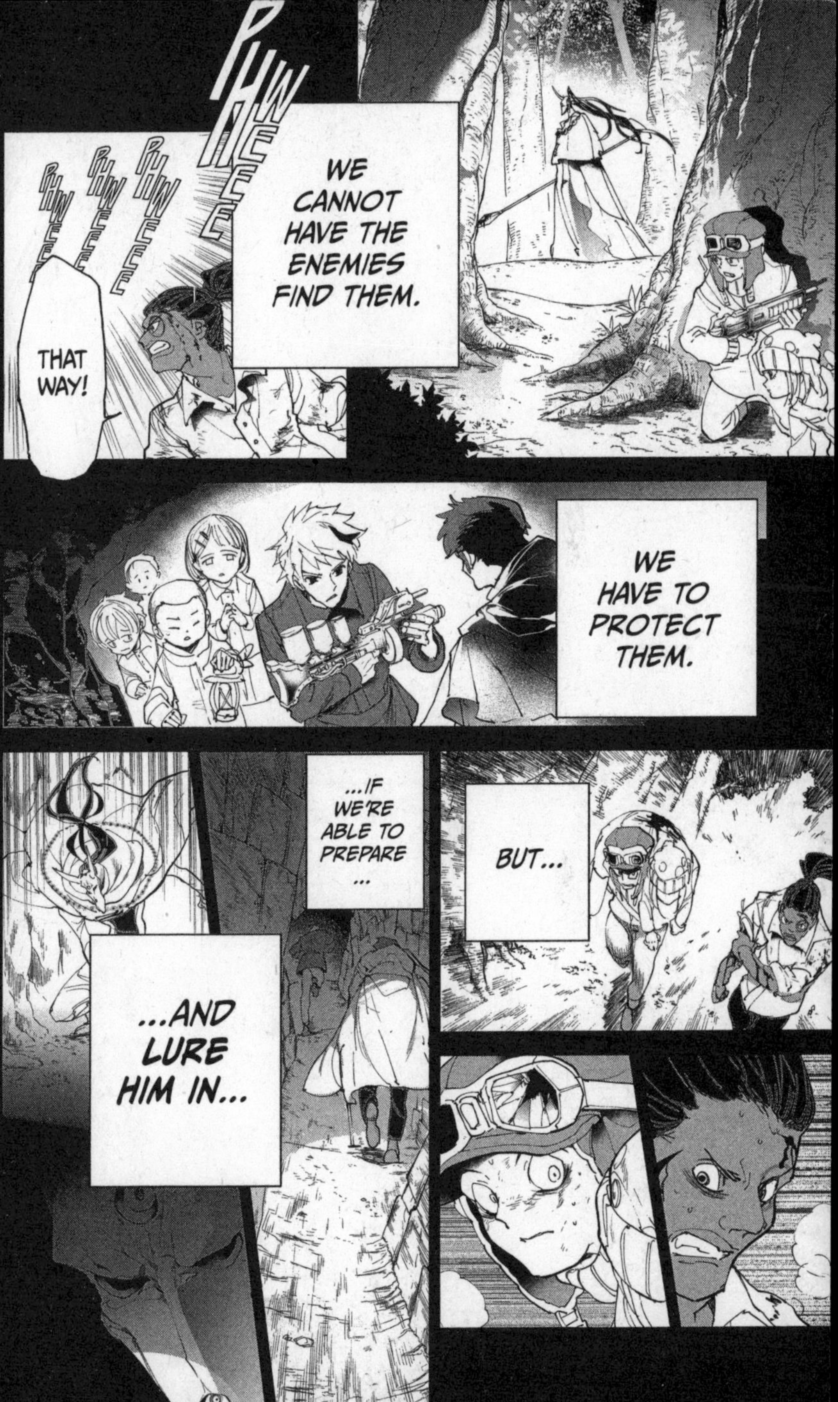
PHWEEEE
PHWEEEE
PHWEEE
PHWEEE
WE CANNOT HAVE THE ENEMIES FIND THEM.
THAT WAY!
WE HAVE TO PROTECT THEM.
...IF WE'RE ABLE TO PREPARE ...
...AND LURE HIM IN...
BUT...

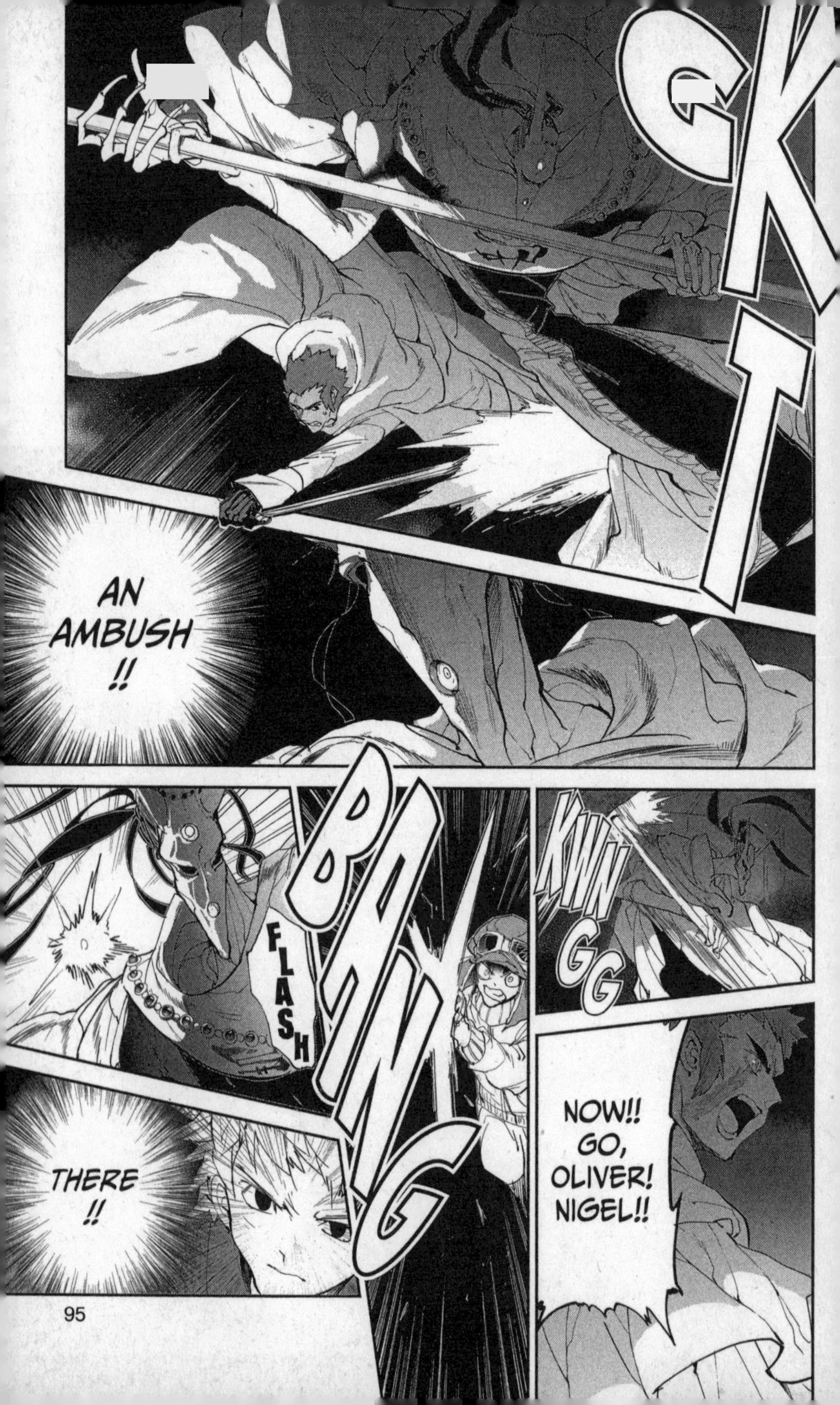
GKT
AN AMBUSH !!
KWINGG
NOW!! GO, OLIVER! NIGEL!!
FLASH
BANG
THERE !!

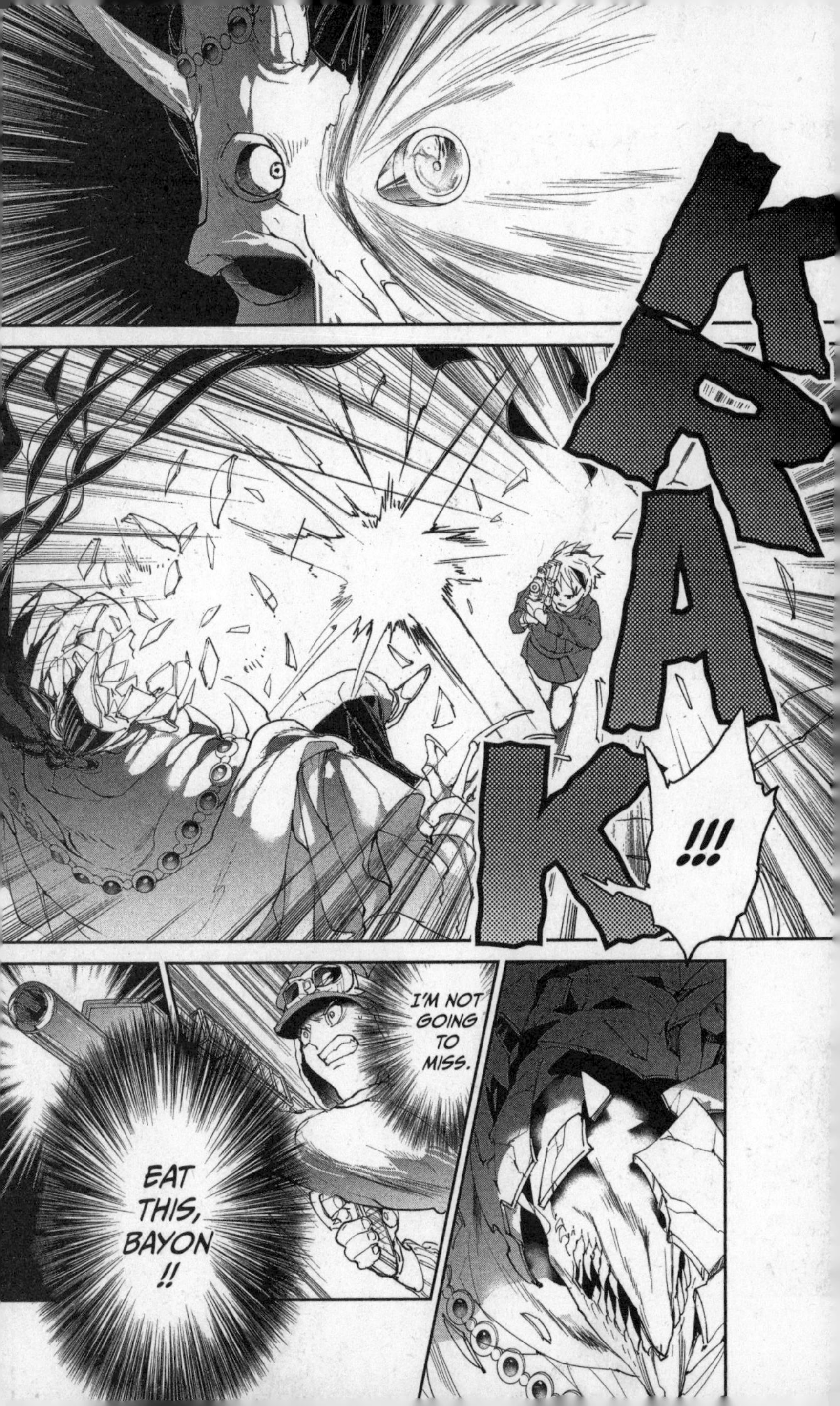
KRAK!!!
I'M NOT GOING TO MISS.
EAT THIS, BAYON!!

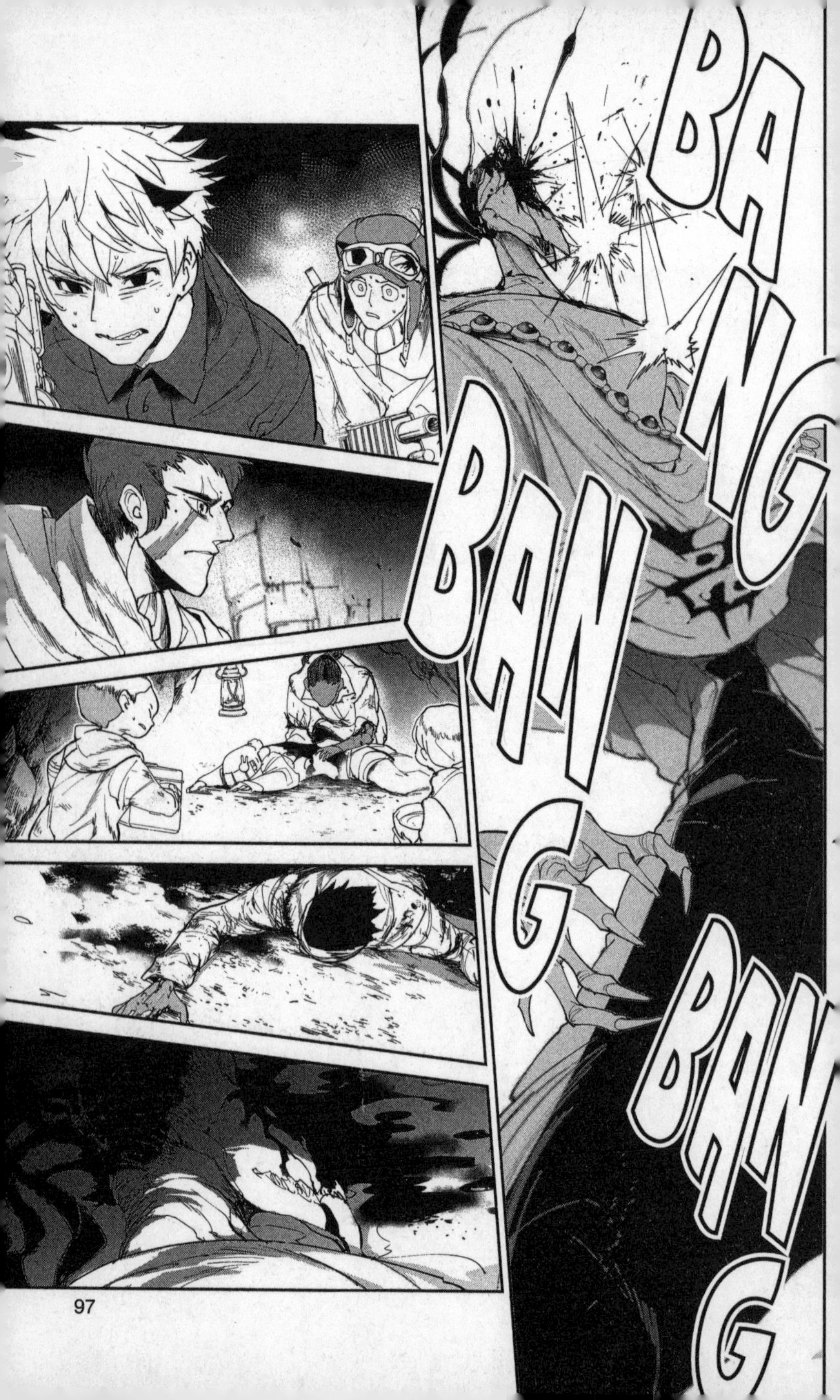

BANG
BANG
BANG

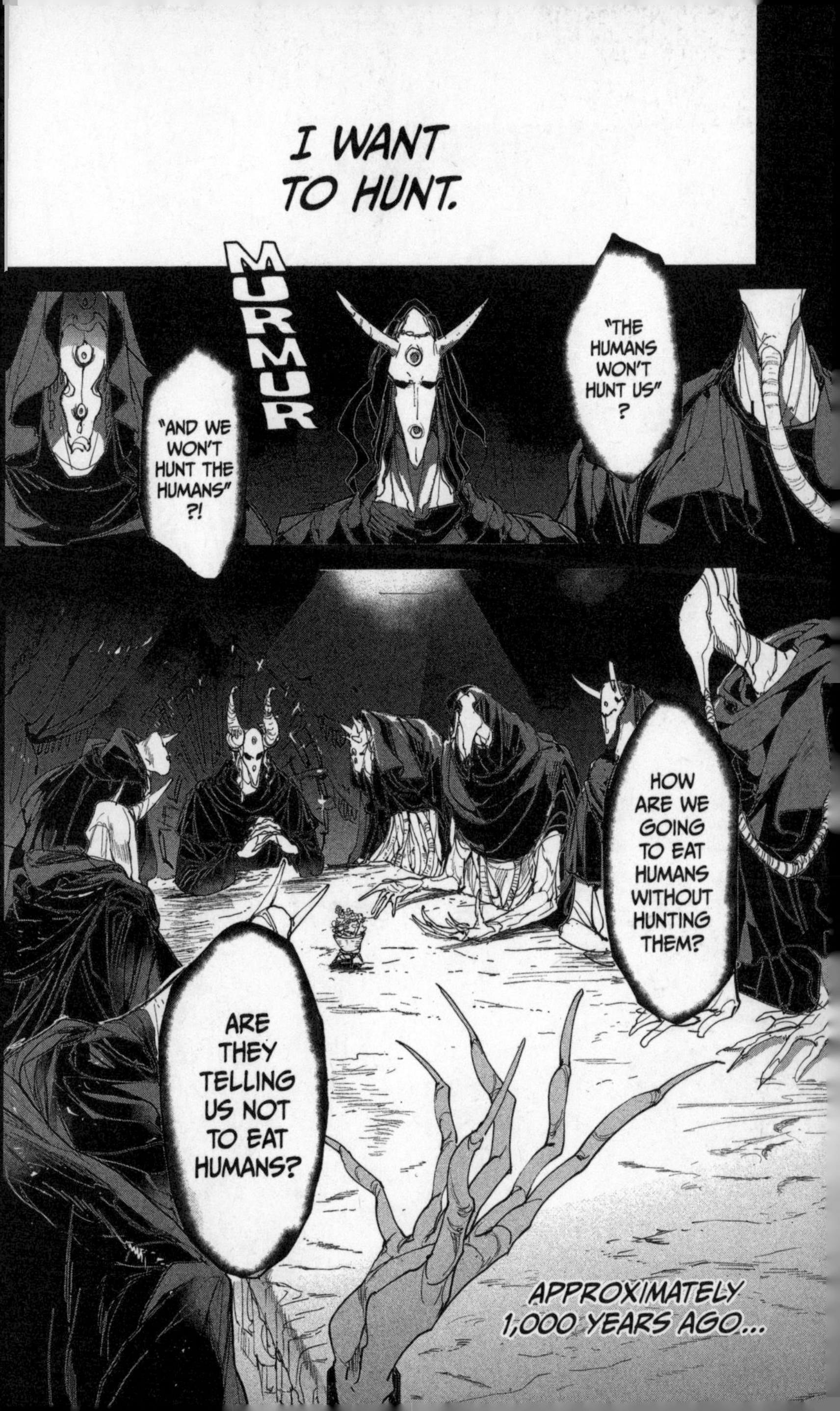
I WANT TO HUNT.
"THE HUMANS WON'T HUNT US"?
MURMUR
"AND WE WON'T HUNT THE HUMANS"?!
HOW ARE WE GOING TO EAT HUMANS WITHOUT HUNTING THEM?
ARE THEY TELLING US NOT TO EAT HUMANS?
APPROXIMATELY 1,000 YEARS AGO...

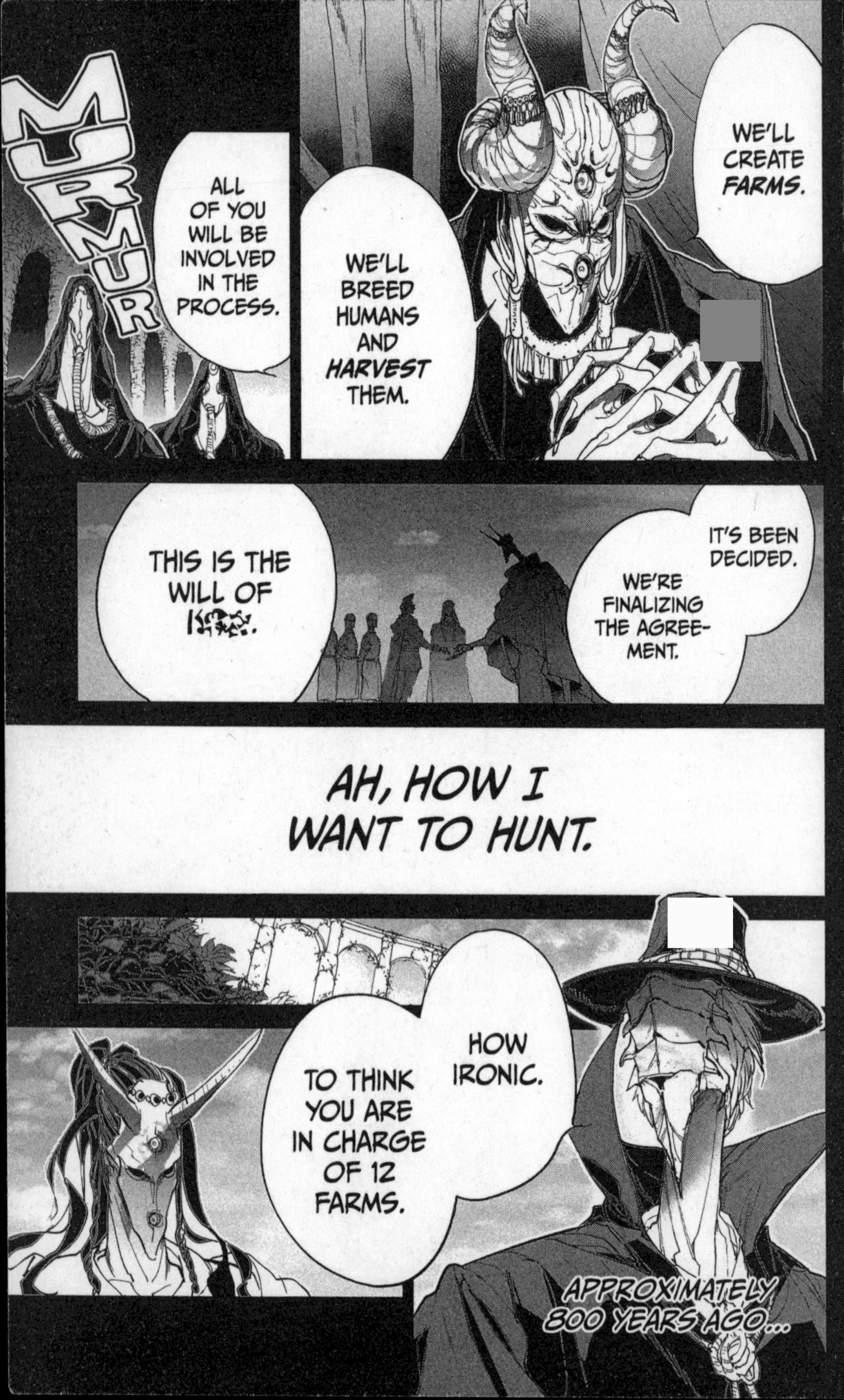
WE'LL CREATE FARMS.
WE'LL BREED HUMANS AND HARVEST THEM.
MURMUR
ALL OF YOU WILL BE INVOLVED IN THE PROCESS.
IT'S BEEN DECIDED.
WE'RE FINALIZING THE AGREE-MENT.
THIS IS THE WILL OF
AH, HOW I WANT TO HUNT.
HOW IRONIC.
TO THINK YOU ARE IN CHARGE OF 12 FARMS.
APPROXIMATELY 800 YEARS AGO...

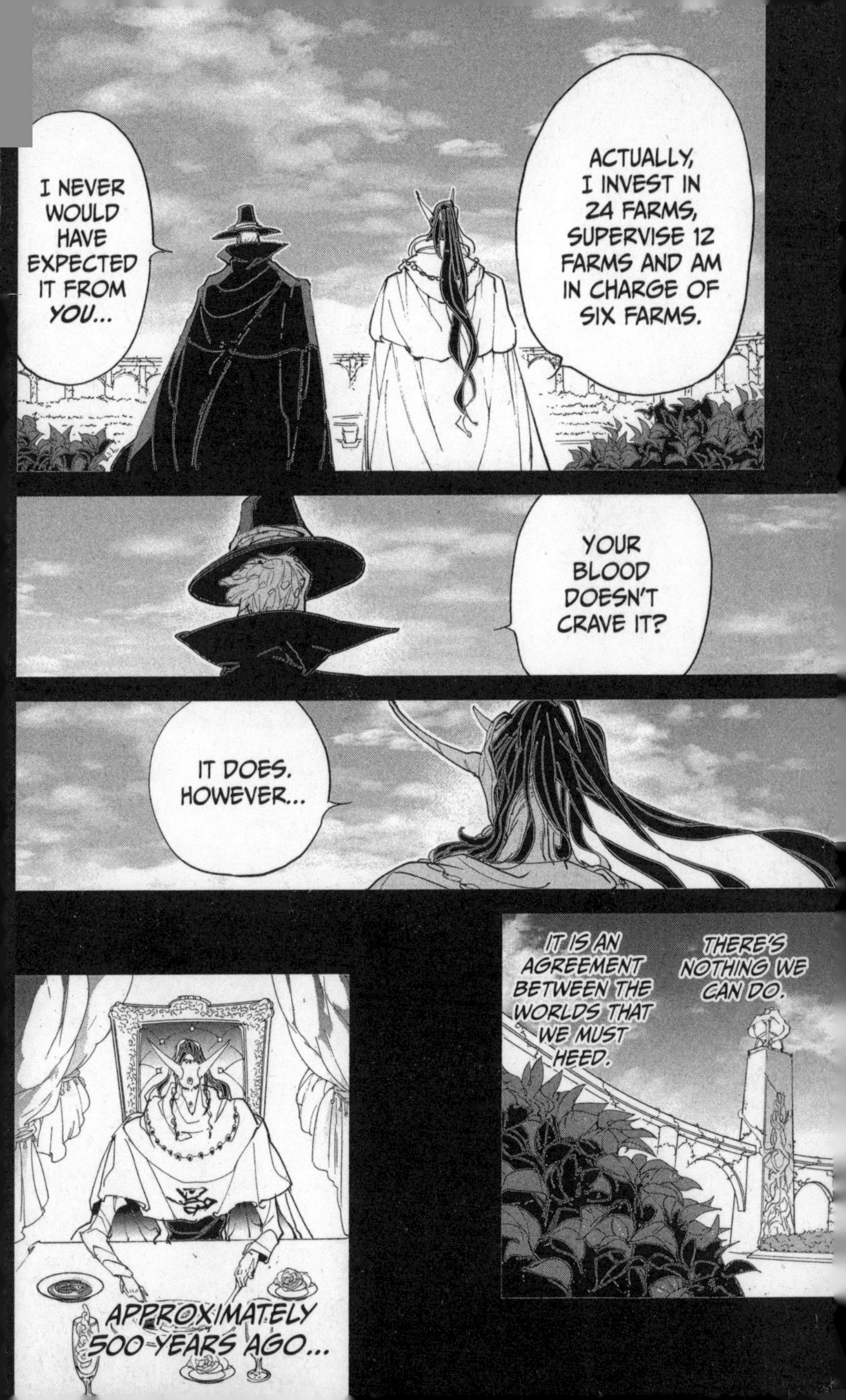
ACTUALLY, I INVEST IN 24 FARMS, SUPERVISE 12 FARMS AND AM IN CHARGE OF SIX FARMS.
I NEVER WOULD HAVE EXPECTED IT FROM YOU...
YOUR BLOOD DOESN'T CRAVE IT?
IT DOES. HOWEVER...
THERE'S NOTHING WE CAN DO.
IT IS AN AGREEMENT BETWEEN THE WORLDS THAT WE MUST HEED.
APPROXIMATELY 500 YEARS AGO...

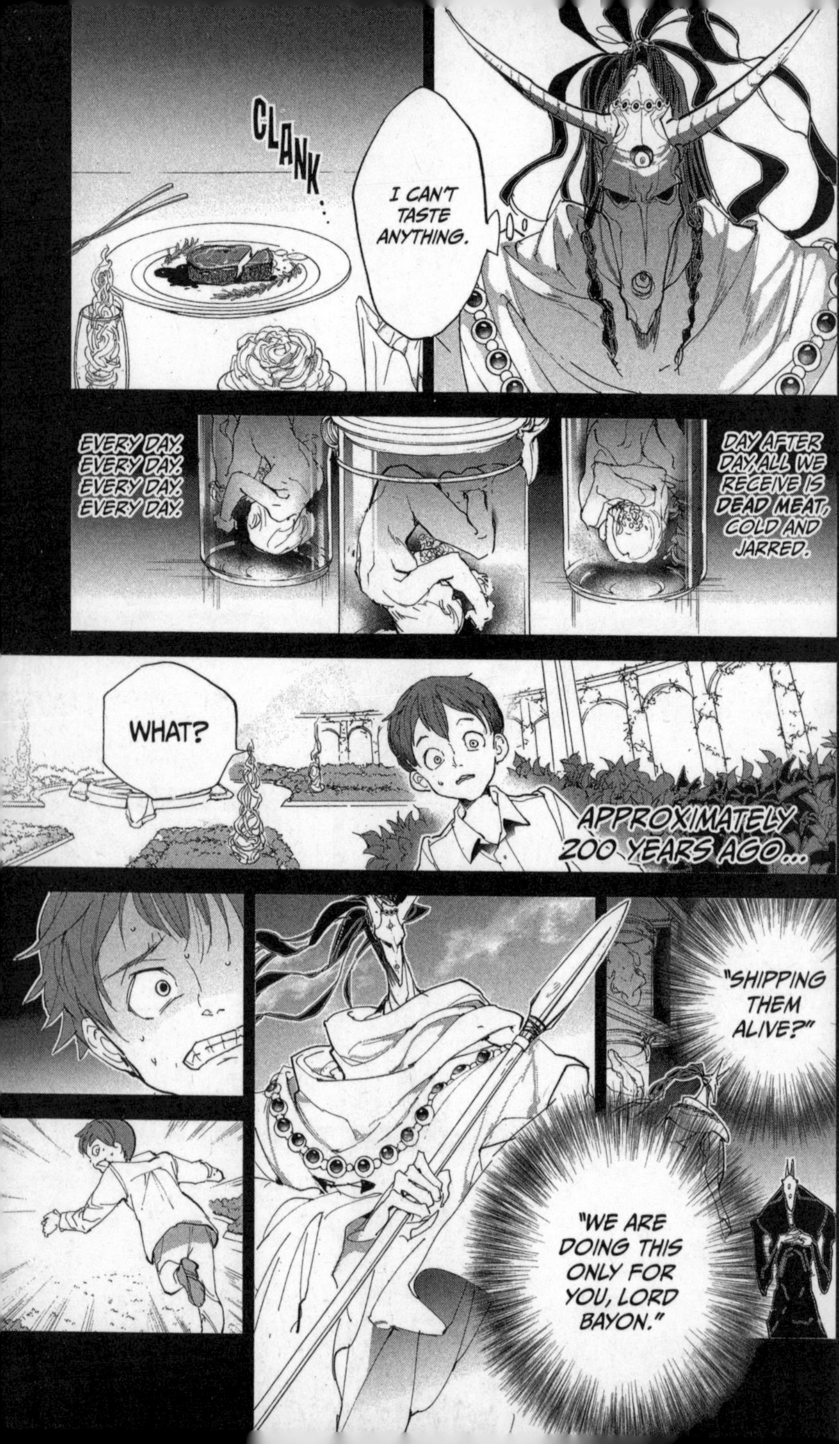
I CAN'T TASTE ANYTHING.
CLANK...
DAY AFTER DAY, ALL WE RECEIVE IS DEAD MEAT, COLD AND JARRED.
EVERY DAY. EVERY DAY. EVERY DAY. EVERY DAY.
APPROXIMATELY 200 YEARS AGO...
WHAT?
"SHIPPING THEM ALIVE?"
"WE ARE DOING THIS ONLY FOR YOU, LORD BAYON."

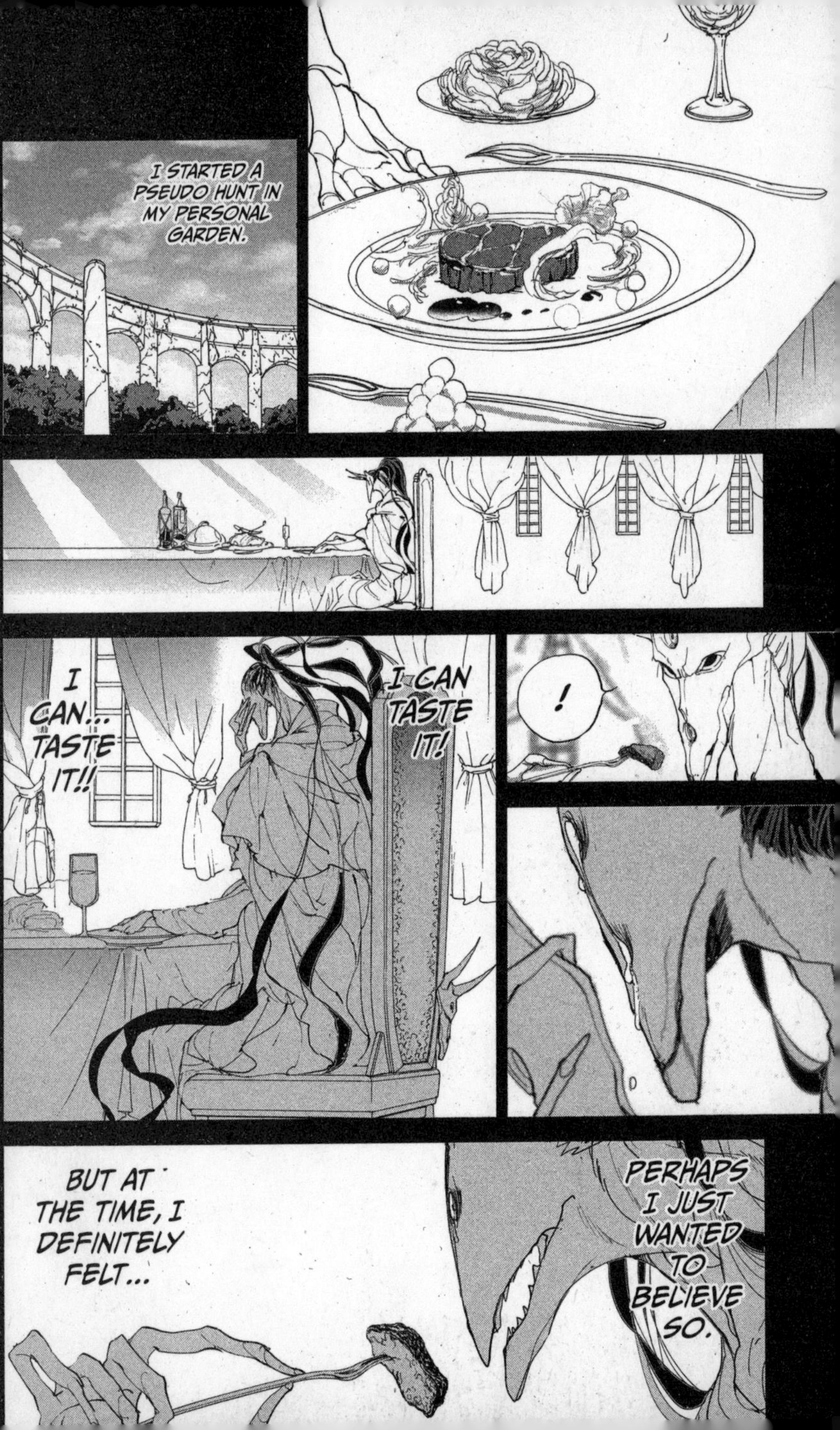
I STARTED A PSEUDO HUNT IN MY PERSONAL GARDEN.
!
I CAN TASTE IT!
I CAN... TASTE IT!!
PERHAPS I JUST WANTED TO BELIEVE SO.
BUT AT THE TIME, I DEFINITELY FELT...

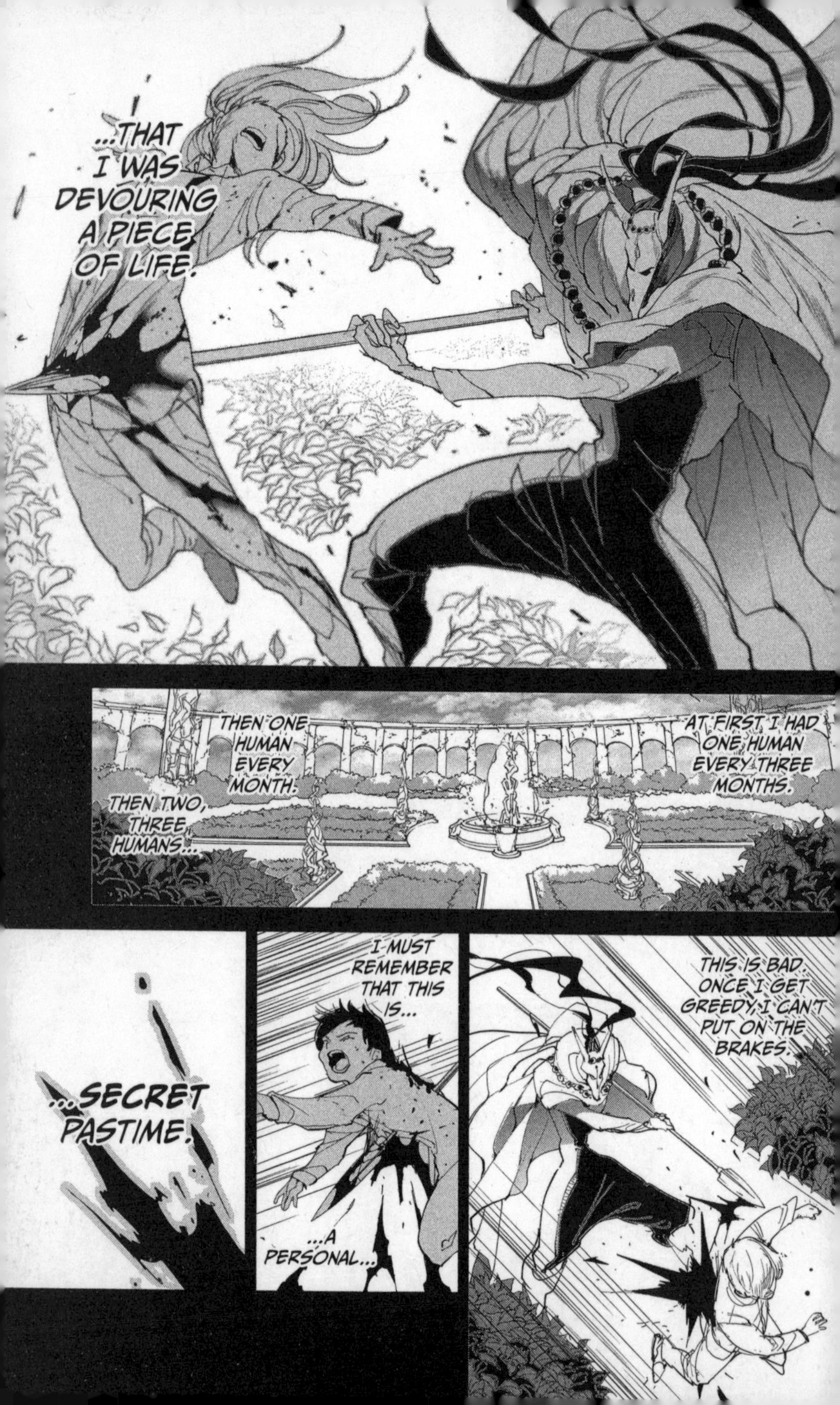
...THAT I WAS DEVOURING A PIECE OF LIFE.
AT FIRST I HAD ONE HUMAN EVERY THREE MONTHS.
THEN ONE HUMAN EVERY MONTH.
THEN TWO, THREE HUMANS...
THIS IS BAD. ONCE I GET GREEDY, I CAN'T PUT ON THE BRAKES.
I MUST REMEMBER THAT THIS IS...
...A PERSONAL...
...SECRET PASTIME.

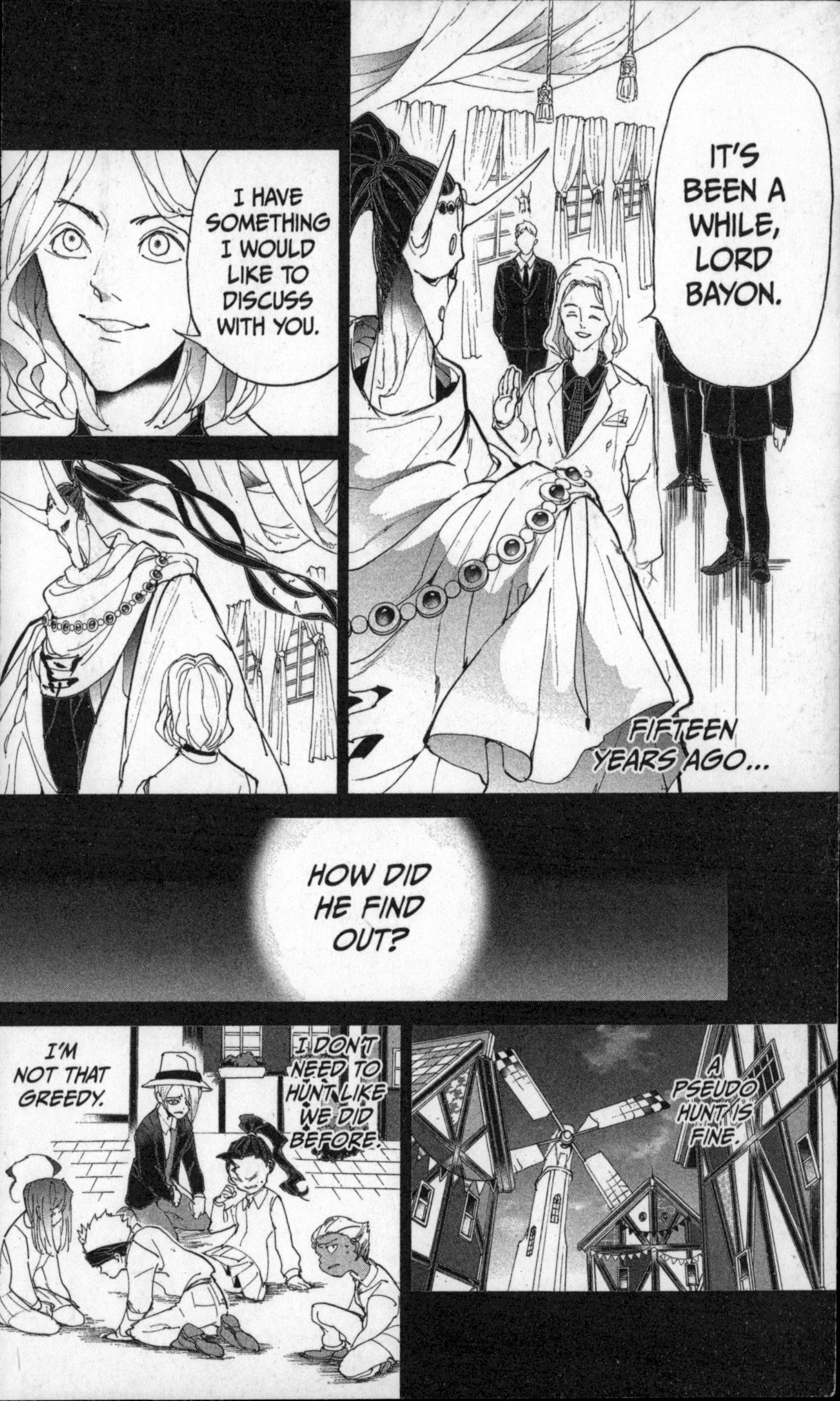

IT'S BEEN A WHILE, LORD BAYON.
FIFTEEN YEARS AGO...
I HAVE SOMETHING I WOULD LIKE TO DISCUSS WITH YOU.
HOW DID HE FIND OUT?
A PSEUDO HUNT IS FINE.
I DON'T NEED TO HUNT LIKE WE DID BEFORE.
I'M NOT THAT GREEDY.

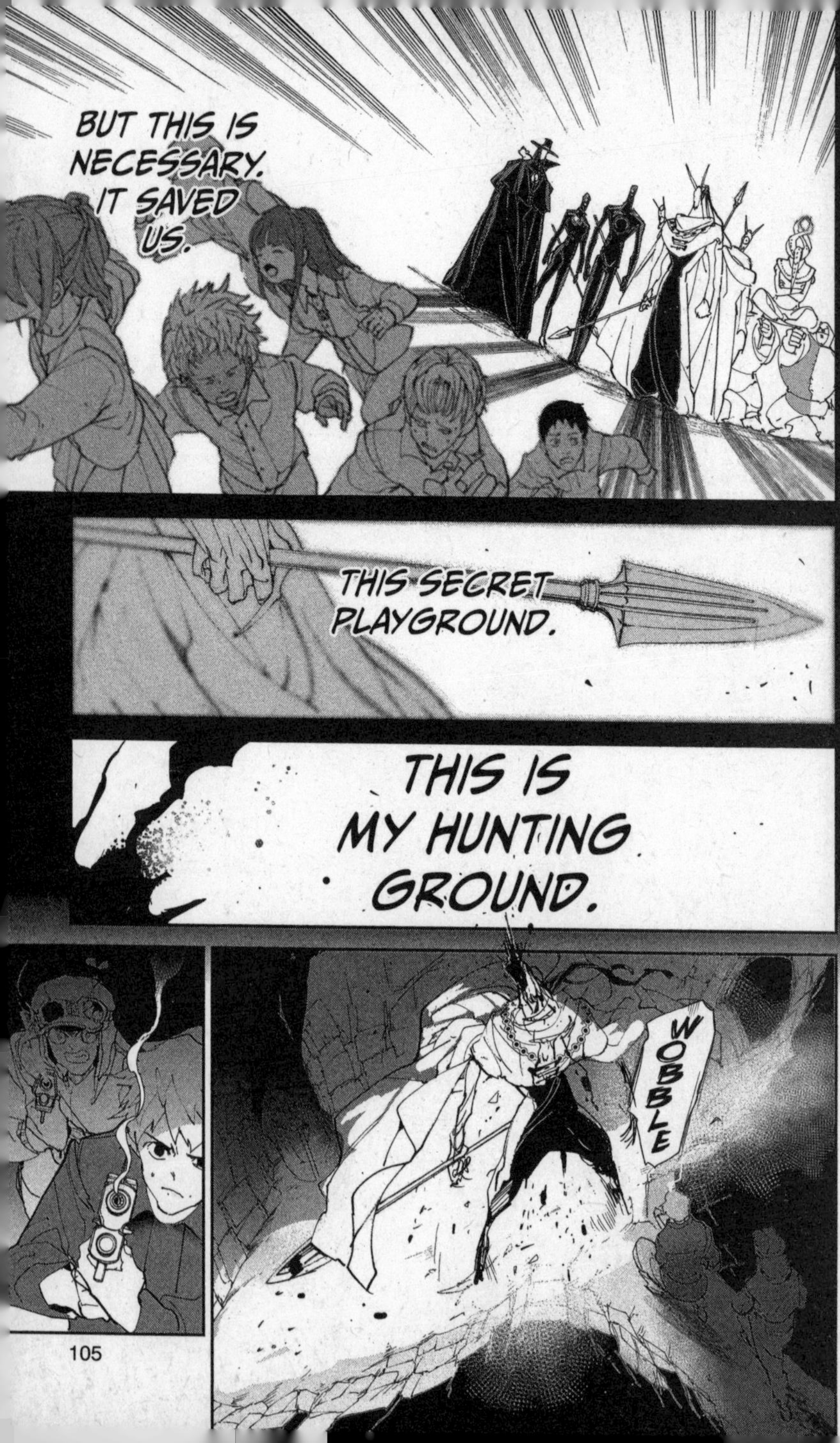
BUT THIS IS NECESSARY. IT SAVED US.
THIS SECRET PLAYGROUND.
THIS IS MY HUNTING GROUND.
WOBBLE

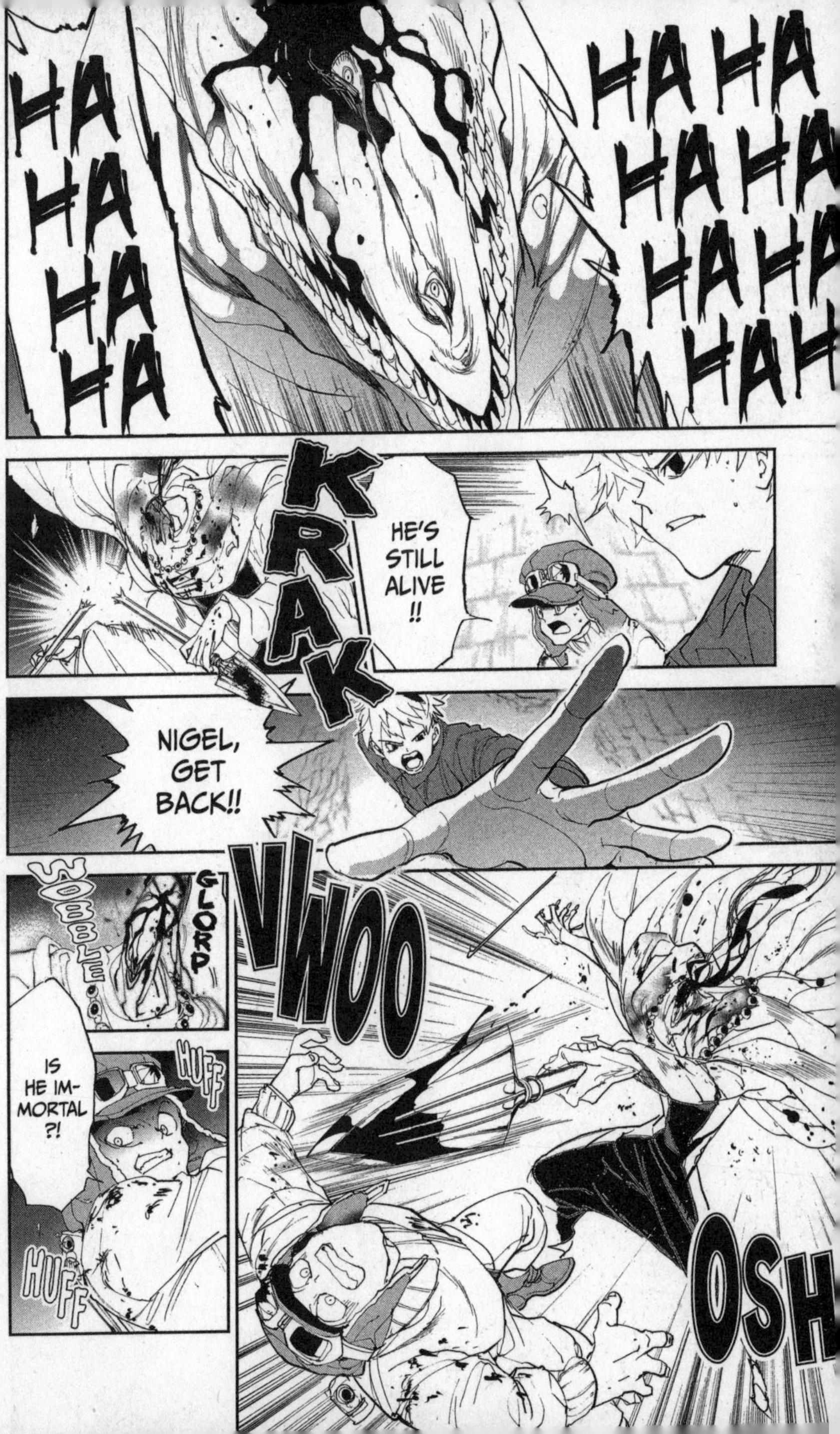
HA HA HA
HA HA HA
HA HA HA
HAH
HA
HA
HA
HA
HA
HE'S STILL ALIVE!!
KRAK
NIGEL, GET BACK!!
VWOO
OSH
GLORP
WOBBLE
IS HE IM-MORTAL?!
HUFF
HUFF

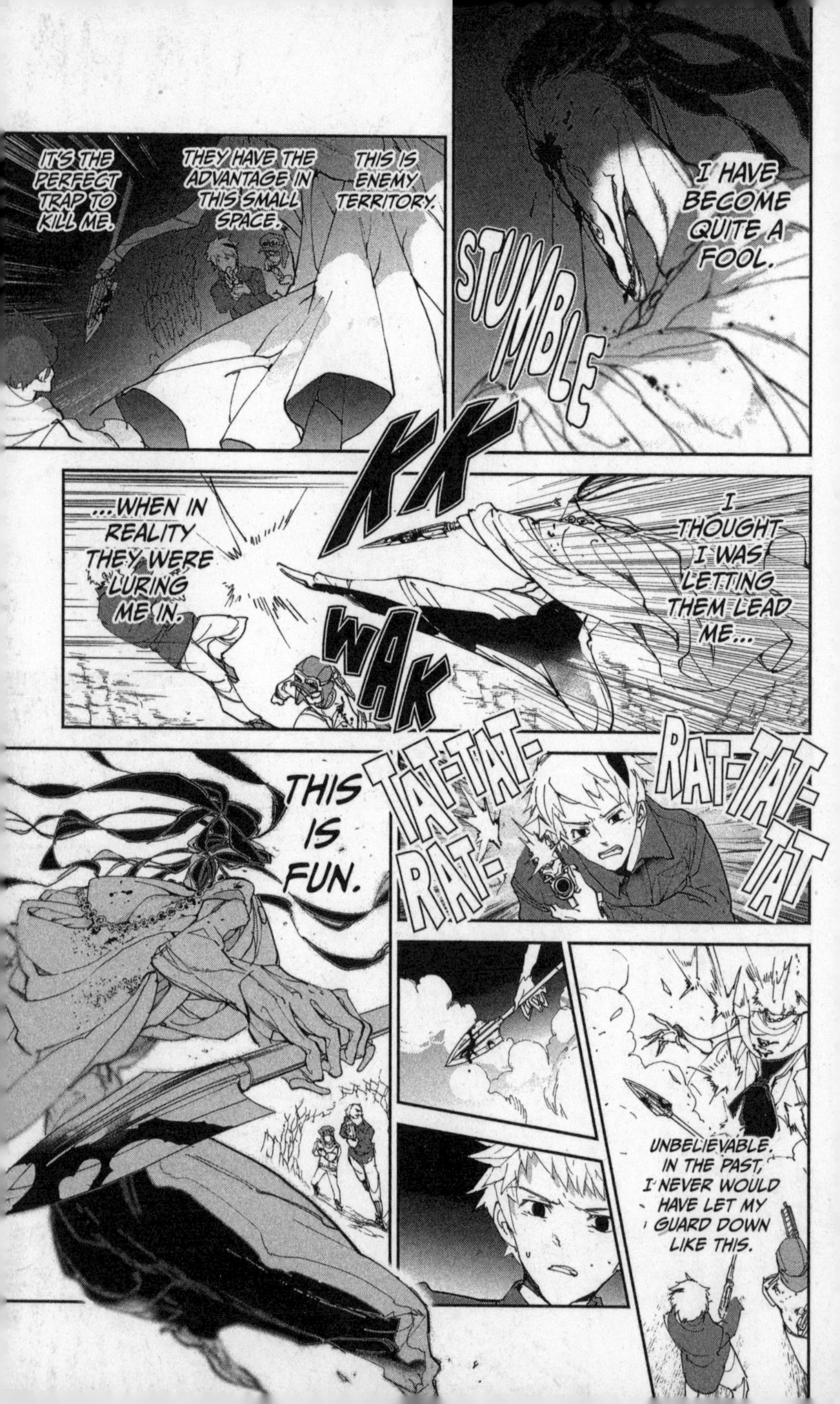
STUMBLE
I HAVE BECOME QUITE A FOOL.
THIS IS ENEMY TERRITORY.
THEY HAVE THE ADVANTAGE IN THIS SMALL SPACE.
IT'S THE PERFECT TRAP TO KILL ME.
KK
I THOUGHT I WAS LETTING THEM LEAD ME...
...WHEN IN REALITY THEY WERE LURING ME IN.
WAK
RAT-TAT-TAT-TAT
TAT-TAT-
RAT-
THIS IS FUN.
UNBELIEVABLE. IN THE PAST, I NEVER WOULD HAVE LET MY GUARD DOWN LIKE THIS.

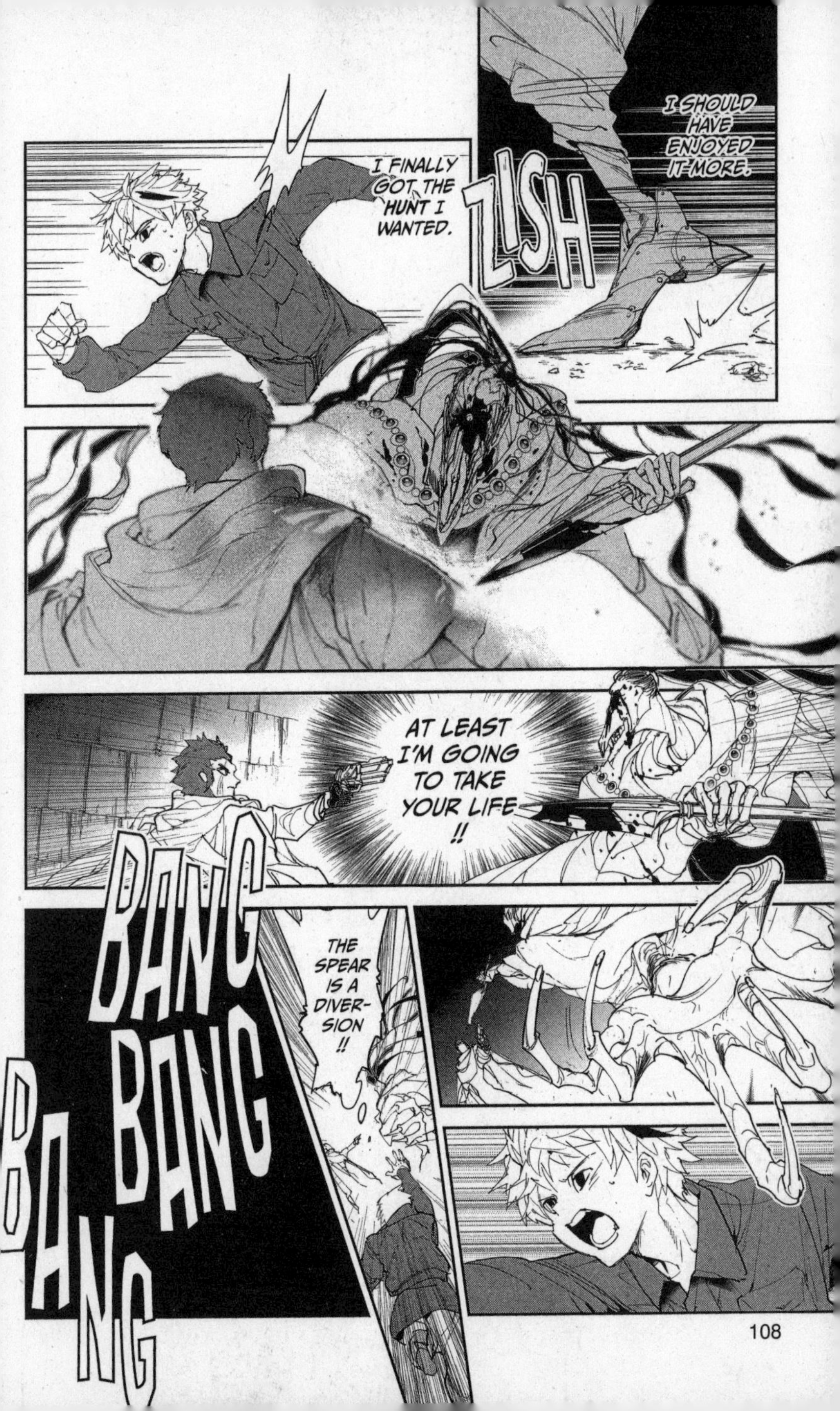
I SHOULD HAVE ENJOYED IT MORE.
ZISH
I FINALLY GOT THE HUNT I WANTED.
AT LEAST I'M GOING TO TAKE YOUR LIFE!!
THE SPEAR IS A DIVER-SION!!
BANG
BANG
BANG

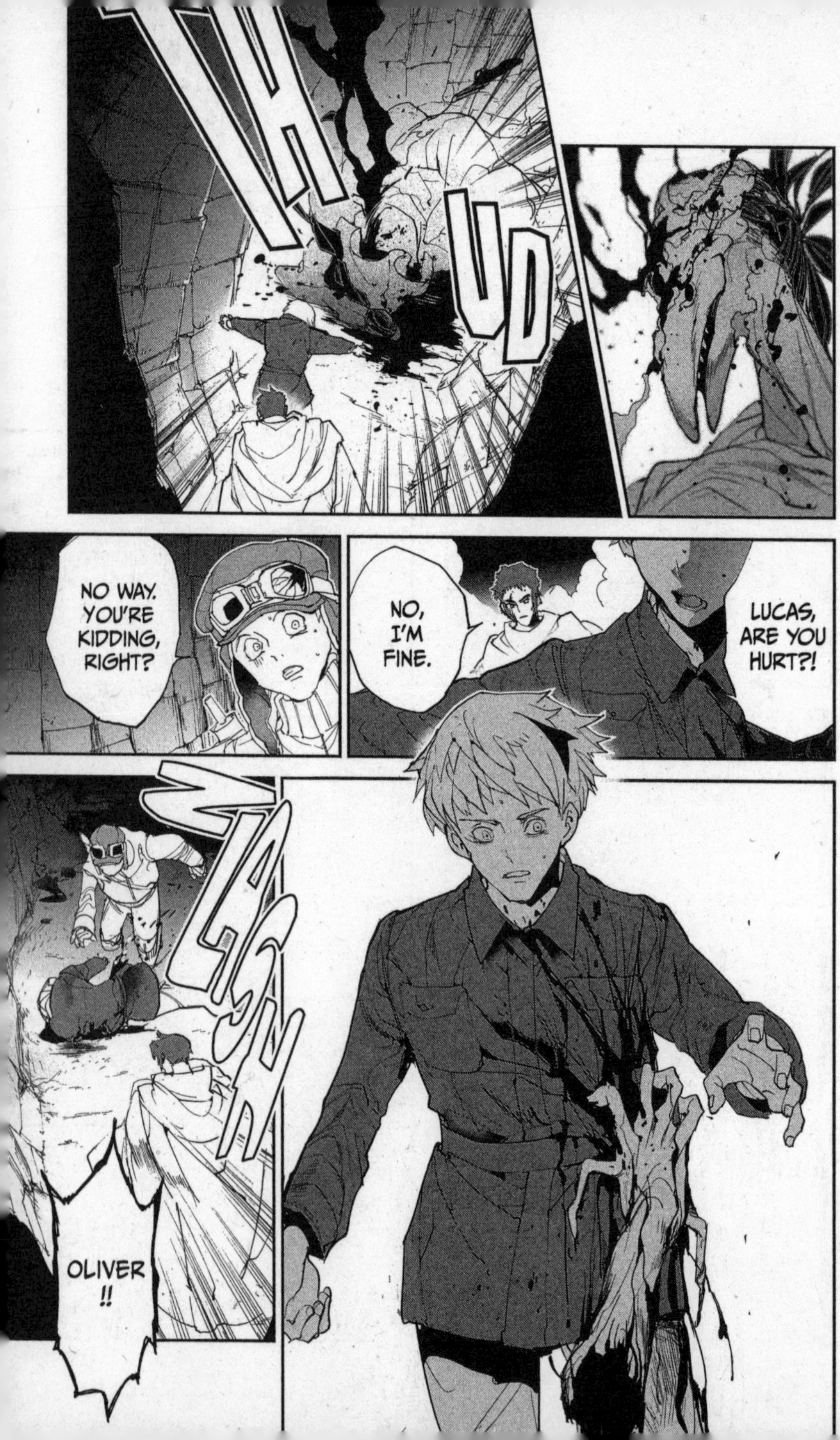
HUD
LUCAS, ARE YOU HURT?!
NO, I'M FINE.
NO WAY. YOU'RE KIDDING, RIGHT?
OLIVER !!

SEASIDE VENDOR 1

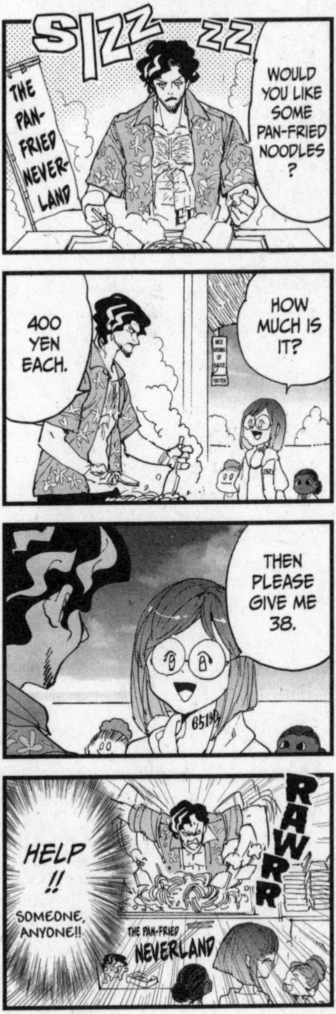
SIZZZZ
THE PAN-FRIED NEVERLAND
WOULD YOU LIKE SOME PAN-FRIED NOODLES?
HOW MUCH IS IT?
400 YEN EACH.
THEN PLEASE GIVE ME 38.
RAWRR
HELP!!
SOMEONE, ANYONE!!
THE PAN-FRIED NEVERLAND

HELP

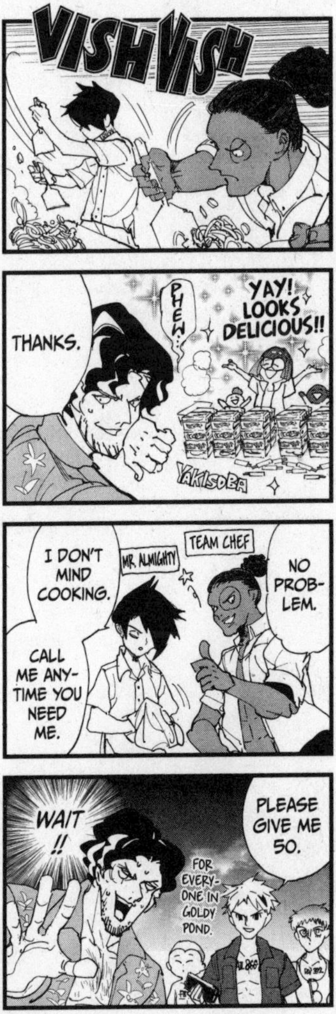
VISH VISH
YAY! LOOKS DELICIOUS!!
PHEW...
THANKS.
YAKISOBA
NO PROBLEM.
TEAM CHEF
MR. ALMIGHTY
I DON'T MIND COOKING.
CALL ME ANYTIME YOU NEED ME.
PLEASE GIVE ME 50.
FOR EVERYONE IN GOLDY POND.
WAIT!!

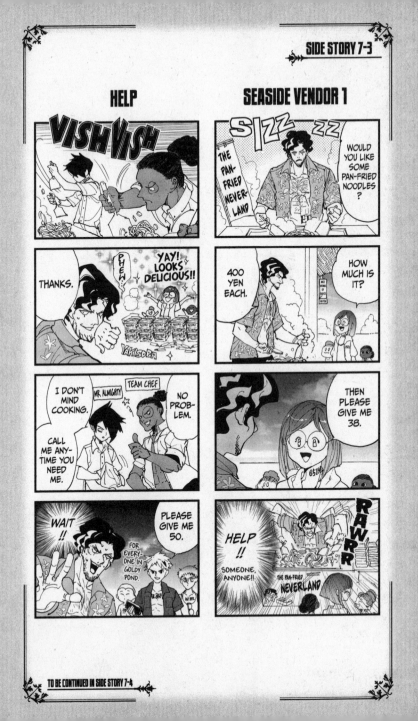

TO BE CONTINUED IN SIDE STORY 7-4

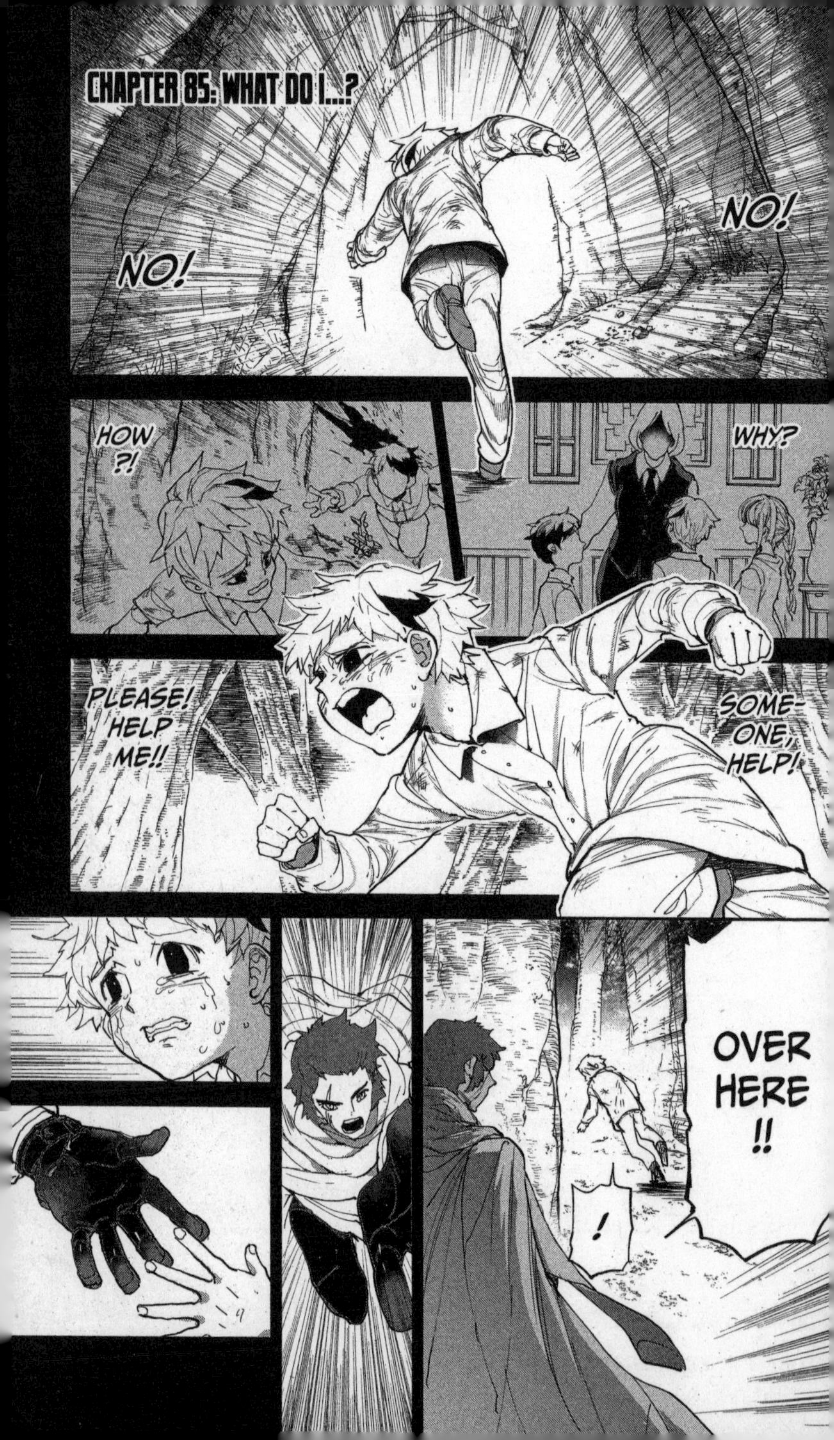
CHAPTER 85: WHAT DO I...?
NO!
NO!
WHY?
HOW ?!
SOME-ONE, HELP!
PLEASE! HELP ME!!
OVER HERE !!
!

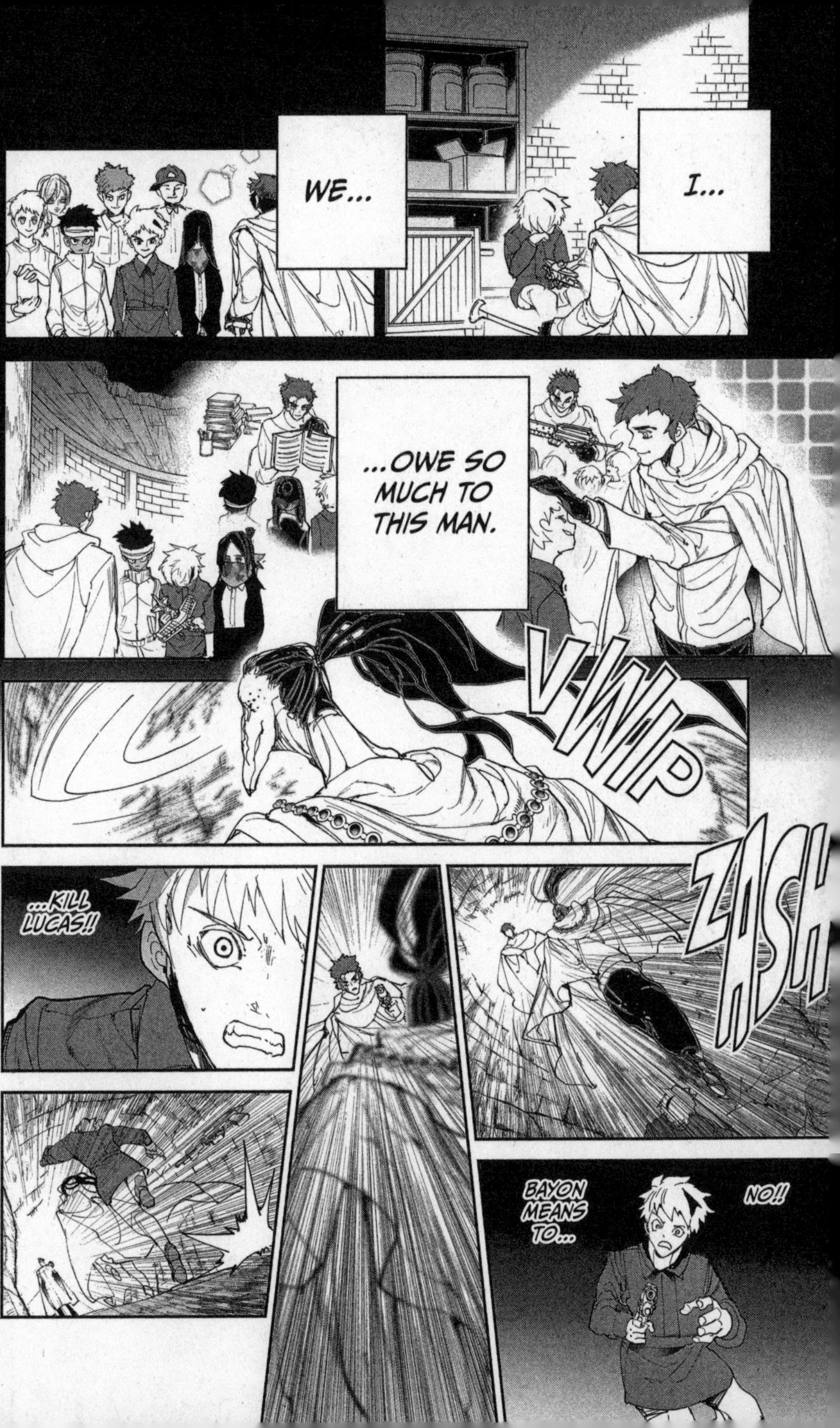
I...
WE...
...OWE SO MUCH TO THIS MAN.
V-WIP
ZASH
NO!!
BAYON MEANS TO...
...KILL LUCAS!!

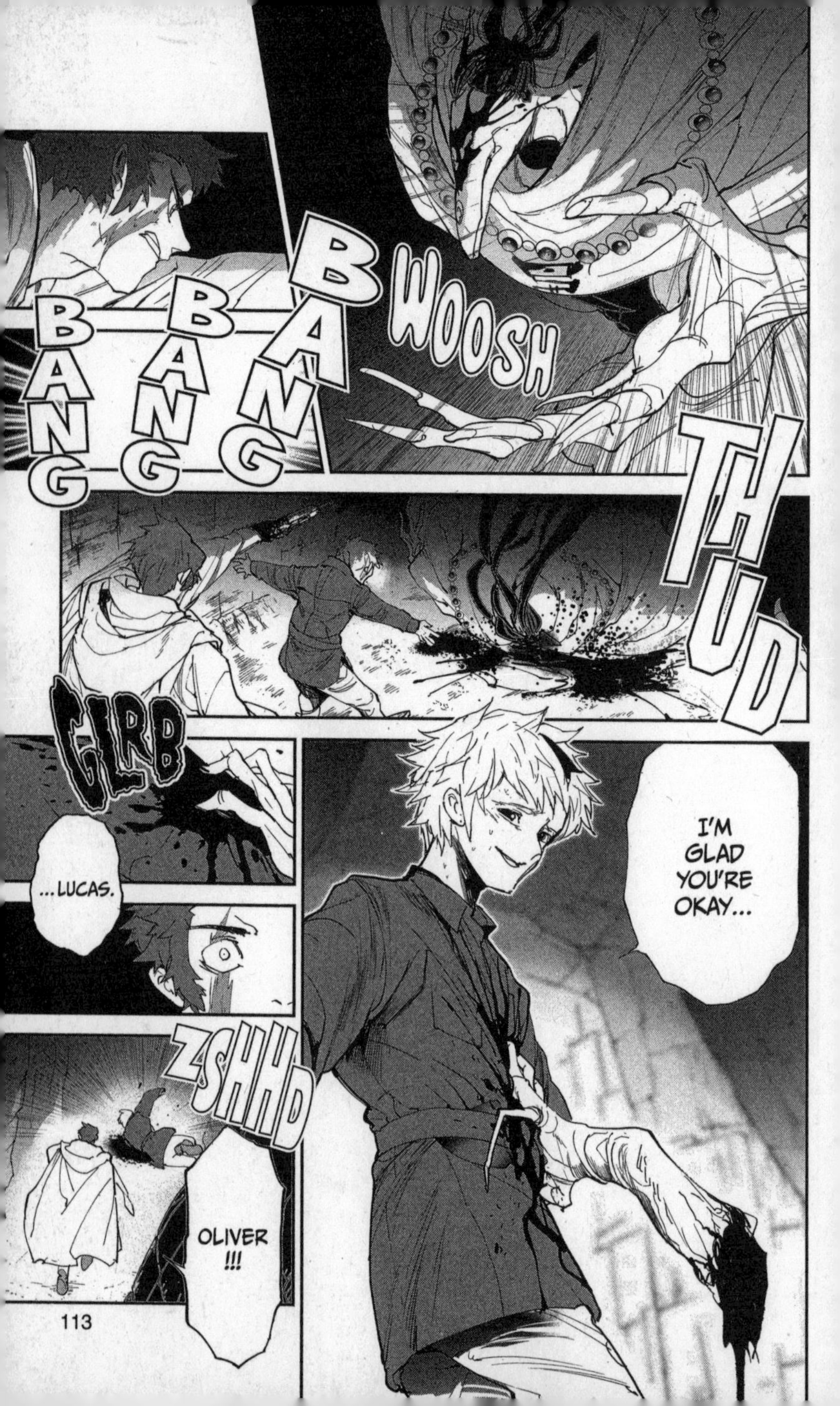
WOOSH
BANG
BANG
BANG
THUD
I'M GLAD YOU'RE OKAY...
GLRB
...LUCAS.
ZSHHD
OLIVER !!!

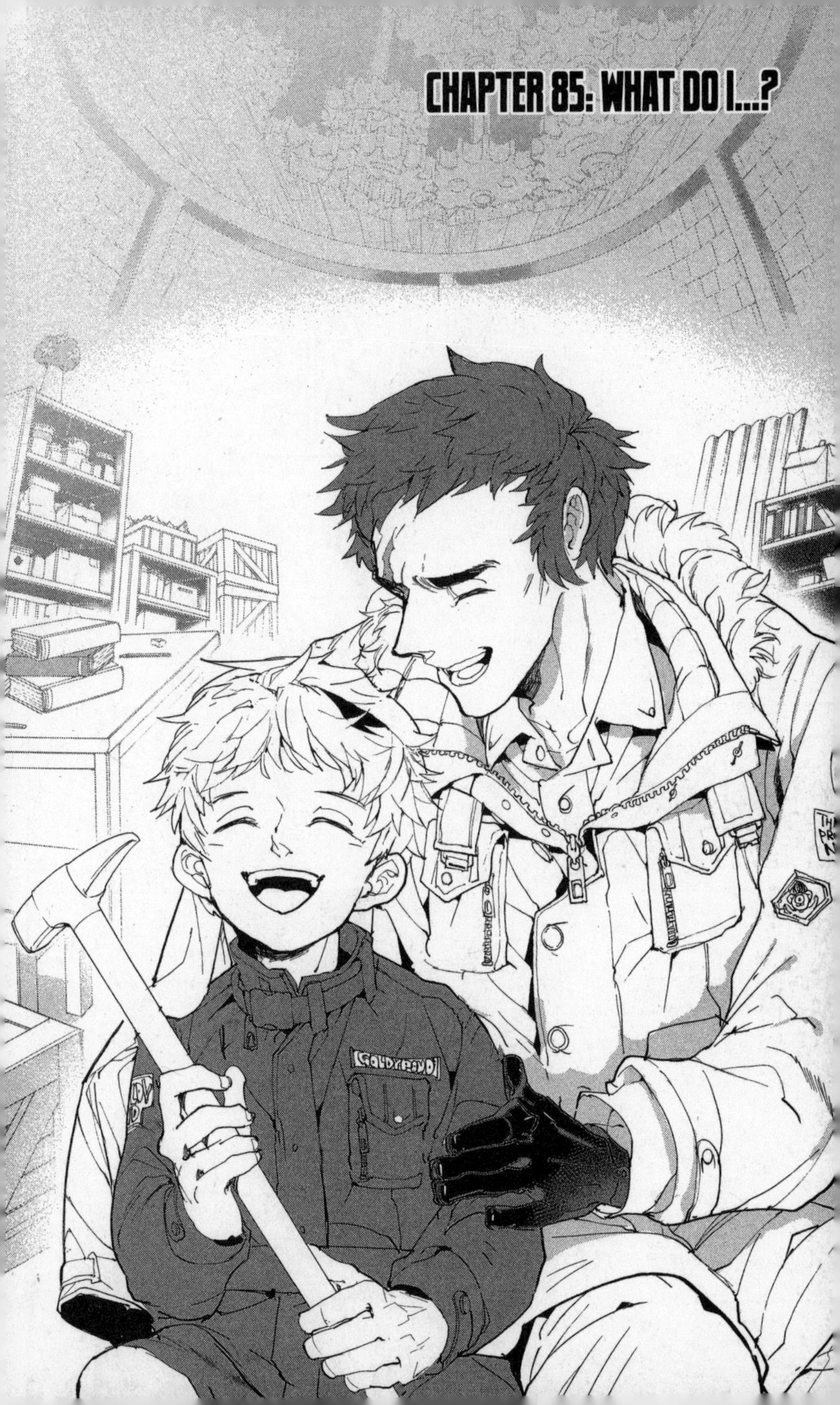
CHAPTER 85: WHAT DO I...?

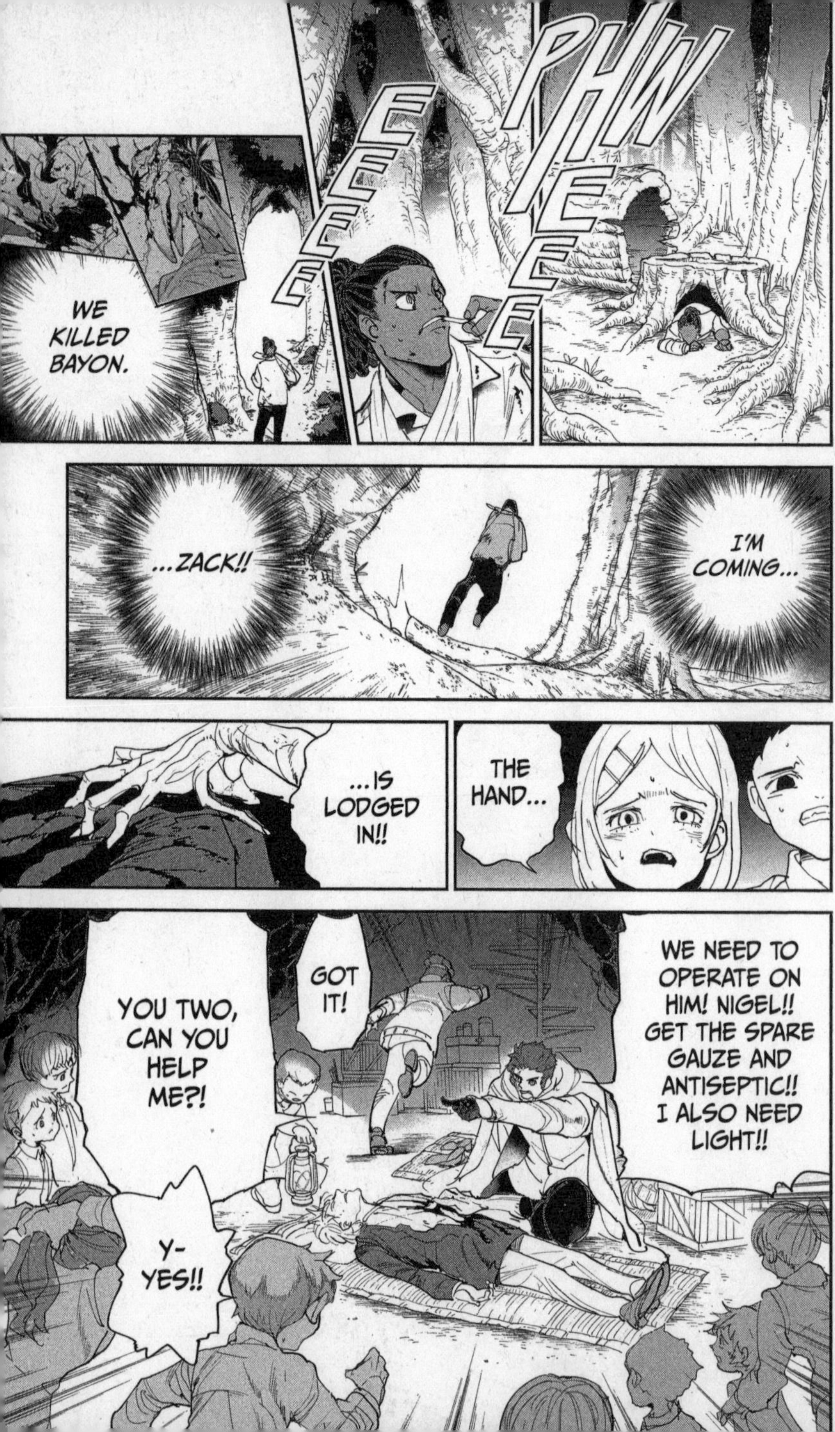
PHWEEEE
EEEEE
WE KILLED BAYON.
I'M COMING...
...ZACK!!
THE HAND...
...IS LODGED IN!!
WE NEED TO OPERATE ON HIM! NIGEL!! GET THE SPARE GAUZE AND ANTISEPTIC!! I ALSO NEED LIGHT!!
GOT IT!
YOU TWO, CAN YOU HELP ME?!
Y- YES!!

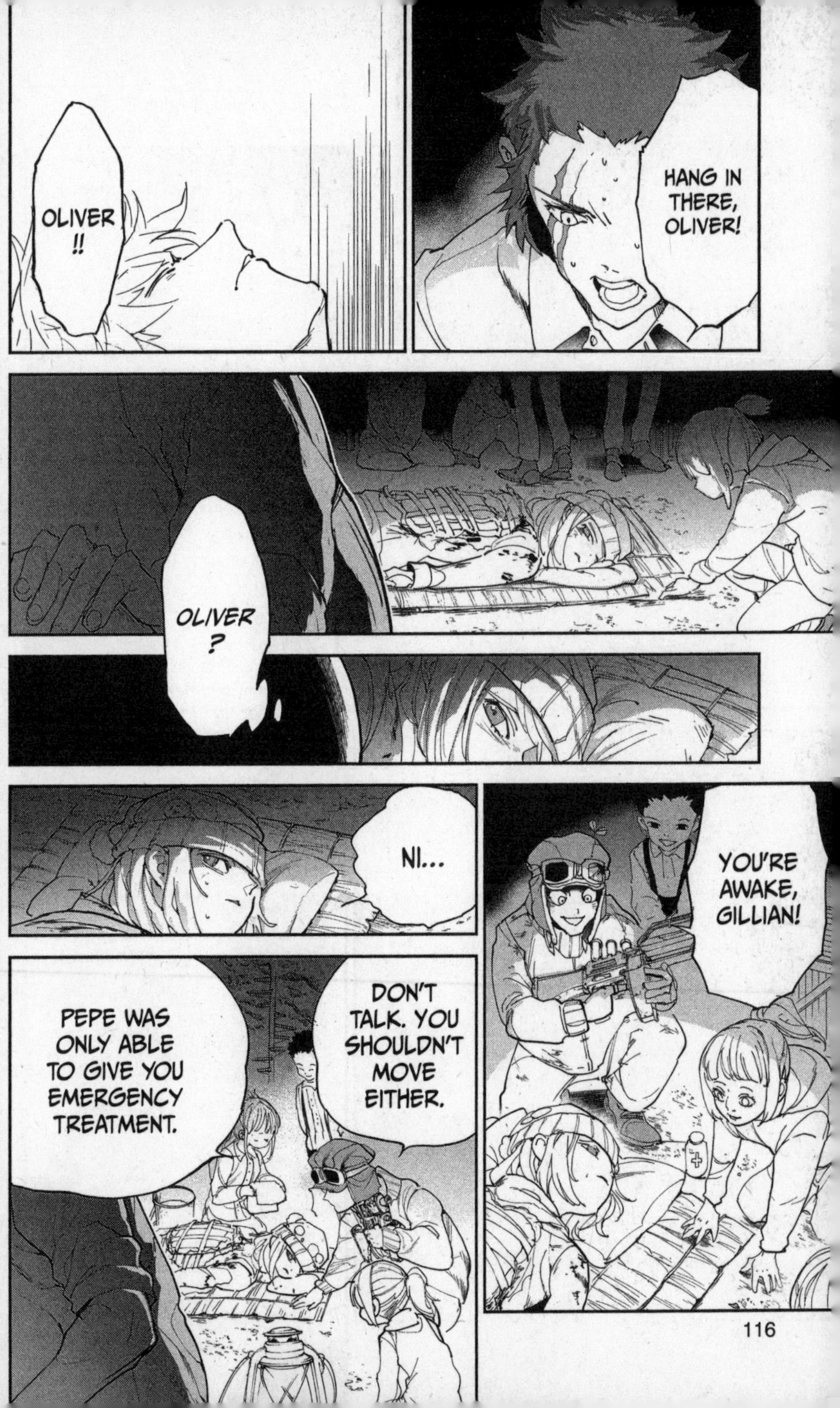
HANG IN THERE, OLIVER!
OLIVER !!
OLIVER ?
YOU'RE AWAKE, GILLIAN!
NI...
DON'T TALK. YOU SHOULDN'T MOVE EITHER.
PEPE WAS ONLY ABLE TO GIVE YOU EMERGENCY TREATMENT.

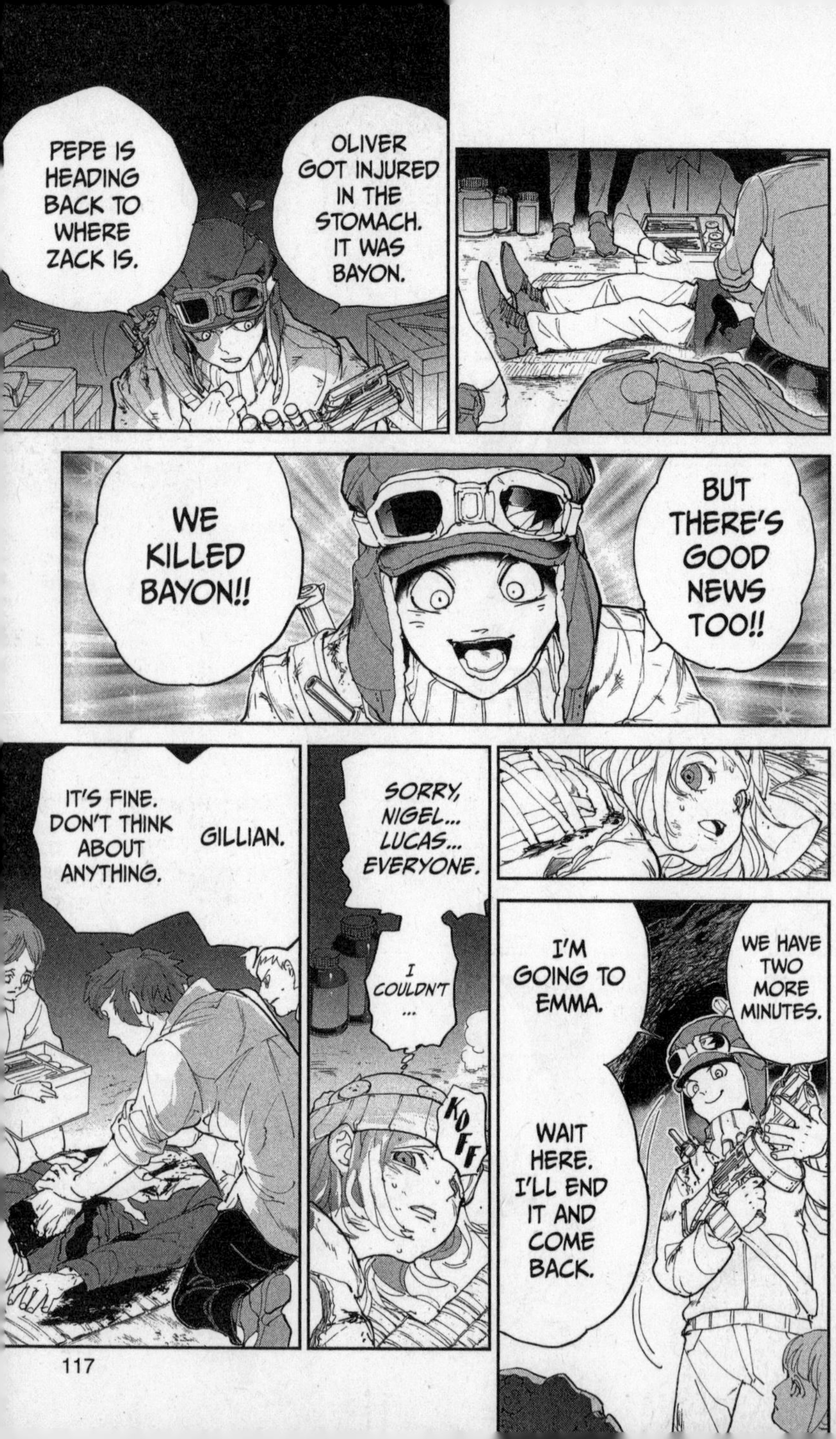
OLIVER GOT INJURED IN THE STOMACH. IT WAS BAYON.
PEPE IS HEADING BACK TO WHERE ZACK IS.
BUT THERE'S GOOD NEWS TOO!!
WE KILLED BAYON!!
WE HAVE TWO MORE MINUTES.
I'M GOING TO EMMA.
WAIT HERE. I'LL END IT AND COME BACK.
SORRY, NIGEL... LUCAS... EVERYONE.
I COULDN'T ...
KOFF
GILLIAN.
IT'S FINE. DON'T THINK ABOUT ANYTHING.

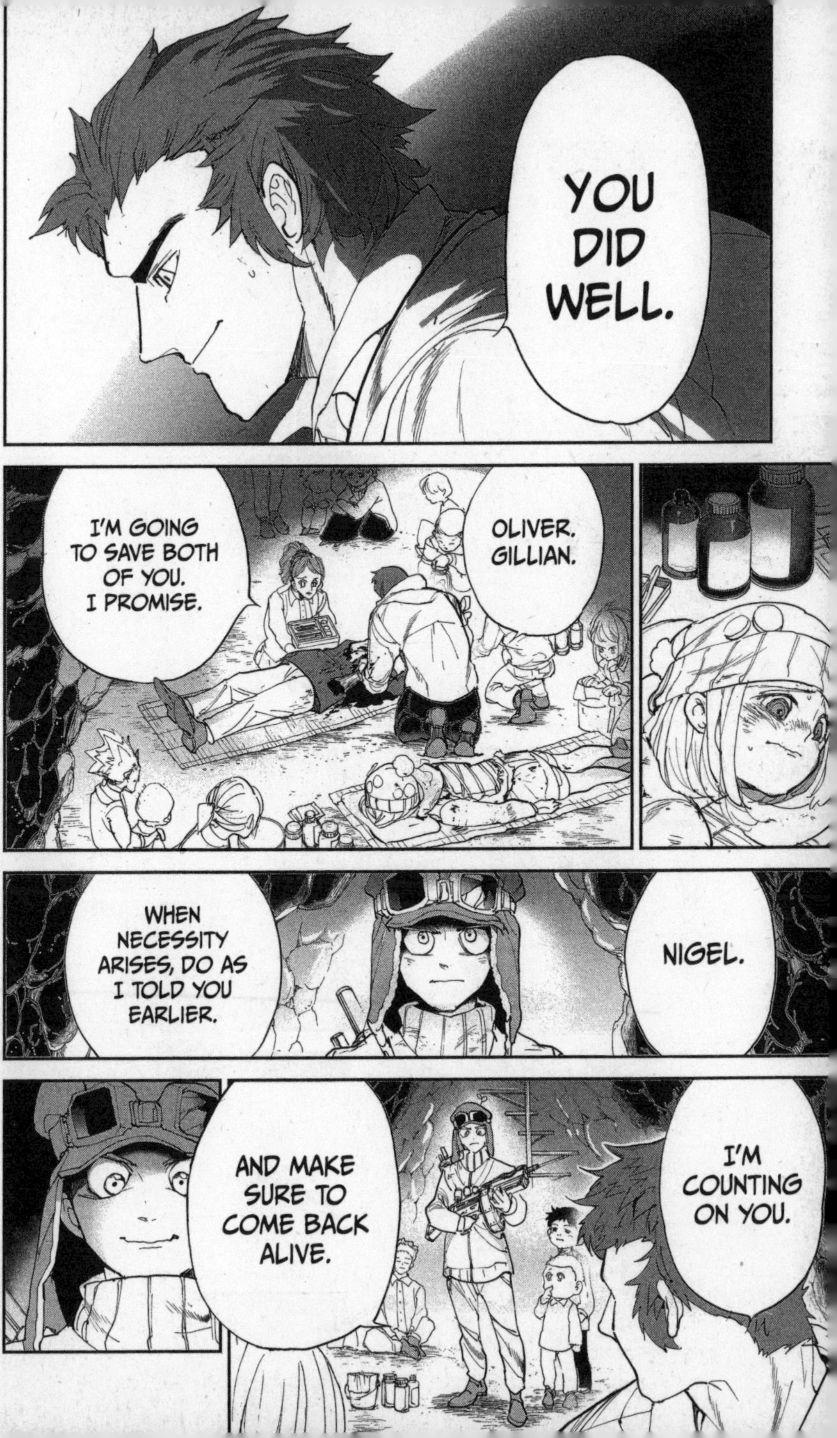
YOU DID WELL.
OLIVER. GILLIAN.
I'M GOING TO SAVE BOTH OF YOU. I PROMISE.
NIGEL.
WHEN NECESSITY ARISES, DO AS I TOLD YOU EARLIER.
I'M COUNTING ON YOU.
AND MAKE SURE TO COME BACK ALIVE.

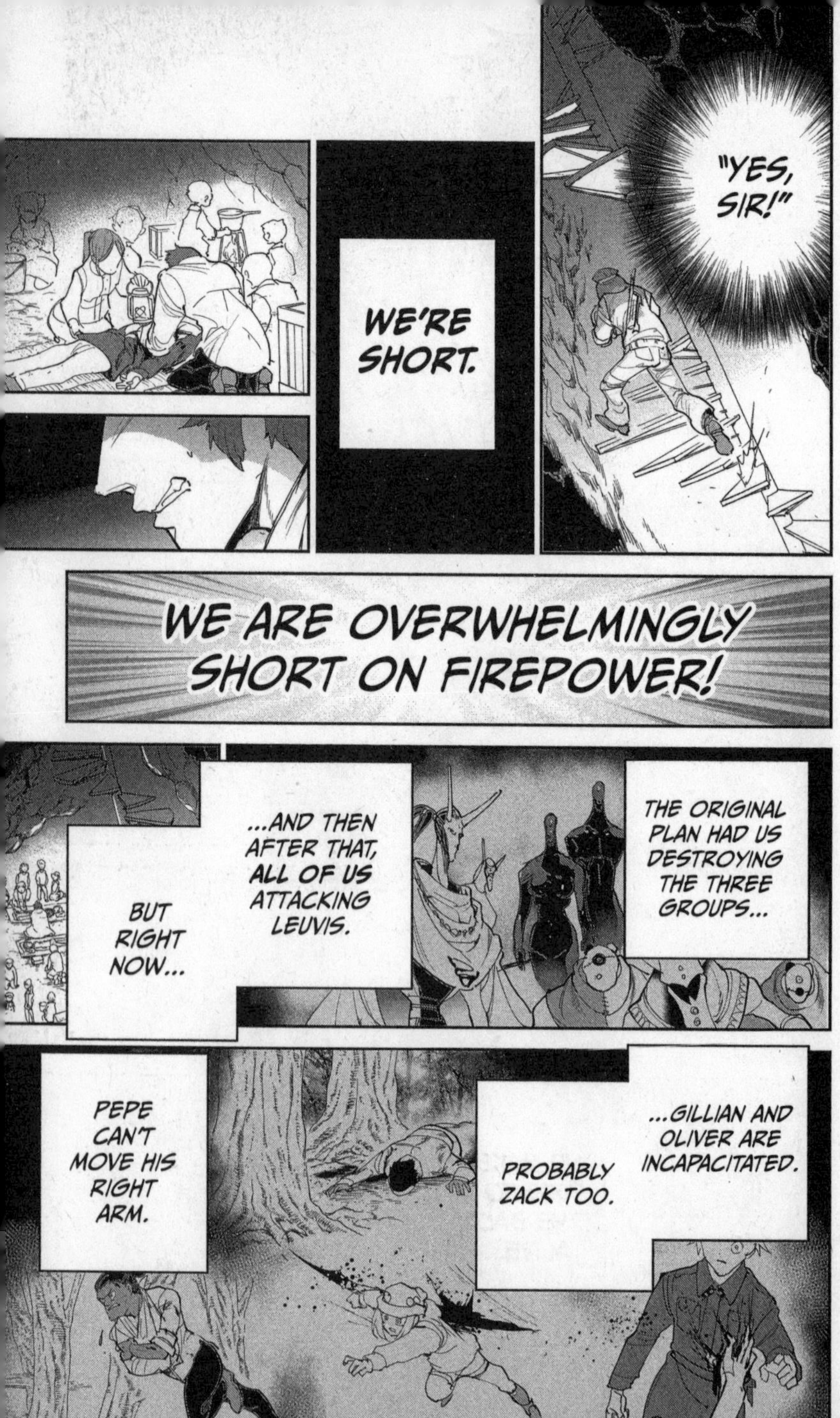
"YES, SIR!"
WE'RE SHORT.
WE ARE OVERWHELMINGLY SHORT ON FIREPOWER!
THE ORIGINAL PLAN HAD US DESTROYING THE THREE GROUPS...
...AND THEN AFTER THAT, ALL OF US ATTACKING LEUVIS.
BUT RIGHT NOW...
...GILLIAN AND OLIVER ARE INCAPACITATED.
PROBABLY ZACK TOO.
PEPE CAN'T MOVE HIS RIGHT ARM.

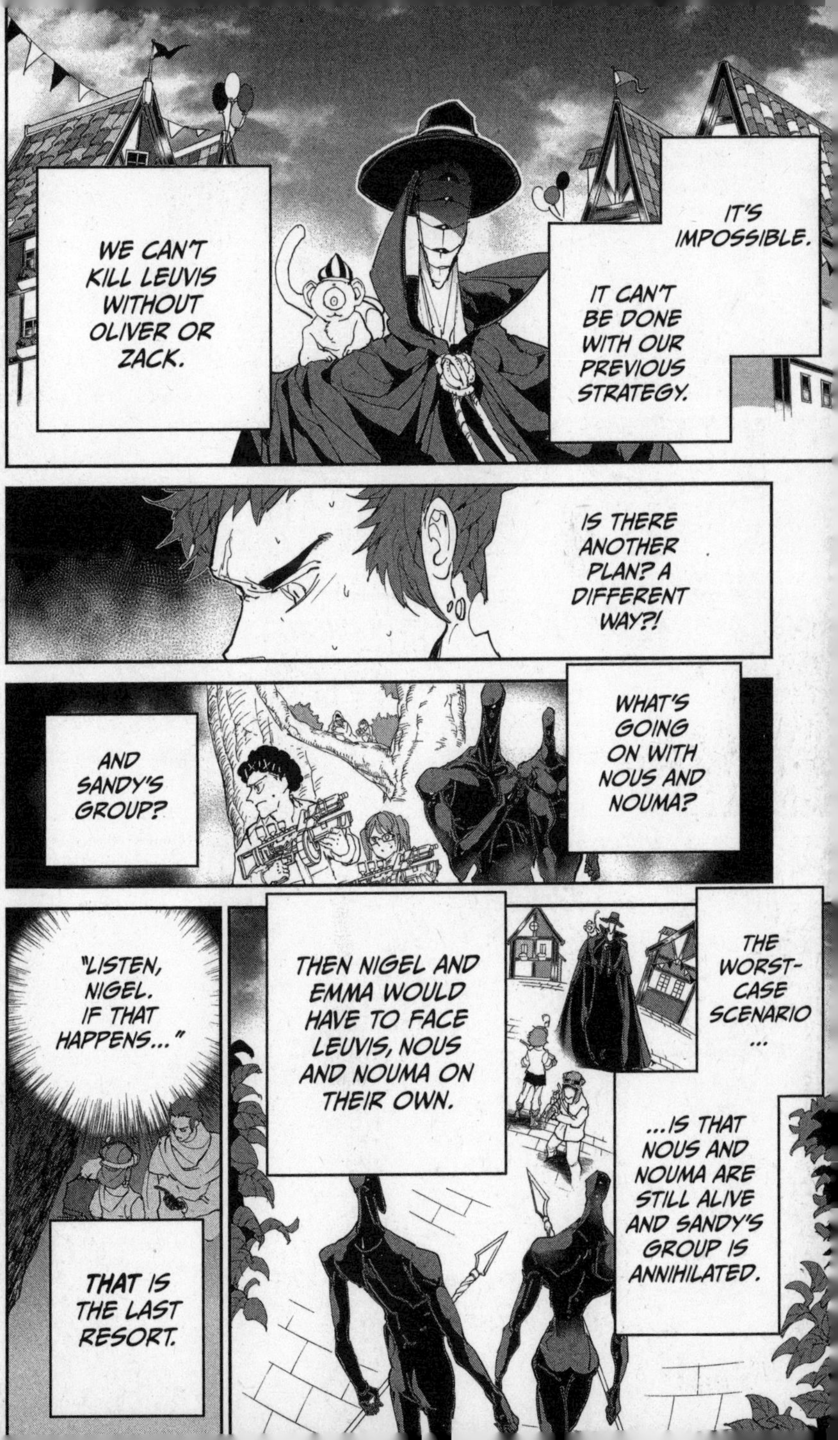
IT'S IMPOSSIBLE.
IT CAN'T BE DONE WITH OUR PREVIOUS STRATEGY.
WE CAN'T KILL LEUVIS WITHOUT OLIVER OR ZACK.
IS THERE ANOTHER PLAN? A DIFFERENT WAY?!
WHAT'S GOING ON WITH NOUS AND NOUMA?
AND SANDY'S GROUP?
THE WORST-CASE SCENARIO...
...IS THAT NOUS AND NOUMA ARE STILL ALIVE AND SANDY'S GROUP IS ANNIHILATED.
THEN NIGEL AND EMMA WOULD HAVE TO FACE LEUVIS, NOUS AND NOUMA ON THEIR OWN.
"LISTEN, NIGEL. IF THAT HAPPENS..."
THAT IS THE LAST RESORT.

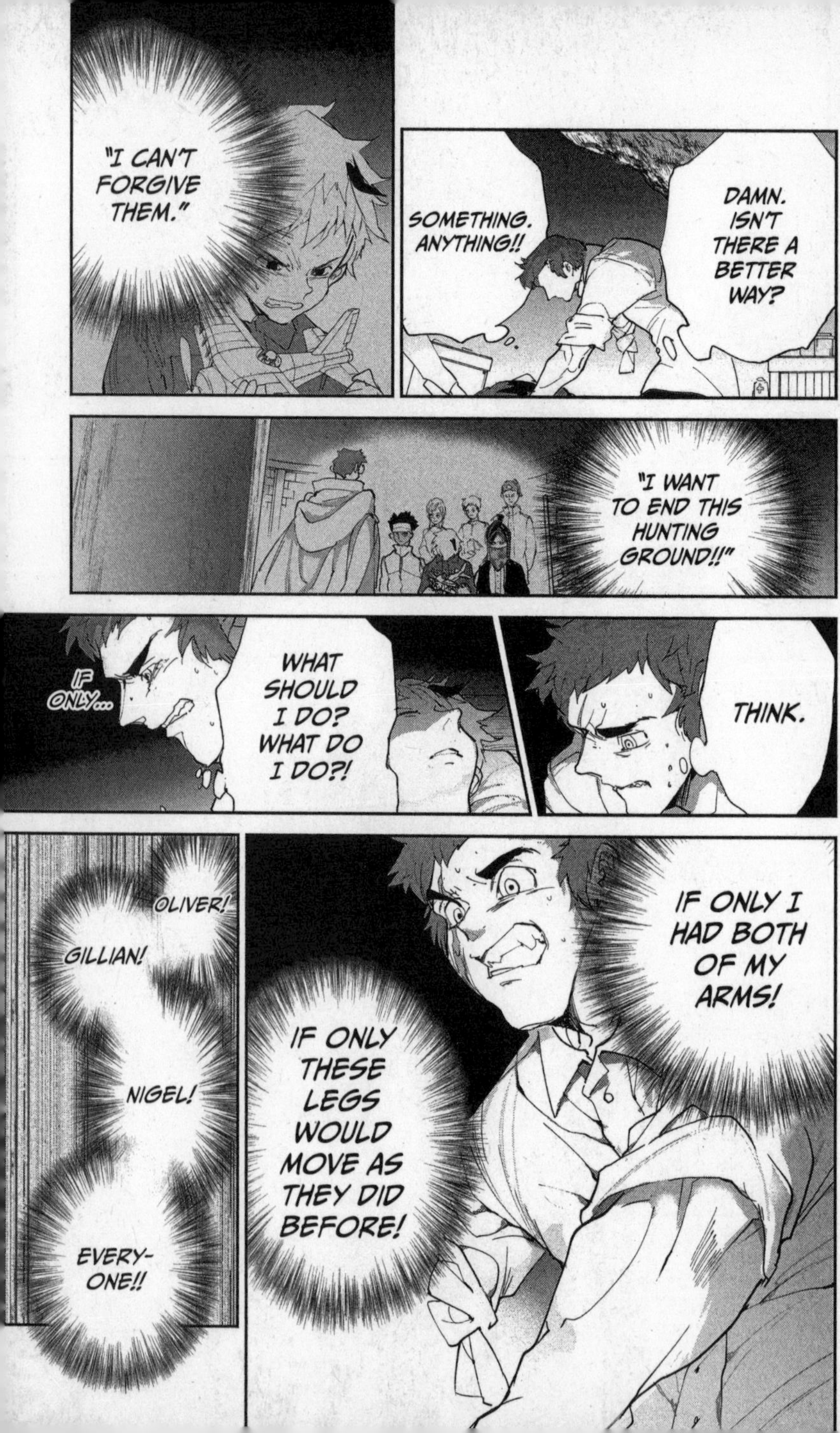
DAMN. ISN'T THERE A BETTER WAY?
SOMETHING. ANYTHING!!
"I CAN'T FORGIVE THEM."
"I WANT TO END THIS HUNTING GROUND!!"
THINK.
WHAT SHOULD I DO? WHAT DO I DO?!
IF ONLY...
IF ONLY I HAD BOTH OF MY ARMS!
IF ONLY THESE LEGS WOULD MOVE AS THEY DID BEFORE!
OLIVER!
GILLIAN!
NIGEL!
EVERY-ONE!!

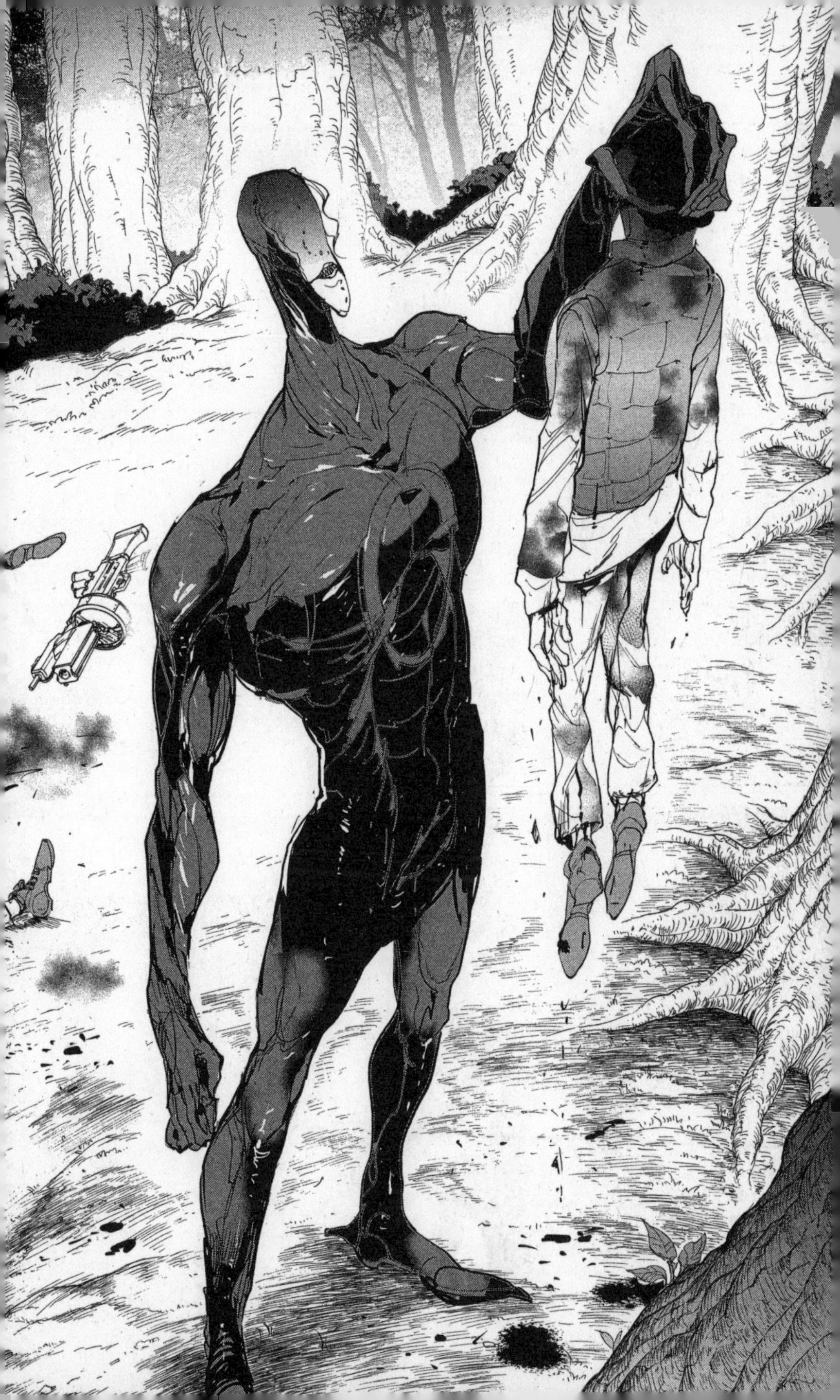

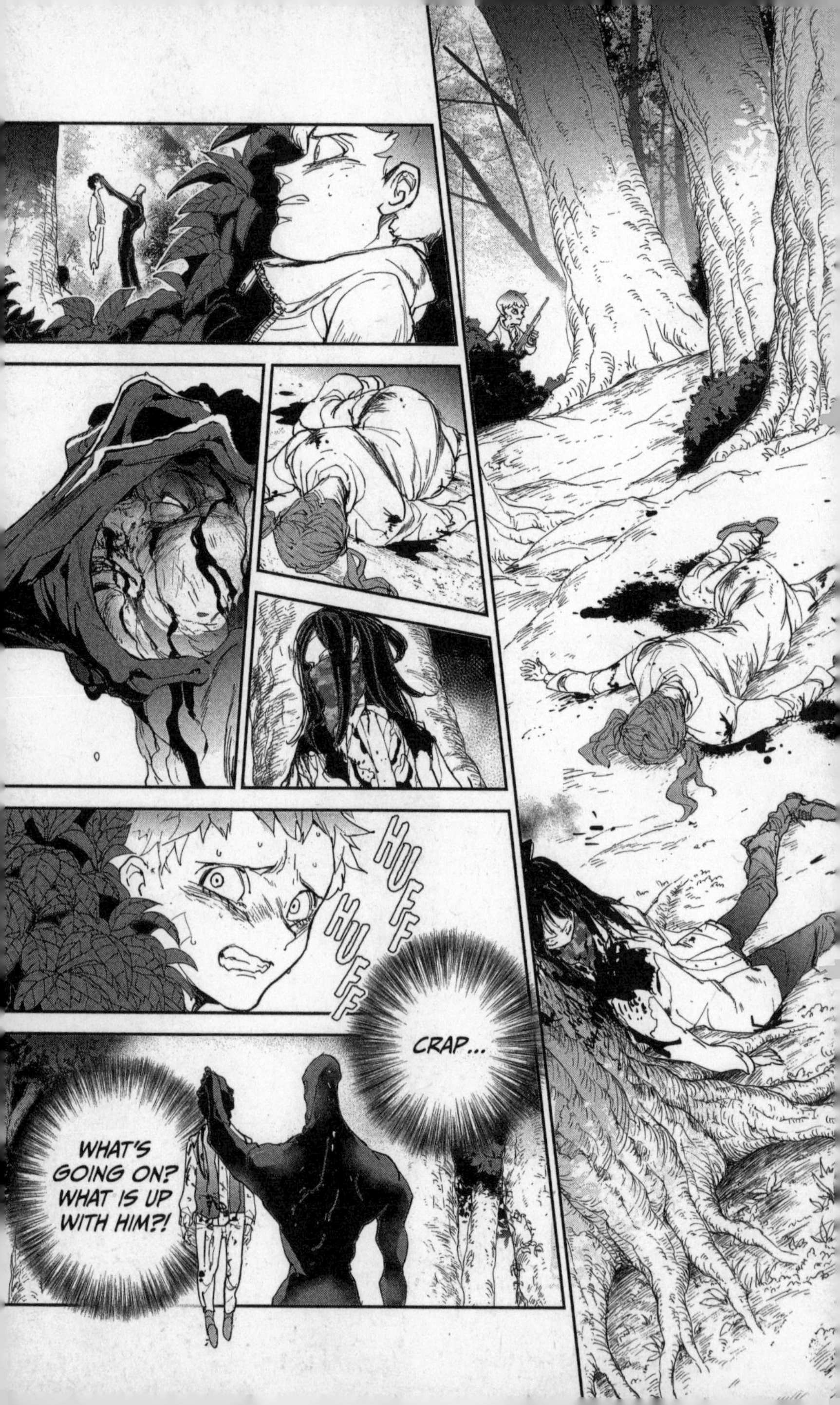
HUFF
HUFF
HUFF
CRAP...
WHAT'S GOING ON? WHAT IS UP WITH HIM?!

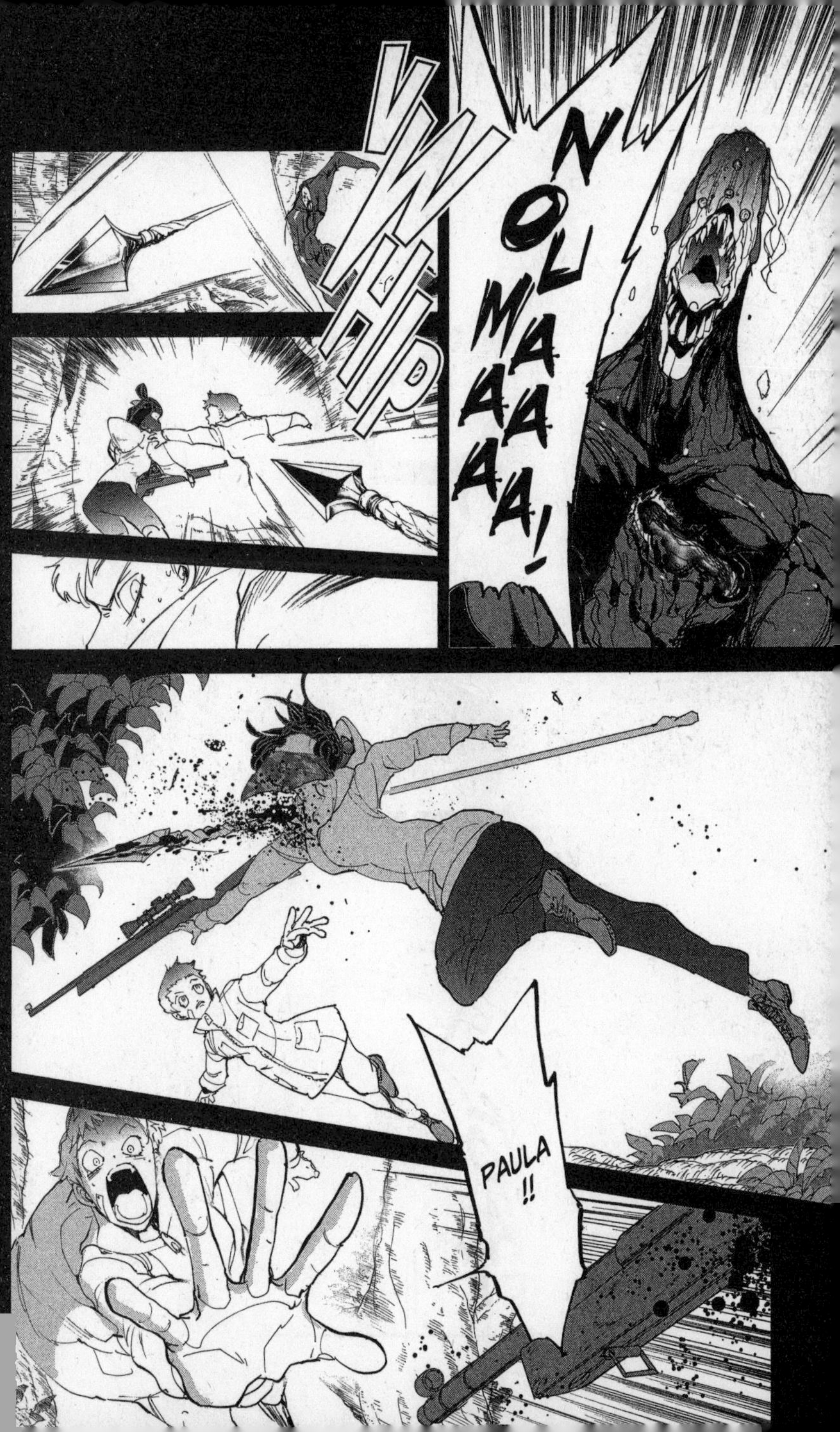
NOUL
MAMAAAAAA!
VWHIP
PAULA!!

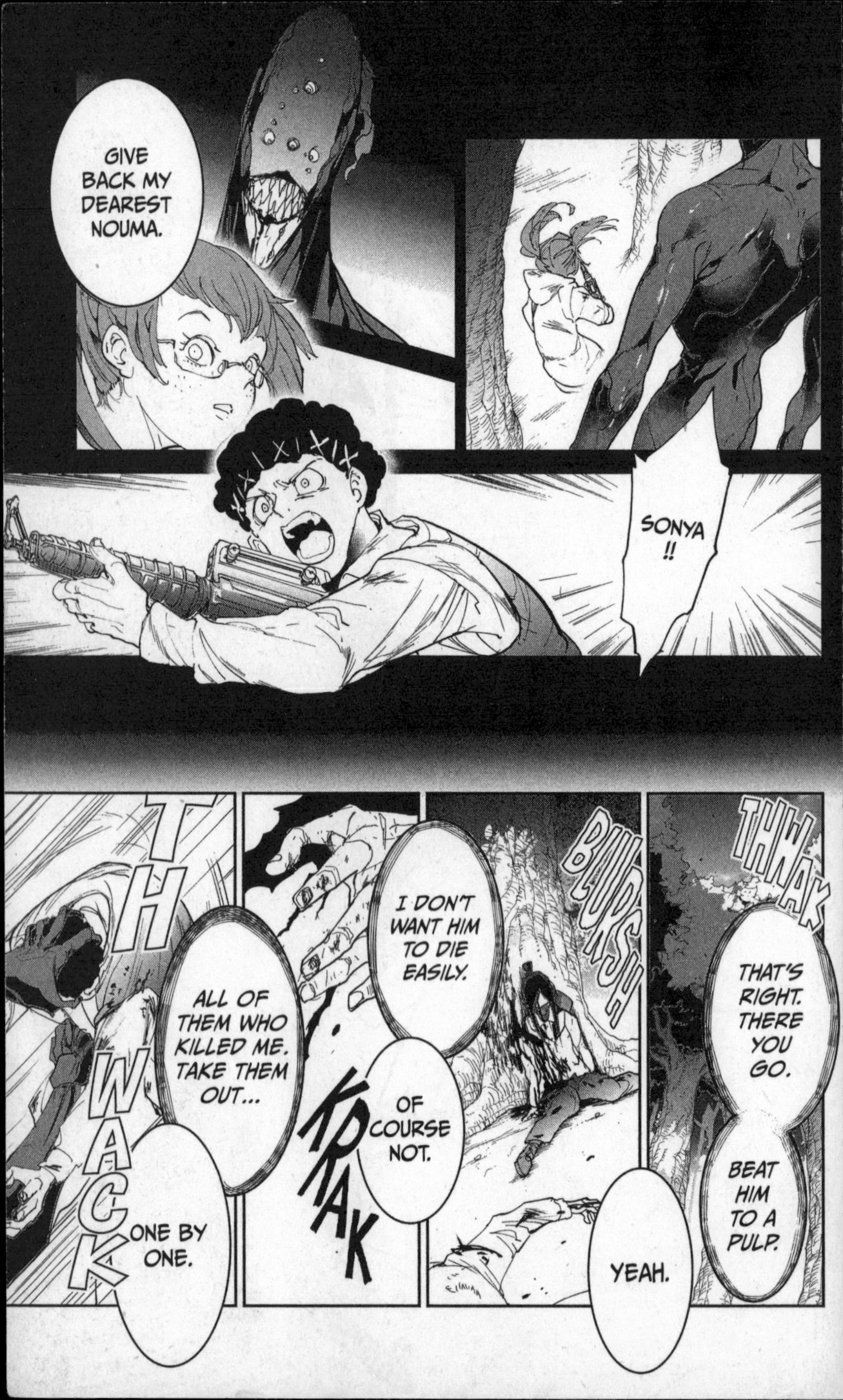
GIVE BACK MY DEAREST NOUMA.
SONYA !!
THWAK
THAT'S RIGHT. THERE YOU GO.
BEAT HIM TO A PULP.
YEAH.
I DON'T WANT HIM TO DIE EASILY.
OF COURSE NOT.
KRAK
THWACK
ALL OF THEM WHO KILLED ME. TAKE THEM OUT...
ONE BY ONE.

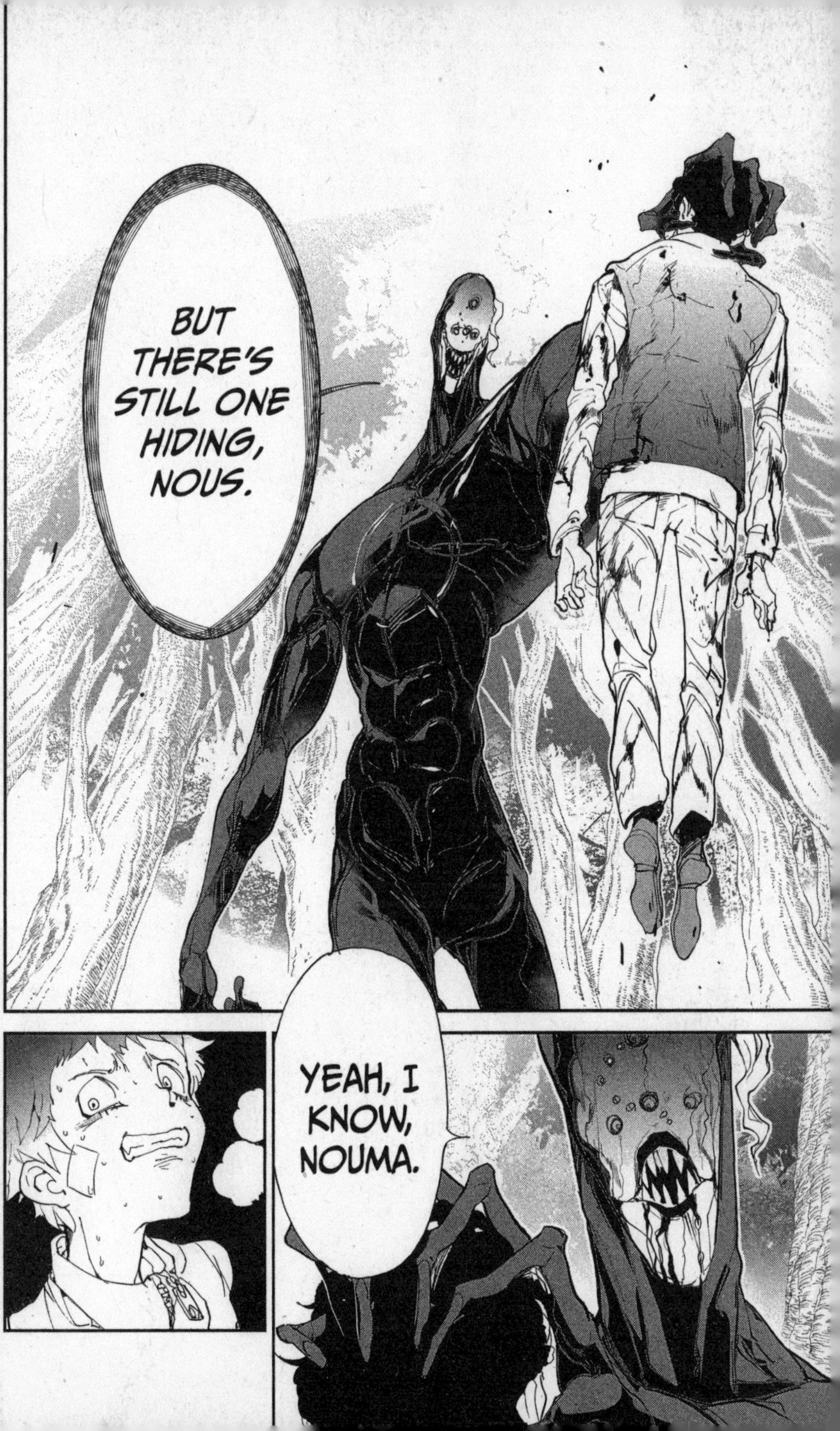
BUT THERE'S STILL ONE HIDING, NOUS.
YEAH, I KNOW, NOUMA.

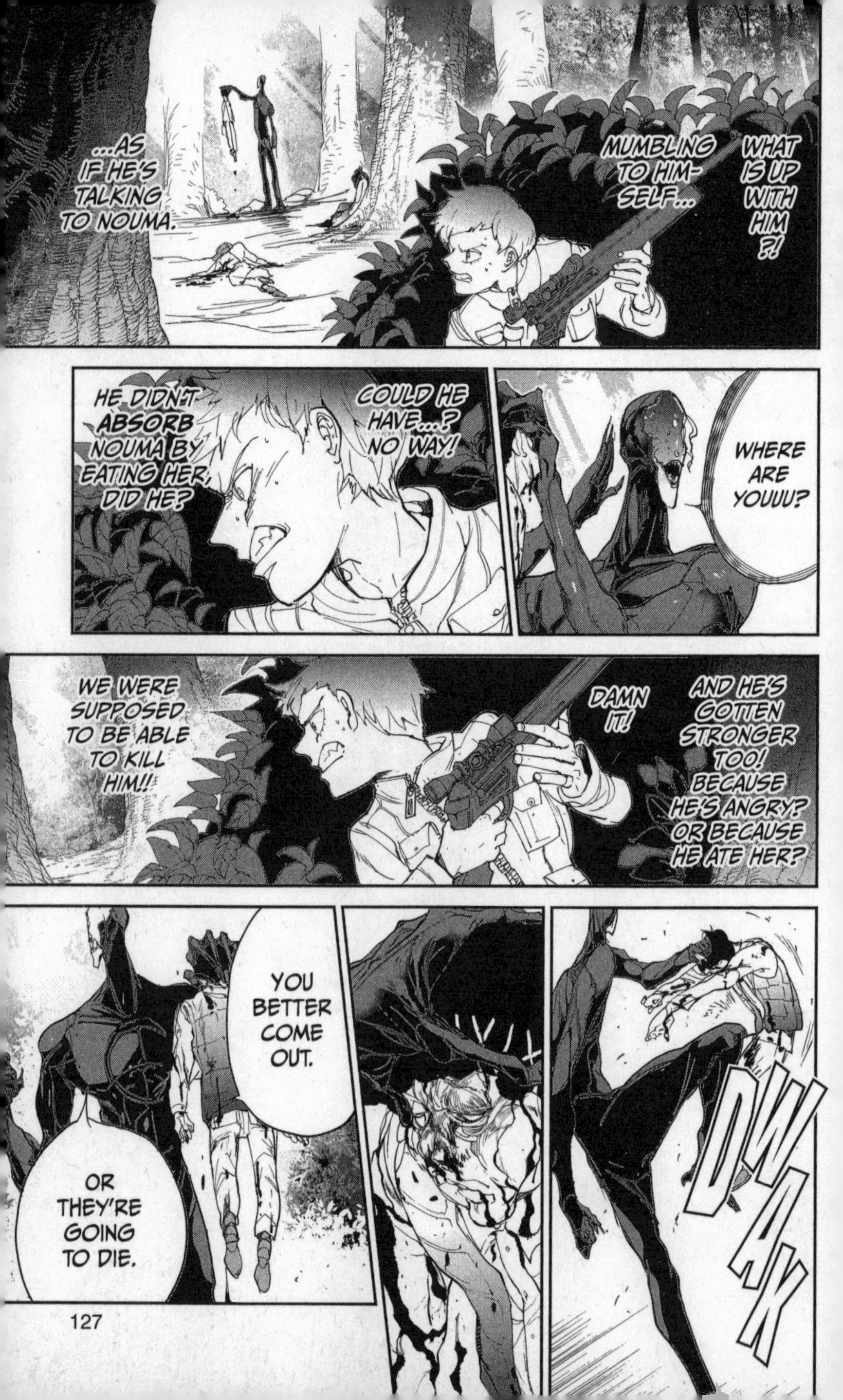
WHAT IS UP WITH HIM?!
MUMBLING TO HIMSELF...
...AS IF HE'S TALKING TO NOUMA.
WHERE ARE YOUUU?
COULD HE HAVE...? NO WAY!
HE DIDN'T ABSORB NOUMA BY EATING HER, DID HE?
AND HE'S GOTTEN STRONGER TOO! BECAUSE HE'S ANGRY? OR BECAUSE HE ATE HER?
DAMN IT!
WE WERE SUPPOSED TO BE ABLE TO KILL HIM!!
DWACK
YOU BETTER COME OUT.
OR THEY'RE GOING TO DIE.

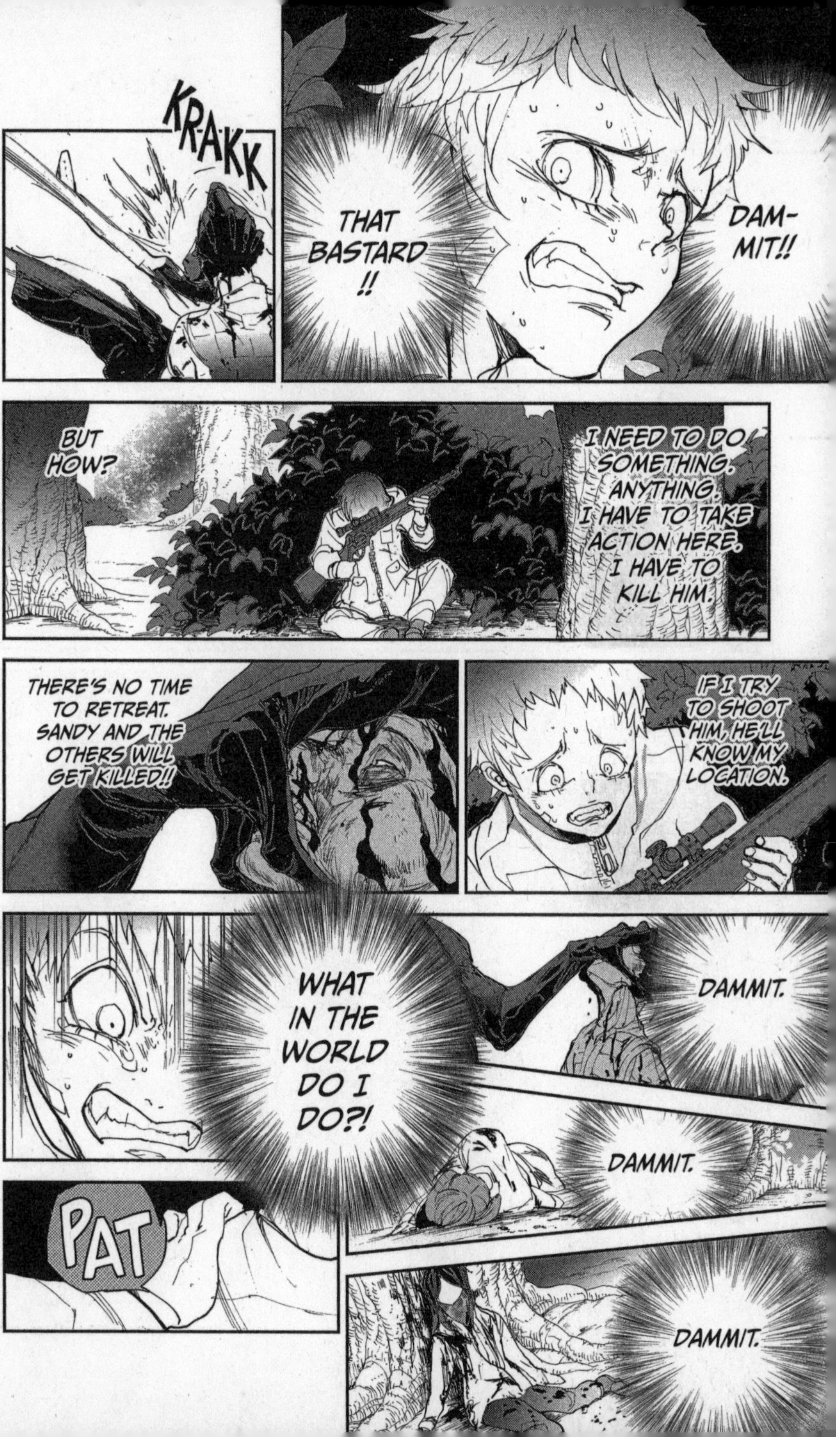
DAM-MIT!!
THAT BASTARD !!
KR-A-KK
I NEED TO DO SOMETHING. ANYTHING. I HAVE TO TAKE ACTION HERE. I HAVE TO KILL HIM.
BUT HOW?
IF I TRY TO SHOOT HIM, HE'LL KNOW MY LOCATION.
THERE'S NO TIME TO RETREAT. SANDY AND THE OTHERS WILL GET KILLED!!
DAMMIT.
DAMMIT.
DAMMIT.
WHAT IN THE WORLD DO I DO?!
PAT

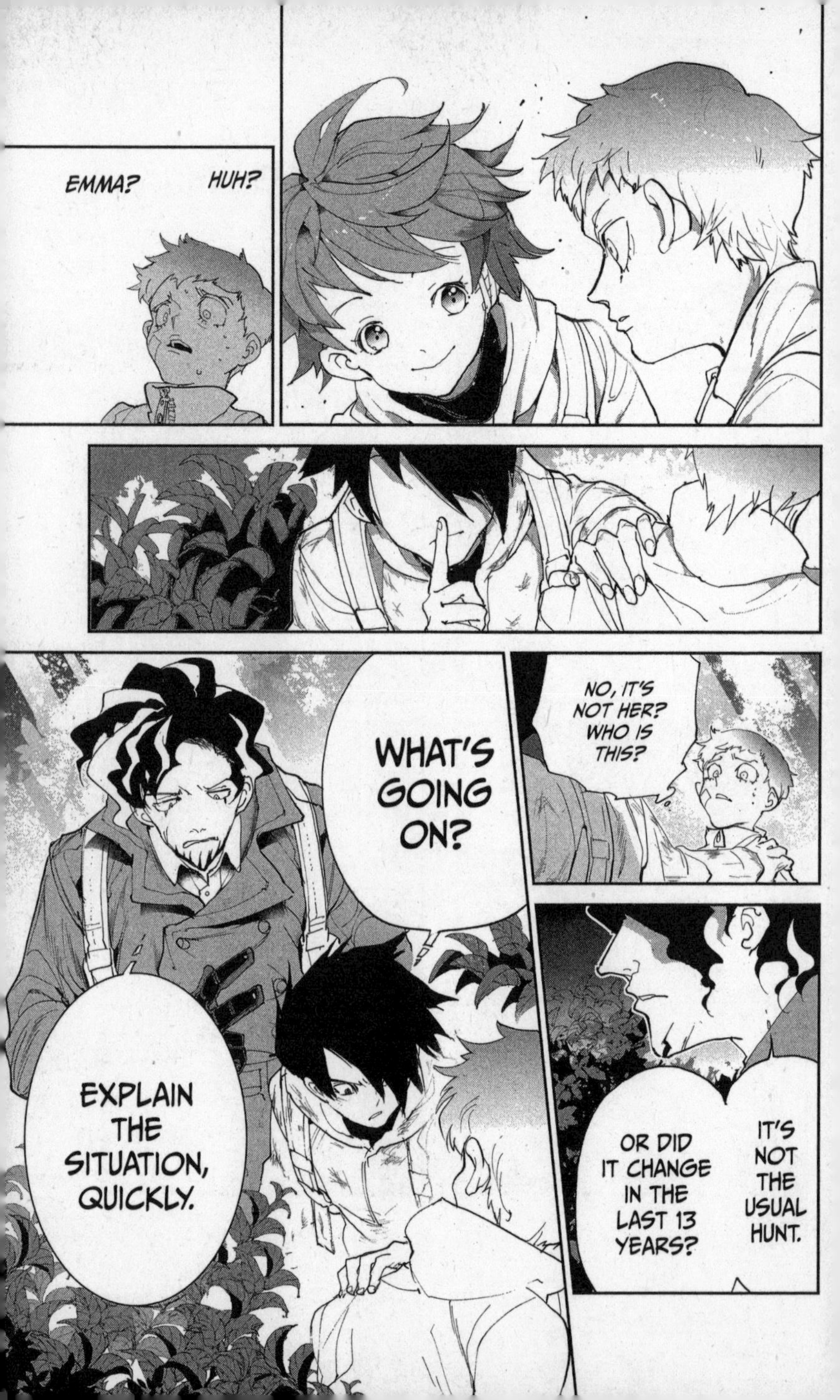
HUH?
EMMA?
NO, IT'S NOT HER? WHO IS THIS?
IT'S NOT THE USUAL HUNT.
OR DID IT CHANGE IN THE LAST 13 YEARS?
WHAT'S GOING ON?
EXPLAIN THE SITUATION, QUICKLY.

YOU'RE ENLISTED!!

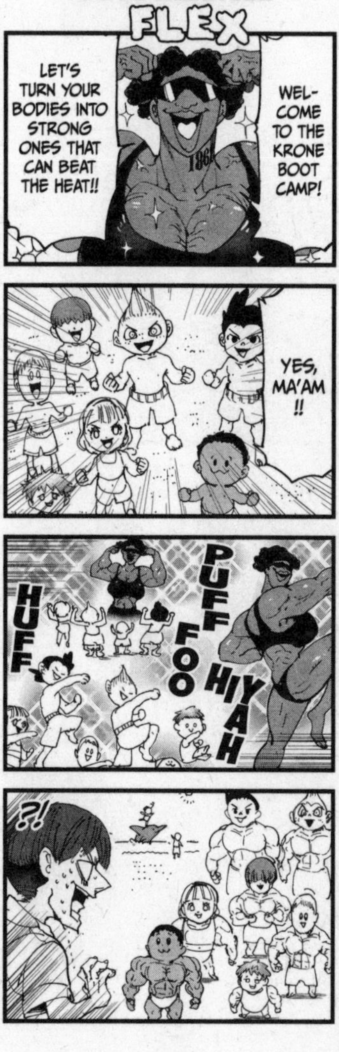
FLEX
WELCOME TO THE KRONE BOOT CAMP!
LET'S TURN YOUR BODIES INTO STRONG ONES THAT CAN BEAT THE HEAT!!
YES, MA'AM !!
PUFF PUFF
HIYAH
FOO
HUFF
?!

HEATSTROKE

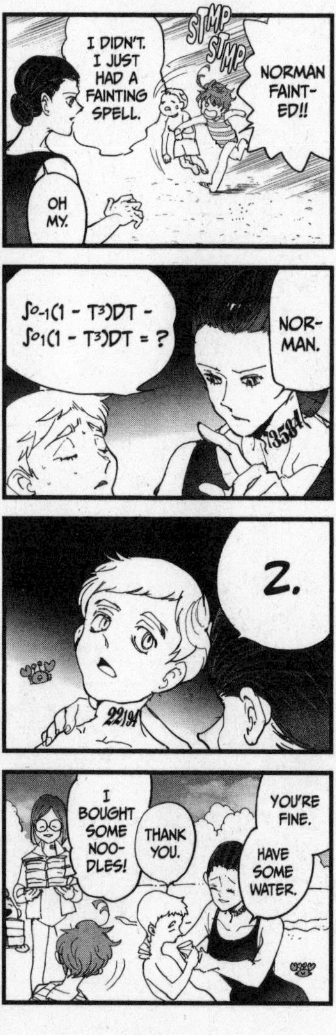
NORMAN FAINTED!!
STMP STMP
I DIDN'T. I JUST HAD A FAINTING SPELL.
OH MY.
NORMAN.
$\int_{-1}^{0}(1 - T^3)DT - \int_{0}^{1}(1 - T^3)DT = ?$
2.
YOU'RE FINE.
HAVE SOME WATER.
THANK YOU.
I BOUGHT SOME NOODLES!

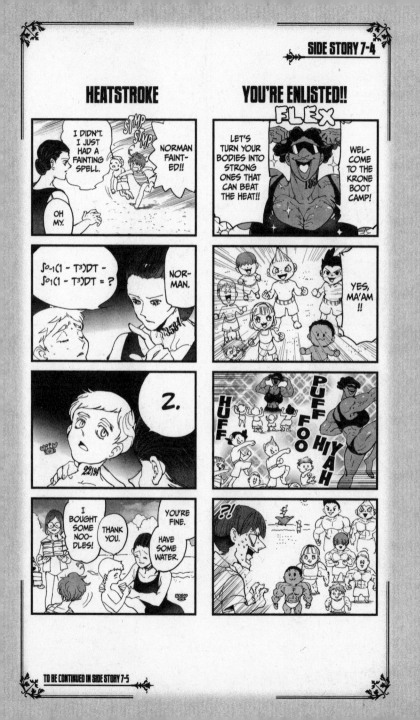

TO BE CONTINUED IN SIDE STORY 7-5

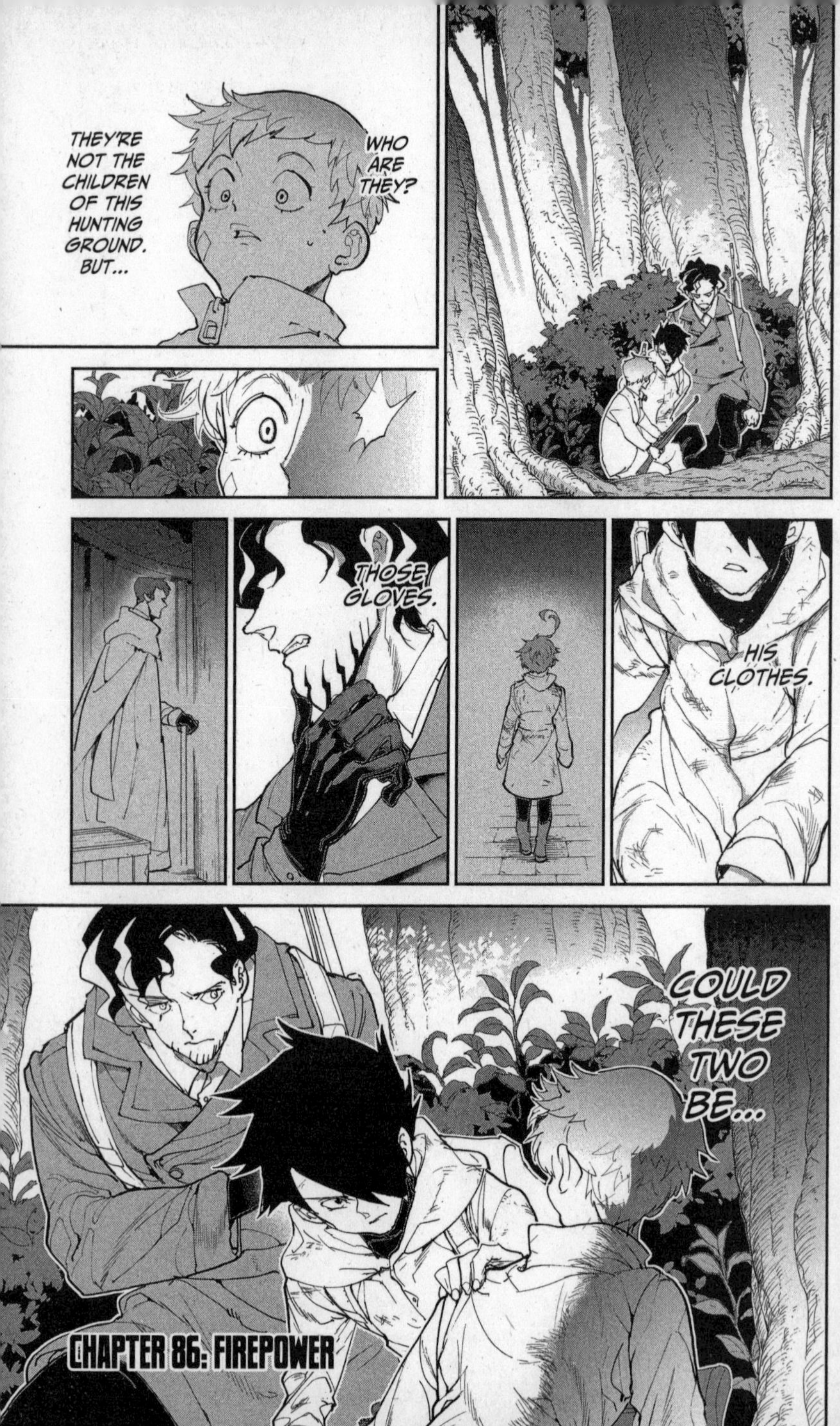
WHO ARE THEY?
THEY'RE NOT THE CHILDREN OF THIS HUNTING GROUND. BUT...
HIS CLOTHES.
THOSE GLOVES.
COULD THESE TWO BE...
CHAPTER 86: FIREPOWER

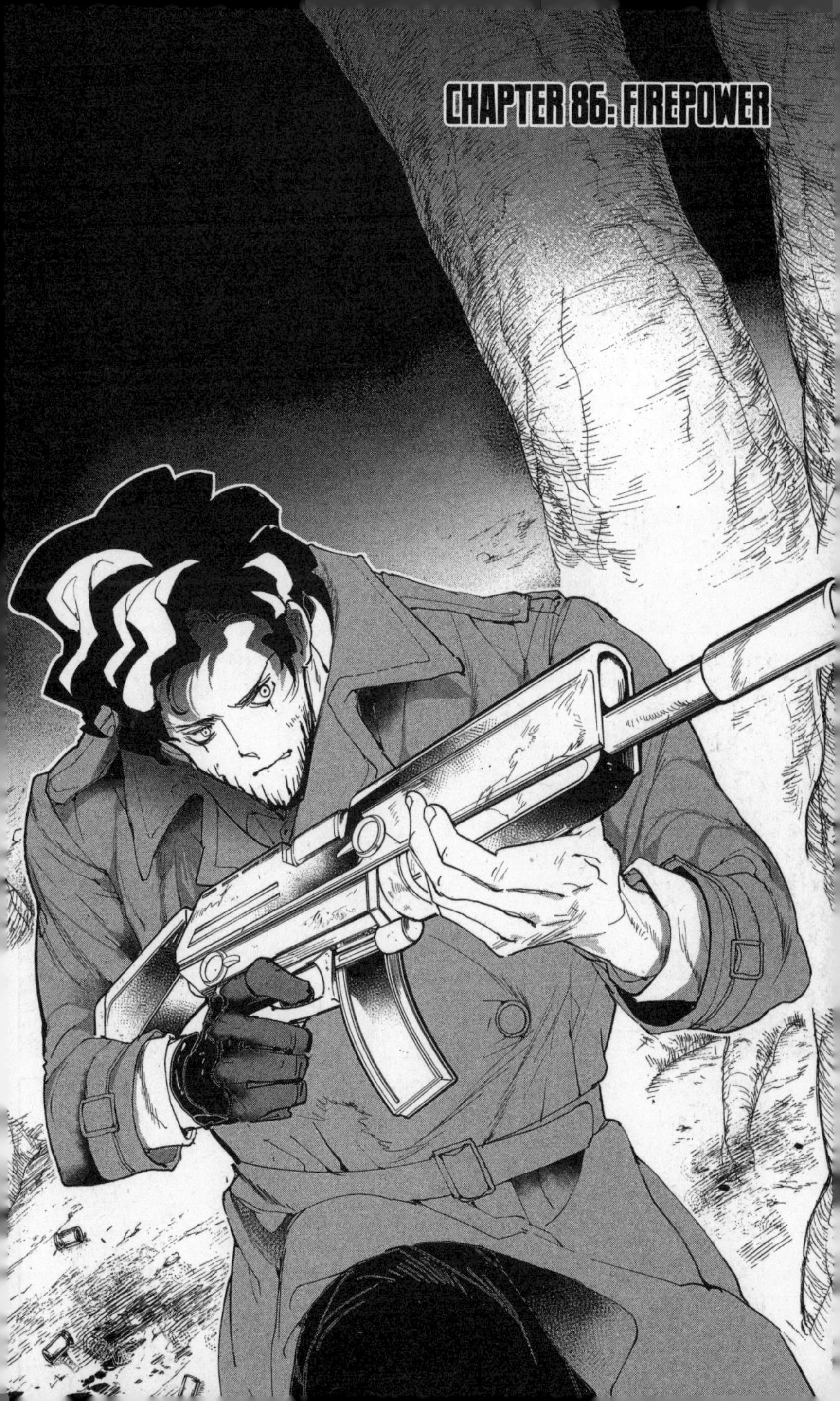
CHAPTER 86: FIREPOWER

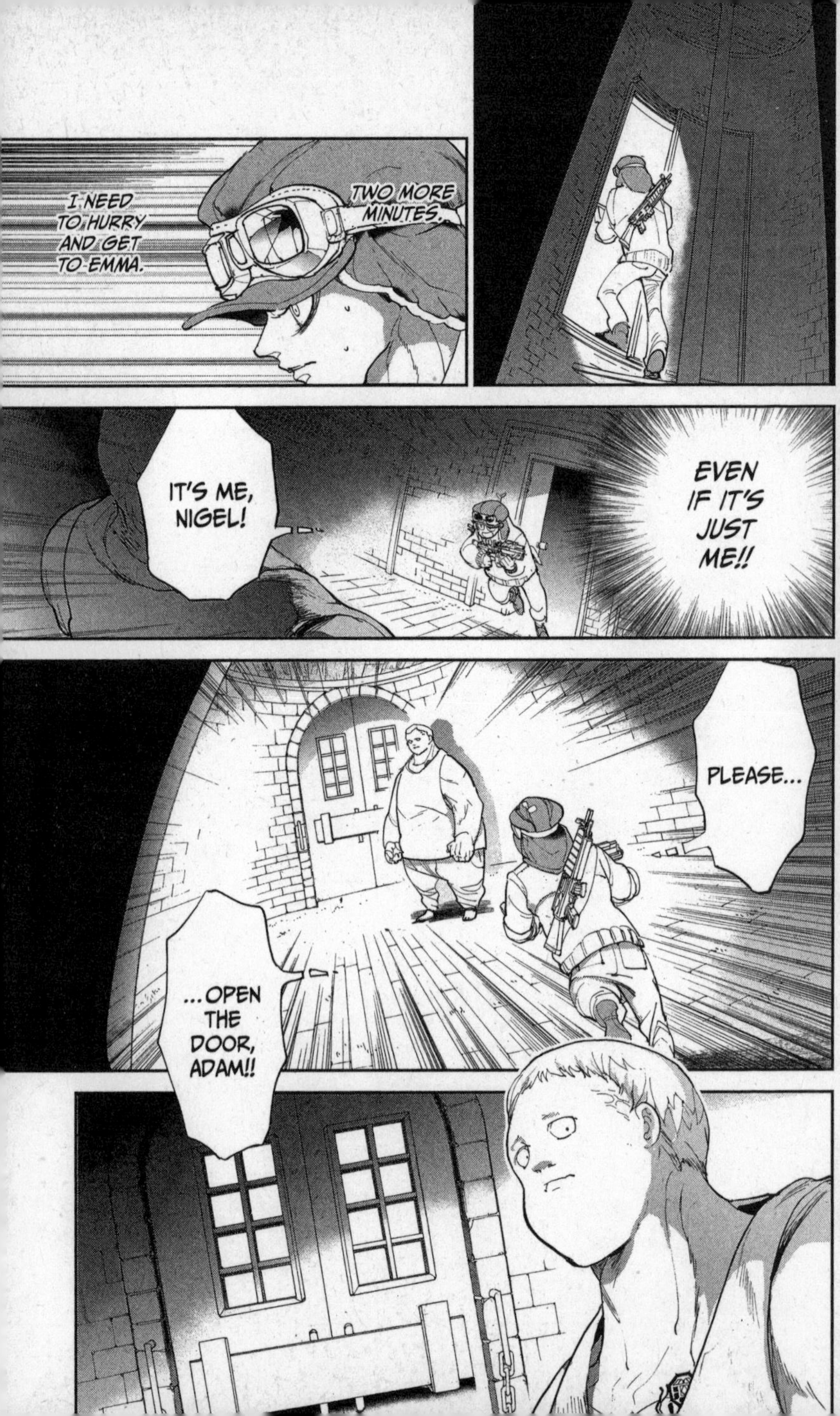
TWO MORE MINUTES.
I NEED TO HURRY AND GET TO EMMA.
EVEN IF IT'S JUST ME!!
IT'S ME, NIGEL!
PLEASE...
...OPEN THE DOOR, ADAM!!

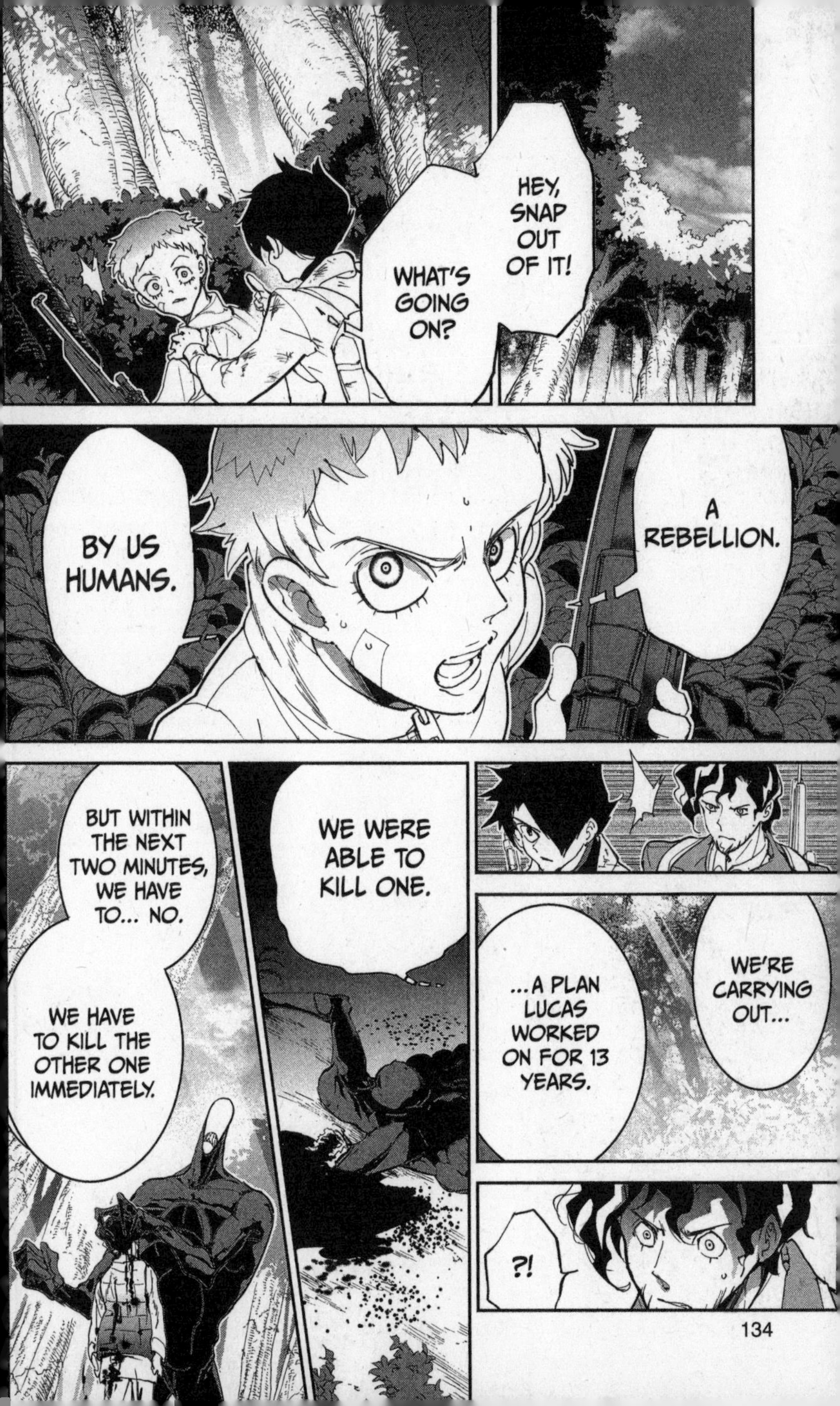
HEY, SNAP OUT OF IT!
WHAT'S GOING ON?
A REBELLION.
BY US HUMANS.
WE'RE CARRYING OUT...
...A PLAN LUCAS WORKED ON FOR 13 YEARS.
?!
WE WERE ABLE TO KILL ONE.
BUT WITHIN THE NEXT TWO MINUTES, WE HAVE TO... NO.
WE HAVE TO KILL THE OTHER ONE IMMEDIATELY.

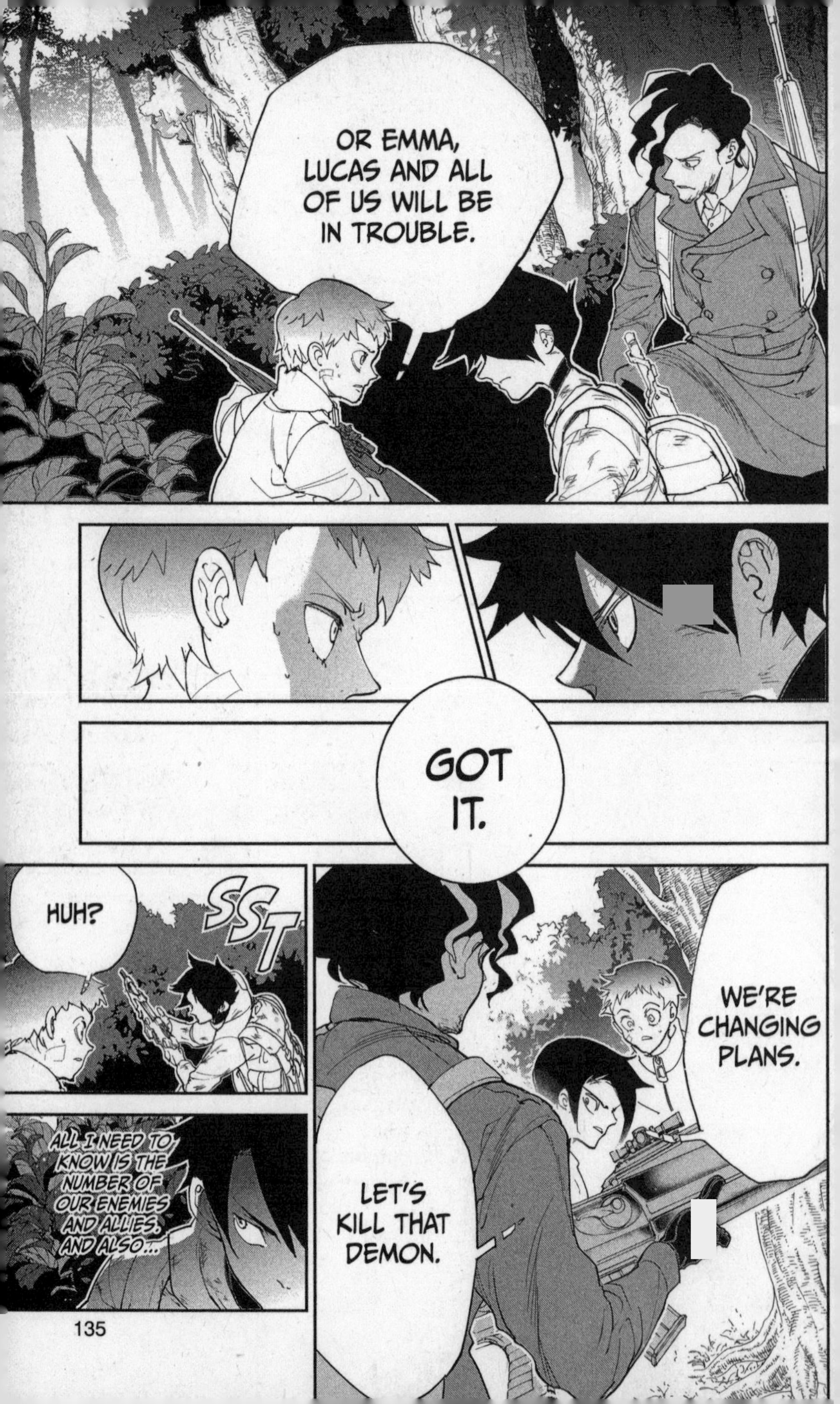
OR EMMA, LUCAS AND ALL OF US WILL BE IN TROUBLE.
GOT IT.
WE'RE CHANGING PLANS.
LET'S KILL THAT DEMON.
HUH?
SST
ALL I NEED TO KNOW IS THE NUMBER OF OUR ENEMIES AND ALLIES. AND ALSO...

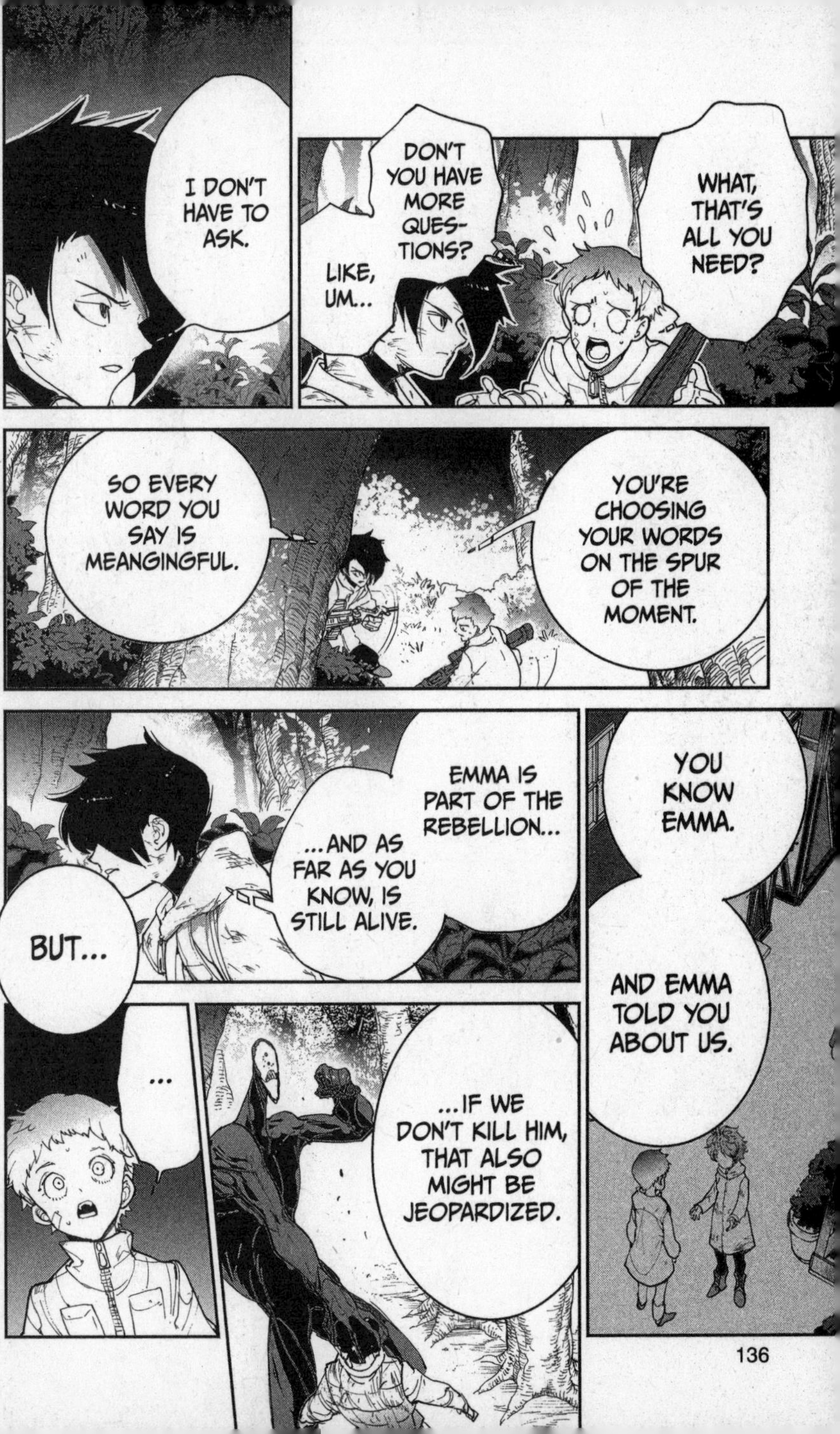
WHAT, THAT'S ALL YOU NEED?
DON'T YOU HAVE MORE QUES-TIONS?
LIKE, UM...
I DON'T HAVE TO ASK.
YOU'RE CHOOSING YOUR WORDS ON THE SPUR OF THE MOMENT.
SO EVERY WORD YOU SAY IS MEANGINGFUL.
YOU KNOW EMMA.
AND EMMA TOLD YOU ABOUT US.
EMMA IS PART OF THE REBELLION...
...AND AS FAR AS YOU KNOW, IS STILL ALIVE.
BUT...
...IF WE DON'T KILL HIM, THAT ALSO MIGHT BE JEOPARDIZED.
...

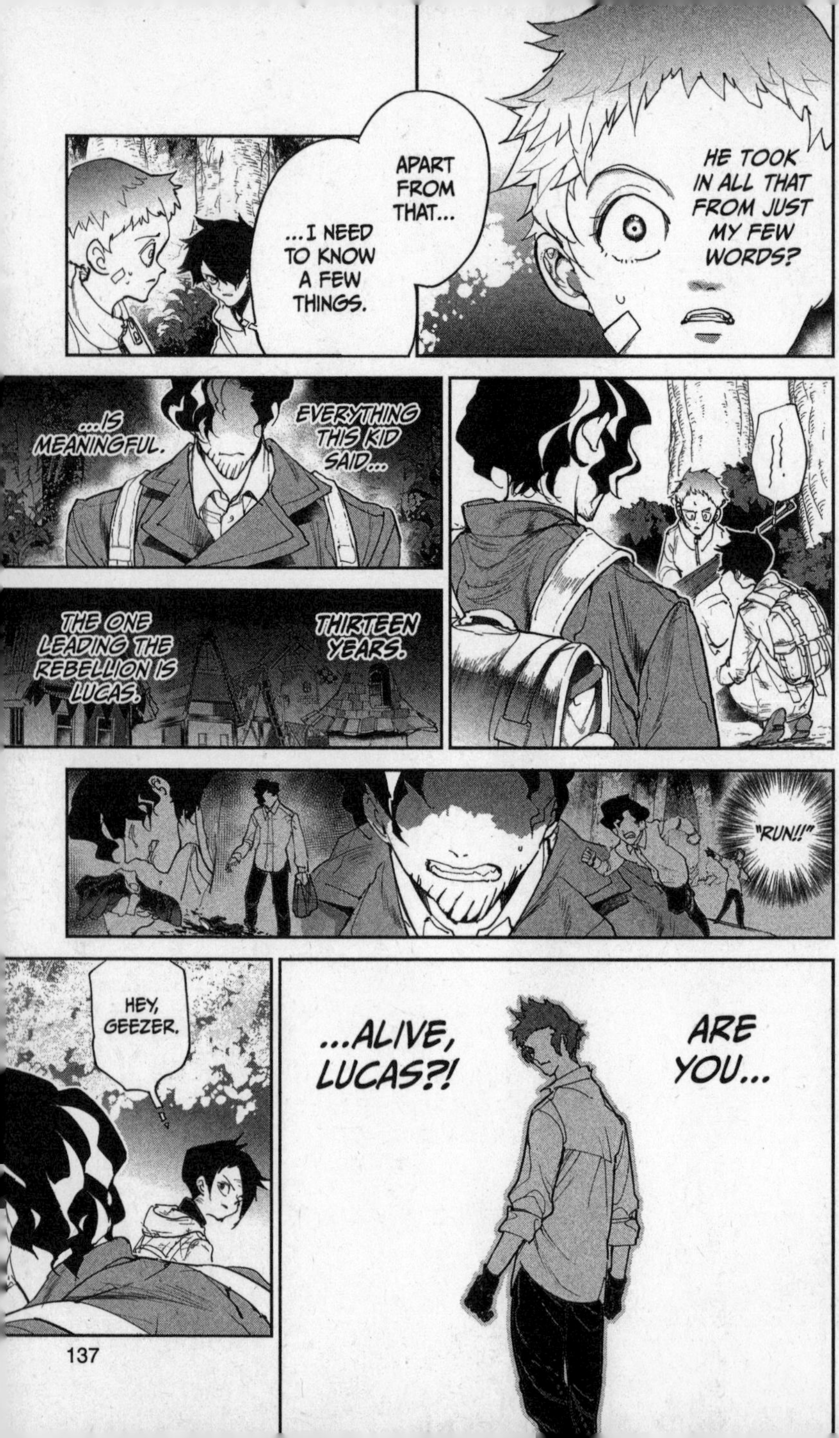
HE TOOK IN ALL THAT FROM JUST MY FEW WORDS?
APART FROM THAT...
...I NEED TO KNOW A FEW THINGS.
......
EVERYTHING THIS KID SAID...
...IS MEANINGFUL.
THIRTEEN YEARS.
THE ONE LEADING THE REBELLION IS LUCAS.
"RUN!!"
ARE YOU...
...ALIVE, LUCAS?!
HEY, GEEZER.

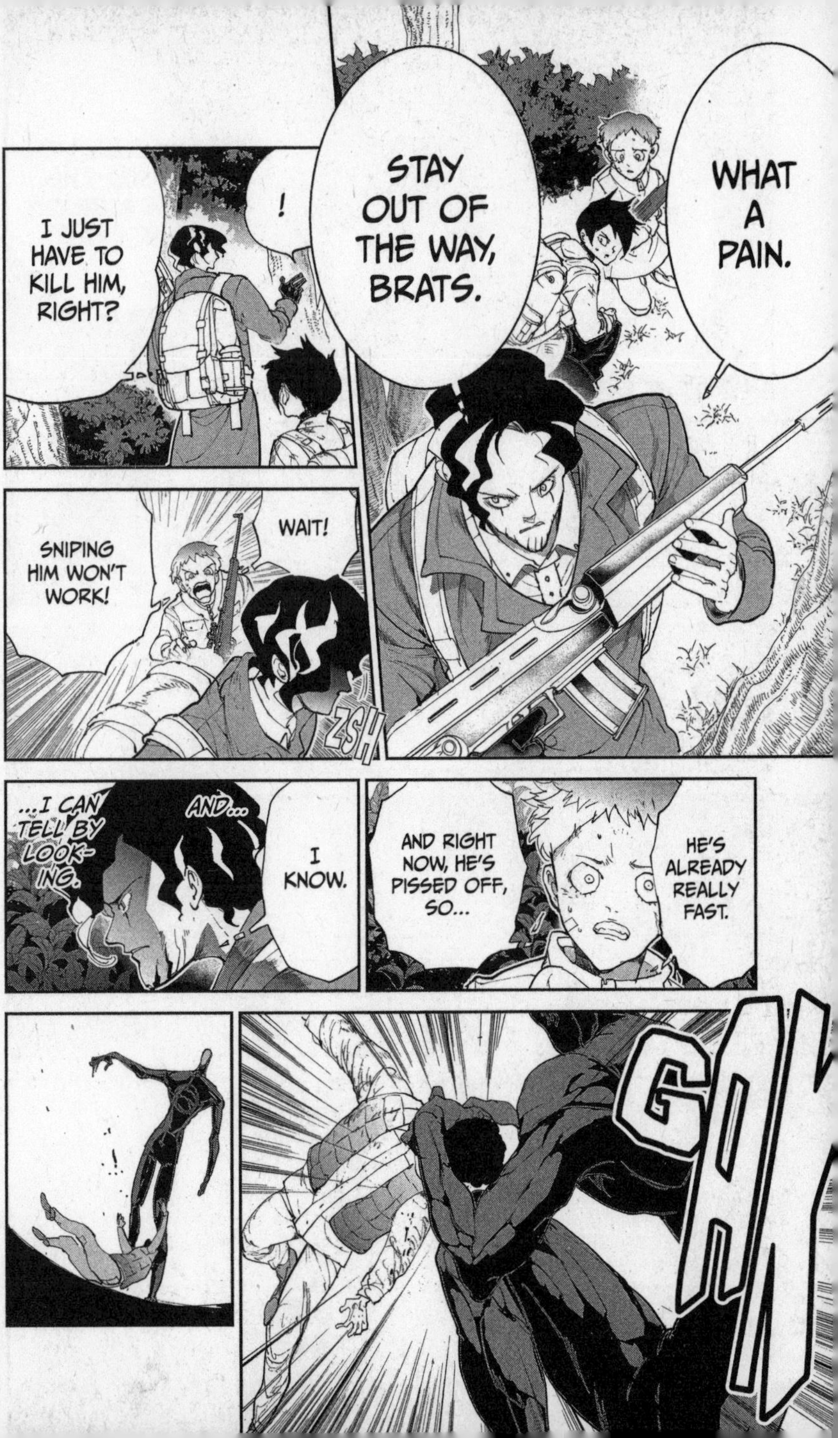
WHAT A PAIN.
STAY OUT OF THE WAY, BRATS.
!
I JUST HAVE TO KILL HIM, RIGHT?
WAIT!
SNIPING HIM WON'T WORK!
ZSH
HE'S ALREADY REALLY FAST.
AND RIGHT NOW, HE'S PISSED OFF, SO...
I KNOW.
AND...
...I CAN TELL BY LOOKING.
GA

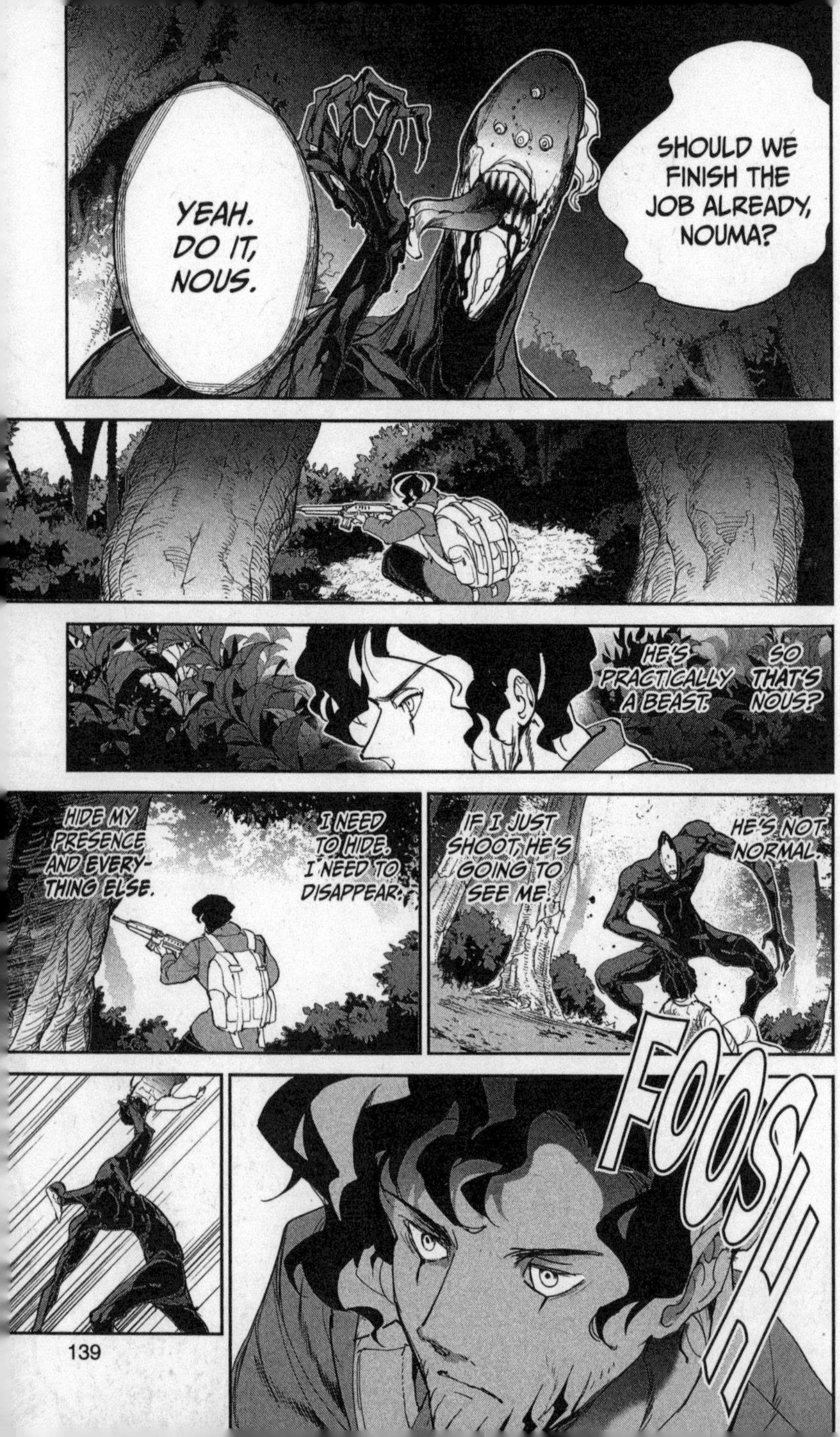
SHOULD WE FINISH THE JOB ALREADY, NOUMA?
YEAH. DO IT, NOUS.
SO THAT'S NOUS?
HE'S PRACTICALLY A BEAST.
HE'S NOT NORMAL.
IF I JUST SHOOT, HE'S GOING TO SEE ME.
I NEED TO HIDE. I NEED TO DISAPPEAR.
HIDE MY PRESENCE AND EVERY-THING ELSE.
FOOSH

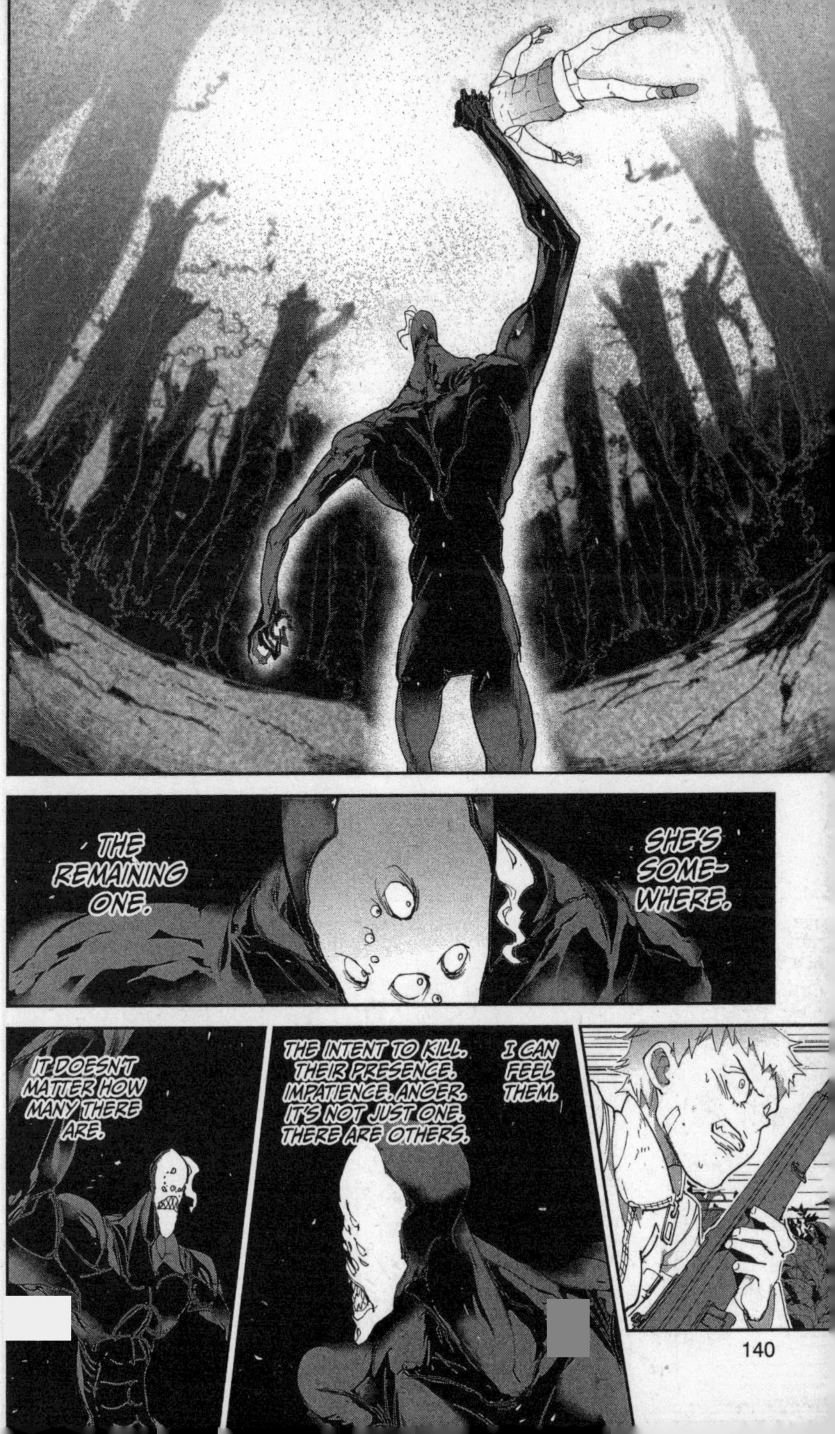
SHE'S SOME-WHERE.
THE REMAINING ONE.
I CAN FEEL THEM.
THE INTENT TO KILL. THEIR PRESENCE. IMPATIENCE. ANGER. IT'S NOT JUST ONE. THERE ARE OTHERS.
IT DOESN'T MATTER HOW MANY THERE ARE.

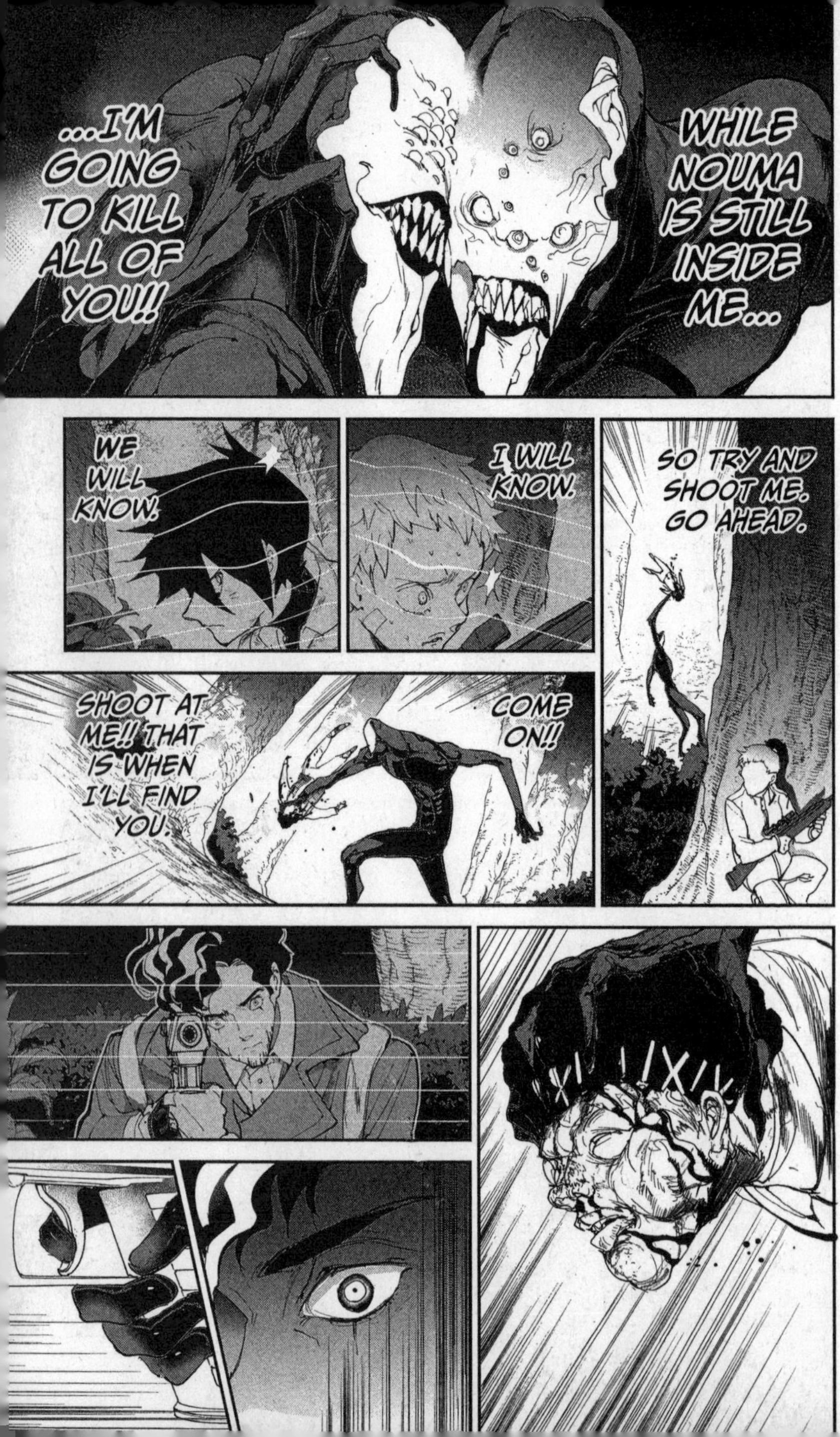
WHILE NOUMA IS STILL INSIDE ME...
...I'M GOING TO KILL ALL OF YOU!!
SO TRY AND SHOOT ME. GO AHEAD.
I WILL KNOW.
WE WILL KNOW.
COME ON!!
SHOOT AT ME!! THAT IS WHEN I'LL FIND YOU.

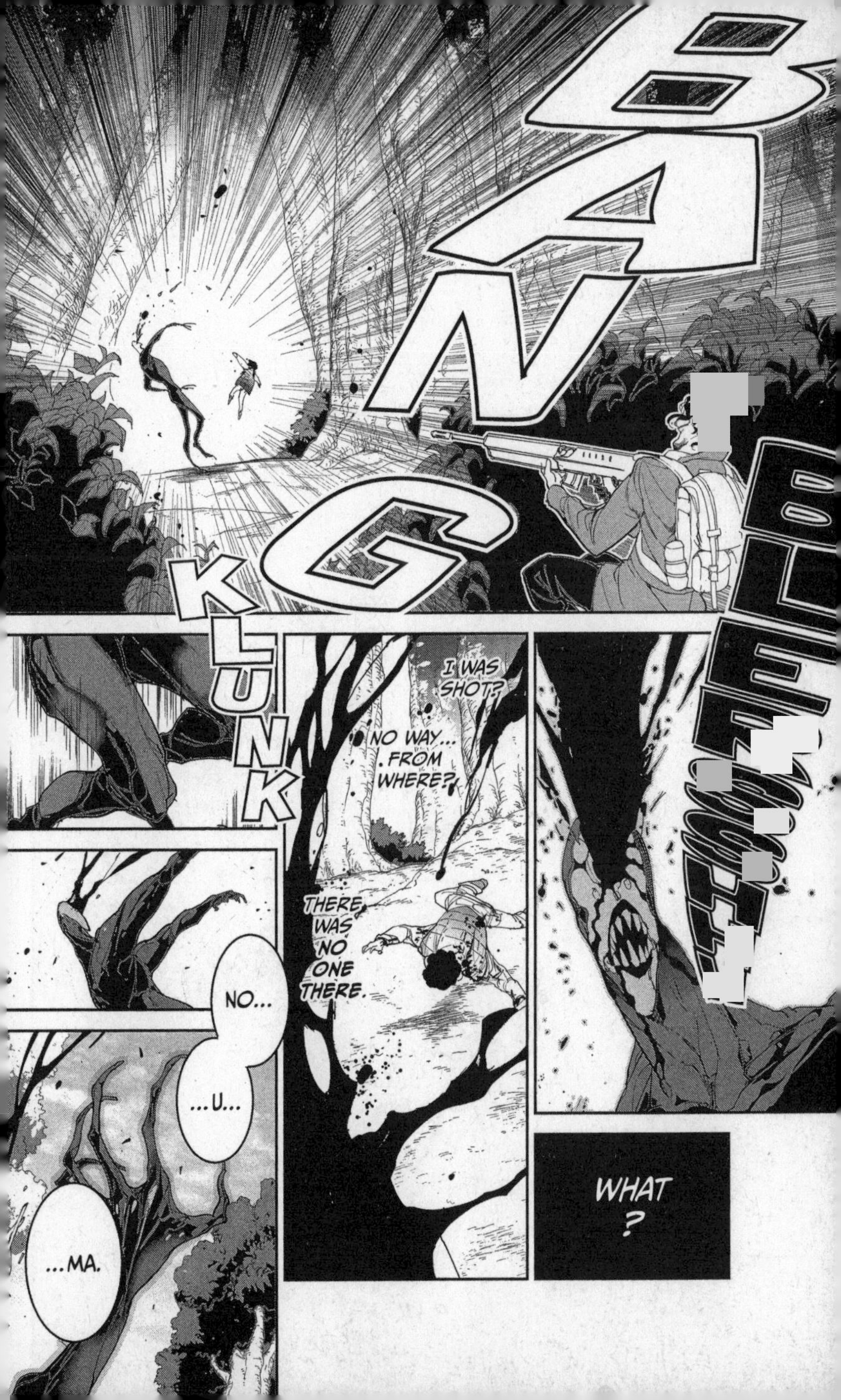
BANG
KLUNK
WHAT ?
I WAS SHOT?
NO WAY... FROM WHERE?
THERE WAS NO ONE THERE.
NO...
...U...
...MA.

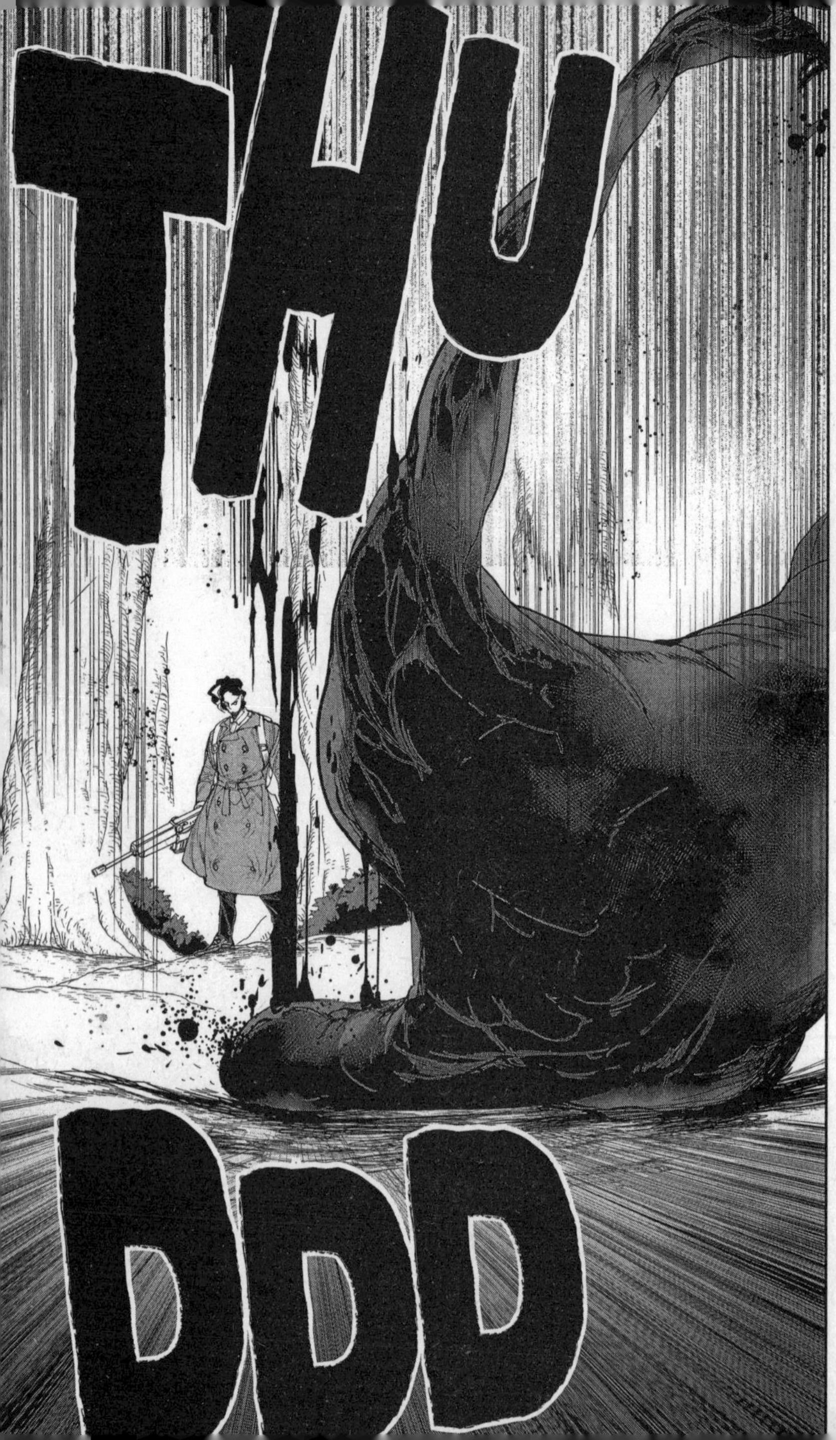
THUDDD

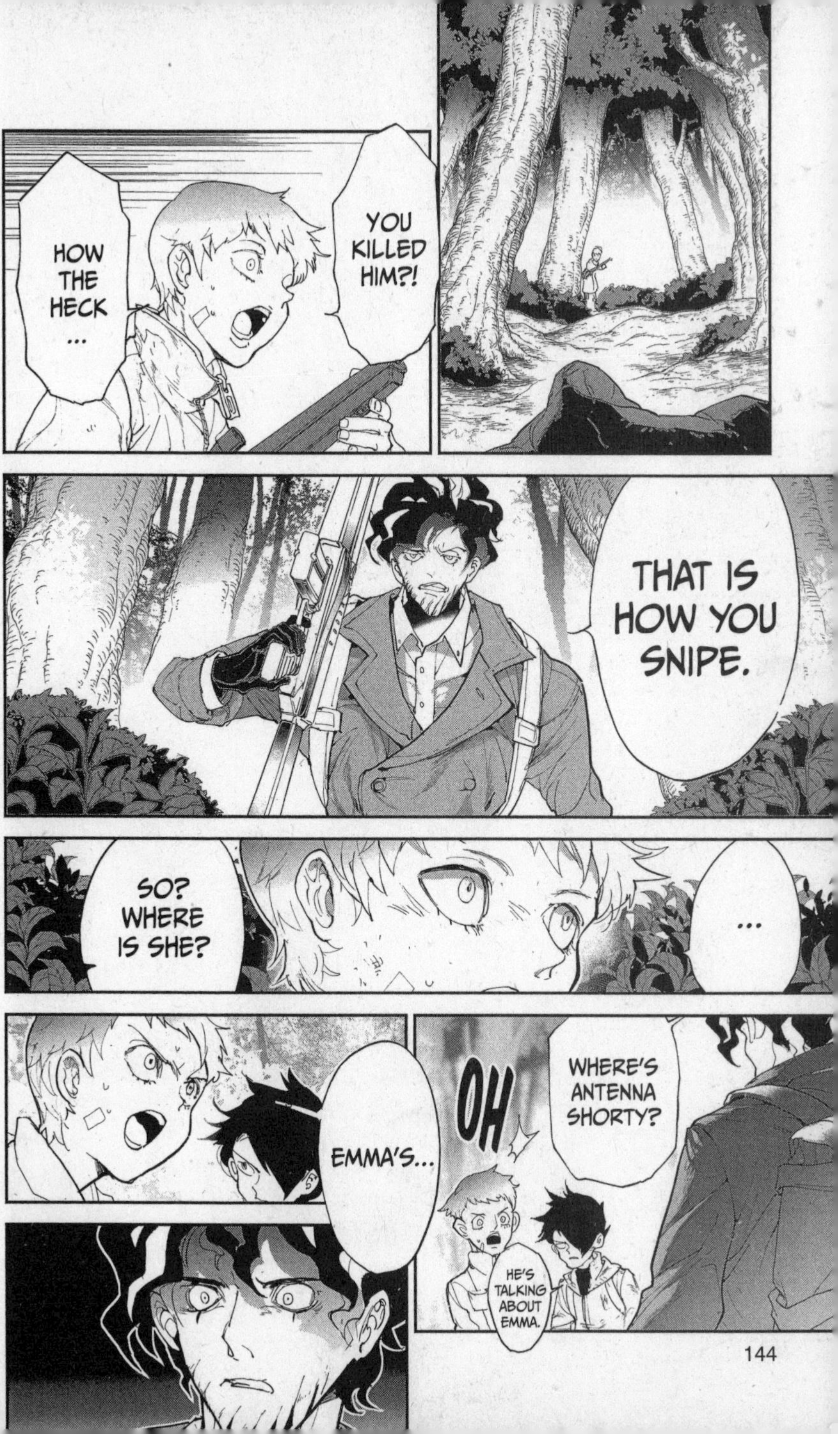
YOU KILLED HIM?!
HOW THE HECK ...
THAT IS HOW YOU SNIPE.
...
SO? WHERE IS SHE?
WHERE'S ANTENNA SHORTY?
OH
HE'S TALKING ABOUT EMMA.
EMMA'S...

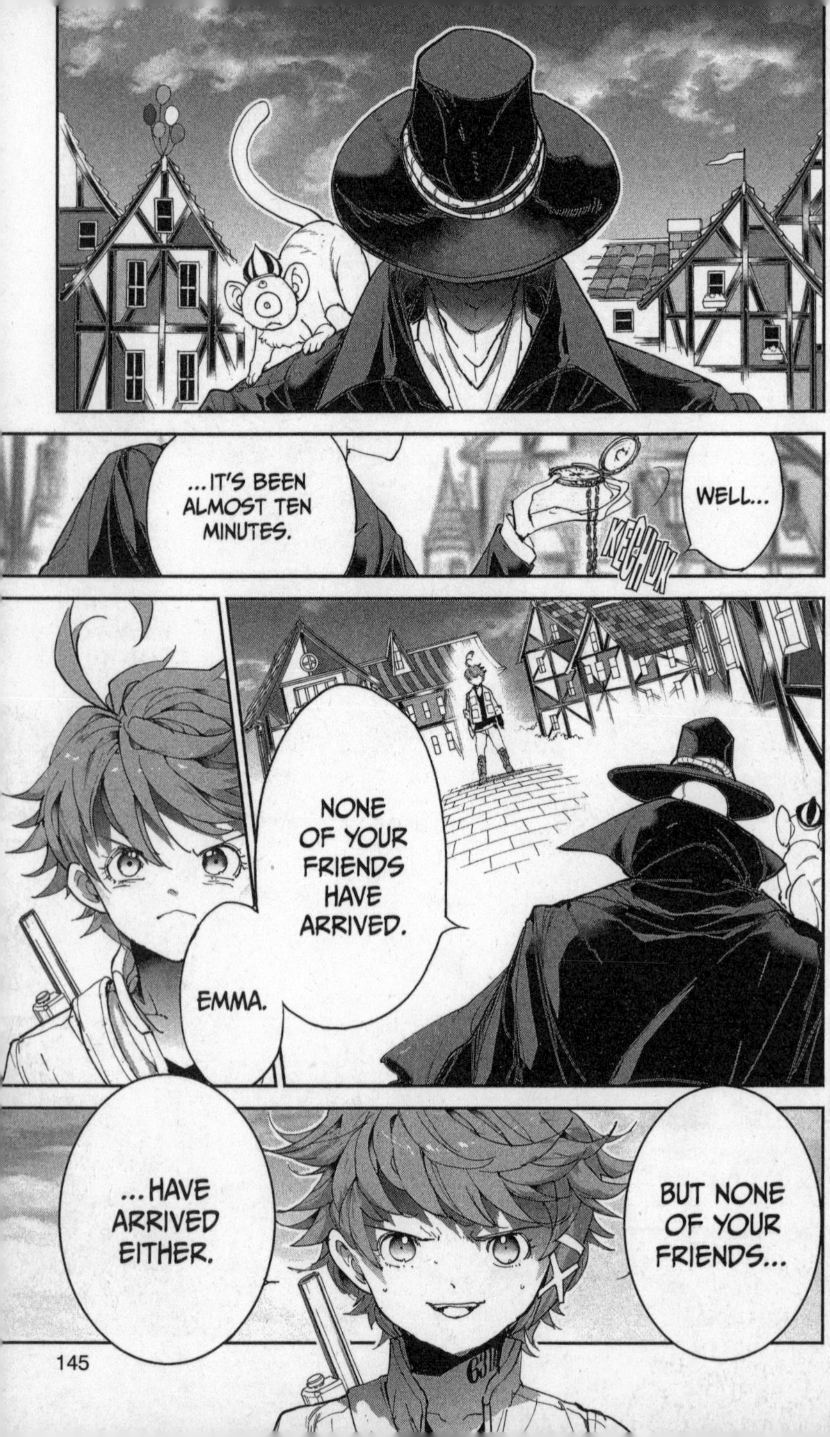
WELL...
KECHUK
...IT'S BEEN ALMOST TEN MINUTES.
NONE OF YOUR FRIENDS HAVE ARRIVED.
EMMA.
BUT NONE OF YOUR FRIENDS...
...HAVE ARRIVED EITHER.

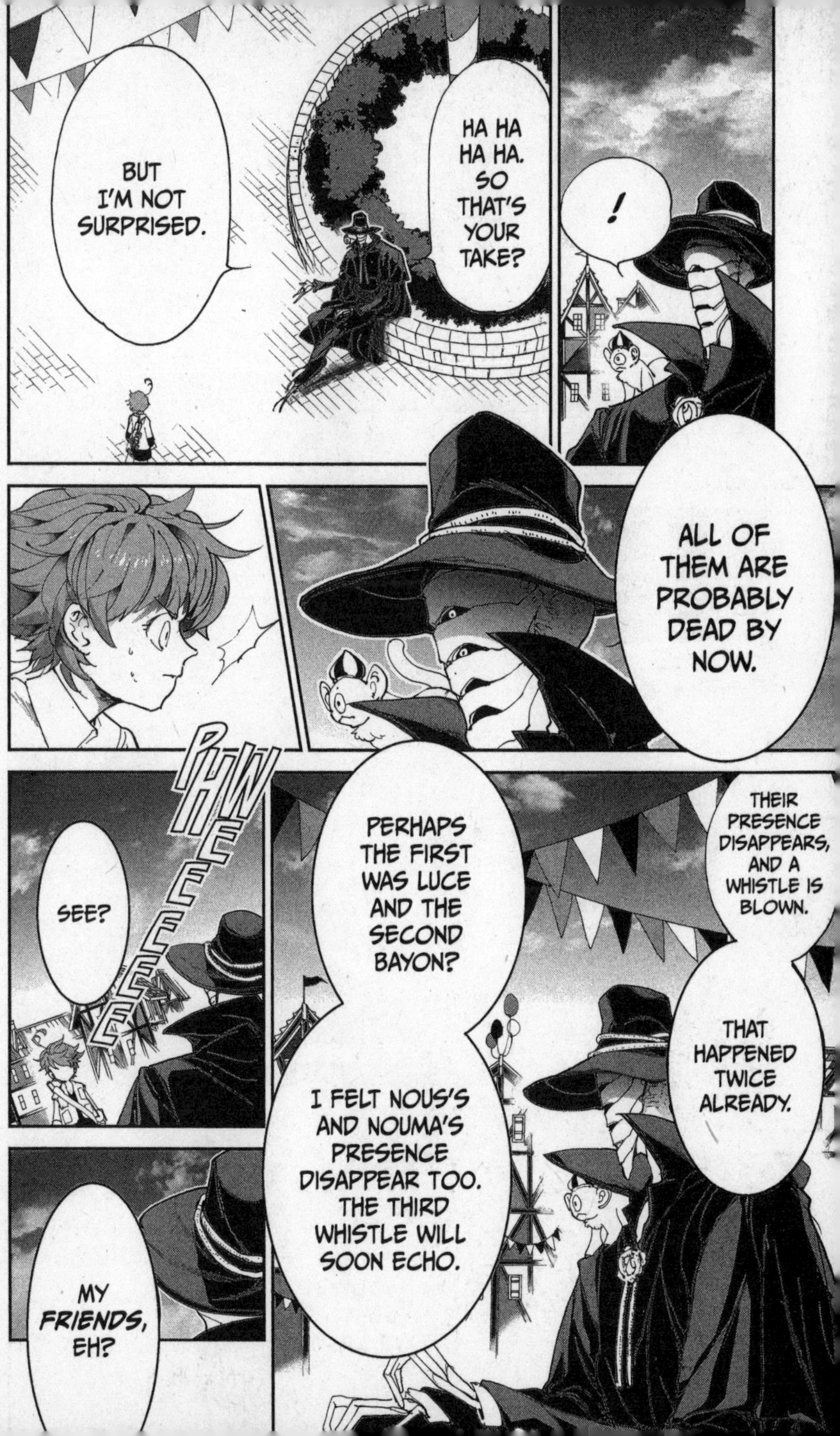
!
HA HA HA HA. SO THAT'S YOUR TAKE?
BUT I'M NOT SURPRISED.
ALL OF THEM ARE PROBABLY DEAD BY NOW.
THEIR PRESENCE DISAPPEARS, AND A WHISTLE IS BLOWN.
THAT HAPPENED TWICE ALREADY.
PERHAPS THE FIRST WAS LUCE AND THE SECOND BAYON?
I FELT NOUS'S AND NOUMA'S PRESENCE DISAPPEAR TOO. THE THIRD WHISTLE WILL SOON ECHO.
SEE?
PHWEEEEEE
MY FRIENDS, EH?

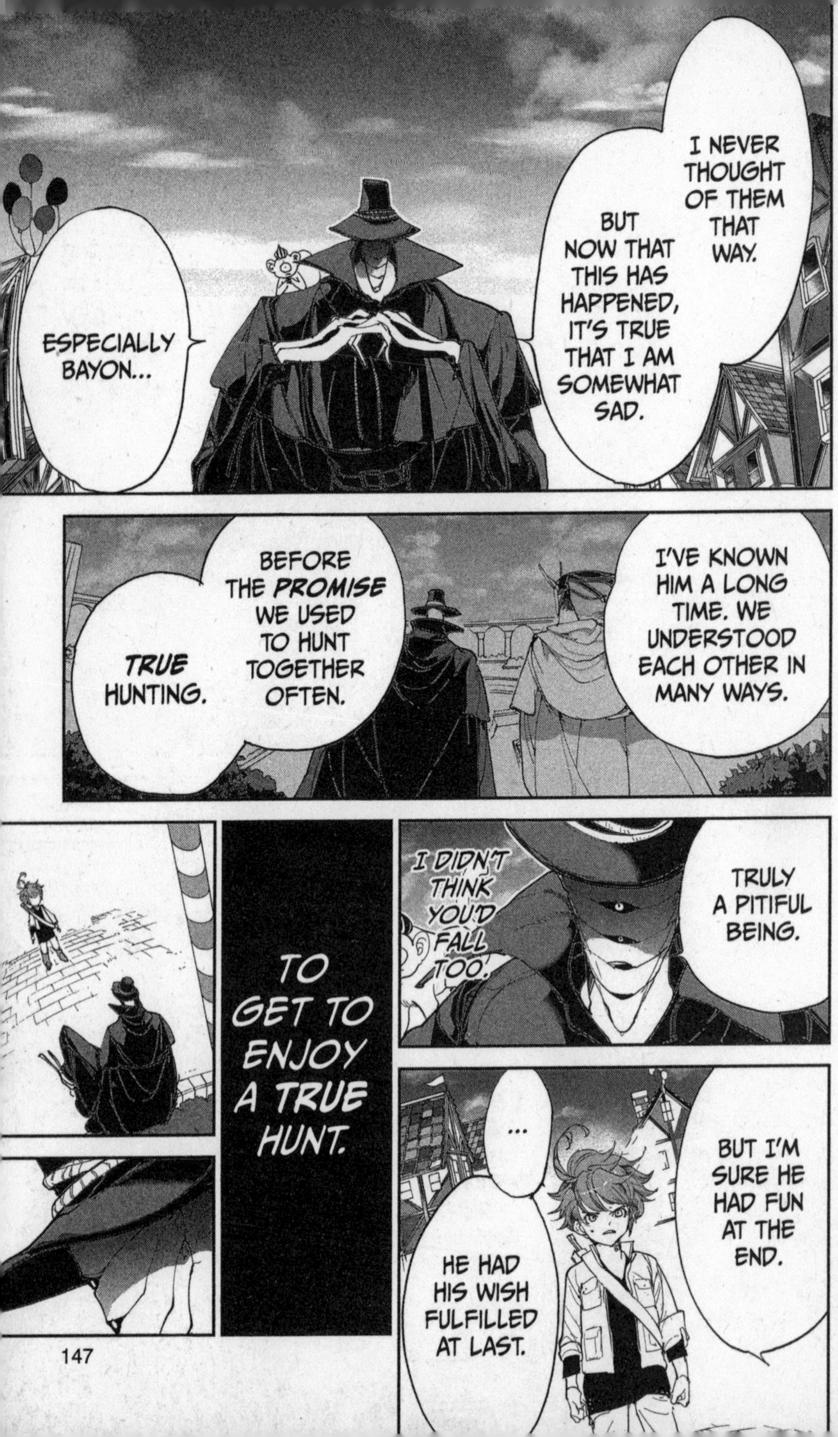

I NEVER THOUGHT OF THEM THAT WAY.
BUT NOW THAT THIS HAS HAPPENED, IT'S TRUE THAT I AM SOMEWHAT SAD.
ESPECIALLY BAYON...
I'VE KNOWN HIM A LONG TIME. WE UNDERSTOOD EACH OTHER IN MANY WAYS.
BEFORE THE *PROMISE* WE USED TO HUNT TOGETHER OFTEN.
TRUE HUNTING.
TRULY A PITIFUL BEING.
I DIDN'T THINK YOU'D FALL TOO.
BUT I'M SURE HE HAD FUN AT THE END.
...
HE HAD HIS WISH FULFILLED AT LAST.
TO GET TO ENJOY A TRUE HUNT.

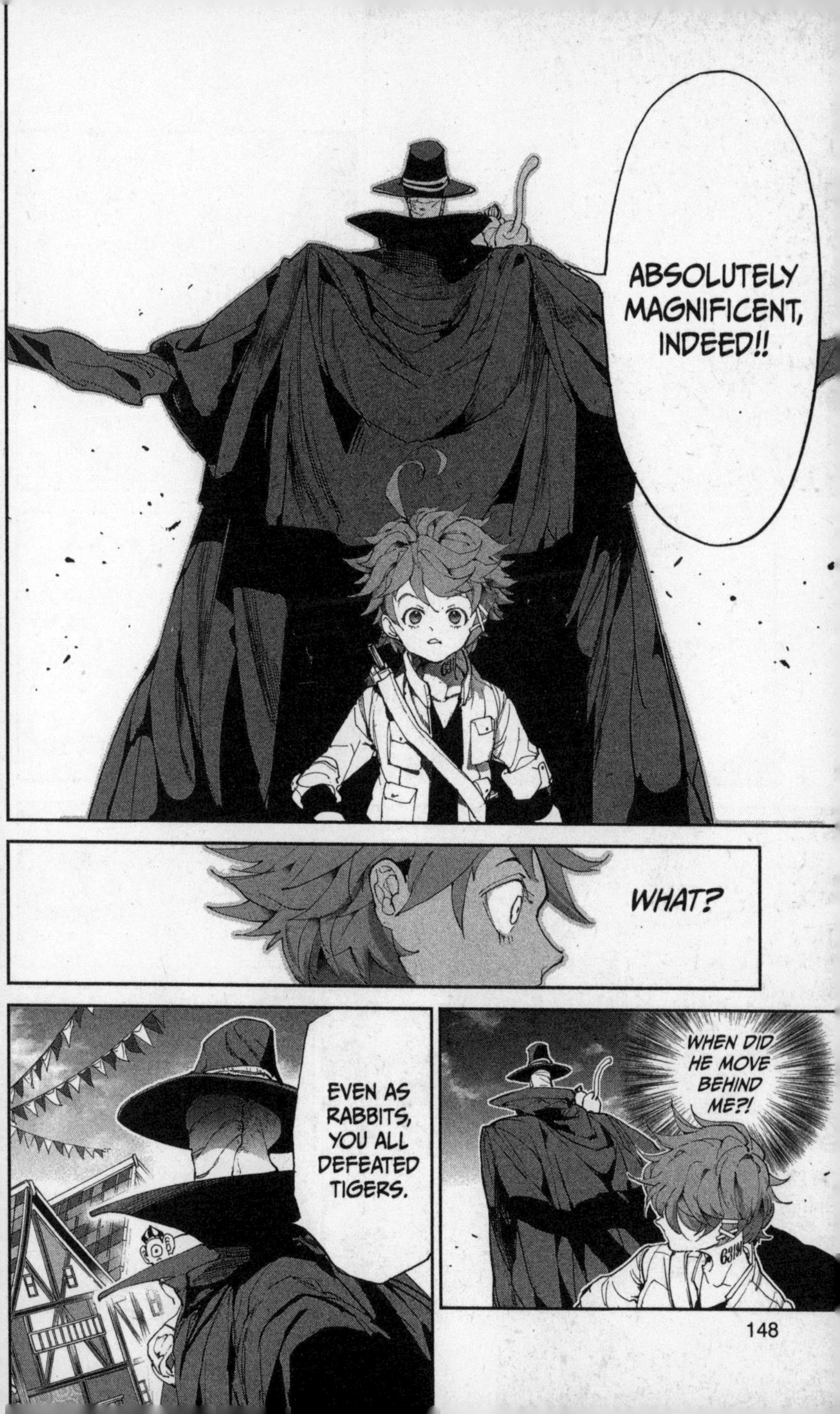
ABSOLUTELY MAGNIFICENT, INDEED!!
WHAT?
WHEN DID HE MOVE BEHIND ME?!
EVEN AS RABBITS, YOU ALL DEFEATED TIGERS.

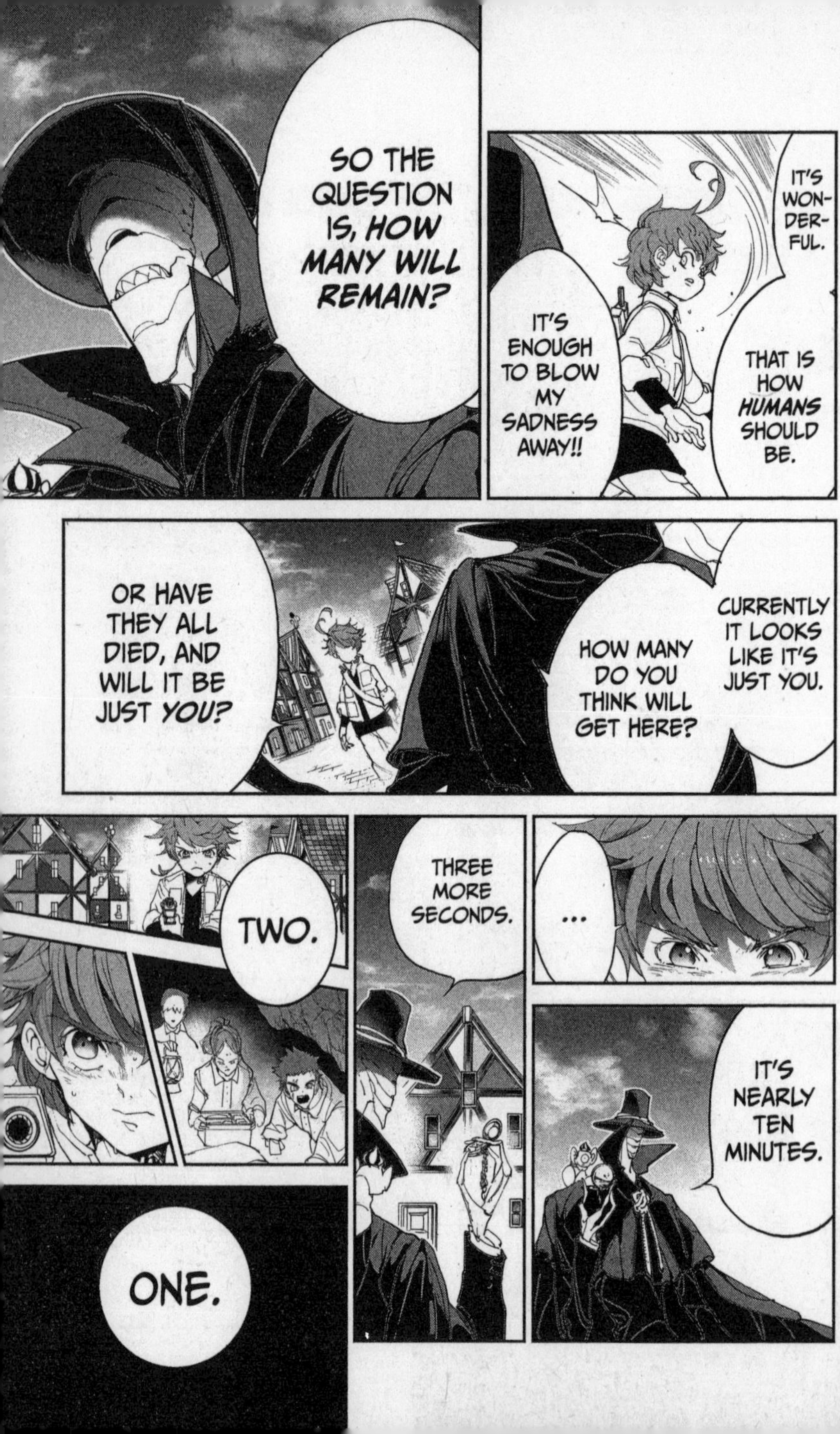
IT'S WON-DER-FUL.
THAT IS HOW *HUMANS* SHOULD BE.
IT'S ENOUGH TO BLOW MY SADNESS AWAY!!
SO THE QUESTION IS, *HOW MANY WILL REMAIN?*
CURRENTLY IT LOOKS LIKE IT'S JUST YOU.
HOW MANY DO YOU THINK WILL GET HERE?
OR HAVE THEY ALL DIED, AND WILL IT BE JUST *YOU?*
...
IT'S NEARLY TEN MINUTES.
THREE MORE SECONDS.
TWO.
ONE.

SEASIDE VENDOR 2

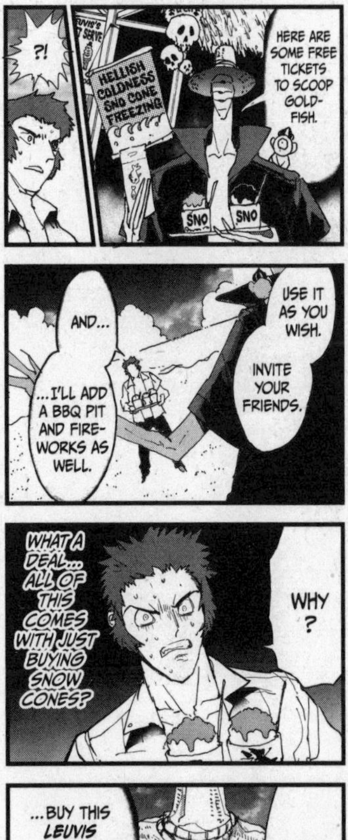
HERE ARE SOME FREE TICKETS TO SCOOP GOLD-FISH.
?!
HELLISH COLDNESS SNO CONE FREEZING
SNO
SNO
USE IT AS YOU WISH.
INVITE YOUR FRIENDS.
AND...
...I'LL ADD A BBQ PIT AND FIRE-WORKS AS WELL.
WHY ?
WHAT A DEAL... ALL OF THIS COMES WITH JUST BUYING SNOW CONES?
FOR A THRILLING EXPERI-ENCE...
...BUY THIS LEUVIS SUMMER ENJOYMENT SET FOR JUST FIVE EASY PAYMENTS OF 360 YEN.
HANABI
SST
SST

NOT JUST A DREAM

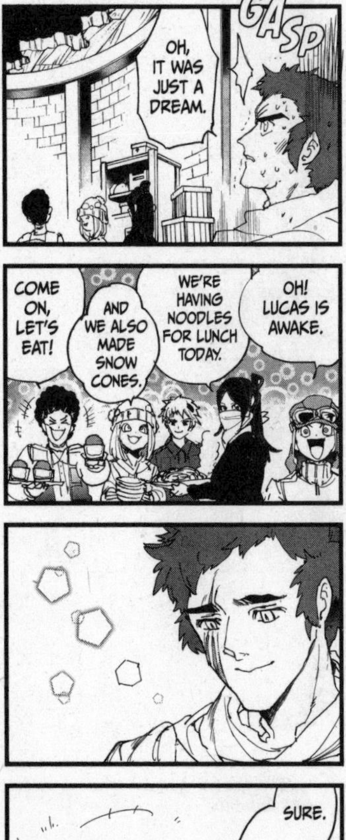
GASP
OH, IT WAS JUST A DREAM.
OH! LUCAS IS AWAKE.
WE'RE HAVING NOODLES FOR LUNCH TODAY.
AND WE ALSO MADE SNOW CONES.
COME ON, LET'S EAT!
SURE.
THANKS.

SIDE STORY 7 FIN

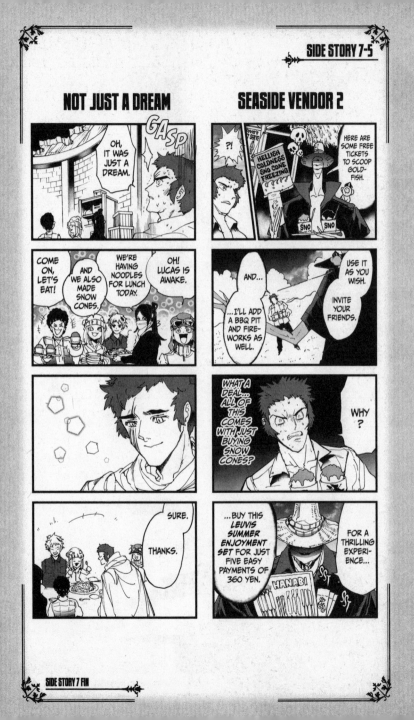

CHAPTER 87: BOUNDARY

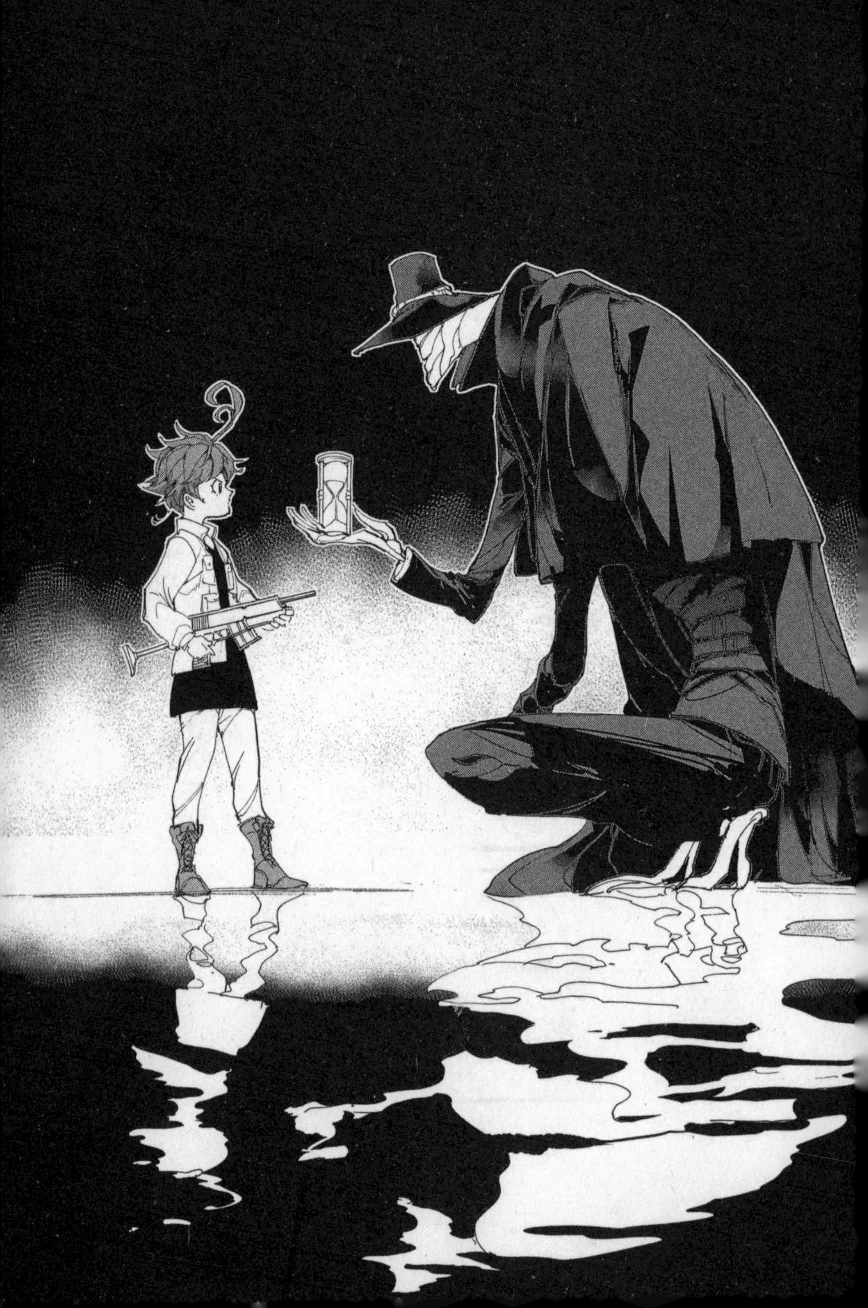

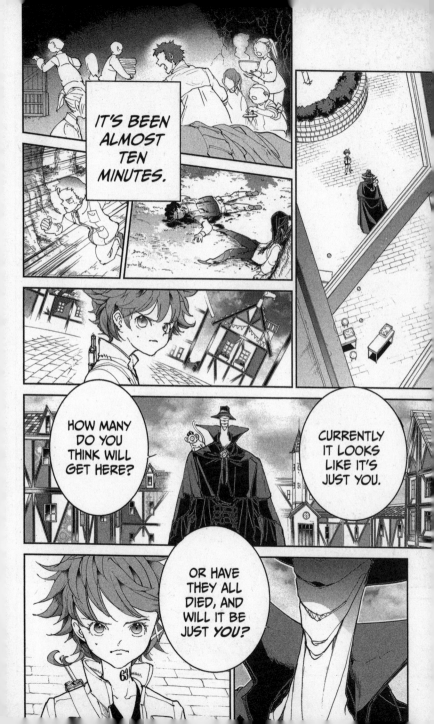

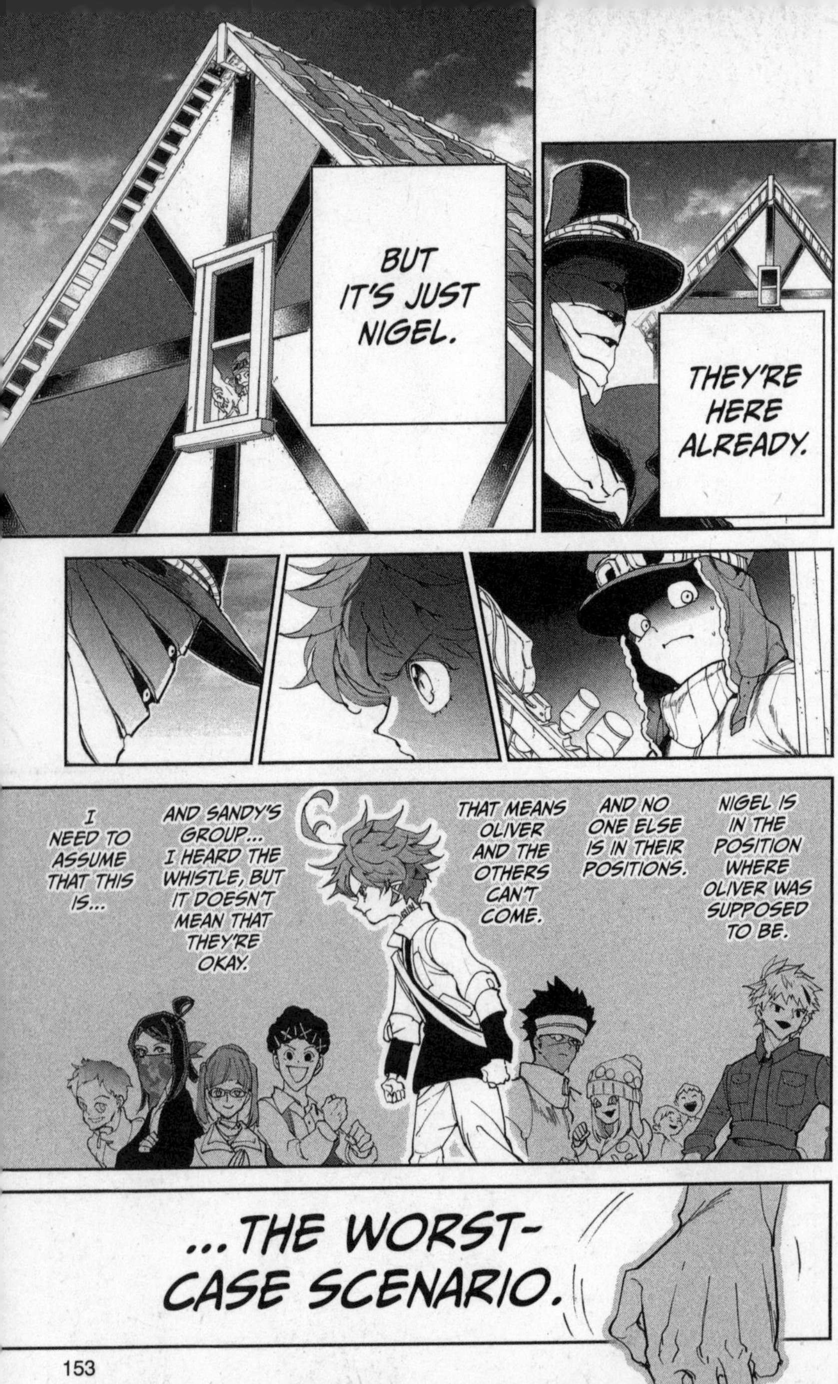
THEY'RE HERE ALREADY.
BUT IT'S JUST NIGEL.
NIGEL IS IN THE POSITION WHERE OLIVER WAS SUPPOSED TO BE.
AND NO ONE ELSE IS IN THEIR POSITIONS.
THAT MEANS OLIVER AND THE OTHERS CAN'T COME.
AND SANDY'S GROUP... I HEARD THE WHISTLE, BUT IT DOESN'T MEAN THAT THEY'RE OKAY.
I NEED TO ASSUME THAT THIS IS...
...THE WORST-CASE SCENARIO.

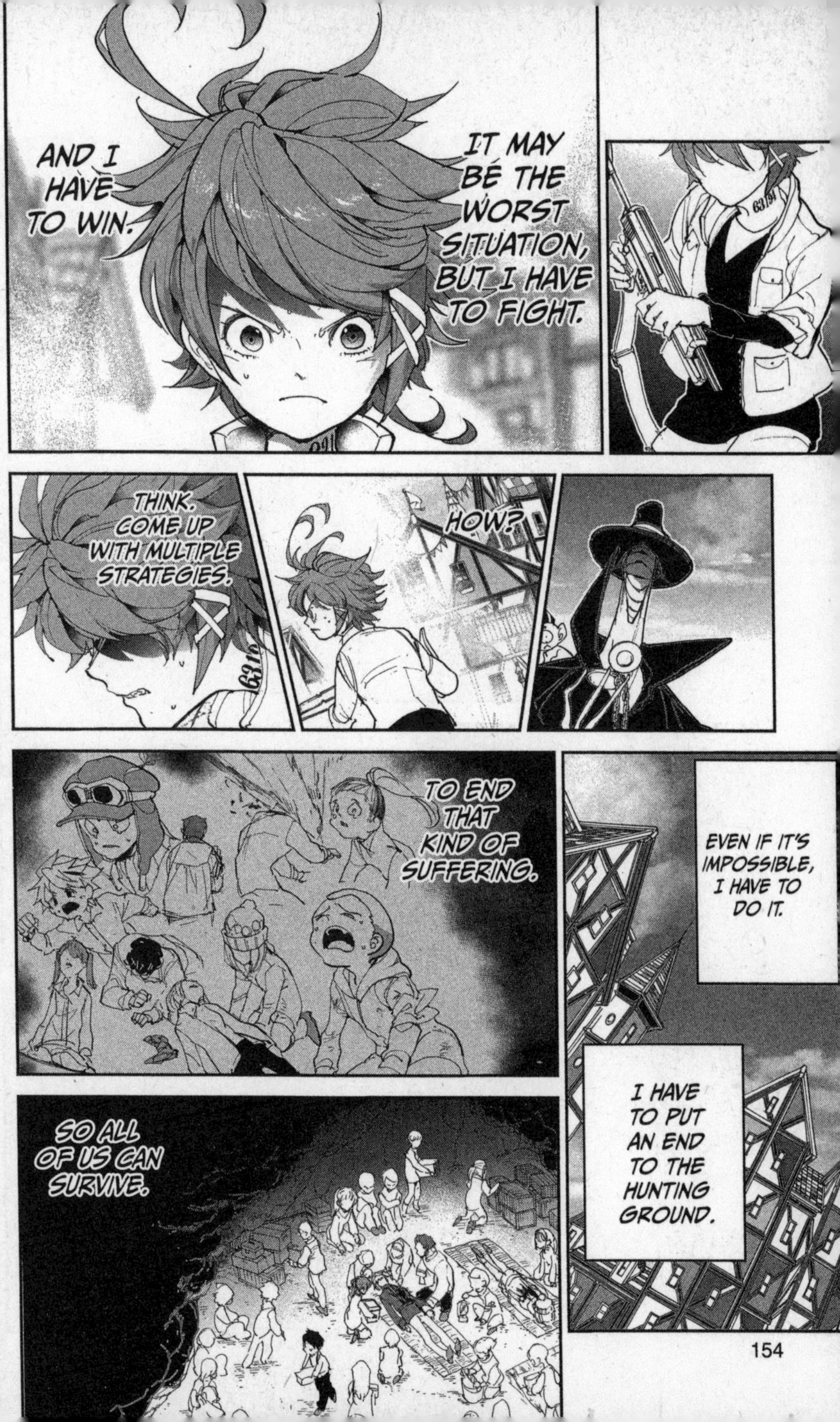
IT MAY BE THE WORST SITUATION, BUT I HAVE TO FIGHT.
AND I HAVE TO WIN.
HOW?
THINK. COME UP WITH MULTIPLE STRATEGIES.
EVEN IF IT'S IMPOSSIBLE, I HAVE TO DO IT.
I HAVE TO PUT AN END TO THE HUNTING GROUND.
TO END THAT KIND OF SUFFERING.
SO ALL OF US CAN SURVIVE.

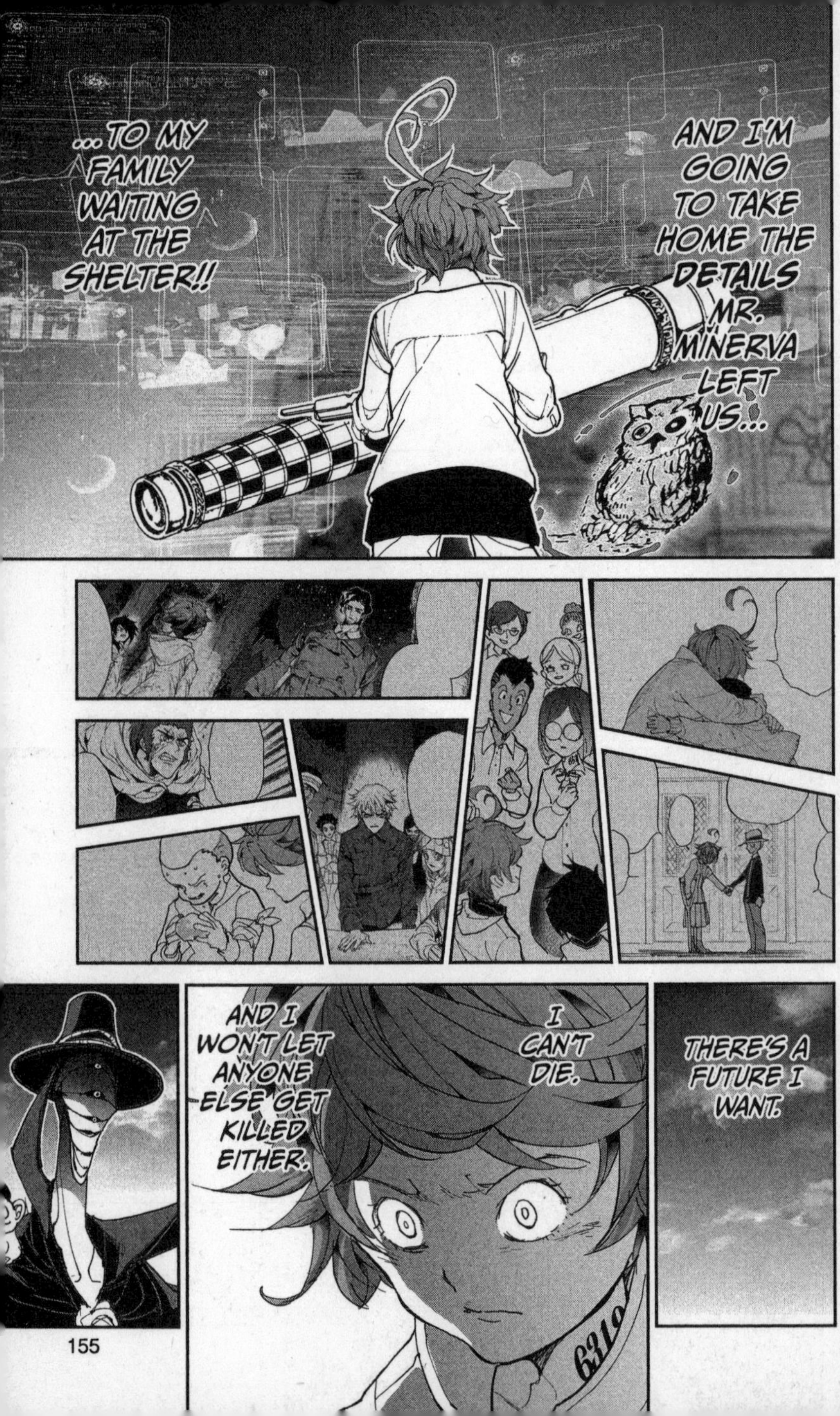
AND I'M GOING TO TAKE HOME THE DETAILS MR. MINERVA LEFT US...
...TO MY FAMILY WAITING AT THE SHELTER!!
THERE'S A FUTURE I WANT.
I CAN'T DIE.
AND I WON'T LET ANYONE ELSE GET KILLED EITHER.

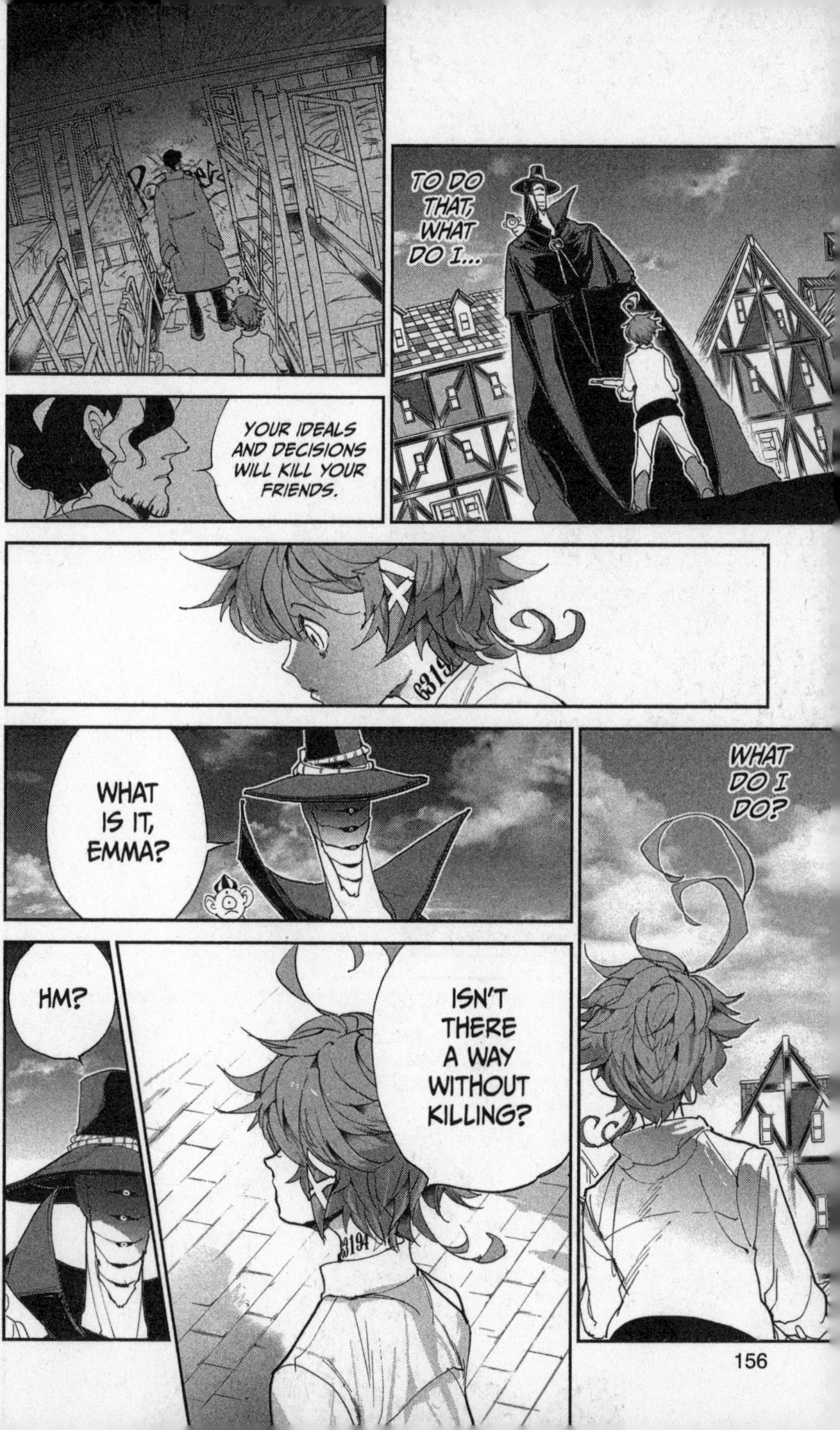
TO DO THAT, WHAT DO I...
YOUR IDEALS AND DECISIONS WILL KILL YOUR FRIENDS.
WHAT DO I DO?
WHAT IS IT, EMMA?
ISN'T THERE A WAY WITHOUT KILLING?
HM?

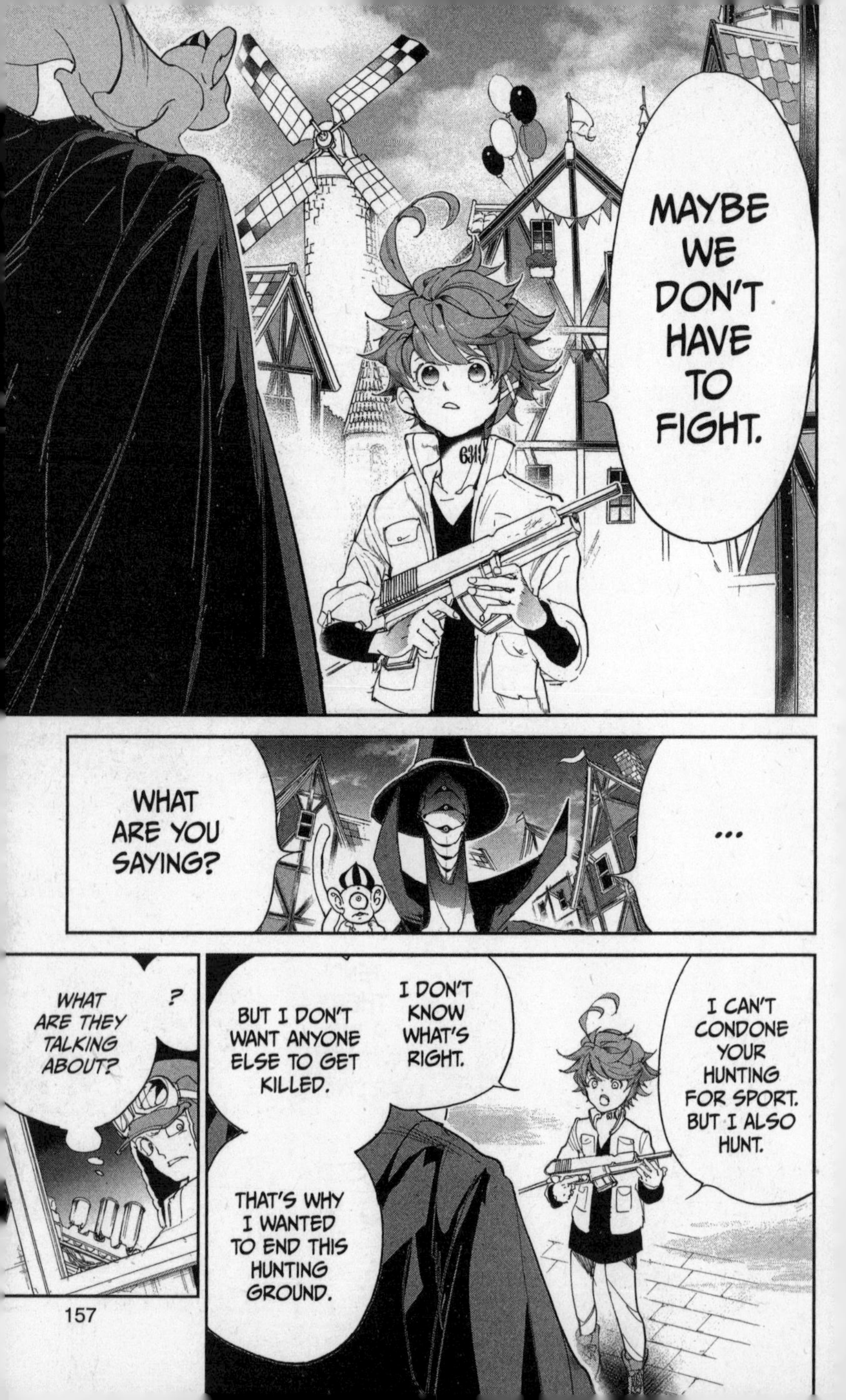
MAYBE WE DON'T HAVE TO FIGHT.
...
WHAT ARE YOU SAYING?
I CAN'T CONDONE YOUR HUNTING FOR SPORT. BUT I ALSO HUNT.
I DON'T KNOW WHAT'S RIGHT.
BUT I DON'T WANT ANYONE ELSE TO GET KILLED.
THAT'S WHY I WANTED TO END THIS HUNTING GROUND.
?
WHAT ARE THEY TALKING ABOUT?

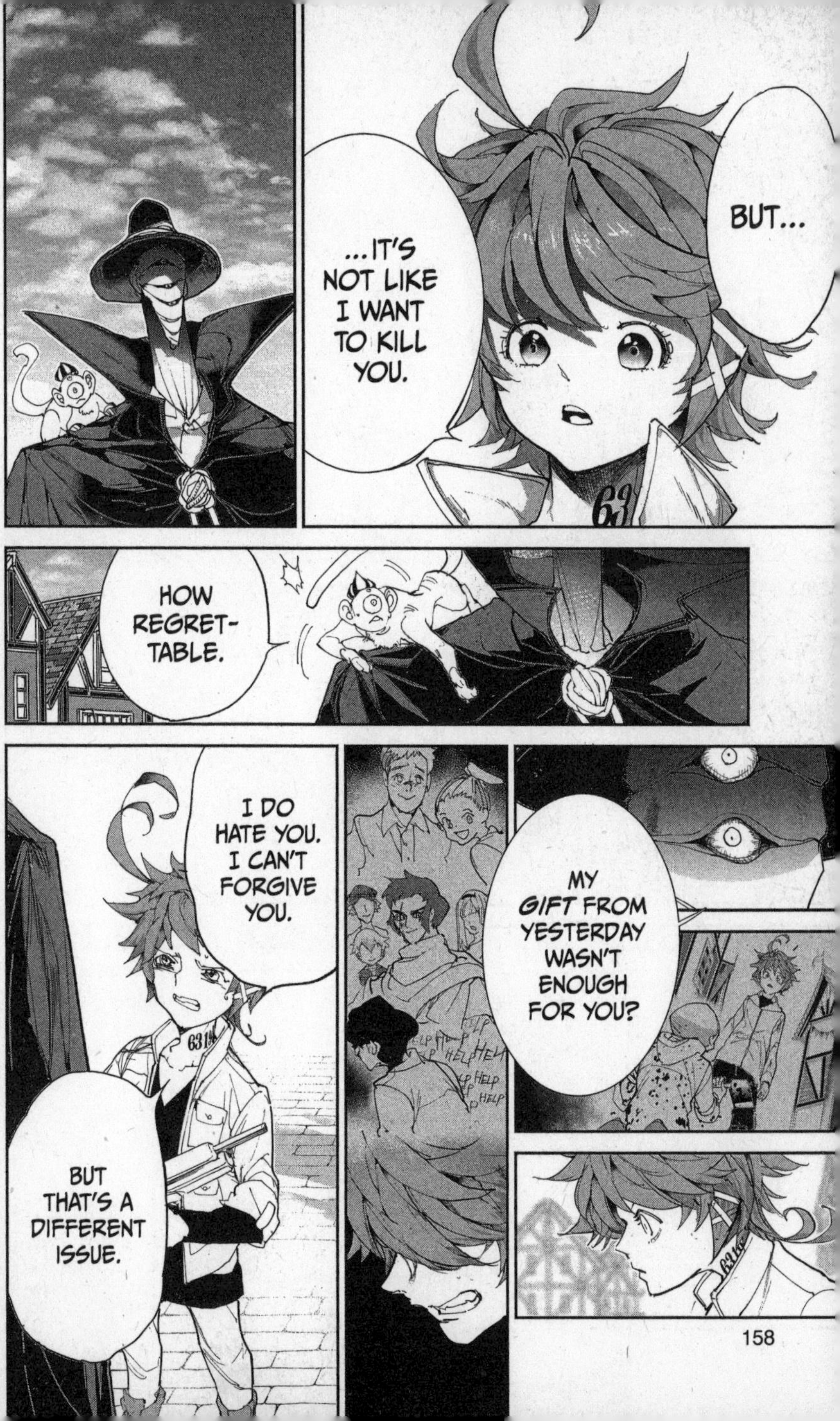
BUT...
...IT'S NOT LIKE I WANT TO KILL YOU.
HOW REGRET-TABLE.
MY GIFT FROM YESTERDAY WASN'T ENOUGH FOR YOU?
I DO HATE YOU. I CAN'T FORGIVE YOU.
BUT THAT'S A DIFFERENT ISSUE.

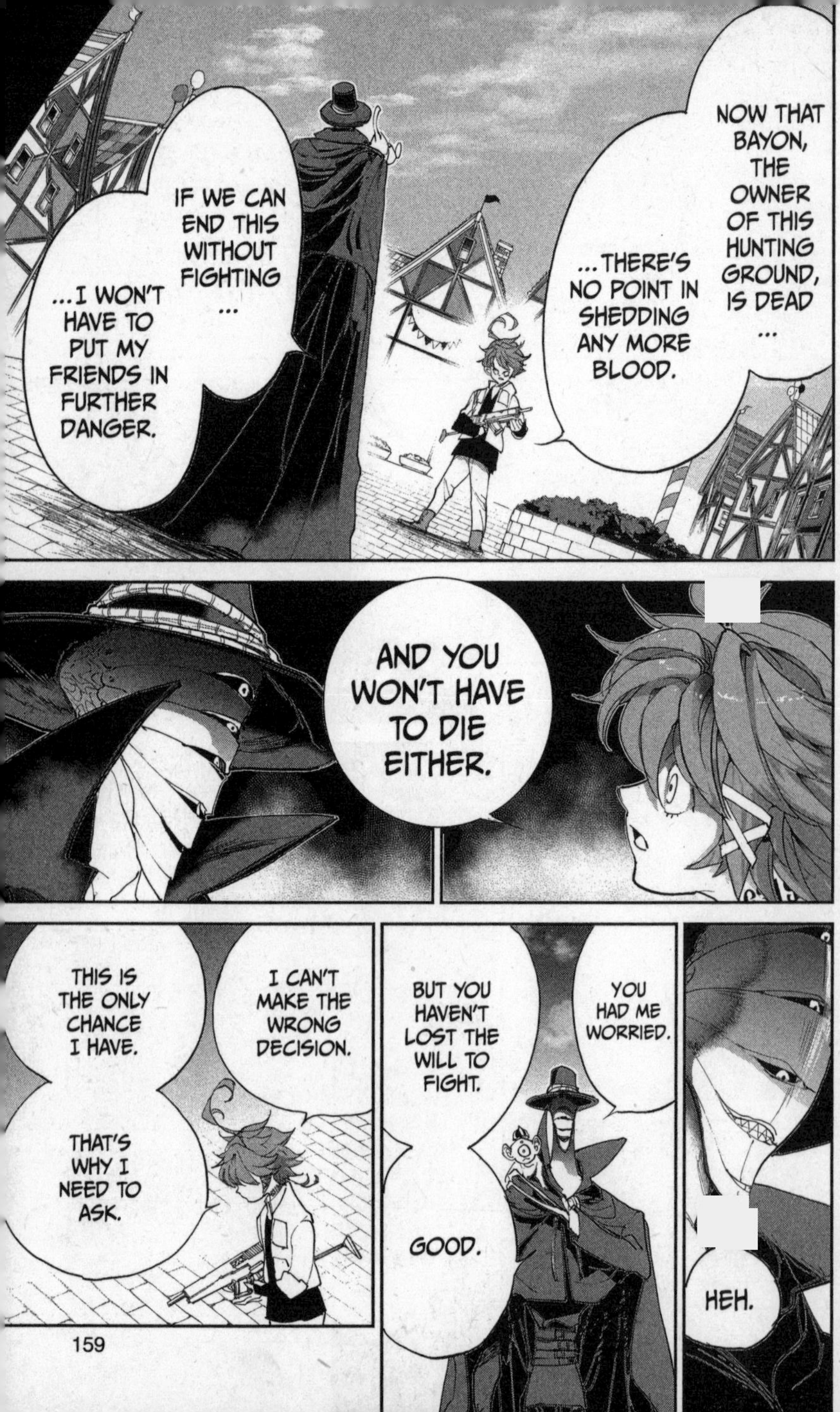
NOW THAT BAYON, THE OWNER OF THIS HUNTING GROUND, IS DEAD...
...THERE'S NO POINT IN SHEDDING ANY MORE BLOOD.
IF WE CAN END THIS WITHOUT FIGHTING...
...I WON'T HAVE TO PUT MY FRIENDS IN FURTHER DANGER.
AND YOU WON'T HAVE TO DIE EITHER.
HEH.
YOU HAD ME WORRIED.
BUT YOU HAVEN'T LOST THE WILL TO FIGHT.
GOOD.
I CAN'T MAKE THE WRONG DECISION.
THIS IS THE ONLY CHANCE I HAVE.
THAT'S WHY I NEED TO ASK.

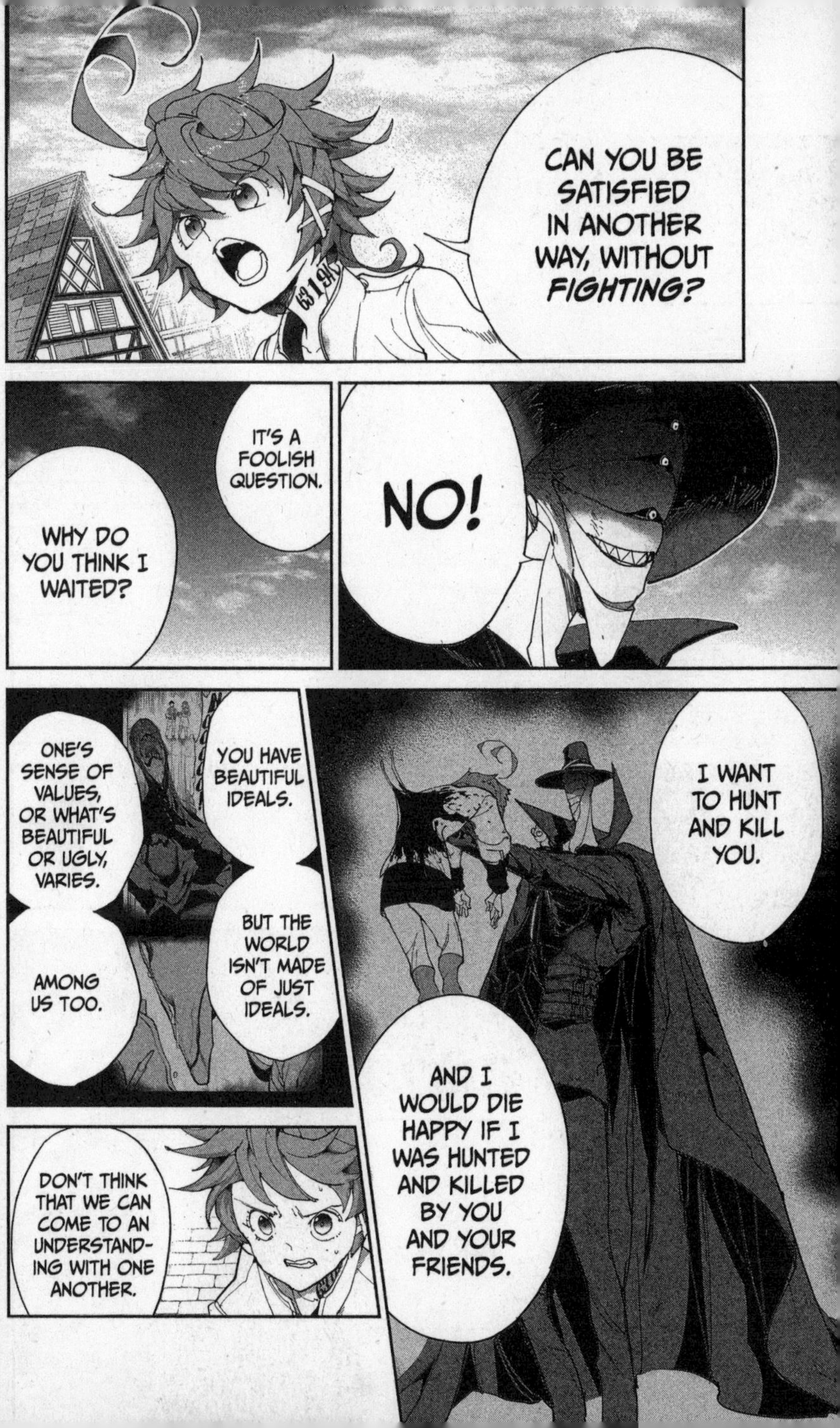
CAN YOU BE SATISFIED IN ANOTHER WAY, WITHOUT FIGHTING?
NO!
IT'S A FOOLISH QUESTION.
WHY DO YOU THINK I WAITED?
I WANT TO HUNT AND KILL YOU.
AND I WOULD DIE HAPPY IF I WAS HUNTED AND KILLED BY YOU AND YOUR FRIENDS.
YOU HAVE BEAUTIFUL IDEALS.
BUT THE WORLD ISN'T MADE OF JUST IDEALS.
ONE'S SENSE OF VALUES, OR WHAT'S BEAUTIFUL OR UGLY, VARIES.
AMONG US TOO.
DON'T THINK THAT WE CAN COME TO AN UNDERSTAND-ING WITH ONE ANOTHER.

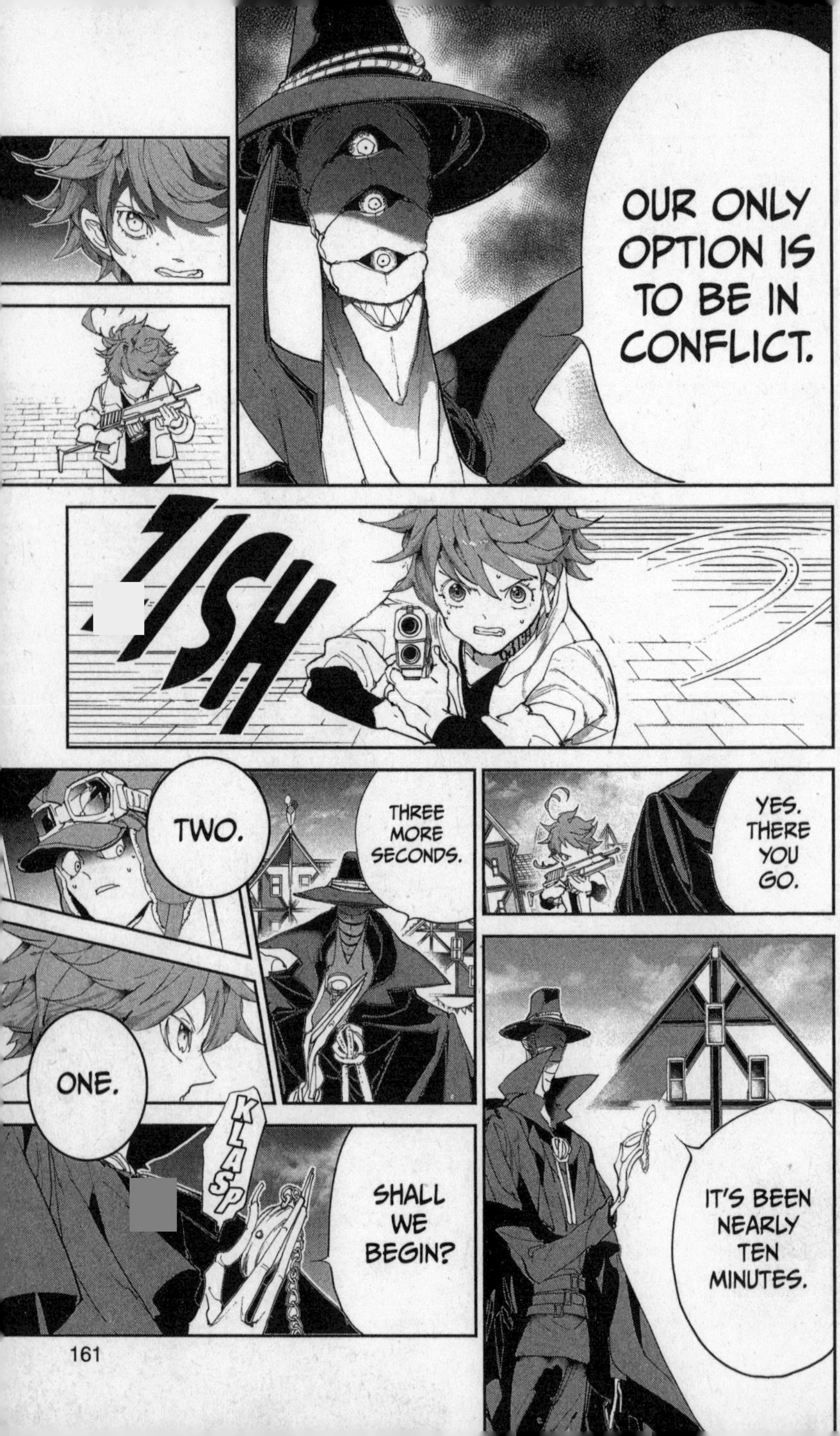
OUR ONLY OPTION IS TO BE IN CONFLICT.
ZISH
YES. THERE YOU GO.
THREE MORE SECONDS.
TWO.
IT'S BEEN NEARLY TEN MINUTES.
ONE.
SHALL WE BEGIN?
KLASP

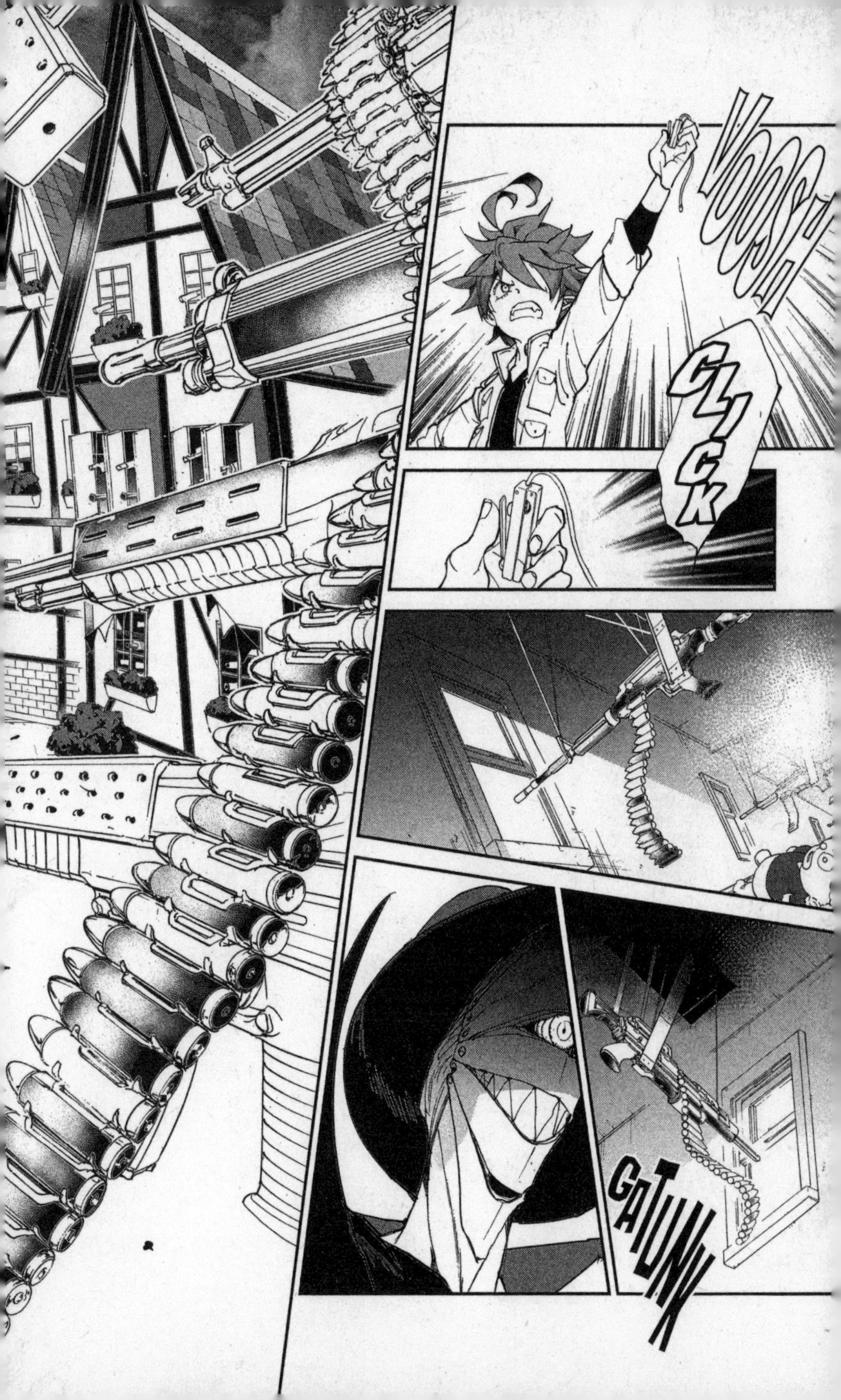
VOOSH
CLICK
GATUNK

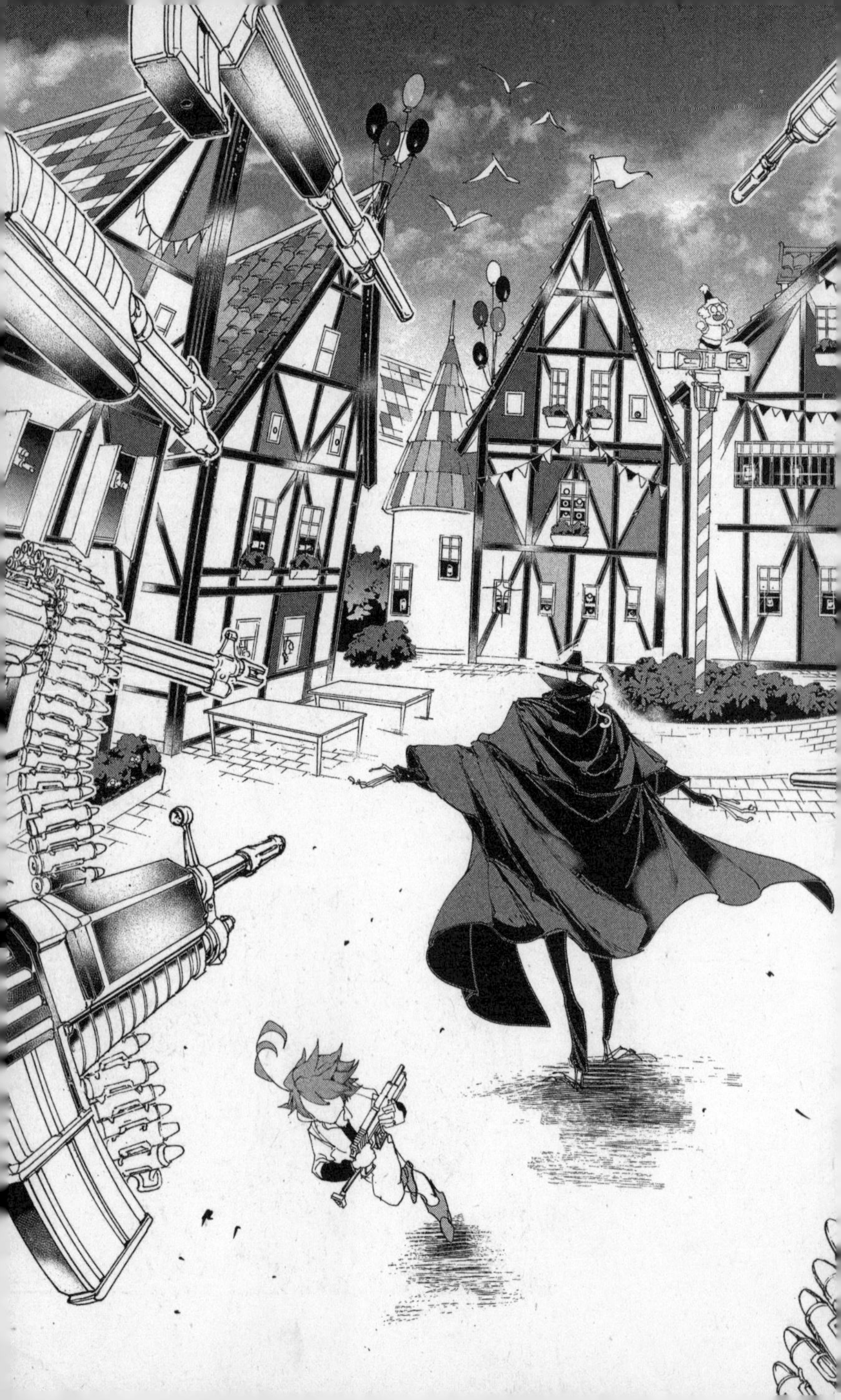

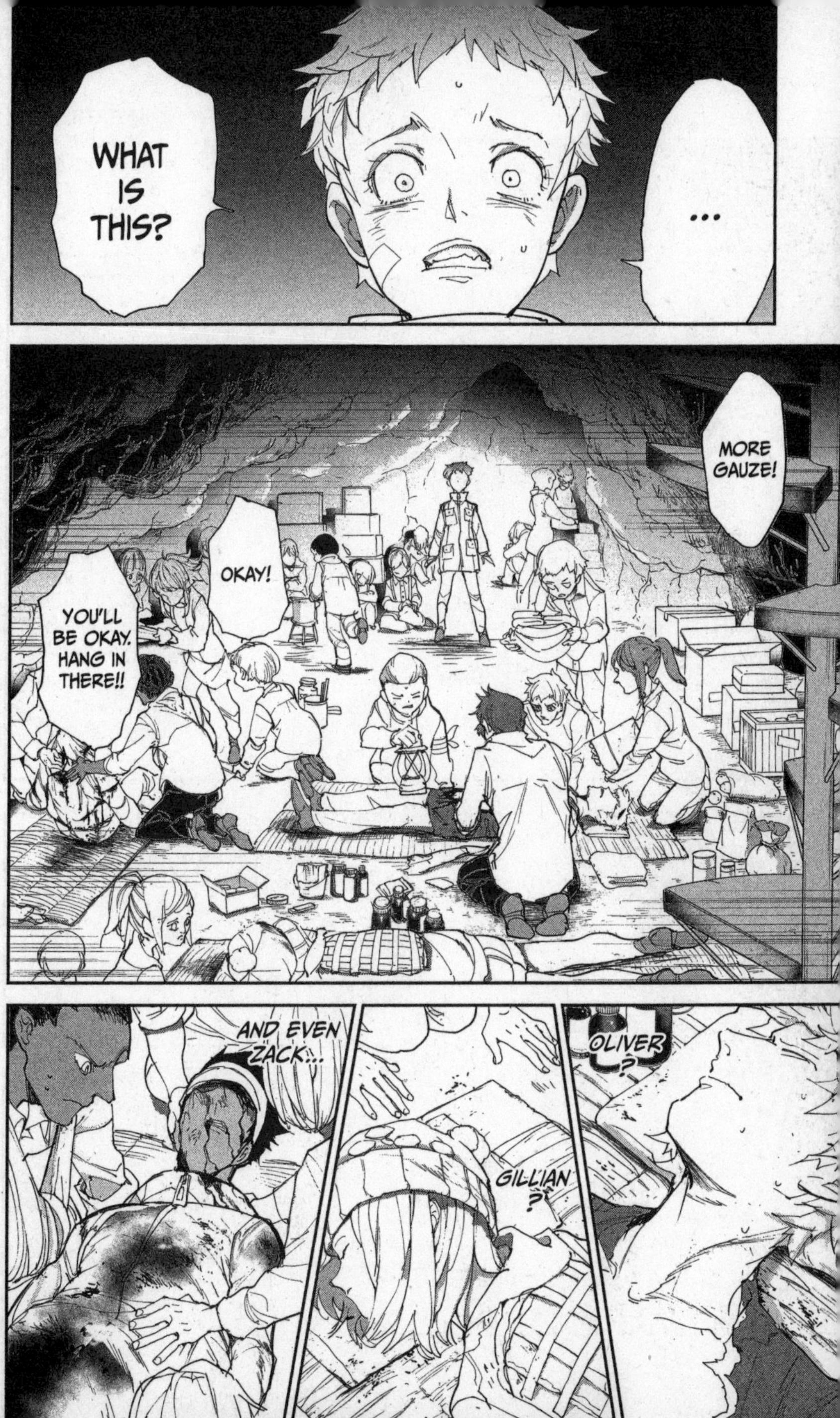
...
WHAT IS THIS?
MORE GAUZE!
OKAY!
YOU'LL BE OKAY. HANG IN THERE!!
OLIVER?
GILLIAN?
AND EVEN ZACK...

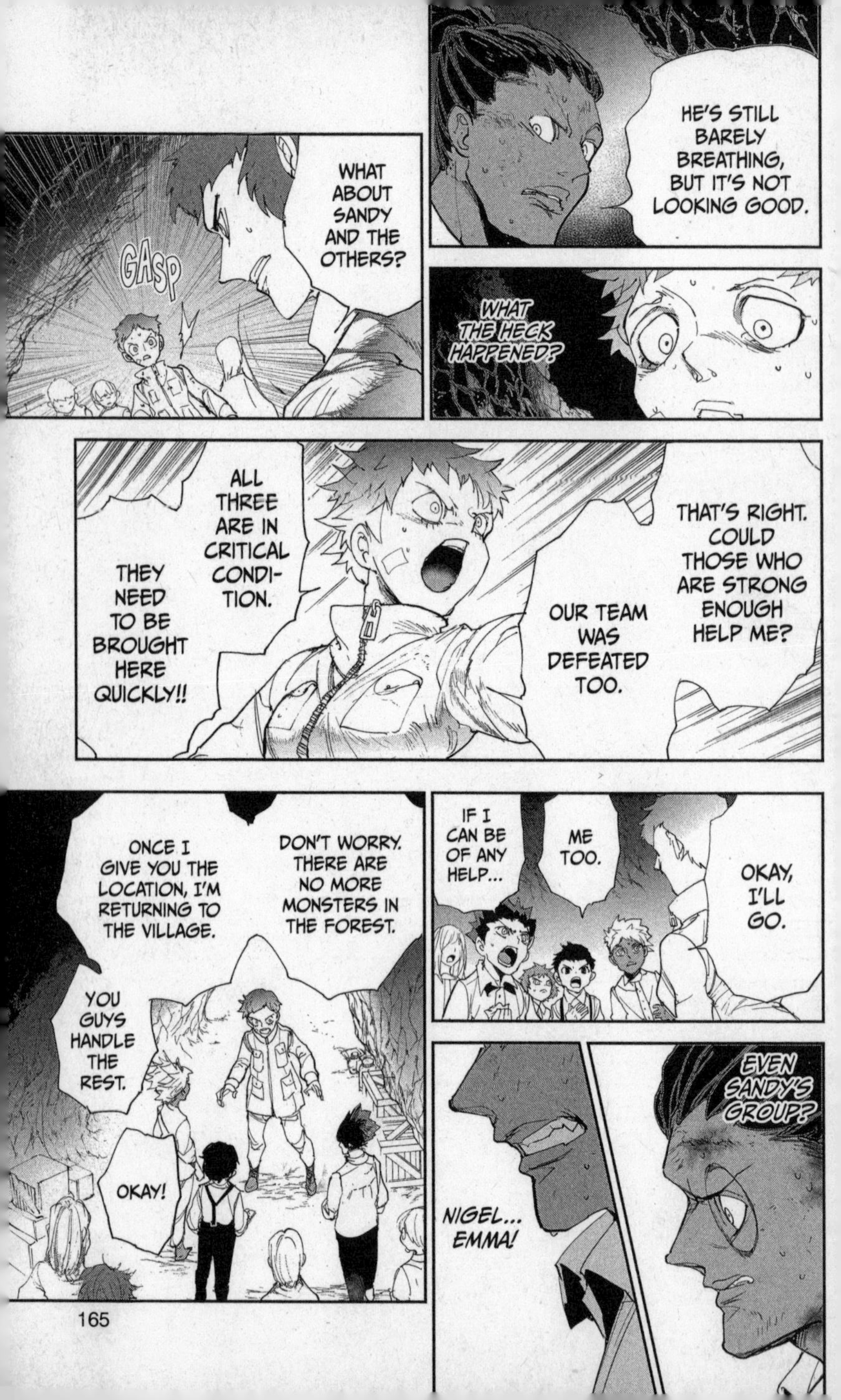
HE'S STILL BARELY BREATHING, BUT IT'S NOT LOOKING GOOD.
WHAT THE HECK HAPPENED?
WHAT ABOUT SANDY AND THE OTHERS?
GASP
THAT'S RIGHT. COULD THOSE WHO ARE STRONG ENOUGH HELP ME?
OUR TEAM WAS DEFEATED TOO.
ALL THREE ARE IN CRITICAL CONDITION.
THEY NEED TO BE BROUGHT HERE QUICKLY!!
OKAY, I'LL GO.
ME TOO.
IF I CAN BE OF ANY HELP...
EVEN SANDY'S GROUP?
NIGEL... EMMA!
DON'T WORRY. THERE ARE NO MORE MONSTERS IN THE FOREST.
ONCE I GIVE YOU THE LOCATION, I'M RETURNING TO THE VILLAGE.
YOU GUYS HANDLE THE REST.
OKAY!

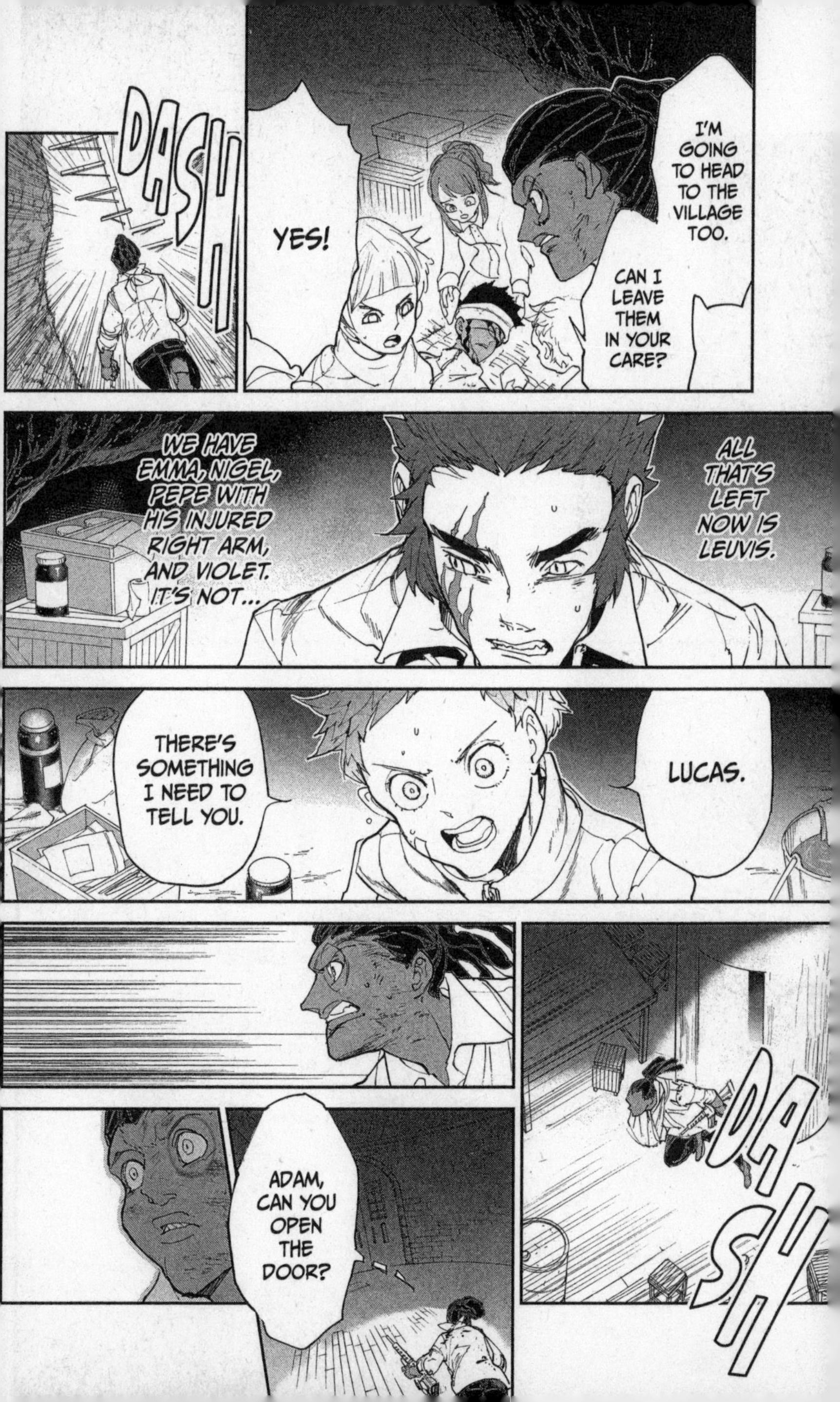
I'M GOING TO HEAD TO THE VILLAGE TOO.
CAN I LEAVE THEM IN YOUR CARE?
YES!
DASH
ALL THAT'S LEFT NOW IS LEUVIS.
WE HAVE EMMA, NIGEL, PEPE WITH HIS INJURED RIGHT ARM, AND VIOLET. IT'S NOT...
LUCAS.
THERE'S SOMETHING I NEED TO TELL YOU.
DASH
ADAM, CAN YOU OPEN THE DOOR?

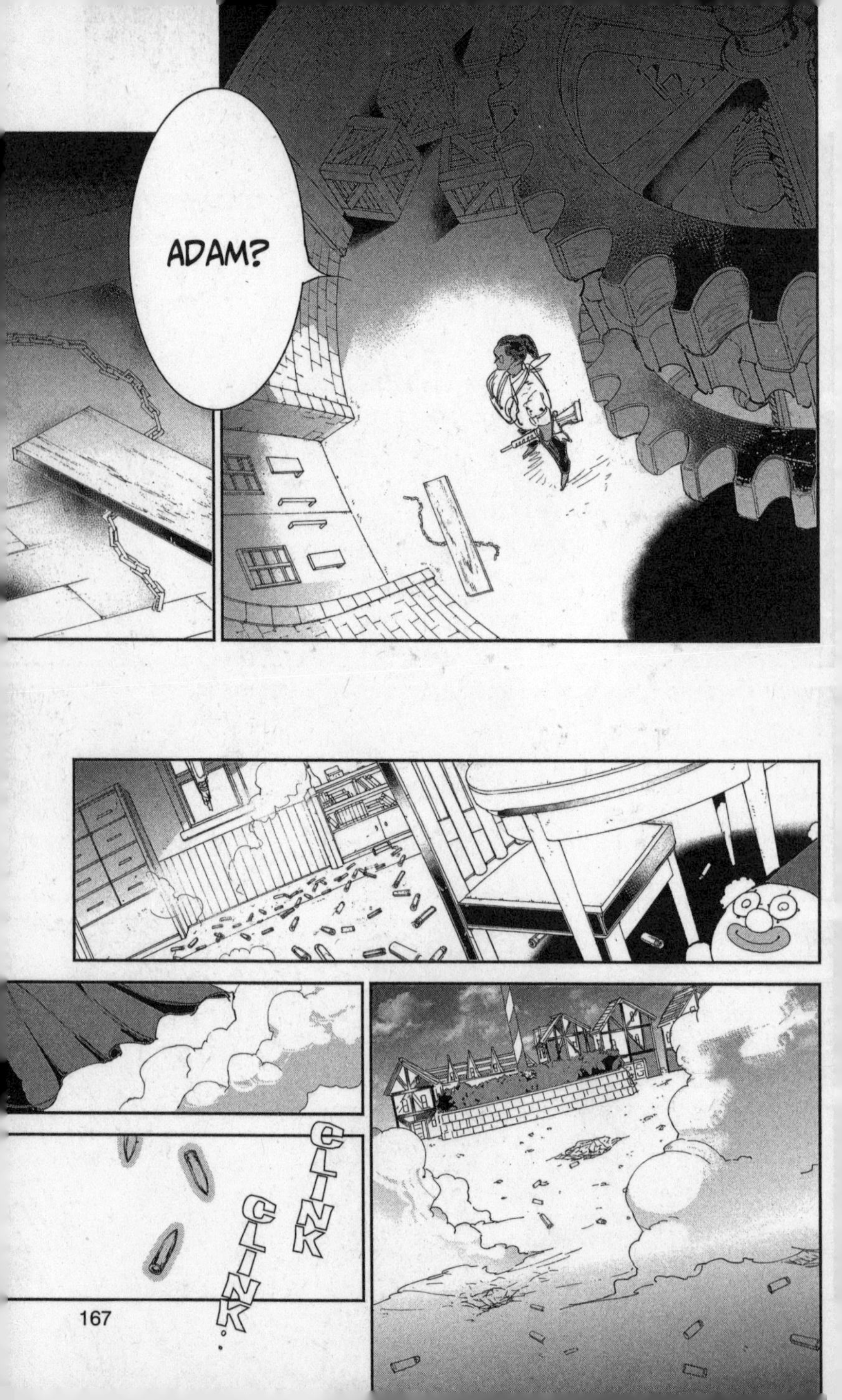
ADAM?
CLINK
CLINK

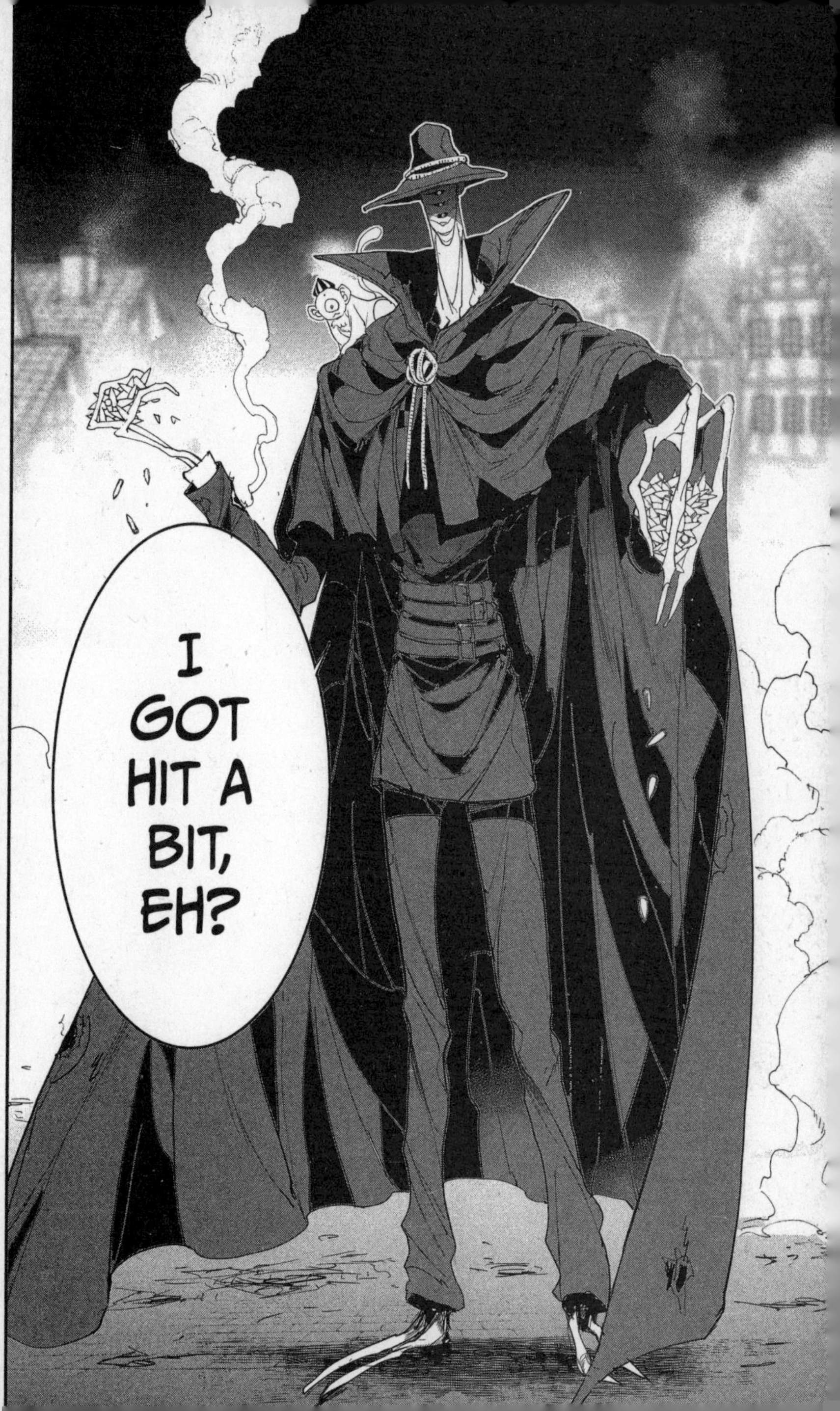
I GOT HIT A BIT, EH?

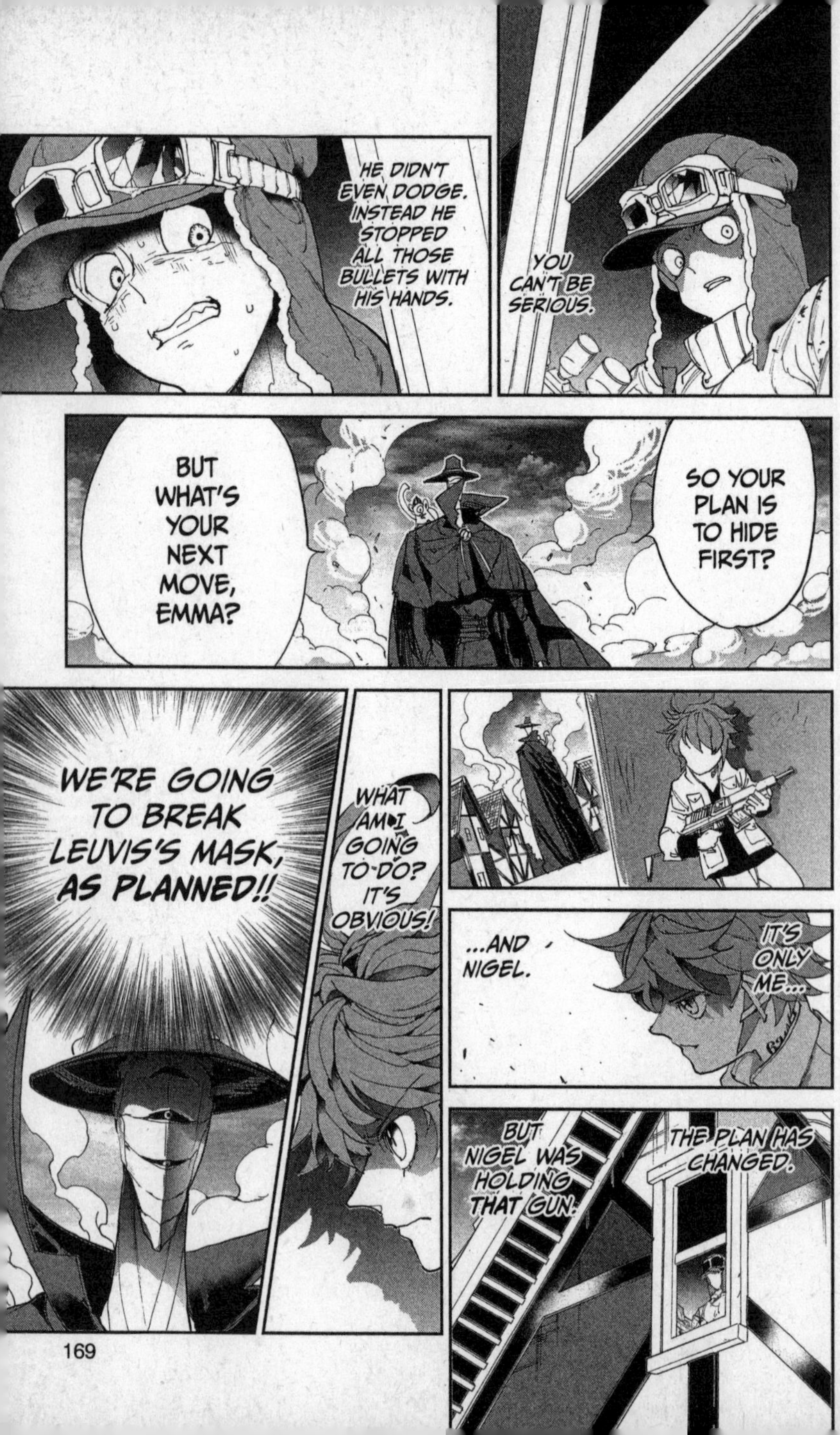
YOU CAN'T BE SERIOUS.
HE DIDN'T EVEN DODGE. INSTEAD HE STOPPED ALL THOSE BULLETS WITH HIS HANDS.
SO YOUR PLAN IS TO HIDE FIRST?
BUT WHAT'S YOUR NEXT MOVE, EMMA?
IT'S ONLY ME...
...AND NIGEL.
THE PLAN HAS CHANGED.
BUT NIGEL WAS HOLDING THAT GUN.
WHAT AM I GOING TO DO? IT'S OBVIOUS!
WE'RE GOING TO BREAK LEUVIS'S MASK, AS PLANNED!!

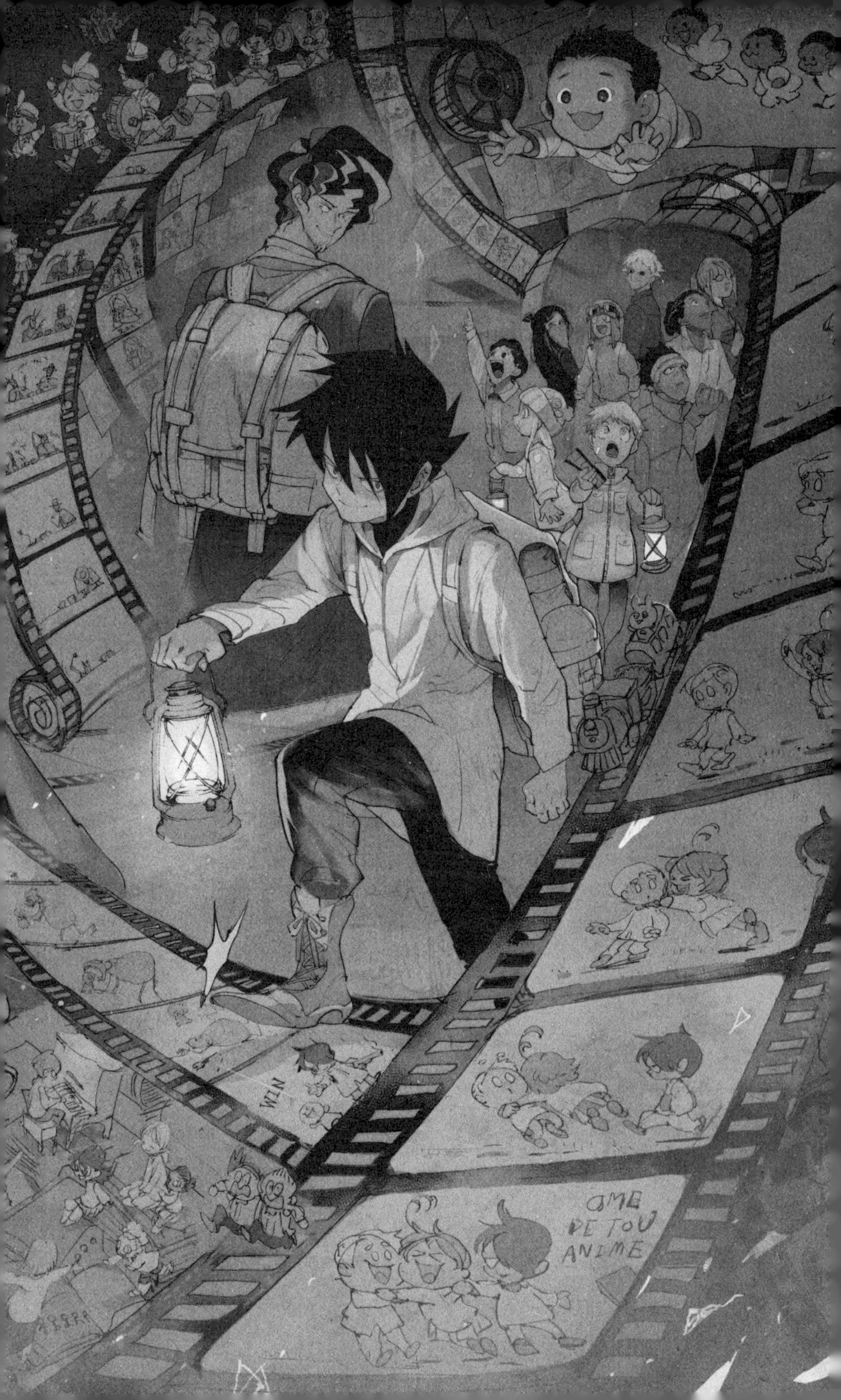
WIN
OME
DE TOU
ANIME

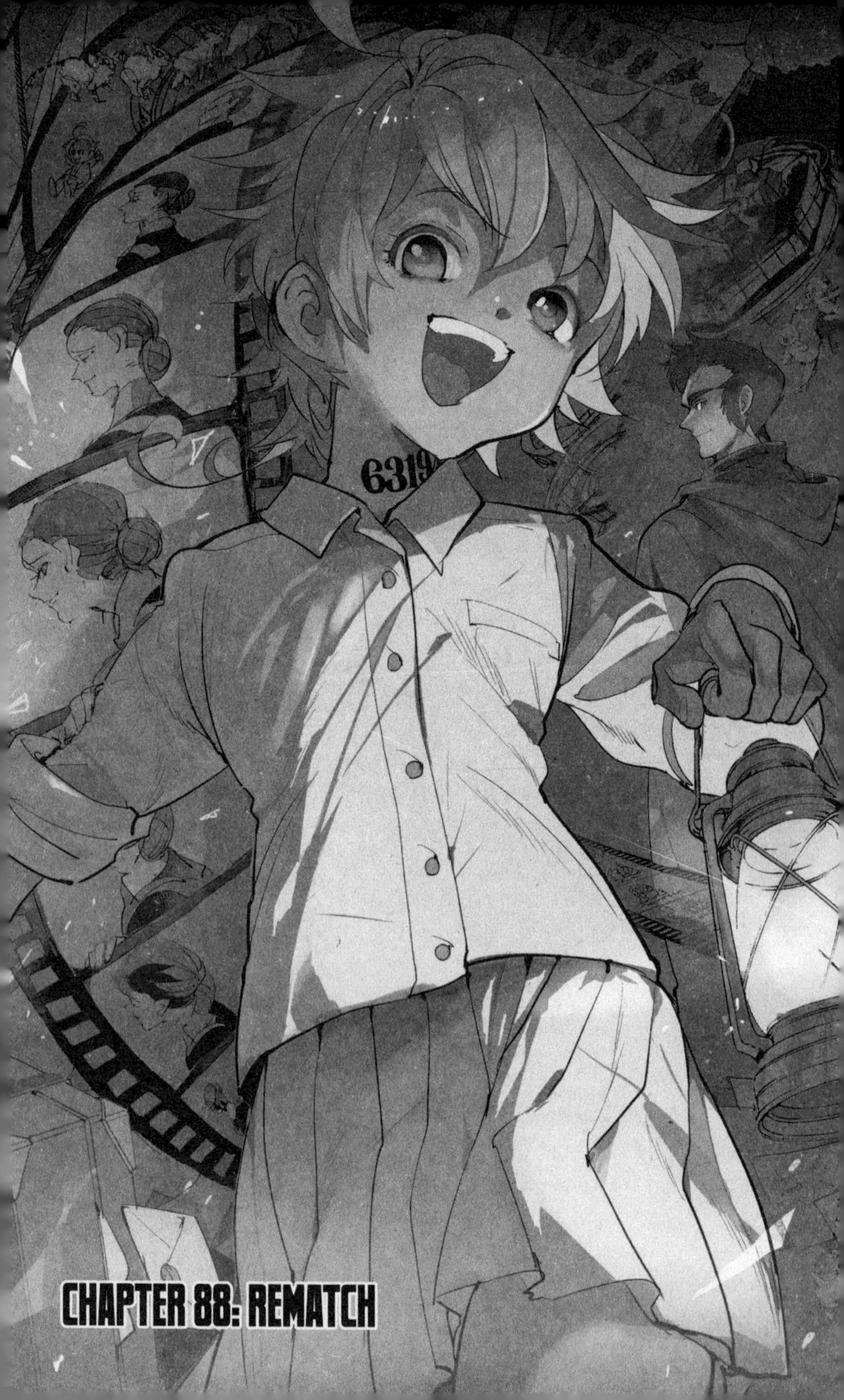
6319
CHAPTER 88: REMATCH

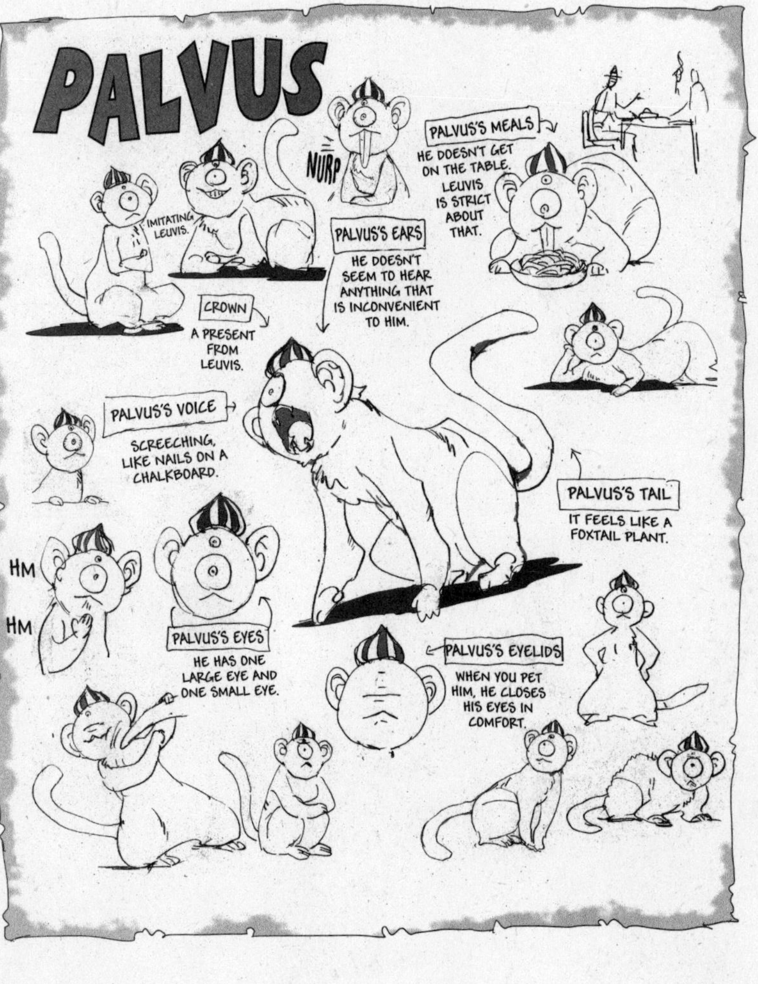

PALVUS
PALVUS'S MEALS
HE DOESN'T GET ON THE TABLE. LEUVIS IS STRICT ABOUT THAT.
NURP
IMITATING LEUVIS.
PALVUS'S EARS
HE DOESN'T SEEM TO HEAR ANYTHING THAT IS INCONVENIENT TO HIM.
CROWN
A PRESENT FROM LEUVIS.
PALVUS'S VOICE
SCREECHING, LIKE NAILS ON A CHALKBOARD.
PALVUS'S TAIL
IT FEELS LIKE A FOXTAIL PLANT.
HM
HM
PALVUS'S EYES
HE HAS ONE LARGE EYE AND ONE SMALL EYE.
PALVUS'S EYELIDS
WHEN YOU PET HIM, HE CLOSES HIS EYES IN COMFORT.

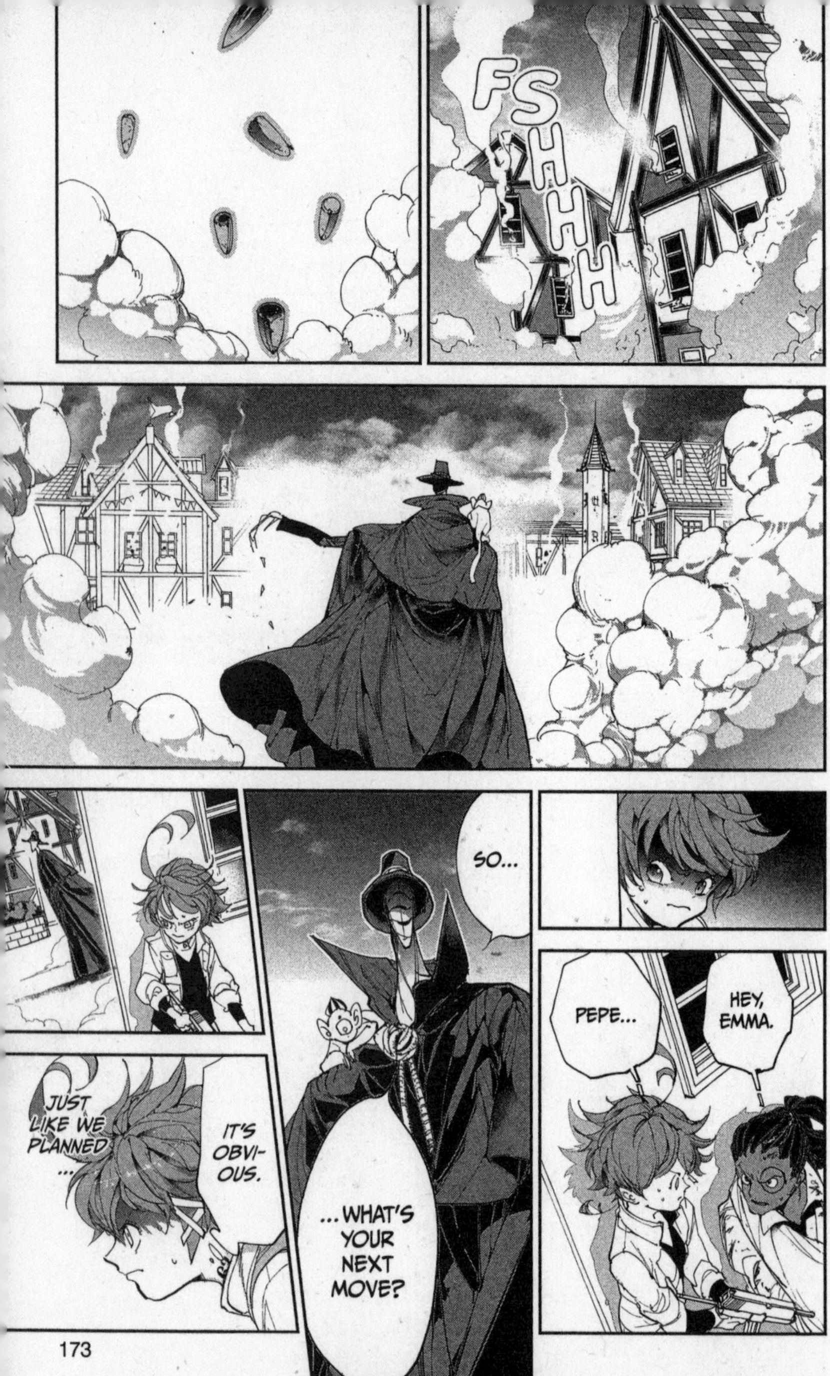
FSHHHH
HEY, EMMA.
PEPE...
SO...
...WHAT'S YOUR NEXT MOVE?
IT'S OBVI-OUS.
JUST LIKE WE PLANNED...

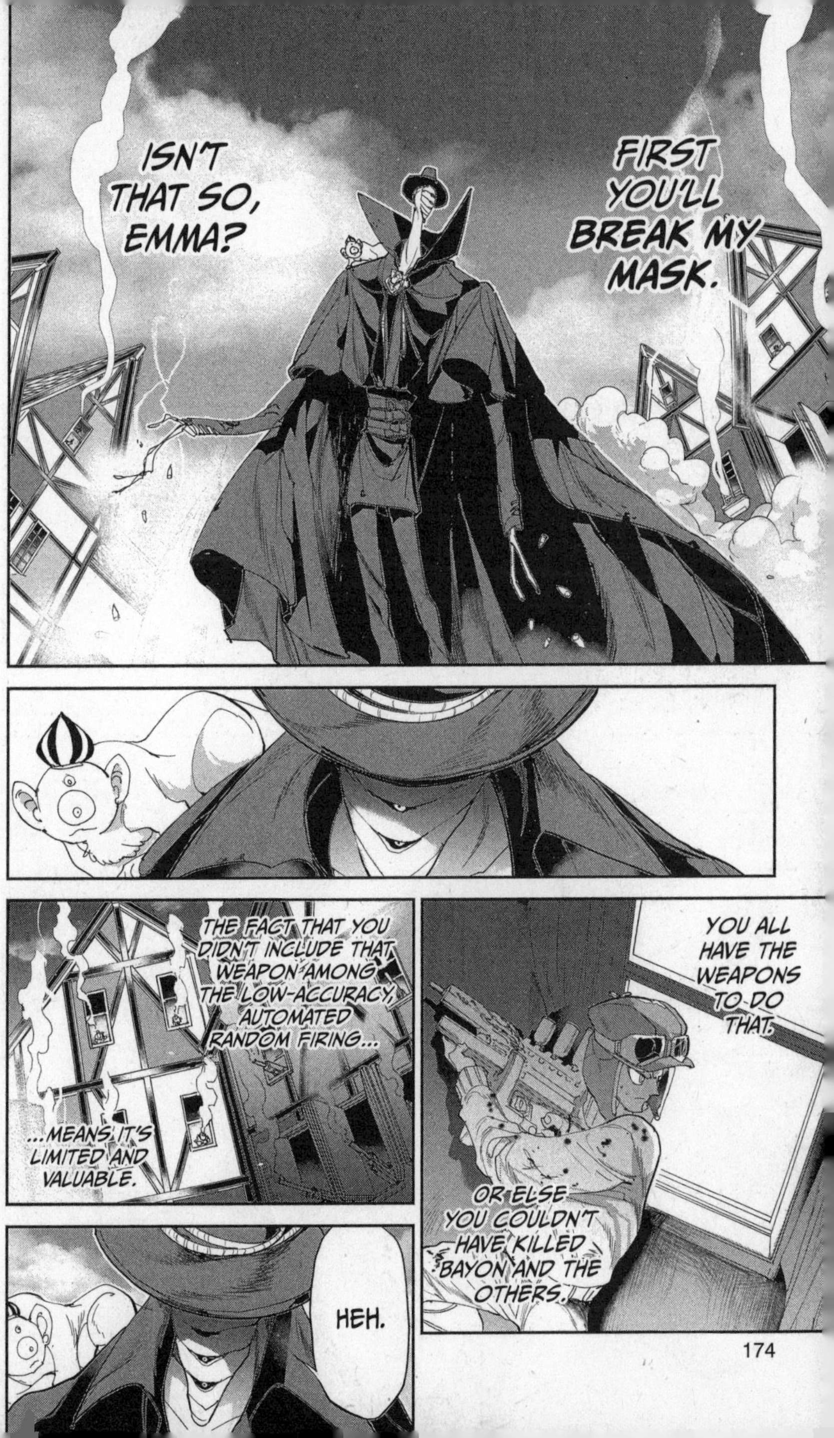
FIRST YOU'LL BREAK MY MASK.
ISN'T THAT SO, EMMA?
YOU ALL HAVE THE WEAPONS TO DO THAT.
OR ELSE YOU COULDN'T HAVE KILLED BAYON AND THE OTHERS.
THE FACT THAT YOU DIDN'T INCLUDE THAT WEAPON AMONG THE LOW-ACCURACY, AUTOMATED RANDOM FIRING...
...MEANS IT'S LIMITED AND VALUABLE.
HEH.

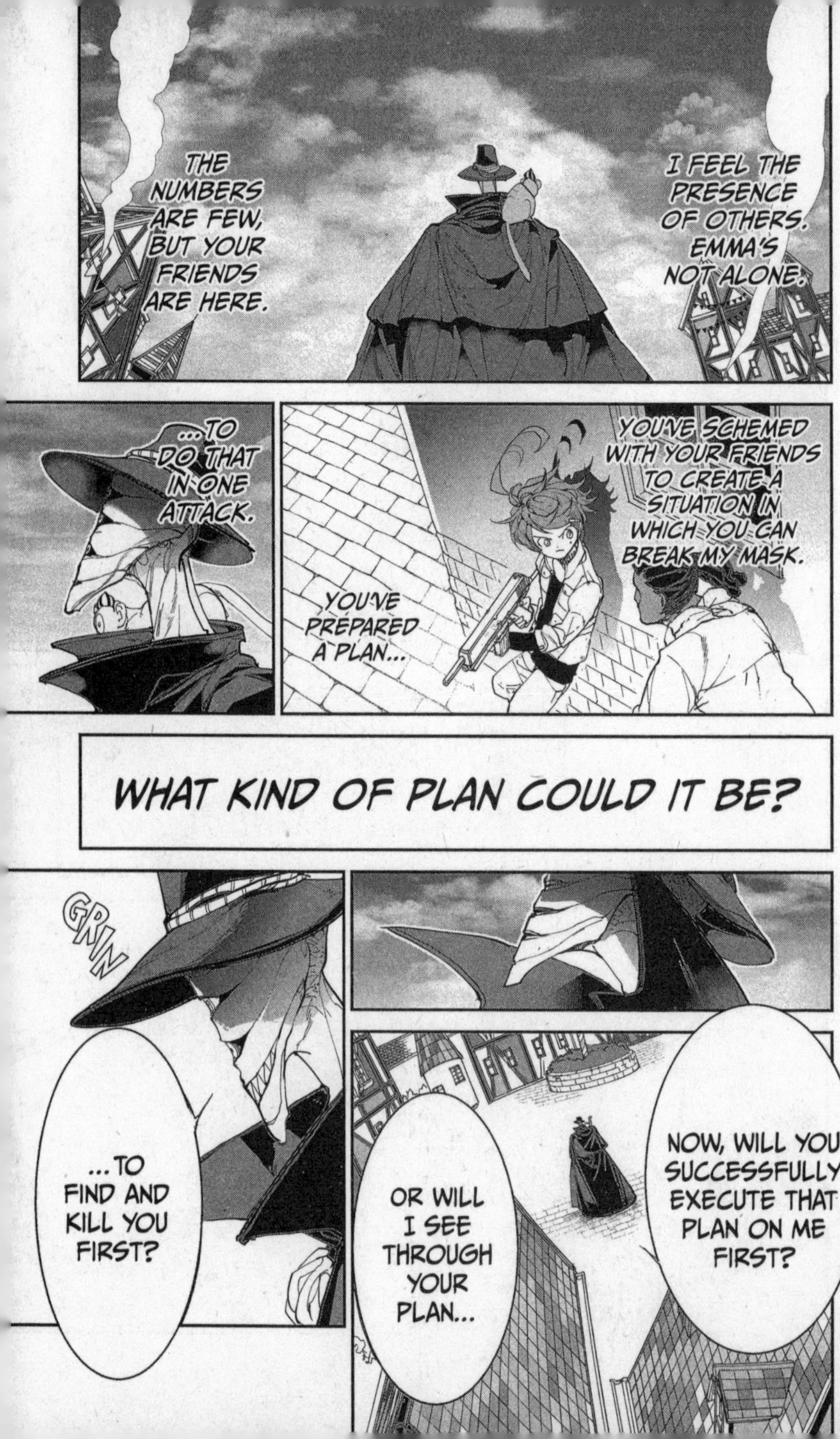
I FEEL THE PRESENCE OF OTHERS. EMMA'S NOT ALONE.
THE NUMBERS ARE FEW, BUT YOUR FRIENDS ARE HERE.
YOU'VE SCHEMED WITH YOUR FRIENDS TO CREATE A SITUATION IN WHICH YOU CAN BREAK MY MASK.
YOU'VE PREPARED A PLAN...
...TO DO THAT IN ONE ATTACK.
WHAT KIND OF PLAN COULD IT BE?
NOW, WILL YOU SUCCESSFULLY EXECUTE THAT PLAN ON ME FIRST?
OR WILL I SEE THROUGH YOUR PLAN...
GRIN
...TO FIND AND KILL YOU FIRST?

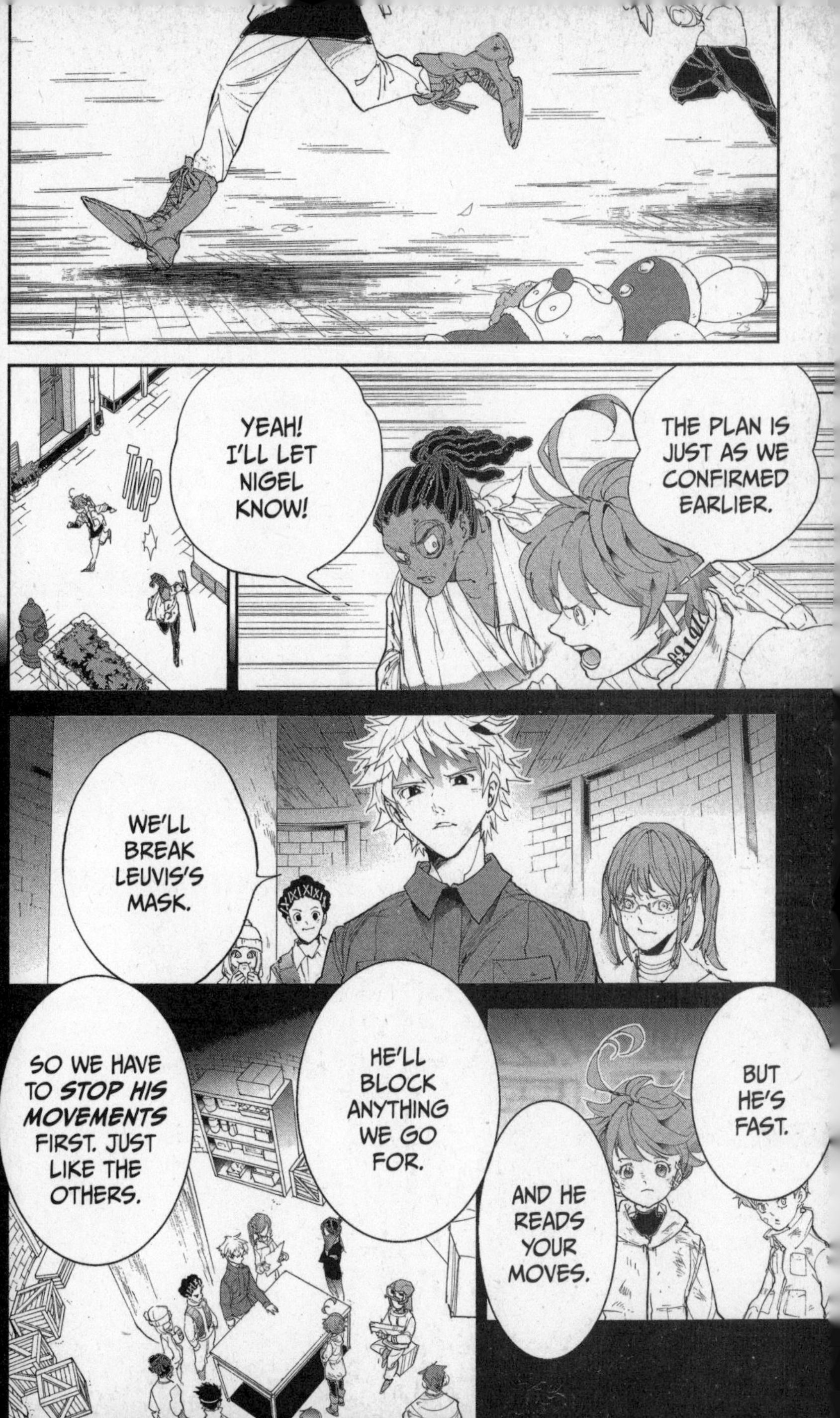
THE PLAN IS JUST AS WE CONFIRMED EARLIER.
YEAH! I'LL LET NIGEL KNOW!
TMP
WE'LL BREAK LEUVIS'S MASK.
BUT HE'S FAST.
AND HE READS YOUR MOVES.
HE'LL BLOCK ANYTHING WE GO FOR.
SO WE HAVE TO *STOP HIS MOVEMENTS* FIRST. JUST LIKE THE OTHERS.

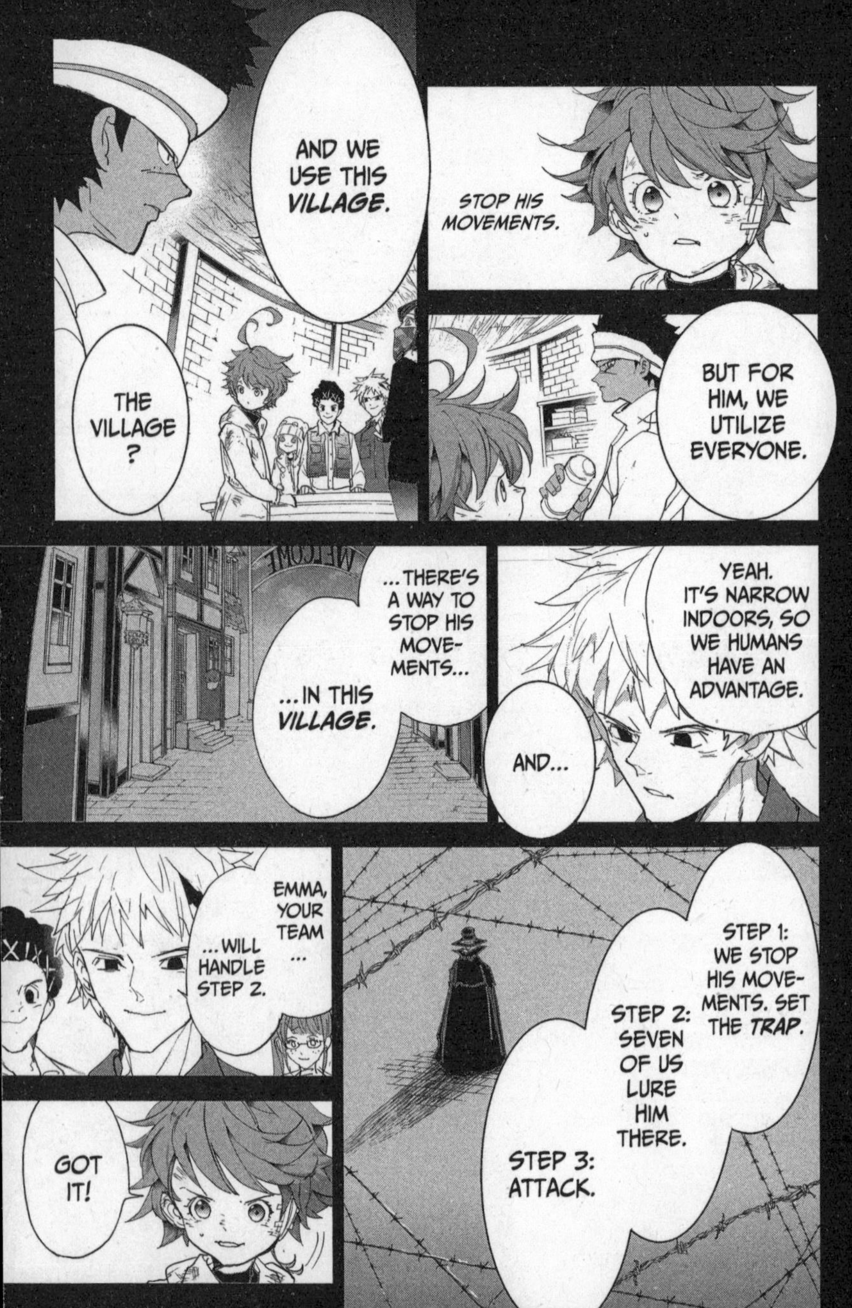
STOP HIS MOVEMENTS.
BUT FOR HIM, WE UTILIZE EVERYONE.
AND WE USE THIS *VILLAGE*.
THE VILLAGE?
YEAH. IT'S NARROW INDOORS, SO WE HUMANS HAVE AN ADVANTAGE.
AND...
...THERE'S A WAY TO STOP HIS MOVE-MENTS...
...IN THIS *VILLAGE*.
STEP 1: WE STOP HIS MOVE-MENTS. SET THE *TRAP*.
STEP 2: SEVEN OF US LURE HIM THERE.
STEP 3: ATTACK.
EMMA, YOUR TEAM...
...WILL HANDLE STEP 2.
GOT IT!

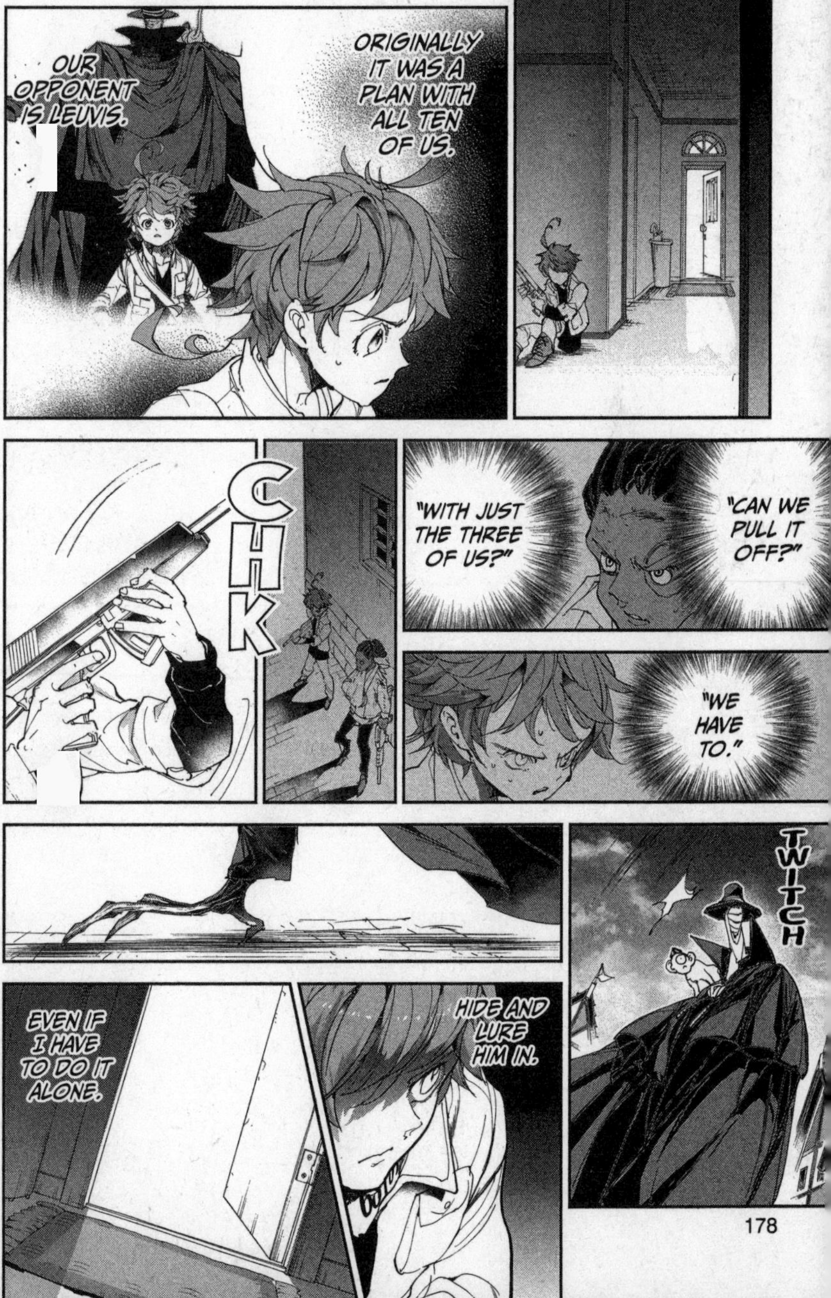

ORIGINALLY IT WAS A PLAN WITH ALL TEN OF US.
OUR OPPONENT IS LEUVIS.
"CAN WE PULL IT OFF?"
"WITH JUST THE THREE OF US?"
"WE HAVE TO."
CHK
TWITCH
HIDE AND LURE HIM IN.
EVEN IF I HAVE TO DO IT ALONE.

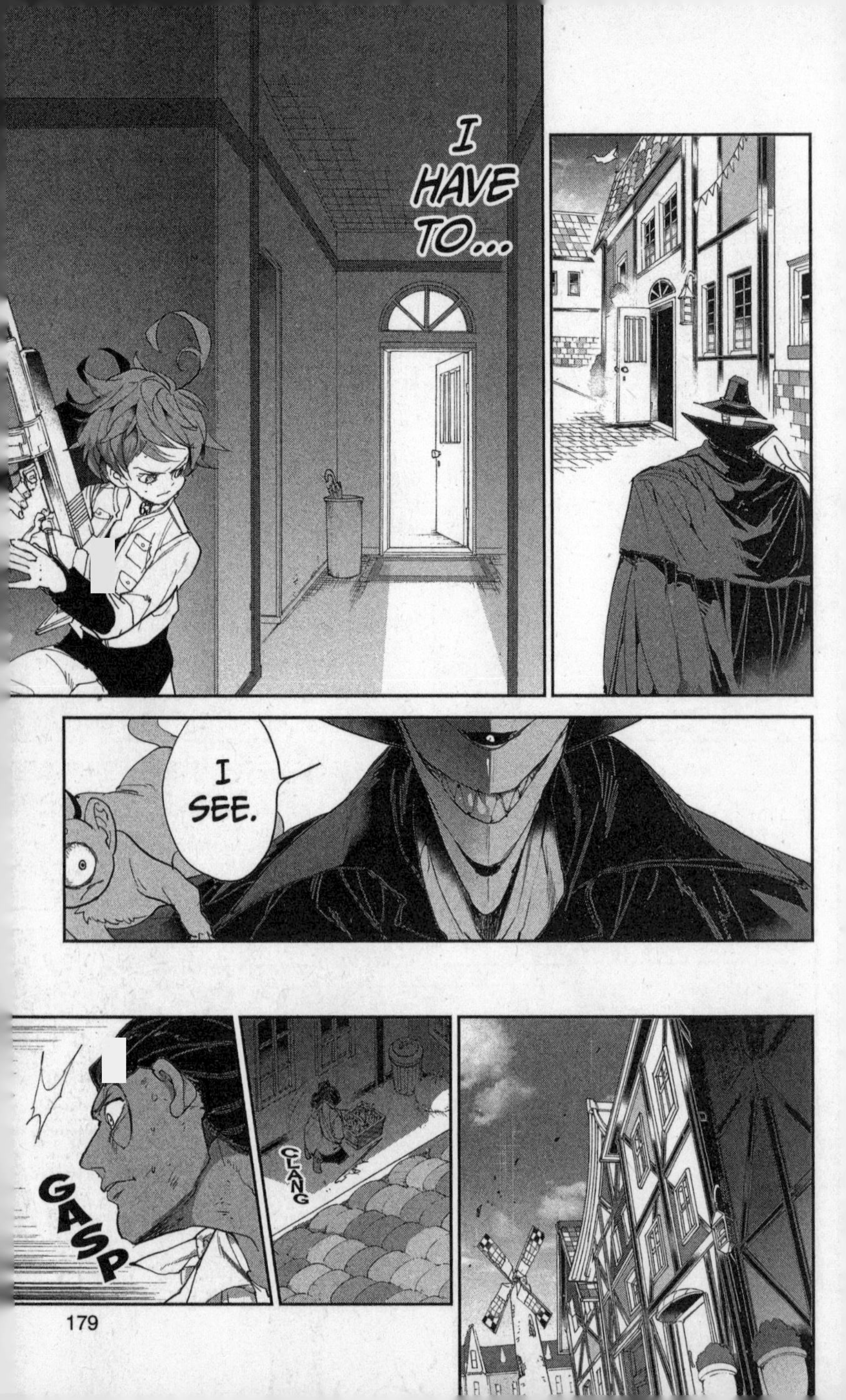
I HAVE TO...
I SEE.
CLANG
GASP

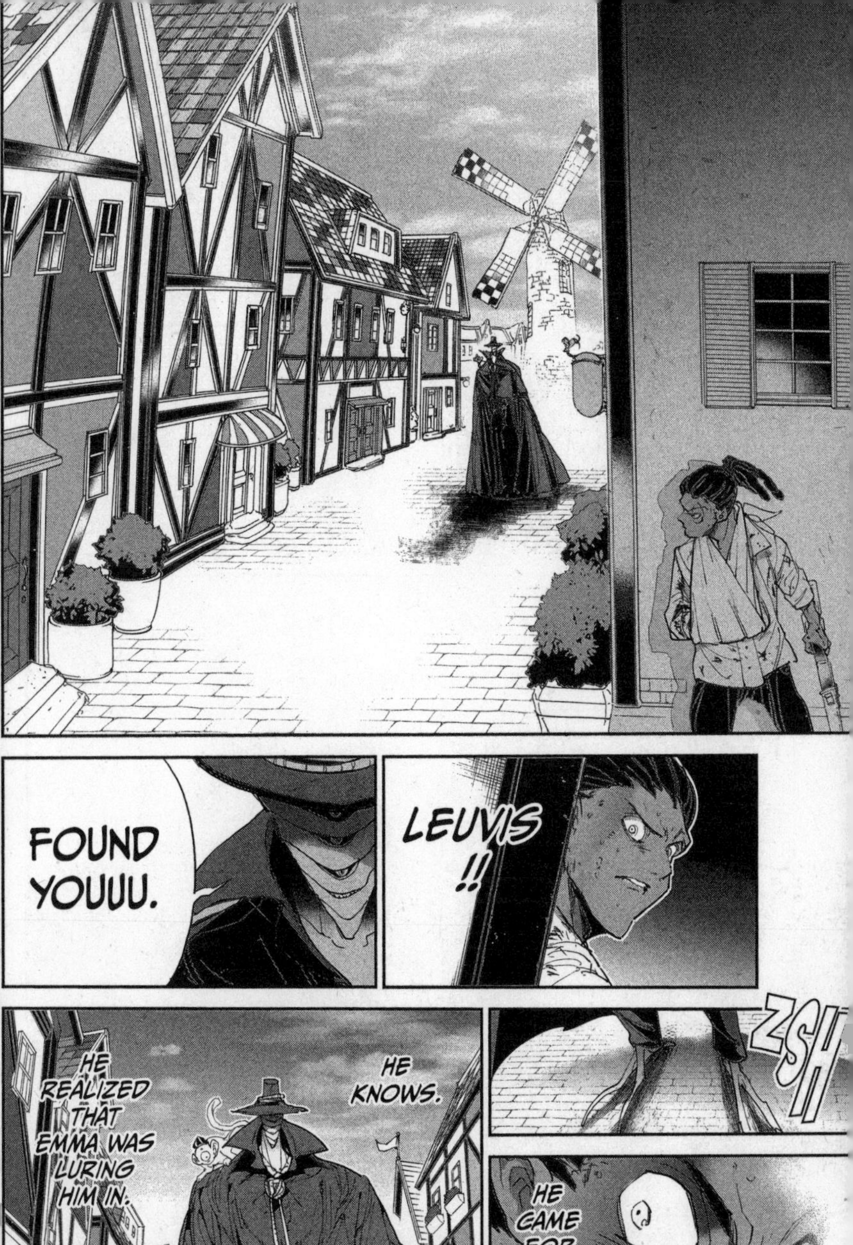
LEUVIS!!
FOUND YOUUU.
ZSH
HE CAME FOR ME?!
HE KNOWS.
HE REALIZED THAT EMMA WAS LURING HIM IN.

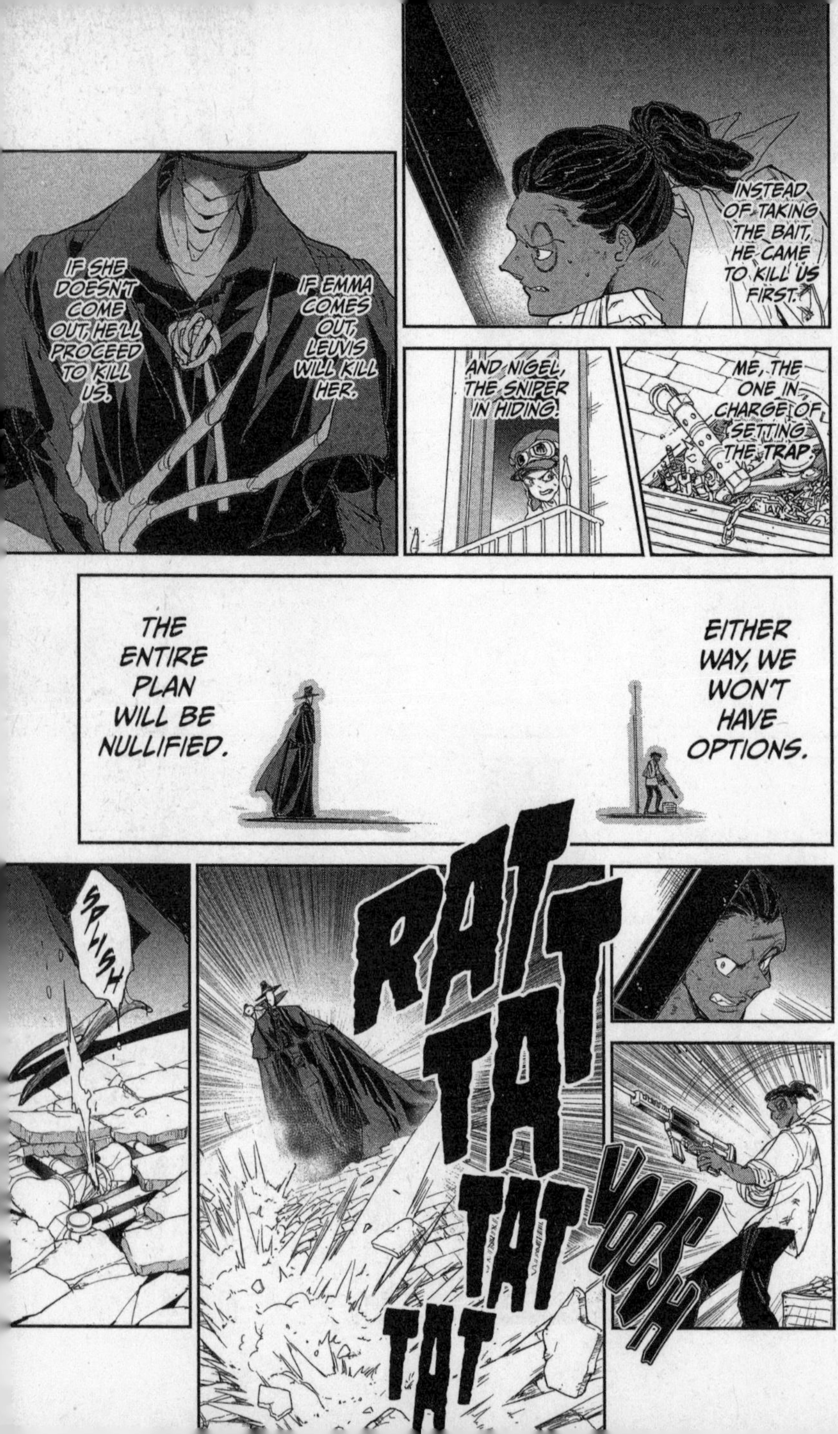
INSTEAD OF TAKING THE BAIT, HE CAME TO KILL US FIRST.
ME, THE ONE IN CHARGE OF SETTING THE TRAP.
AND NIGEL, THE SNIPER IN HIDING.
IF EMMA COMES OUT, LEUVIS WILL KILL HER.
IF SHE DOESN'T COME OUT, HE'LL PROCEED TO KILL US.
EITHER WAY, WE WON'T HAVE OPTIONS.
THE ENTIRE PLAN WILL BE NULLIFIED.
VOOSH
RAT TAT TAT TAT
SPLISH

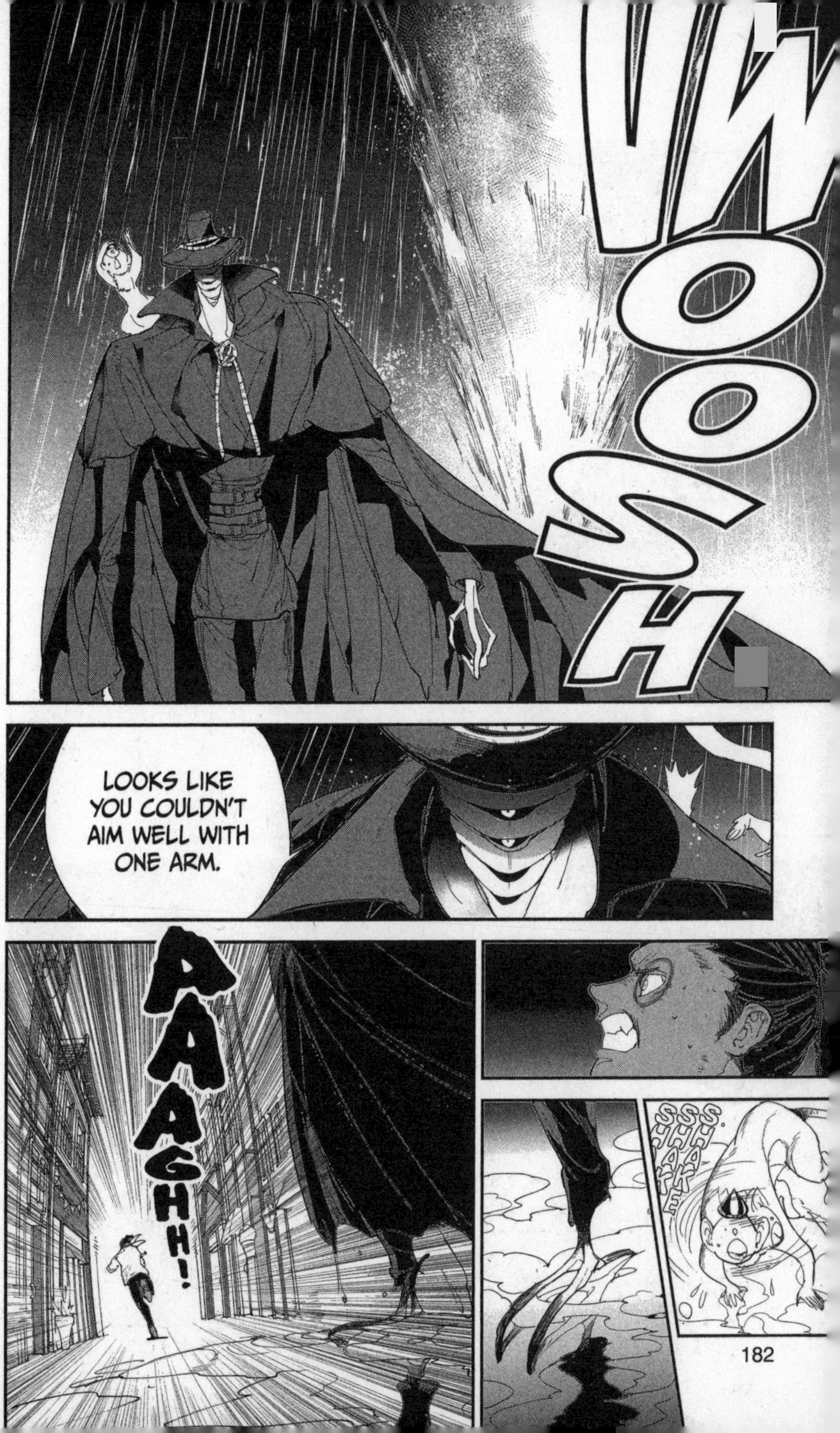
WHOOSH
LOOKS LIKE YOU COULDN'T AIM WELL WITH ONE ARM.
SHAKE SHAKE SHAKE
AAAAGHH!

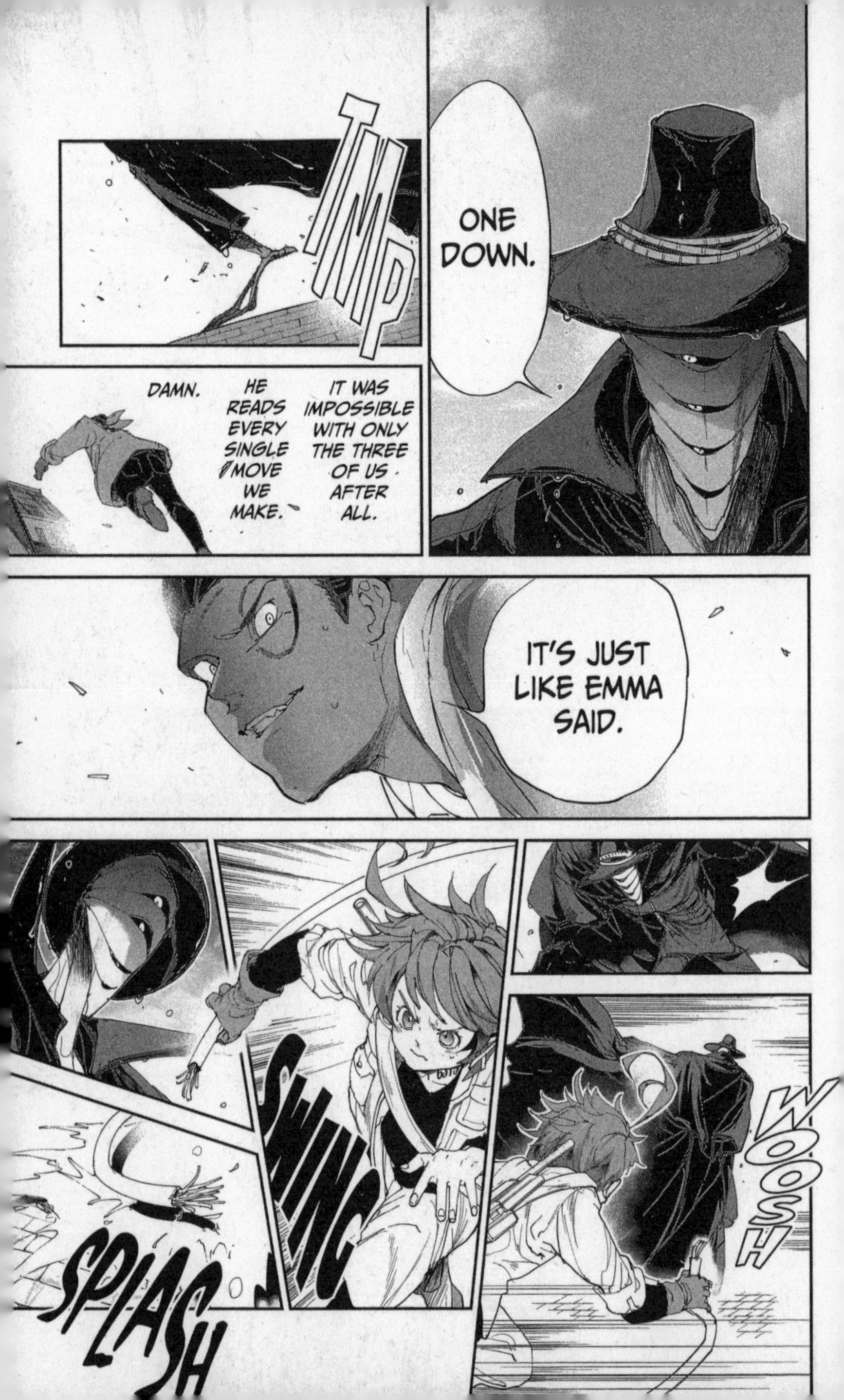
ONE DOWN.
TMP
IT WAS IMPOSSIBLE WITH ONLY THE THREE OF US AFTER ALL.
HE READS EVERY SINGLE MOVE WE MAKE.
DAMN.
IT'S JUST LIKE EMMA SAID.
WOOSH
SWING
SPLASH

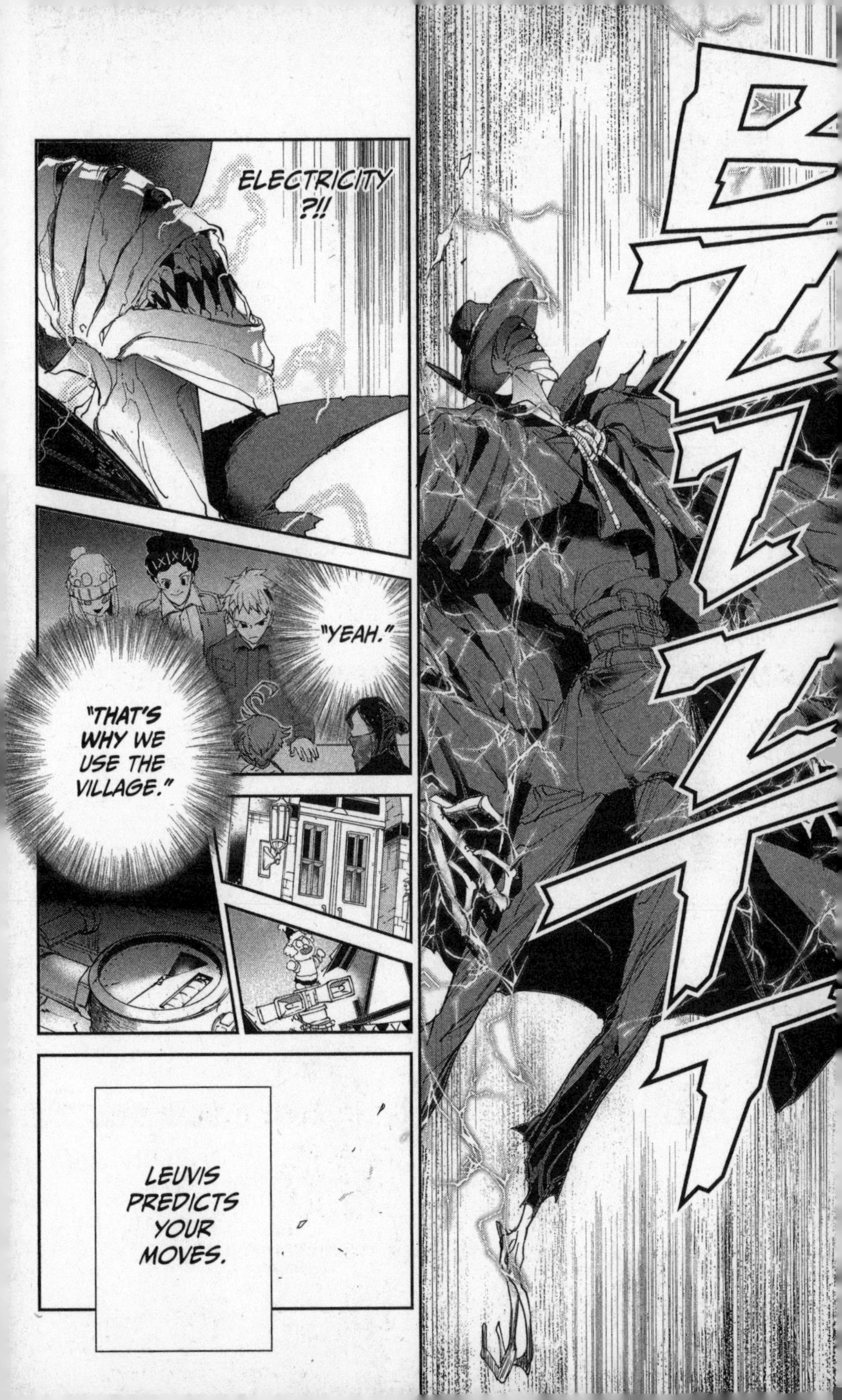
ELECTRICITY ?!!
"YEAH."
"THAT'S WHY WE USE THE VILLAGE."
LEUVIS PREDICTS YOUR MOVES.

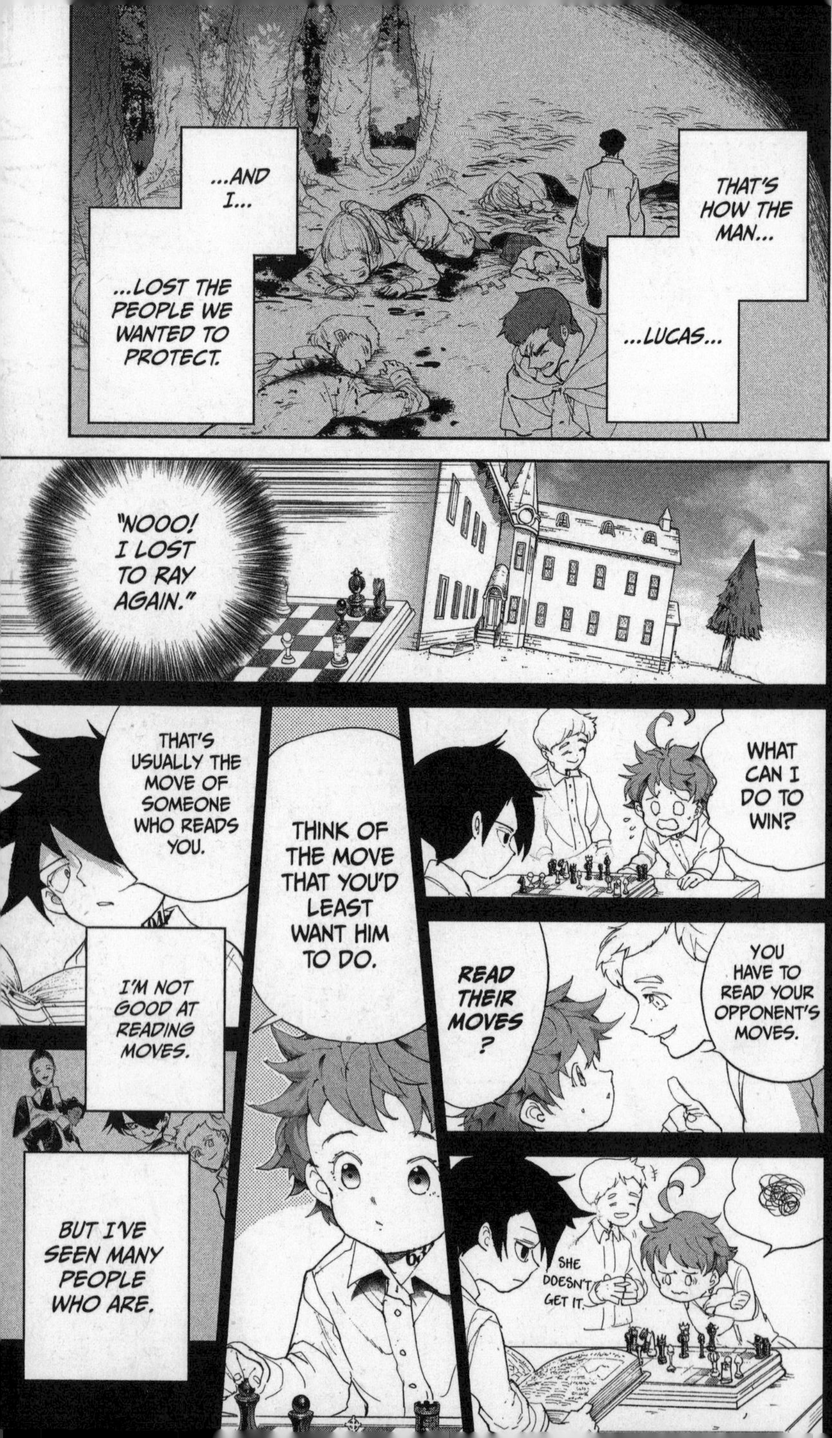
THAT'S HOW THE MAN...
...LUCAS...
...AND I...
...LOST THE PEOPLE WE WANTED TO PROTECT.
"NOOO! I LOST TO RAY AGAIN."
WHAT CAN I DO TO WIN?
YOU HAVE TO READ YOUR OPPONENT'S MOVES.
READ THEIR MOVES?
SHE DOESN'T GET IT.
THINK OF THE MOVE THAT YOU'D LEAST WANT HIM TO DO.
THAT'S USUALLY THE MOVE OF SOMEONE WHO READS YOU.
I'M NOT GOOD AT READING MOVES.
BUT I'VE SEEN MANY PEOPLE WHO ARE.

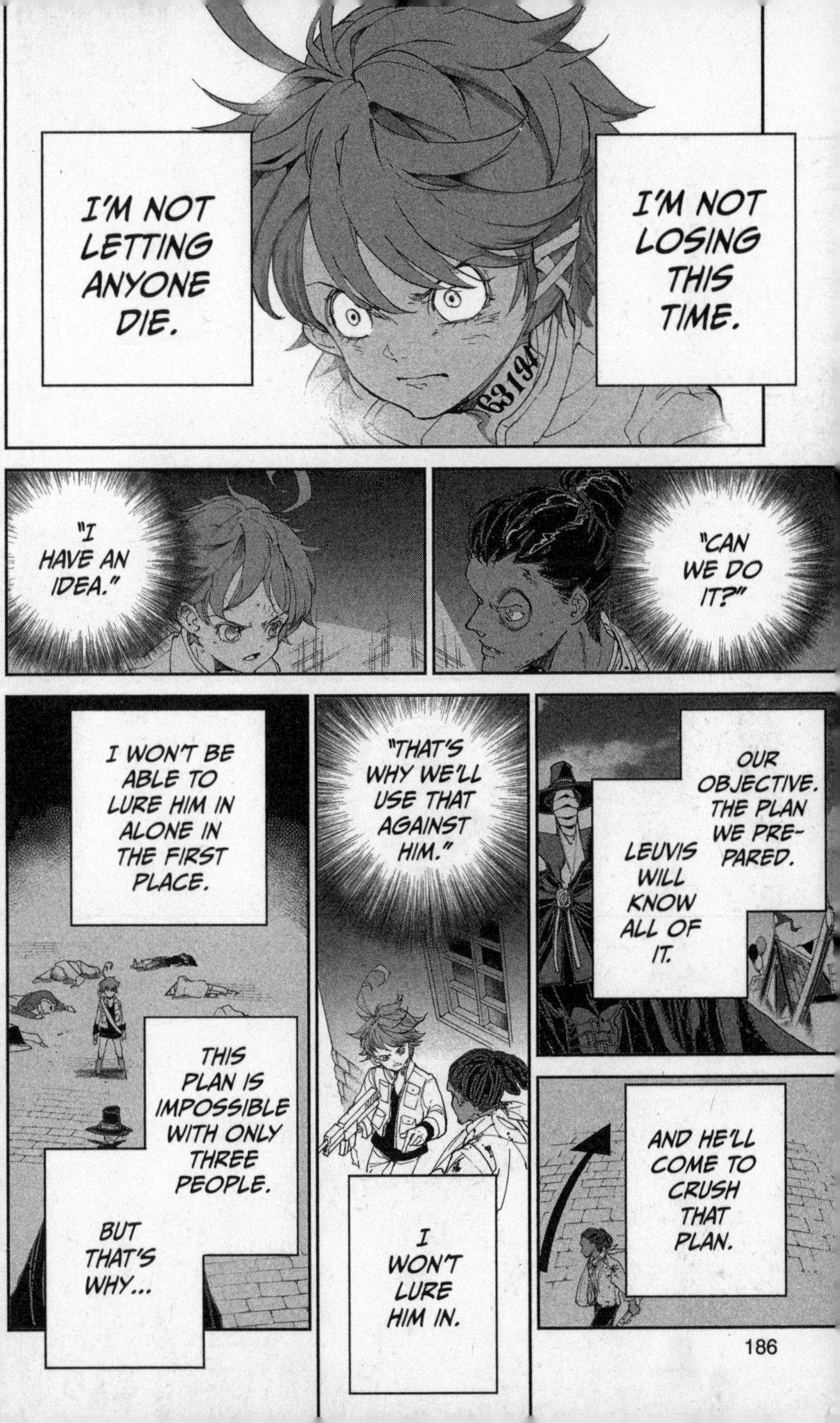
I'M NOT LOSING THIS TIME.
I'M NOT LETTING ANYONE DIE.
"CAN WE DO IT?"
"I HAVE AN IDEA."
OUR OBJECTIVE. THE PLAN WE PRE-PARED.
LEUVIS WILL KNOW ALL OF IT.
AND HE'LL COME TO CRUSH THAT PLAN.
"THAT'S WHY WE'LL USE THAT AGAINST HIM."
I WON'T LURE HIM IN.
I WON'T BE ABLE TO LURE HIM IN ALONE IN THE FIRST PLACE.
THIS PLAN IS IMPOSSIBLE WITH ONLY THREE PEOPLE.
BUT THAT'S WHY...

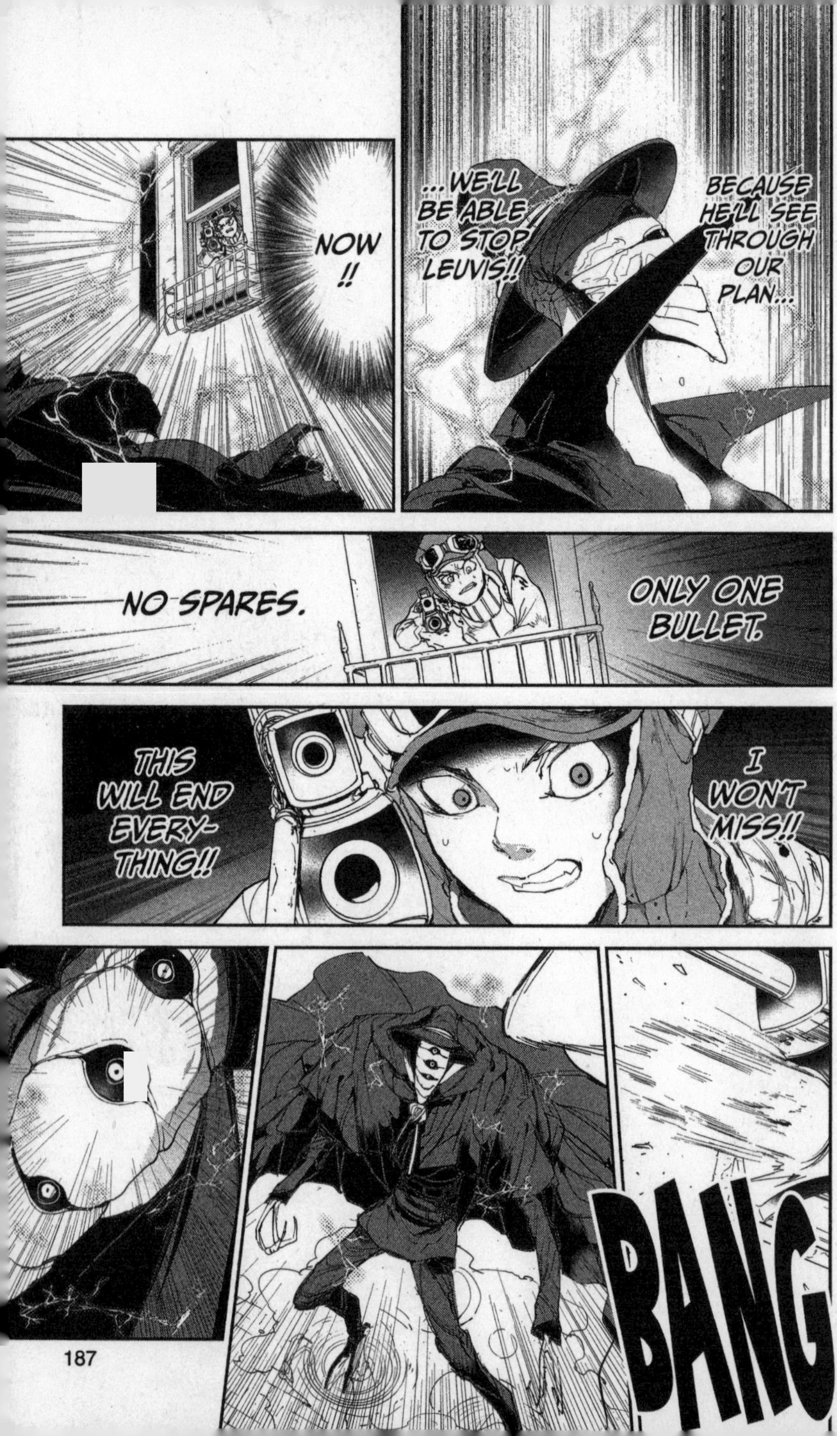
BECAUSE HE'LL SEE THROUGH OUR PLAN...
...WE'LL BE ABLE TO STOP LEUVIS!!
NOW!!
ONLY ONE BULLET.
NO SPARES.
I WON'T MISS!!
THIS WILL END EVERY-THING!!
BANG

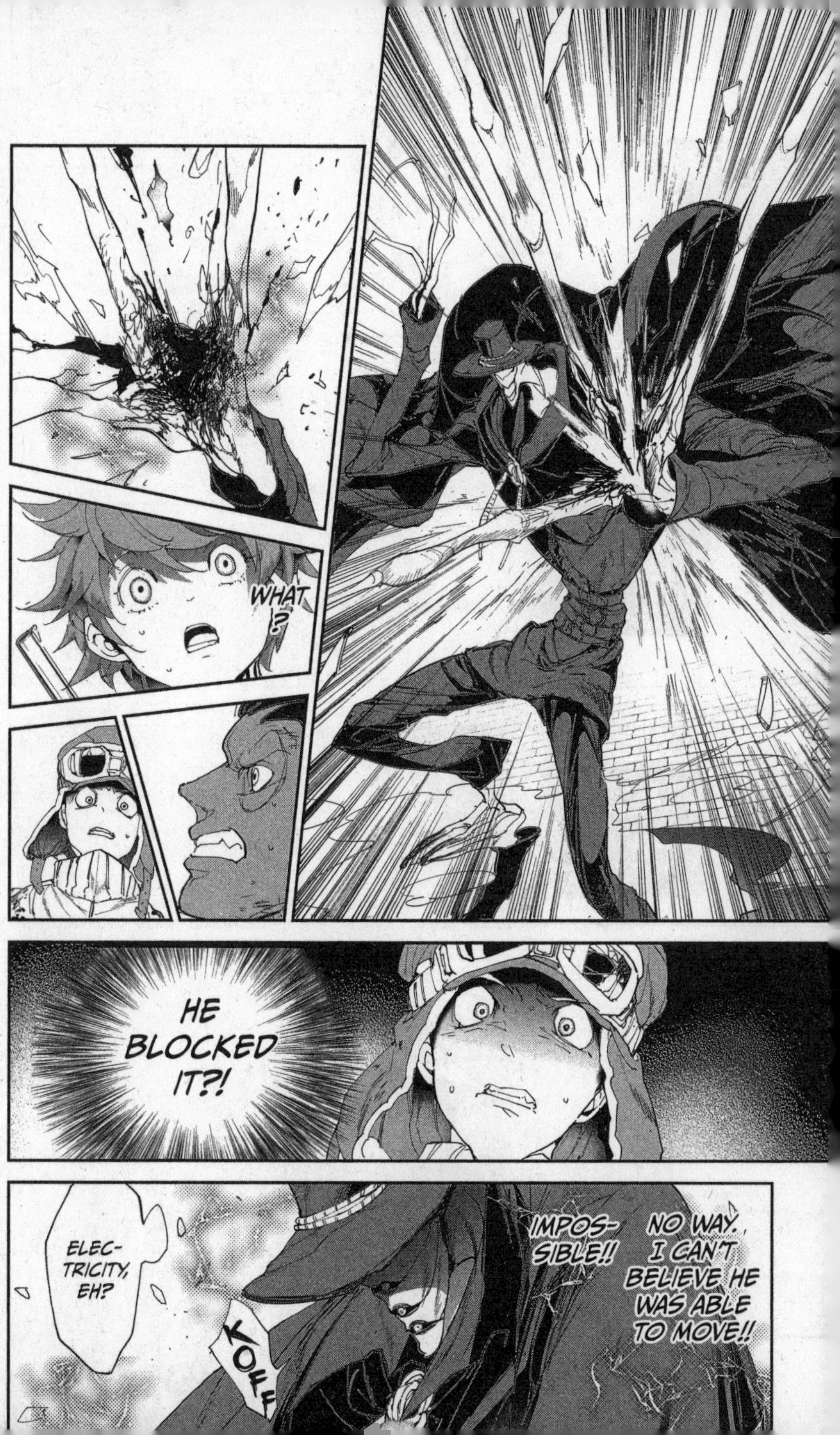
WHAT?
HE BLOCKED IT?!
NO WAY. I CAN'T BELIEVE HE WAS ABLE TO MOVE!!
IMPOSSIBLE!!
ELECTRICITY, EH?
KOFF

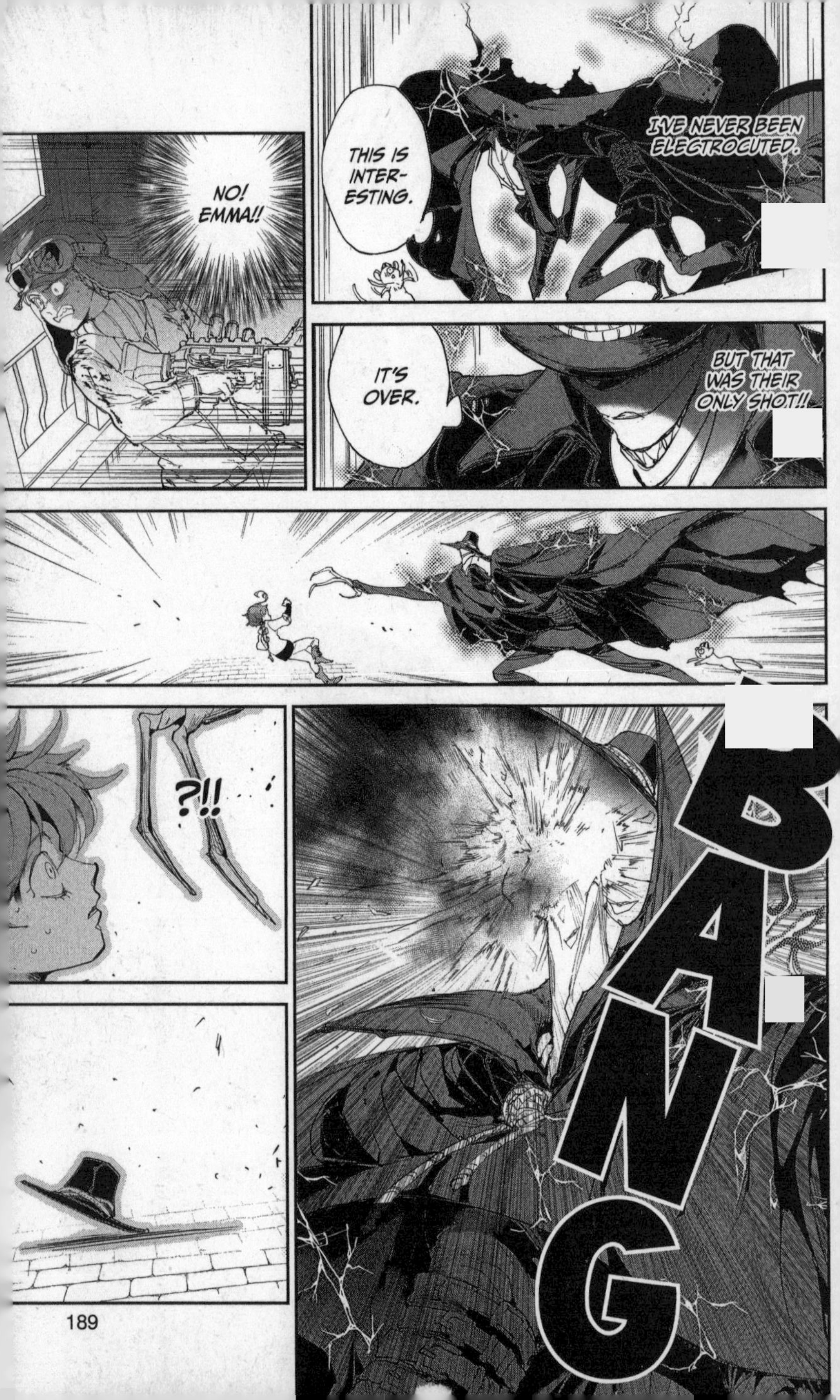
I'VE NEVER BEEN ELECTROCUTED.
THIS IS INTER-ESTING.
BUT THAT WAS THEIR ONLY SHOT!!
IT'S OVER.
NO! EMMA!!
BANG
?!!

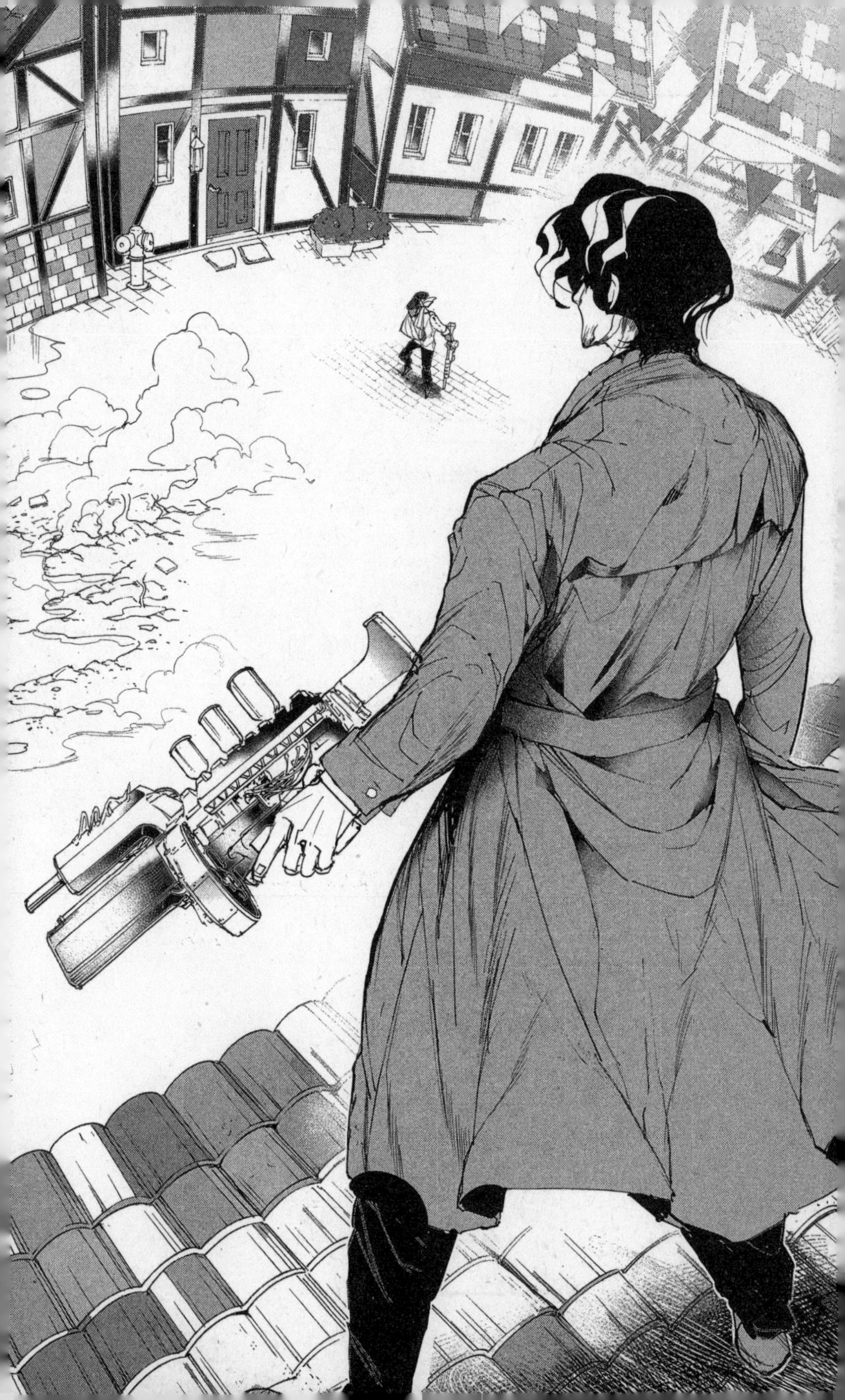

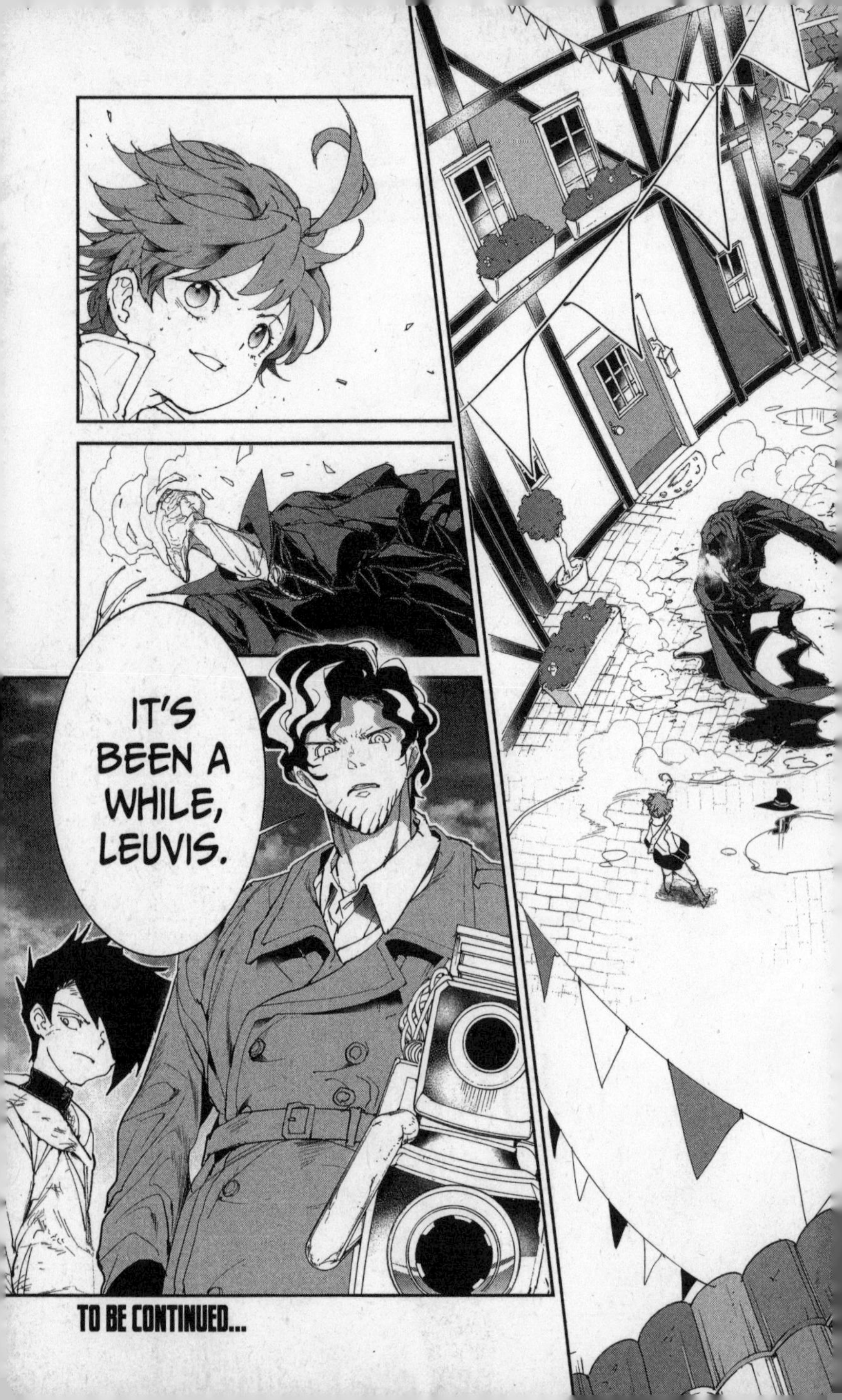
IT'S BEEN A WHILE, LEUVIS.
TO BE CONTINUED...

A SPECIAL EXTRA CHAPTER 3

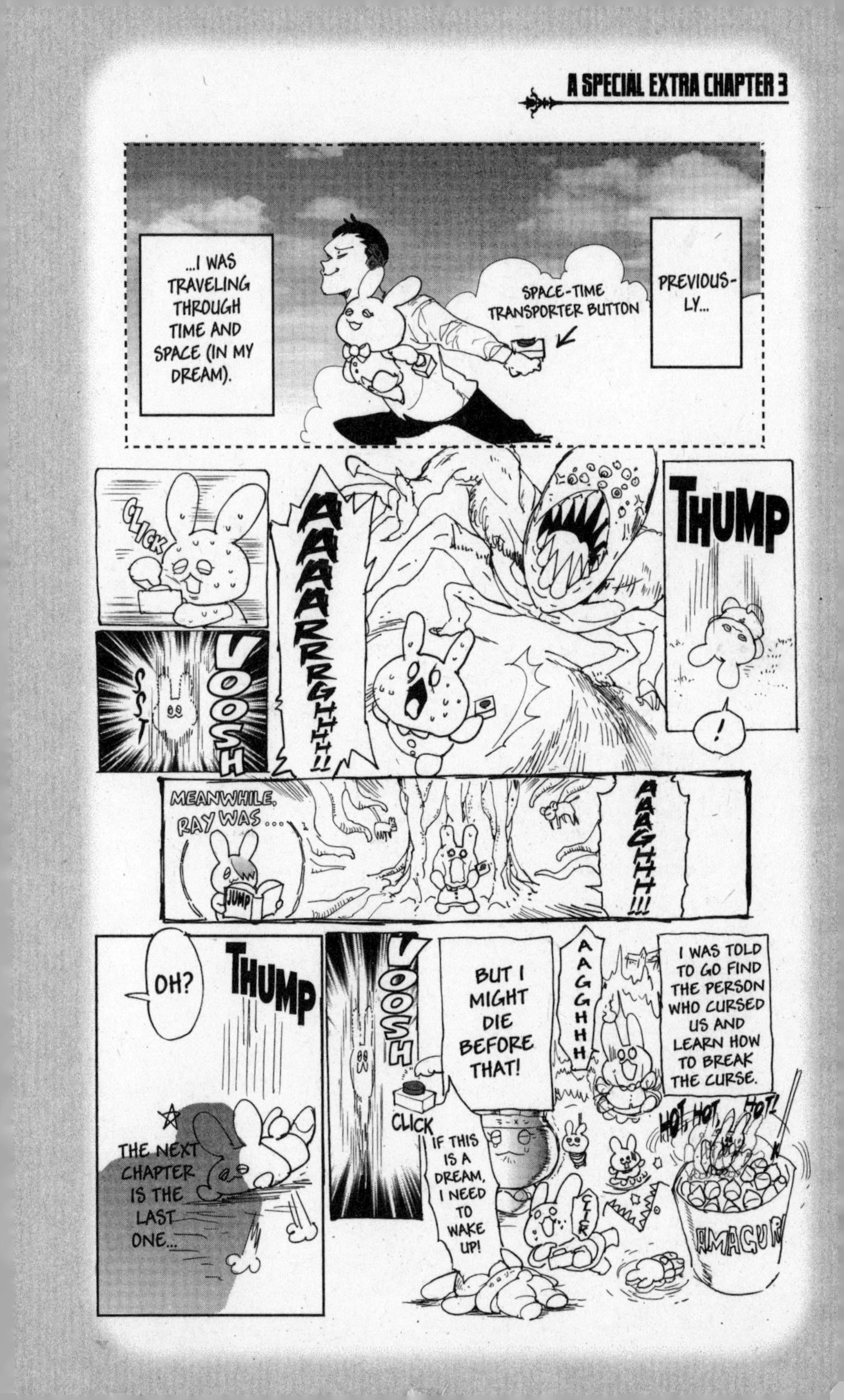
PREVIOUSLY...
SPACE-TIME TRANSPORTER BUTTON
...I WAS TRAVELING THROUGH TIME AND SPACE (IN MY DREAM).
THUMP
!
AAAARRRGHHHH!!
CLICK
VOOSH
SST
AAAGHHH!!!
MEANWHILE, RAY WAS...
JUMP
I WAS TOLD TO GO FIND THE PERSON WHO CURSED US AND LEARN HOW TO BREAK THE CURSE.
AAGGHHH
HOT, HOT, HOT!
AMAGURI
BUT I MIGHT DIE BEFORE THAT!
IF THIS IS A DREAM, I NEED TO WAKE UP!
CLICK
VOOSH
THUMP
OH?
THE NEXT CHAPTER IS THE LAST ONE...

How to Draw?! EMMA's Hair

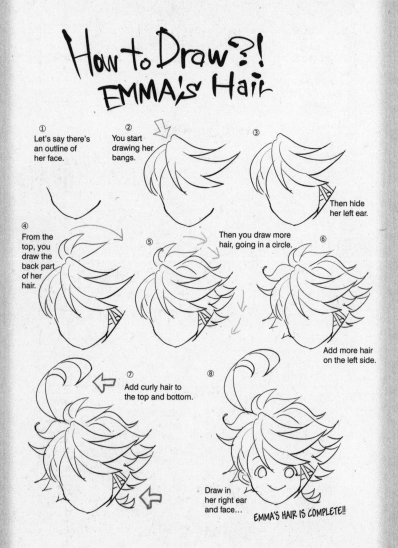

① Let's say there's an outline of her face.

② You start drawing her bangs.

③ Then hide her left ear.

④ From the top, you draw the back part of her hair.

⑤ Then you draw more hair, going in a circle.

⑥ Add more hair on the left side.

⑦ Add curly hair to the top and bottom.

⑧ Draw in her right ear and face...

EMMA'S HAIR IS COMPLETE!!

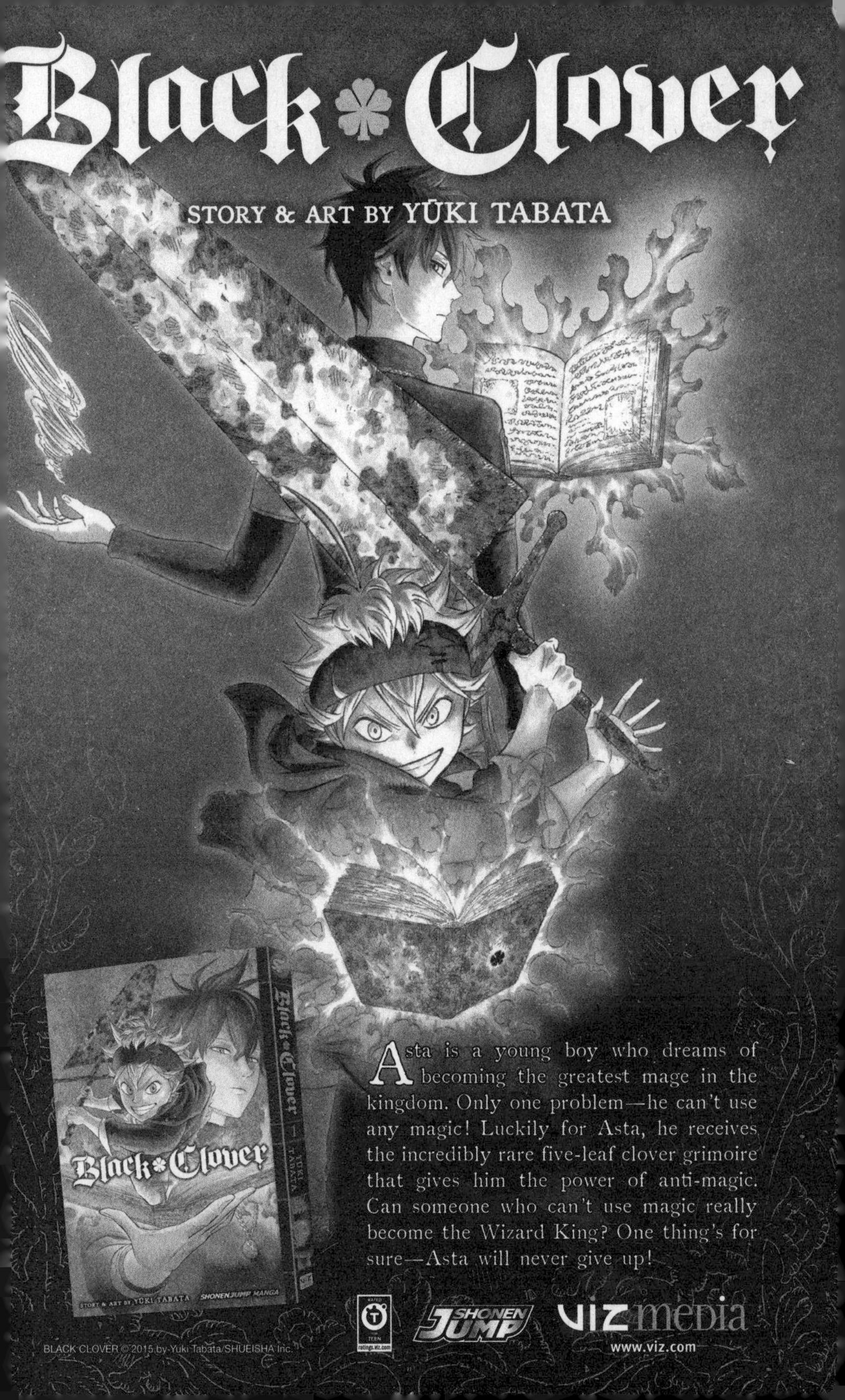
Black Clover
STORY & ART BY YŪKI TABATA
Asta is a young boy who dreams of becoming the greatest mage in the kingdom. Only one problem—he can't use any magic! Luckily for Asta, he receives the incredibly rare five-leaf clover grimoire that gives him the power of anti-magic. Can someone who can't use magic really become the Wizard King? One thing's for sure—Asta will never give up!
Black Clover
STORY & ART BY YŪKI TABATA
SHONEN JUMP MANGA
SHONEN JUMP
VIZ media
www.viz.com
BLACK CLOVER © 2015 by Yuki Tabata/SHUEISHA Inc.

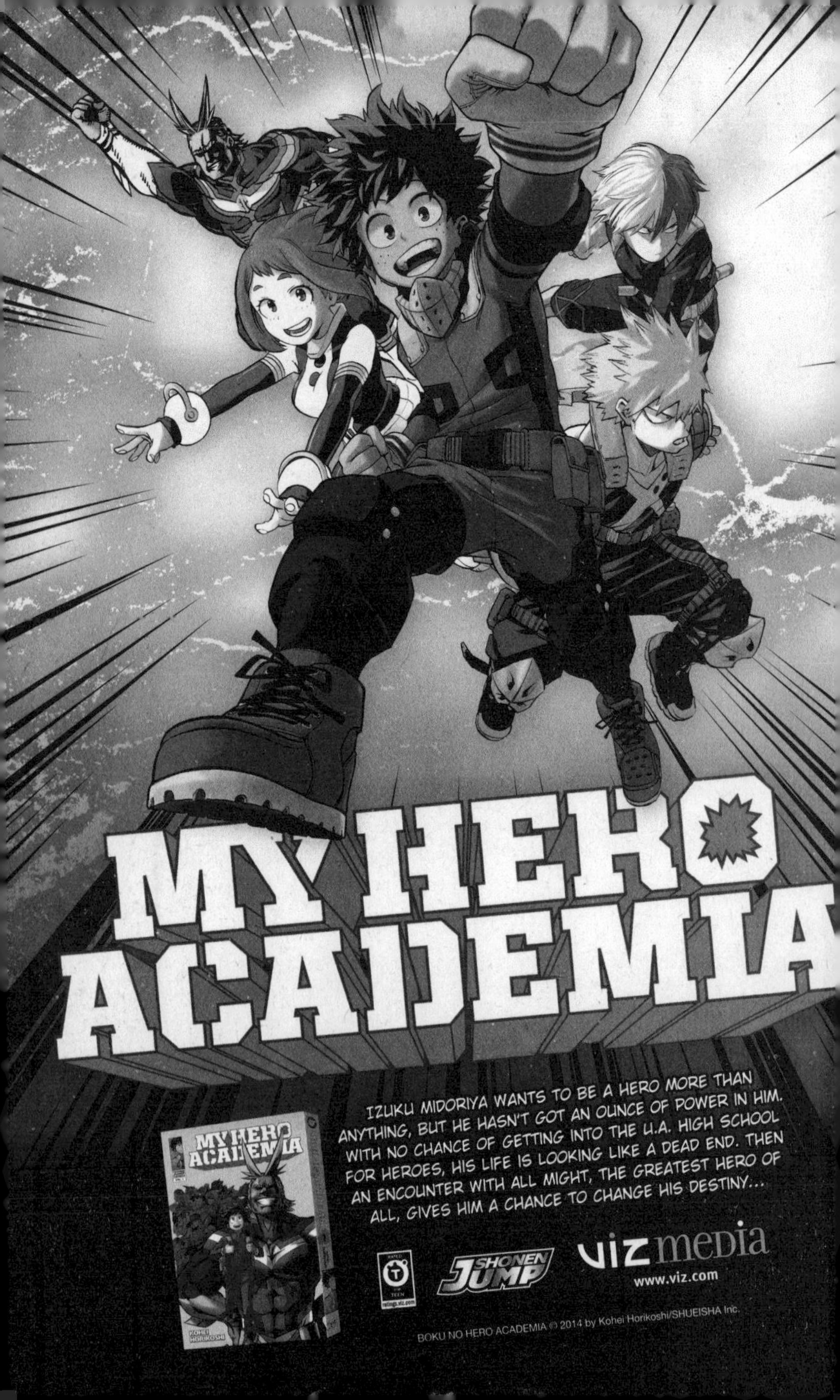
MY HERO ACADEMIA
IZUKU MIDORIYA WANTS TO BE A HERO MORE THAN ANYTHING, BUT HE HASN'T GOT AN OUNCE OF POWER IN HIM. WITH NO CHANCE OF GETTING INTO THE U.A. HIGH SCHOOL FOR HEROES, HIS LIFE IS LOOKING LIKE A DEAD END. THEN AN ENCOUNTER WITH ALL MIGHT, THE GREATEST HERO OF ALL, GIVES HIM A CHANCE TO CHANGE HIS DESTINY...
MY HERO ACADEMIA
KOHEI HORIKOSHI
TEEN
ratings.viz.com
SHONEN JUMP
viz media
www.viz.com
BOKU NO HERO ACADEMIA © 2014 by Kohei Horikoshi/SHUEISHA Inc.

DEATH NOTE
ALL-IN-ONE EDITION

Story by Tsugumi Ohba   **Art by Takeshi Obata**

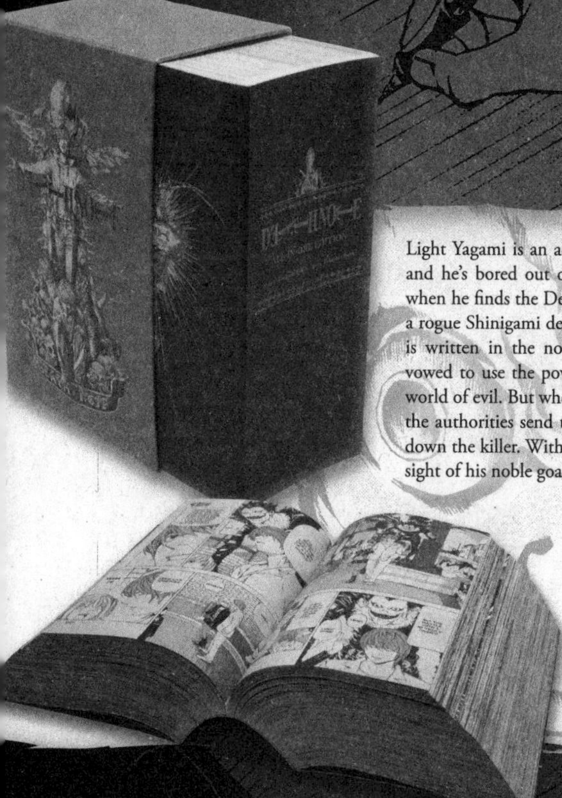

Light Yagami is an ace student with great prospects—
and he's bored out of his mind. But all that changes
when he finds the Death Note, a notebook dropped by
a rogue Shinigami death god. Any human whose name
is written in the notebook dies, and now Light has
vowed to use the power of the Death Note to rid the
world of evil. But when criminals begin dropping dead,
the authorities send the legendary detective L to track
down the killer. With L hot on his heels, will Light lose
sight of his noble goal...or his life?

Includes a NEW epilogue chapter!

All 12 volumes in ONE monstrously large edition!

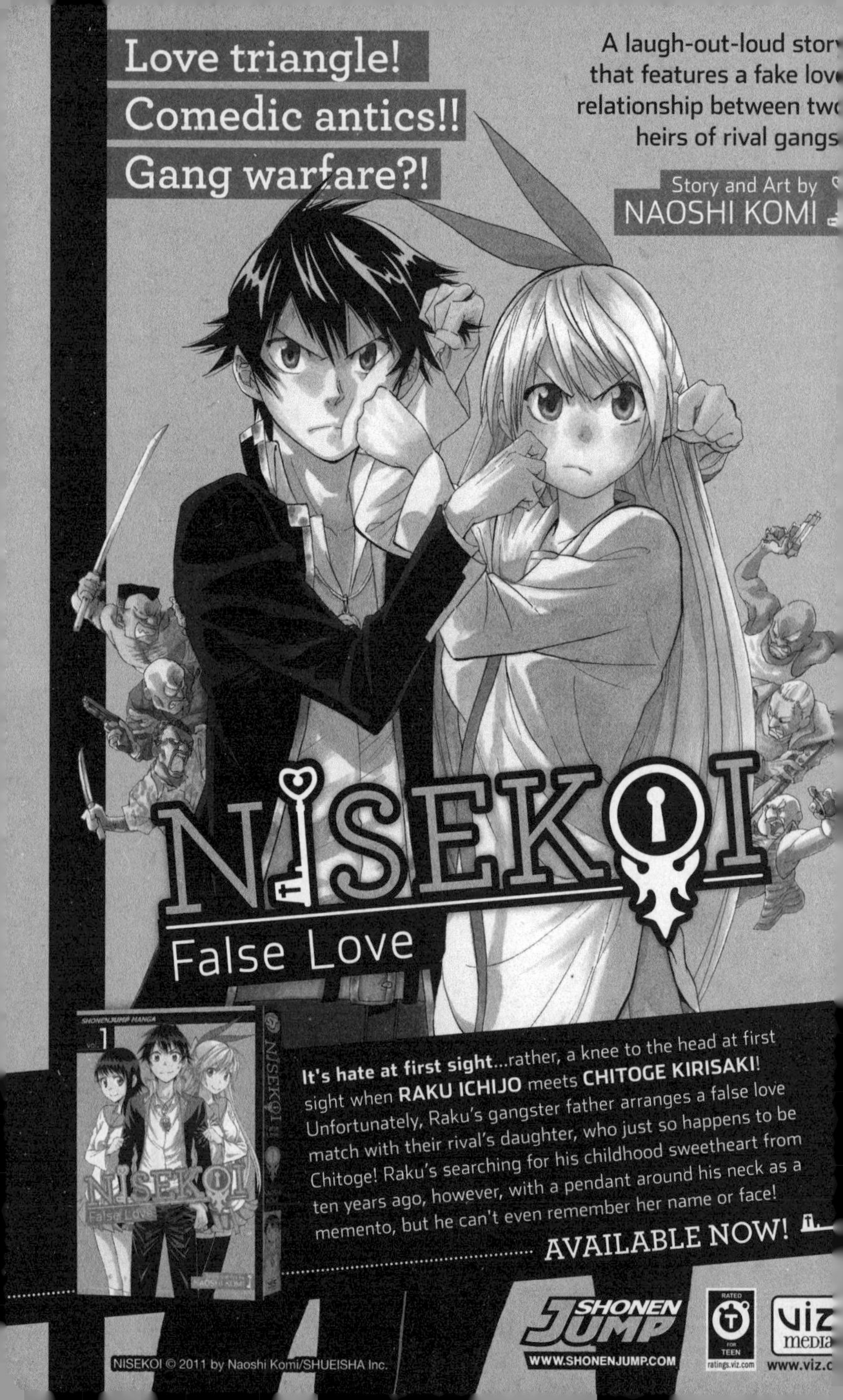

Love triangle!
Comedic antics!!
Gang warfare?!
A laugh-out-loud stor
that features a fake lov
relationship between tw
heirs of rival gangs
Story and Art by
NAOSHI KOMI
NISEKOI
False Love
SHONEN JUMP MANGA
vol. 1
NISEKOI
False Love
NAOSHI KOMI
It's hate at first sight...rather, a knee to the head at first sight when RAKU ICHIJO meets CHITOGE KIRISAKI! Unfortunately, Raku's gangster father arranges a false love match with their rival's daughter, who just so happens to be Chitoge! Raku's searching for his childhood sweetheart from ten years ago, however, with a pendant around his neck as a memento, but he can't even remember her name or face!
AVAILABLE NOW!
SHONEN JUMP
WWW.SHONENJUMP.COM
RATED T FOR TEEN
ratings.viz.com
viz media
www.viz.c
NISEKOI © 2011 by Naoshi Komi/SHUEISHA Inc.

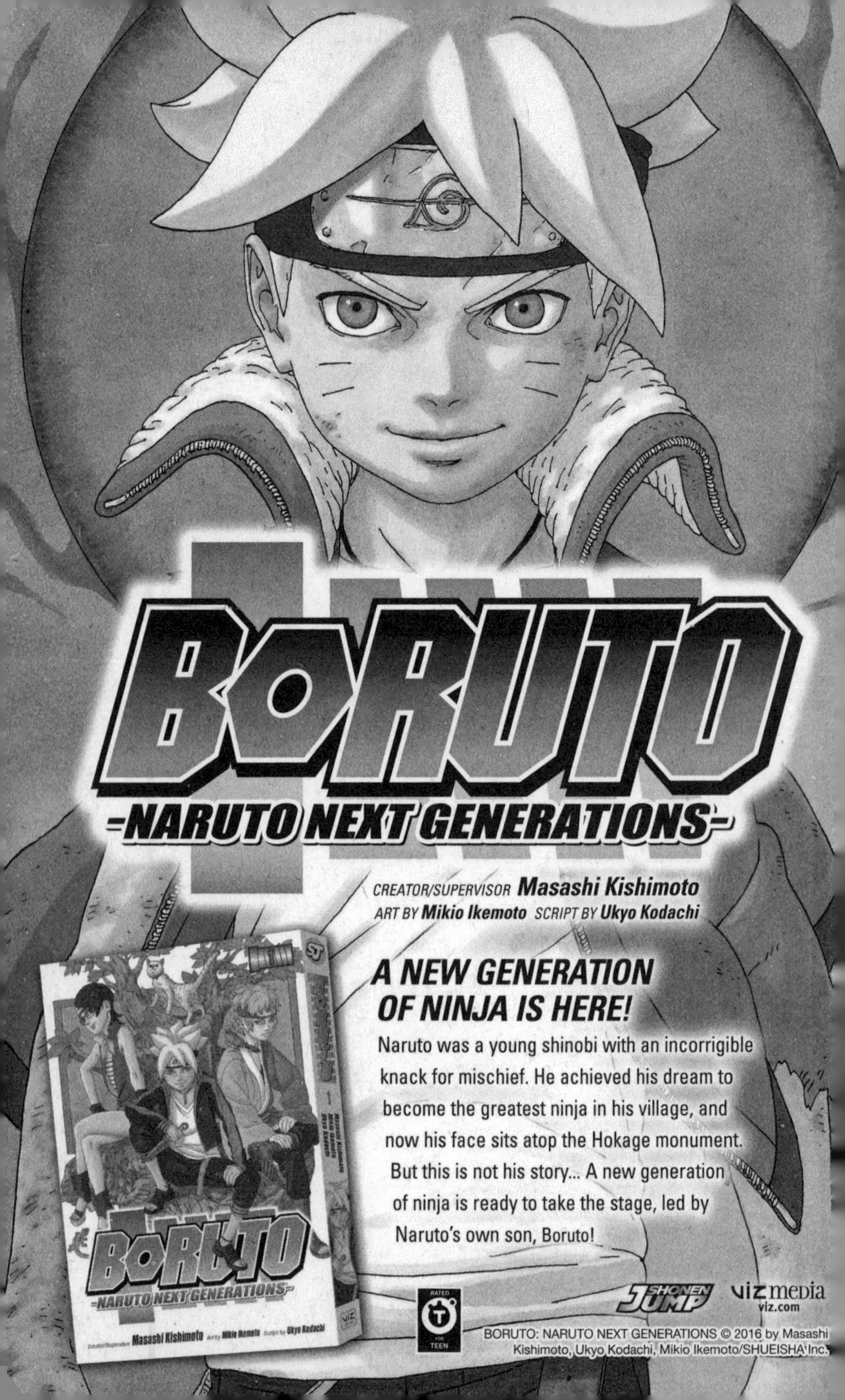
BORUTO
-NARUTO NEXT GENERATIONS-
CREATOR/SUPERVISOR Masashi Kishimoto
ART BY Mikio Ikemoto SCRIPT BY Ukyo Kodachi
A NEW GENERATION OF NINJA IS HERE!
Naruto was a young shinobi with an incorrigible knack for mischief. He achieved his dream to become the greatest ninja in his village, and now his face sits atop the Hokage monument. But this is not his story... A new generation of ninja is ready to take the stage, led by Naruto's own son, Boruto!
BORUTO
-NARUTO NEXT GENERATIONS-
Masashi Kishimoto Art by Mikio Ikemoto Script by Ukyo Kodachi
RATED T FOR TEEN
SHONEN JUMP
viz media
viz.com
BORUTO: NARUTO NEXT GENERATIONS © 2016 by Masashi Kishimoto, Ukyo Kodachi, Mikio Ikemoto/SHUEISHA Inc.

YOU'RE READING THE WRONG WAY!

The Promised Neverland reads from right to left, starting in the upper-right corner. Japanese is read from right to left, meaning that action, sound effects and word-balloon order are completely reversed from English order.

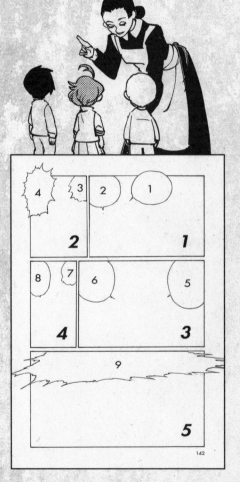